Oriental Memoirs

Selected from a Series of Familiar Letters Written During Seventeen Years Residence in India

James Forbes

A new introduction by W.H. SIDDIQUI

In 4 Vols.

VOL. II

GYAN PUBLISHING HOUSE
Delhi-110 007

GYAN PUBLISHING HOUSE
Publishers of Books on Human Civilization
5, Ansari Road, Daryaganj, Delhi

First Published in 1813 (London)
First reprint in India, 1988

ISBN: 9788121201117 (Set)
ISBN: 9788121201827(Vol 2)

Published by Smt. Gayatri Garg for Gyan Publishing House, Delhi-110007, and Printed at Goyal Offset Printers, Delhi-110035

CHAPTER XVIII.

CHAPTER XIX.

CHAPTER XX.

CHAPTER XXII.

CHAPTER XXIII.

CHAPTER XXIV.

CHAPTER XXV.

CHAPTER XXVI.

CHAPTER XXVII.

CONTENTS.

ness and superstition of the latter—narrow policy and cruelty of oriental courts—noble character of the emperor Acbar—fatal effects of unlimited power, and want of moral obligation among the higher classes of society—punishments at Cambay—asylum of many Persian emigrants—etiquette and ceremonies at an oriental court—general effects of opium—diversions of the nabob and nobles at Cambay—literature—sentiment of Omar on burning the Alexandrian library.

Pleasant situation of the English head-quarters at Narranseer—beauty of the country—game—wild beasts and reptiles—nabob's gardens—heat in the English camp—luxury of cool water—roses and rose water—news of Ragobah's army marching towards Cambay—the English encampment at Narranseer struck; the detachment proceed to Darah; the junction effected—number and condition of our allies—unpleasant encampment at Darah—want of water—delight of shady groves and living streams.

Engraved by T. Wageman

RAGONATH ROW, BALLAJEE; PUNDIT PURDHAN,

PESHWA OF THE MAHRATTA EMPIRE.

Jam. Forbes 1775.

Published by Richard Bentley 8 New Burlington St. 1834

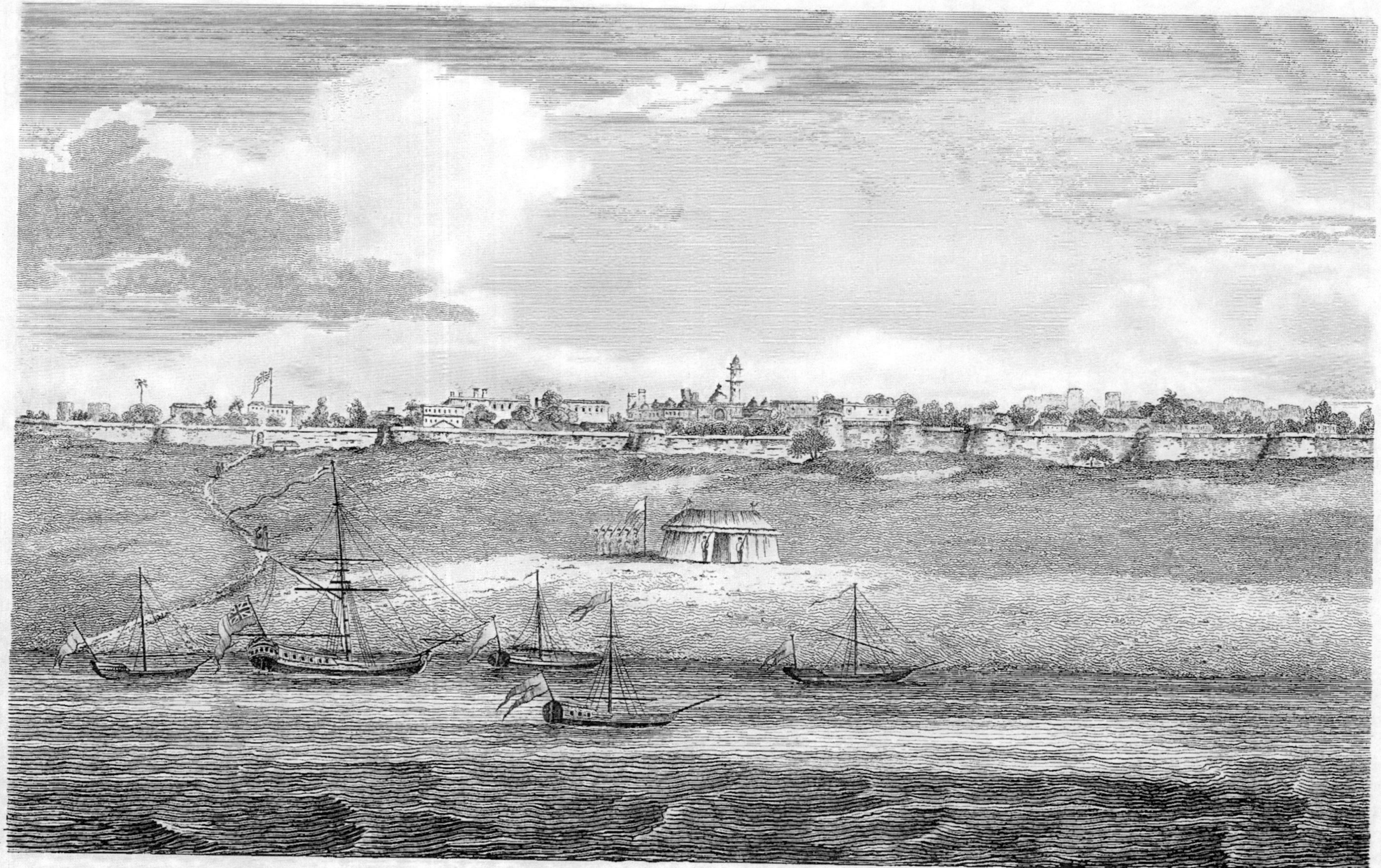

Engraved by J. Storer

View of CAMBAY, from the South.

Jam. Forbes 1770

Published by White Cochrane & Co. Fleet Street June 1st. 1812.

CHAPTER XVI.

When the English detachment sailed from Bombay, we were in expectation of forming a speedy junction with Ragobah's army in Guzerat; but on our arrival at Surat, we found he had experienced a sad reverse of fortune; the confederate generals had engaged him a few weeks before on the plains of Arras, near the banks of the Myhi, and gained a decisive victory. Ragobah's army was entirely dispersed, great part of his artillery, elephants, and camp-equipage taken; and himself with some of his women, Emrut Row, an adopted son, and a few confidential friends, entrusted with his jewels, fled precipitately from the plains of Arras, on elephants and camels, escorted by a troop of cavalry.

Ragobah first halted at the gates of Cambay, in the hope that by means of Sir Charles Malet, the Company's resident at that durbar, he might be enabled to embark for Surat; but the nabob, dreading the vengeance of the victorious army, refused to receive the fugitive prince. The resident immediately procured guides to conduct him to Bownagur, and sent vessels thither which conveyed him in safety to Surat. At parting, Ragobah left with Sir Charles Malet all his remaining treasure and jewels; among the latter were some valuable strings of pearl, with diamonds and precious stones belonging to the peshwa family, amounting to six lacs of rupees: the whole value in money, bonds, and government securities, was said to exceed forty-three lacs, upwards of half a million sterling. Perhaps some of the latter might be of imaginary worth; but the deposit shews the confidence placed by the unfortunate prince in an English individual, in preference to an independent oriental sovereign, surrounded by his army and fortifications.

The arrival of the English forces at Surat gave Ragobah consequence; he cherished hope, and soon after our landing had his first interview with the nabob, who visited him at the house allotted for his residence, and from thence accompanied him in state to one of his summer-palaces, with the usual magnificence: to shew Ragobah the greater honour, his body-guard consisted of a battalion of English sepoys. In the hall of audience he was placed on an elevated throne covered with cloth of gold, while the nabob and his sons sat on the carpet. The nabob on this occasion presented Ragobah with gold and silver coin as a mark of respect; and afterwards with an elephant, an Arabian horse, and a profusion of shawls and keemcobs, in token of friendship.

We passed some time in suspense at Surat: at length Ragobah receiving intelligence that his generals in Guzerat had collected his scattered forces at Copperwanje, resolved to proceed to Cambay with the English detachment, and from thence endeavour to effect a junction with his army. We embarked at Surat, and procceded in boats down the Taptee; but Ragobah deeming it necessary to perform some religious ceremonies at a Hindoo temple near Domus, a village not far from the entrance of the river, he landed there with his family. Several of us followed his example, from a wish to explore the country. No tents were pitched, nor any accommodation provided for the ladies of his zenana, who were obliged to pass some time under the humble roof of the English serjeant posted at Domus. There I first saw these females, seven in number, besides their attendants: one of them was handsome, all richly drest, and covered with jewels; they appeared distressed at their situation, and were much struck by the novelty of Europeans. While we gratified their curiosity, we enjoyed no common opportunity of indulging our own; but a jealous eunuch soon deprived us of this mutual satisfaction, and hurried them to the temple, whither Ragobah had retired.

The next morning some splendid tents were pitched for the reception of the chief and council at Surat, who came to pay a visit of ceremony to Ragobah at Domus: on taking leave the chief presented him, in the name of the English company, with three Arabian horses, some bales of the finest scarlet broad-cloth, and a valuable assortment of shawls, keemcobs, and muslin. The English gentlemen accompanied Ragobah from the tent of audience to the water-side; where, previous to his entering the boat, he stood for some time, without his turban, gazing steadfastly at the sun; he then prostrated himself on the ground, and continued a few minutes in silent prayer.

On reaching Surat-bar the weather was boisterous, and we encountered so rough a sea that it was impossible to reach our respective vessels. While attempting to gain the yacht appropriated to the colonel and his staff, we were obliged to take refuge in the vessel destined for Ragobah and his family, where we had another opportunity of seeing his concubines and female attendants in a state of terror and distress to which the Hindoo women are seldom accustomed. We lamented the pride, vanity, and want of feeling in the Asiatics thus exposing the tender sex to the fatigues and dangers of war.

Many religious brahmins and strict professors among the high castes of Hindoos censured Ragobah for undertaking a voyage by sea, in which they alleged he not only deviated from the established laws and customs of his tribe, but thought he acted contrary to the divine injunction. He might have pleaded that "necessity has no law," for he certainly had no other alternative. The religious Hindoos, like the ancient Magi, and many of their followers among the modern Parsees, consider the sea as a sacred element; and, as Tacitus observes of the Parthian magi, "to spit in it, or to defile the purity of the waters by the superfluities of the human body, was held to be profane and impious."

The Greeks and Romans seem also to have had a natural dread, if not an aversion to the sea, and a horror of dying, or being shipwrecked on that element, and by that means deprived of the funeral rites and ceremonies which they deemed essential. Ovid, miserable as he was on his banishment, seemed to prefer even death itself to the danger of a voyage by sea, most probably from a fear of being consigned to the deep without the rites of burial.

> "Demite naufragium, mors mihi munus erit."
>
> "Death would my soul from anxious troubles ease,
> "But that I fear to perish by the seas."

The voyage from Surat to Cambay was uninteresting; hazy

weather prevented our seeing any thing of the surrounding shores on the first day: the next morning we passed the low sandy plains near the entrance of the river Nerbudda, in the Baroche Purgunna; there were no enclosures, and only a few trees round the villages. As we proceeded up the gulf, the atmosphere cleared, and we distinguished the western hills at Bownagur: the eastern view continued to present a flat country, richly cultivated. We anchored that evening with the ebb tide near Gongwa, a village embosomed in mango and tamarind trees, surrounded by cornfields, pasturage, flocks of sheep, herds of cattle, and large ricks of wheat; monkeys, squirrels, peacocks, doves, and smaller birds cheered the groves; the plains were animated by an immense number of antelopes.

This village belongs exclusively to the Gosaings, or Senassees, a caste of religious Hindoo mendicants, described in another place, who march in large bodies through the provinces of Hindostan, and levy heavy contributions: they are sometimes hired as auxiliaries, being an athletic race, brave and hardy, seldom encumbered with drapery, and often entirely naked: these gymnosophists at Gongwa acknowledge a superior of their own tribe, and seem contented with their fertile district, which they enjoy unmolested by paying an annual tribute to the Mahrattas. Some of us landed and were hospitably entertained with milk, butter, and a variety of fruit. Unlike the generality of Hindoos, these Gosaings do not burn their dead, but bury them, and, what is more extraordinary, often inhume them before they expire. On this occasion, when a patient is deemed past recovery, his friends dig a grave, and placing him in a perpendicular posture, put an earthen pot over his head, fill the grave with mould, and immediately erect a tomb of masonry over the devoted victim. A living wife is sometimes thus interred with her dead husband. These superstitious rites seem to be more cruel and absurd than those on the banks of the Ganges, where the Hindoos carry their dying friends, that its sacred stream may receive their last breath.

When the tide had ebbed a few hours, we were left aground; and before the flood made, the gulf was perfectly dry for many leagues around us. The tides flow there with amazing rapidity, and occasion fatal accidents; when the south-west monsoon blows strong, they are said to rush faster than the swiftest horse can gallop, and sometimes rise to the height of forty feet. The flood carried us on with wonderful velocity, but with a fair wind, fine weather, and skilful pilots, we were not apprehensive of danger. The quicksands in the Cambay gulf are frequently alarming; constantly shifting by the conflux of the tides, they render the navigation difficult, and form large banks entirely across, which prevent ships and vessels of heavy burden sailing higher than the Nerbudda; the small craft, convoyed by light gallivats, proceed to Cambay.

Our anchorage, when the flood rushed up the gulf, like the bore of the Ganges, resembled Alexander's fleet at the mouth of the Indus; which probably consisted of the same kind of vessels, employed for a similar purpose, the embarkation of troops and warlike stores, on an expedition to the peaceful provinces of Hindostan. Arnan mentions several Grecian vessels that were left dry on the sands by the ebb-tide, being overset by the velocity of the flood. Our fleet would have shared the same fate had not each vessel been supported by strong poles. When the water retires the mud and sands of the Cambay gulf swarm with millions of a small fish called a nutee, in taste resembling an eel, but not in form; it seldom exceeds four or five inches in length; and when washed from the slimy mud, in which it delights, the body appears beautifully spotted, and the fins variegated with shades of blue.

We anchored on the 17th in Cambay road, about a mile and a half from the city. Ragobah and his family immediately landed, and proceded to the tents pitched near the water-side for their accommodation. The next morning I accompanied the commanding officer and his staff on shore, to be present at the nabob's first visit to Ragobah, who was now before his gates in a different character from that of a fugitive. When the etiquette and ceremonials of this interview were arranged, the nabob left his durbar, and came in state to Ragobah's tents, accompanied by Sir Charles Malet, the English resident at Cambay, and many Persian noblemen. After the usual formalities, the nabob offered him gold and silver coin; the acknowledgment from an inferior to his superior: he then presented him with an elephant richly caparisoned, two Arabian horses, with a variety of keemcobs, shawls, and muslin. Emrut Row and the English gentlemen received presents according to their respective rank. The conversation, as customary on such visits, was ceremonious and polite; and on the part of the nabob particularly respectful, as if desirous of obliterating the unfavorable impression of his conduct when Ragobah, flying from a conquering army, was denied protection in his capital, and the means of embarkation from it: while Sir Charles, on his own responsibility, supplied him with guides and vessels to convey him out of reach of his pursuers. Ragobah's behaviour to the nabob sufficiently indicated that he had not forgot his treatment; especially when addressing Sir Charles, he said aloud in full durbar, "You are indeed my friend! you did far more for me than my father Badjerow: he gave me life; you saved that life, and with it, preserved my honour and my life!" Having made this speech, Ragobah presented each guest with a leaf of spices and betel nut, and sprinkling us with rose-water, concluded the visit.

At this interview Ragobah was dressed in a short muslin vest, rich drawers, and a profusion of jewels; the nabob wore a plain muslin robe, and small white turban, adorned only with a fresh gathered rose. State elephants, led horses, and all kind of Asiatic pomp had been prepared for Ragobah's procession from the tents to a house provided for him in the city, whither the nabob, the commander in chief, and the principal English gentlemen then attended him. The heat and dust during the cavalcade were almost insupportable, and the crowd of spectators immense. On leaving Ragobah, the commander and his staff repaired to the factory, and remained for several days with Sir Charles Malet, until a camp was formed on the plains of Narranseer, a little distance from the city. The nabob, in the style of Eastern hospitality, sent us a superb dinner of fifty covers, cooked in the Mogul taste; consisting of pilaurs, keb-abs, curries, and other savoury dishes, with a profusion of rice variously dressed in the most delicate manner. This was repeated for several days.

Ragobah afterwards removed to a summer-palace belonging

Engraved by T. Wageman

The MAHRATTA PESHWA, *and his* MINISTERS *at* POONAH.

Drawn from an original Sketch belonging to Sir Charles Malet Bart.

[illegible] Richard Bentley 8, New Bur[illegible]

MOHMAN KHAUN, NABOB *of* CAMBAY.

to the nabob, without the city walls; where he established a sort of court, as peshwa of the Mahratta empire, in which character the field and staff officers, and a few other gentlemen of the British army, were introduced to him by the commanding officer. The ceremonies at the Mahratta durbar were similar to the Mogul visits already described, and the presents of the same nature; shawls, muslins, and rich stuffs, differing in quality and quantity according to the station of the visitors.

This custom of making presents prevails throughout Asia, and has done so from the remotest antiquity; no public visits are made without this ceremony: in many parts, among the inferior classes, a flower, fruit, or a cardamom, is offered out of respect at familiar visits: an Indian never requests a favour from his superior with an empty hand. When the aged patriarch sent his sons before the ruler of Egypt, he said, " Take of the best fruits in the land, and carry the man a present; a little balm, a little honey; spices, and myrrh, nuts, and almonds." Solomon remarks that a man's gift maketh room for him, and bringeth him before great men; and there is an Arabian proverb to this effect, " tokens accompany love; presents are the vehicles of friendship."

It is not so much the custom in India to present dresses ready made to the visitors, as to offer the materials, especially to Europeans: in Turkey, Persia, and Arabia, it is generally the reverse. We find in Chardin that the kings of Persia had great wardrobes, where there were always many hundred habits, sorted, ready for presents; and that the intendant of the wardrobe sent them to those persons for whom they were designed by the sovereign: more than forty taylors were always employed in this service. In

Turkey they do not attend so much to the richness, as to the number of the dresses, giving more or fewer, according to the dignity of the persons to whom they are presented, or the marks of favour the prince would confer on his guests: thus in primeval times Joseph gave to each of his brethren changes of raiment, but to his favourite Benjamin, he gave three hundred pieces of silver, and five changes of raiment. Among the honourable distinctions conferred by a Persian monarch on Mordecai, he ordered him to be clothed with his own royal apparel: the same honour was granted by the king of Babylon to Daniel, who for his excellent wisdom was commanded to be clothed in scarlet, and to have a chain of gold about his neck. In modern times, when Charles the twelfth was made a prisoner by the Turks setting fire to his house at Bender, the dresses, tents, horse-caparisons richly ornamented with gold and jewels, and other valuable articles which had been given him in presents, amounted to fifty thousand pounds.

On our first public visit to Ragobah, it was intimated to me, that acting in the double capacity of chaplain to the British troops, and secretary to the commander in chief, the peshwa being a brahmin, and associating an idea of priesthood or brahminism to the former appointment, the presents allotted to me were on that account superior in quality and quantity to those of the other staff-officers.

One part of Ragobah's behaviour on these public visits, was extremely offensive to the gravity and politeness of the Nabob, and the high-born Moguls and Persians who attended him. On our first introduction to the brahmin sovereign, the English gentlemen were equally astonished and disgusted: a repetition of such uncourtly manners in some degree reconciled us to a succession of windy explosions from the royal musnud, or elevated cushions on which he was seated; we wondered in silence at such an extraordinary dereliction from every idea of delicacy and decorum: the nabobs of Surat and Cambay publicly expressed their abhorrence of such unprincely conduct.

In a Mogul durbar outward manners and etiquette are carried to the greatest extent of ceremonious refinement. Orme says "that persons of distinction have been known, through a sense of shame, to make away with themselves after having committed an involuntary indecorum in the presence of their superiors. There the prince is seated in the center of two rows of courtiers, ranged according to their respective degrees of station or favour: all is attention to his countenance; if he ask a question, it is answered with the turn that will please him; if he asserts, all applaud the truth; does he contradict, all tremble. A multitude of domestics appear in waiting, as silent and immoveable as statues. That tribute of obedience which a man pays to his superior, he naturally exacts from his inferior; and where every man is obliged to pay, and expects to receive this obedience, it is natural that a check should be put to all outward indecorum."

Such refinements are not expected in a Mahratta durbar, although their public visits and political councils are always conducted with ceremony and politeness. The indecorous behaviour of Ragonauth Row was a prerogative peculiar to himself.

We found very few of Ragobah's troops at Cambay, but were informed his army was in the Bisnagar province, about eighty miles from thence, and that the confederate forces were encamped twenty miles nearer, in hopes of preventing a junction with the English. The enemy amounted to forty thousand cavalry, and twelve thousand infantry; bazar-men, foragers, women, and various camp followers, swelled the number to an hundred thousand.

Thus circumstanced, the English detachment landed the next day and marched to the plains of Narranseer, on the north side of Cambay, or Cambaut, an ancient city terminating the gulf of that name in 22° 16′ north latitude and 72° 32′ east longitude: it is now only three miles in circumference, surrounded by a brick wall perforated for musquetry, flanked with fifty-two irregular towers, without fosse or esplanade: the works are out of repair, and the cannon in the towers of little consequence. It is built on uneven ground, which on the whole may be termed an eminence; the houses, mosques, and tombs reach to the walls, and were formerly a part of the city founded near twelve hundred years ago, on the site of Camanes, mentioned by Ptolemy.

Cambay, or Cambaut, once famous in oriental history, is now entirely changed, and its grandeur mingled with poverty and desolation; uninhabited streets, falling mosques, and mouldering palaces, indicate its ancient magnificence and the instability of human structures: formerly every street was fortified, and defended by gates; a few in the principal streets still remain, but the greater part have shared the common fate of the city.

The durbar, or nabob's palace, is almost the only large edifice in good repair, its exterior appearance is far from elegant; within it abounds with small rooms and porticos, surrounding open squares, embellished with gardens and fountains, in the Mogul taste.

Adjoining the durbar is a handsome mosque, called the Jumma Mosseid; it was anciently a Hindoo Pagoda, converted into a mosque when the Moguls conquered Guzerat; the idols which then adorned it are buried beneath the pavement. It forms a square of two hundred and ten feet; a succession of domes of different dimensions, supported by pillars, compose a grand colonnade round the interior area. This temple was once paved with white marble, the greater part is now removed, and replaced with stone: over the south entrance was a handsome minaret; its companion having been destroyed by lightning, was never replaced.

Cambay is also celebrated for a curious Hindoo temple, which I frequently visited. I was first conducted into an open court, its walls adorned with a variety of small sculpture, and images in separate niches; on the east side is an inner temple, the whole length of the outer square, but only six feet wide, in which are placed a number of statues, nearly of the human size, many of white marble, some of black basalt, and a few of yellow antique; inferior deities in the Hindoo mythology, cast in silver, brass, and other metals, were ranged below them. After a present to the brahmins, we lighted candles, and descended thirty feet into a large subterraneous temple, covered by a dome, and entirely dark: on three sides of this temple are a number of empty niches, a little above the floor; and on the east is an opening into another narrow temple, the length of the large one, which contains five images of white marble sitting in the eastern manner, two on each side of a throne placed under a magnificent canopy in the center, which contains the celebrated statue of Parisnaut, one of the principal Hindoo deities. I cannot praise the artist's skill although superior to most

I have seen in India; the countenances express no character, the limbs have neither strength nor elegance, and are destitute of the graces which characterize the sculpture of ancient Greece.

In the suburbs of Cambay are some large mausoleums and Mahometan tombs, in the form of octagon and circular temples, many in a beautiful style of architecture, and the marble sculpture of some exquisitely fine. I was informed the dust that worked out in finishing the flowers and ornaments were weighed against gold, as a compensation to the artist. The grandest was erected to the memory of an eminent Mogul, who died of hunger during a grievous famine, which almost depopulated this part of Guzerat; it appears from the inscription, that during this dreadful scarcity the deceased offered a measure of pearls for an equal quantity of grain, which not being able to procure, he perished by hunger.

From the quantity of wrought stones, and scattered relicks of marble at Cambay, we may judge of its former wealth and magnificence; the charge of transporting them thither must have been immense, the mountains from whence they are hewn being very distant.

The trees which shade the houses are filled with monkeys, squirrels, doves, and parrots: the monkeys are the only mischievous part of these curious citizens; they occupy the roofs of the houses, and swarm all over the town, unmolested by the inhabitants.

Cambay was formerly celebrated for manufactures of chintz, silk and gold stuffs; the weavers are now few and poor, nor is there a merchant of eminence to be met with, except the brokers under the English protection. The population and opulence of this city must have been considerable, when the duties on tamarinds alone amounted annually to twenty thousand rupees: two principal causes for its decline are the oppressive government of the nabob, and the retreat of the sea, which once washed the city walls, but now flows no nearer than a mile and a half from the south gate.

Indigo was always a staple commodity at Cambay, where a large quantity is still manufactured; its cultivation employs many hands in the adjacent districts. When the plant has attained maturity, the leaves are stripped from the stalks, and infused in a certain quantity of water, with a small proportion of sweet oil, for thirty or forty hours; the water, which has by that time acquired a blue tint, being poured off, is left in large flat troughs, until by exhalation there remains only a thick sediment; which is made into small cakes, and dried in the sun for use. This is the pure indigo: it is frequently adulterated with red earth, which adds to its weight, but renders it coarse and dull.

The country in the vicinity of Cambay is fertile and pleasant, abounding with wheat and different grain, peculiar to Hindostan; many acres are sown with carrots and other vegetables, and extensive fields of cotton, erinda, and various shrubs for extracting lamp oil, which is much used. Guzerat is naturally one of the most fruitful provinces in India; but in the Cambay districts, from the indolence of the inhabitants, and the oppressions of the government, they plant only from hand to mouth, and cultivate neither grain nor fruits that require trouble: mangos and tamarinds, which grow spontaneously, are almost the only fruit-trees; in some of the nabob's gardens are a few pomegranates, grapes, and limes.

Cambay is amply supplied with provisions at a reasonable rate;

for a rupee you purchase twenty pounds of excellent beef; mutton, veal, and kid, in the same proportion; poultry not so plentiful, and fish is a rarity; pork in Mahometan towns is never to be met with. In this city and its surrounding domain are fifty thousand wells, and some very fine tanks; but the nabob, to prevent the Mahratta armies from encamping near his capital, drained most of the lakes, and cut off their resources.

Cornelians, agates, and the beautifully variegated stones improperly called mocha-stones, form a valuable part of the trade at Cambay. The best agates and cornelians are found in peculiar strata, thirty feet under the surface of the earth, in a small tract among the Rajepiplee hills, on the banks of the Nerbudda: they are not to be met with in any other part of Guzerat, and are generally cut and polished in Cambay. On being taken from their native bed they are exposed to the heat of the sun for two years: the longer they remain in that situation the brighter and deeper will be the colour of the stone; fire is sometimes substituted for the solar ray, but with less effect, as the stones frequently crack, and seldom acquire a brilliant lustre. After having undergone this process, they are boiled for two days, and sent to the manufacturers at Cambay. The agates are of different hues; those generally called cornelians are black, white, and red, in shades from the palest yellow to the deepest scarlet. The variegated stones with landscapes, trees, and water, beautifully delineated, are found at Copperwange, or more properly Cubbeer-punge, the five tombs, a place sixty miles distant.

While the English troops were detained at Cambay, I resided at head-quarters; but spent much of my time with my kind friend the

English resident in the city, which, with the surrounding district, was then under the dominion of a Mogul prince named Mohman Caun, styled nabob of Cambay; his father was nabob of Ahmedabad, the capital of Guzerat, when it was conquered by the Mahrattas; on that catastrophe he fled to Cambay, then only a sea-port to Ahmedabab; there he established his government, and at his death was succeeded by his son, whose tyranny had lessened the number of his subjects, and reduced the remainder to poverty and degradation. His territory was small, and badly cultivated; after paying the Mahratta choute, or tribute, his annual revenue did not exceed two lacs of rupees: which enabled him to keep only a small establishment, and to maintain two thousand Scindian and Arabian infantry, and five hundred cavalry.

The nabob was a Mogul of the middle stature, well made, and with good features; but his countenance was a true index to a heart cruel, revengeful, and suspicious; to this malevolent disposition, it was said, his only son had a few months before fallen a sacrifice. The nabob was then about fifty years of age, a good soldier, and reckoned a consummate politician, on the narrow system of oriental manœuvring. These are the distinguishing characteristics in an eastern sovereign, who is generally a stranger to magnanimity, generosity, and all the nobler virtues which constitute a good prince. Far from aspiring after the happy title of the "father of his people," an Asiatic despot studies every mode of oppression which avarice can suggest, or intrigue and craftiness carry into execution.

The nabob of Cambay seemed at length to have ingratiated himself into Ragobah's good opinion, and made him an offer of taking the field and joining the allied army. Few characters could be more constrasted than these sovereigns: had the heart of the nabob been equal to his abilities, he might have swayed the imperial sceptre, while Ragobah daily exhibited more superstition and fanaticism than Aurungzebe ever pretended to, and equalled the sanctity of the visionaries and mystics in the professional castes of Hindoo devotees. Duing the detention of the British forces at Cambay, when anxiously expecting a junction with Ragobah's army, an express arrived from his principal general, containing intelligence of importance: the British commander, after waiting a proper time, sent an aid-du-camp to the Mahratta durbar, for the necessary information; who was told Ragobah was at his devotions, and the lucky moment for opening the dispatches not arrived. On sending again the next morning the colonel received for answer that the Mahratta sovereign had not finished his religious ceremonies. One day in the month of March occurred, during our detention at Cambay, which was marked in Ragobah's horoscope as peculiarly unlucky: an inauspicious planet would on that day affect his destiny, unless averted by a variety of rites and ceremonies: the most pious priests and eminent astrologers were convened to assist the brahmin sovereign; on this eventful day " big with the fate of Cæsar and of Rome," Ragobah came forth at day-break bare-headed, and naked, except a cloth round his loins, watching the rising of the sun, and remained until noon with his eyes stedfastly fixed on the glorious orb, which shone with uncommon fervency;

he then retired to the tent set apart for worship, where the ceremonies continued until midnight: the malignant star had then lost its influence, and the next morning opened brighter prospects.

Cunning generally usurps the place of wisdom and prudence in an oriental durbar; superstition assisted in Ragobah's councils, and weakened a mind conscious of possessing unlimited power. Its fatal effects are not confined to Asiatic courts; the page of history presents the same picture in every age: after the corruption of the wise and free governments of Greece and Rome, with what tyranny and wanton violations of justice and humanity are their annals crowded! Although the limits of most Asiatic princes are now comparatively small, yet is each licentious nabob too commonly the Nero or Tiberius of his own domain, and his contracted court presents a scene of ambition, sensuality, and cruelty.

The oriental annals afford some amiable exceptions; Acber stands high in the roll of fame, and vies in every princely virtue with a Titūs, and an Alfred; his memory is revered throughout Hindóstan. Often have I heard the wise and the good speak of this emperor in as warm language and high colouring as we find in the portrait of the son of Onias, one of the finest characters in ancient history. I introduce it not only for its truth, but the beauty of its figurative language. " How was he honoured among his people! as the morning star in the midst of a cloud, and as the moon at the full: as the sun shining upon the temple of the Most High, and as the rainbow giving light in the bright clouds; as the flowers of roses in the spring, and as lilies by the waters; as fire and incense in the censer, and a vessel of gold set with precious stones; as a fair olive-tree, budding forth fruit, and as a cypress which groweth up to the clouds!"

Such is the voice of a grateful people to a wise and beneficent prince; the Asiatics still know how to estimate such a character, and use the same language: the names of Hastings, Cornwallis, and other eminent Englishmen, are dear to their hearts; and, however gradual the progress, the good effect of British legislation, blended with a due regard to ancient manners and customs, will in time be fully appreciated in our extensive empire. The exertions of government for the happiness of millions are already felt and acknowledged throughout the fertile provinces of Bengal, notwithstanding the most deeply-rooted prejudices and attachment to *caste:* if peace continues to extend her olive over British India, we shall see commerce, agriculture, art, and science, once more adorn and enrich those realms, from whence they emigrated to the western world, through the channels of Egypt, Phenicia, and Greece.

At present, in the courts of the nabobs, petty rajahs, and other independent despots of India, there is so little sense of moral obligation, that no stigma attaches to the man who plots the most base and villainous means for attaining the ends of venality and corruption; the odium is incurred for not being properly executed. Perhaps this censure should be limited to the verge of the durbars, courts of justice, and revenue departments of these princes; we will hope that the moral sense operates in general amongst the natives of India, as in those of other countries, although often vitiated by the relaxed state of government and society.

Under these despotic princes, a suspected person is seldom arraigned in a court of justice, confronted with his accusers, or permitted the shadow of a trial; so that judgment and condemnation are synonimous; and execution prompt, though silent. This is certainly a less degree of misery than some European despots have inflicted on their subjects, by confinement in the dungeons of a Bastile, Inquisition, or a Venetian prison; where the unfortunate sufferer drags on a wretched life in solitude and suspense; a prey to that weight of misery emphatically styled the sickness of the heart arising from hope deferred.

Capital punishments are seldom inflicted under these administrations; fines are more frequent, and more acceptable to all parties; pardons can generally be purchased for the most atrocious crimes between man and man, where the prince or his rulers are not affected. It was formerly customary for the nabob to dedicate some time every morning to administer justice; that power now devolved on a deputy, called the cutwall, who inflicted punishments, and superintended the inferior officers of police.

When the English troops landed at Cambay, although fallen from its former importance, it was the residence of many Shah Zadas, descendants of the Persian kings, and other nobles who left that unfortunate country the beginning of the eighteenth century, when Shah Hussein was murdered by Mir Mahmud, and the Afghans usurped the sovereign authority: these were followed by many more who abandoned Persia when Nadir Shah seized the throne, and destroyed the royal line of Saffies. Ahmedabad, then under the Mogul government, and Cambay, were the favourite asylum of those unfortunate emigrants, and of many Persians who accompanied Nadir Shah in his memorable expedition to India, and remained there with their plunder; Cambay has also been the retreat of others who quitted Persia during subsequent distractions.

The Persian language was spoken in great purity at Cambay, and there was as much etiquette and ceremony at the durbar, as in the most refined courts of Europe; as in other oriental palaces, officers in waiting receive a visitor of distinction at their respective stations. He is met at the outer gate by one of inferior rank, who attends him to the inner court, where he is received by one of higher authority, and so in gradation, until he is presented to the prince on the musnud, or throne. The reception by the sovereign varies also according to the rank of the visitors; to those of exalted birth or station, he advances a few paces, and embraces; to others he simply rises, and exchanges the salam, or salutation; while the general throng of civil and military officers, and other visitors of the durbar, are received with a return of the salem from the prince, sitting; when they are conducted by the chopdars, gold-sticks, and silver-sticks in waiting, to the station where they are to stand or sit during the levee. In a Mogul durbar, while the servants are attending with coffee, which is always served, the conversation is general; they afterwards proceed to business: if presents are intended, they are next produced; ottar of roses, betel-nut, or rose-water, offered to each visitor, concludes the ceremony.

At visits of the Rajpoots, Gracias, and many other Hindoo tribes, opium is presented in liquid and solid preparations with the same familiarity as the snuff-box in Europe: the Asiatics are so accustomed to this intoxicating drug, that half the quantity which they take for recreation, would compose an European into the sleep of death. On the Indian it seems to produce the most delightful reveries, transports him in idea to elysium, and fascinates him with the joys of paradise; makes him gay, lively, and good humoured, and his imagination wantons in voluptuous pleasures. These dreams of rapture soon terminate, but the fatal consequences of the enervating drug are permanent; it soon undermines the constitution, debilitates the system, and brings on premature old-age. Taken before a battle it inspires temporary courage, or rather a dreadful phrenzy; among apparent friends its effects are often fatal, by causing those who think themselves injured by their superiors, to speak and act under its influence with an unguarded freedom, which is afterwards recollected and punished: there are many instances of officers, thus intoxicated, upbraiding an oppressive despot when surrounded by his courtiers in full durbar.

The principal diversions of the nabob and his courtiers were hawking and hunting, for which the Cambay districts afford fine sport; the game of chess was also very fashionable, but smoking the hooka, chewing betel, regaling with opium, and attending to the songs and dances of the courtezans, engrossed most of their time, not dedicated to business or the retirement of the haram; there they pass many hours, and there, under the most oppressive government, they remain unmolested: the severest despot respects the female apartment, where none but a husband enters, where a brother does not even visit his married sister.

The Asiatics in general prefer a sedentary life, and are surprised to see a European walk for exercise or pleasure; much more so to behold the English ladies and gentlemen take the trouble of dancing themselves, when they can have a variety of dancers and singers for money: the men like to be well mounted, and give a high price for a good horse and sumptuous furniture; they attend very little to the fine arts, useful improvements, or literary fame; their libraries in general contain only a few tracts of oriental history, Persian poetry, and Arabian tales, with voluminous commentaries on the Koran, but they have little knowledge of general history and the belles-lettres. When the caliph Omar was solicited to spare the Alexandrian library, he replied that its contents either did, or did not, agree with what was written in the holy pages of the Koran; if the former, he alleged the Koran to be sufficient; if the latter, other books were pernicious, and ought to be destroyed. Omar was an ignorant and furious bigot, but many of the succeeding caliphs encouraged letters, and even caused the Greek and Latin classics to be translated, when Europe was enveloped in barbarism and monkish ignorance.

My situation at camp was always at head-quarters: in a beautiful summer palace belonging to the nabob, on the border of the spacious lake at Narranseer, which was always appropriated to the use of the commanding officer and his family, we passed our time as pleasantly as the extreme heat of the weather and anxiety respecting the junction with Ragobah's forces would admit. The tank was surrounded by groves of mango and tamarind trees, surmounted by the minarets and domes of Cambay: the adjacent plains, cultivated and enclosed, produced fine crops of cotton, indigo, wheat, and other grain; the wilder tracts abounded with deer, antelopes, hares, jackals, wolves, and hyenas; the lakes and rivers with flamingos, pelicans, ducks, and water fowl in great variety; peacocks, partridges, quails, doves and green-pigeons supplied our table, and with the addition of two stately birds, called the sahras and cullum, added much to the animated beauty of the country; while monkeys and squirrels, posted in numbers on the trees, approached us with the greatest familiarity. The former are very large, and when sitting in groups at a little distance might have been mistaken for the ryuts, or common peasants, who, except a turban and cloth round the middle, are as naked as themselves. When all these enliveners of the day retired to rest, the camp was surrounded by hyenas, wolves, and jackals; the latter hunted in large herds, making a dismal and incessant howl. Tigers, wild-hogs, and porcupines sometimes sallied forth from the forests, and the camp was much infested by serpents, centipedes and scorpions.

Ragobah and his family resided in another of the nabob's villas, situated on the banks of Narranseer lake, in the midst of luxuriant gardens, which abounded on the borders of that extensive water; after sun-set, the atmosphere was filled with fragrance from the orange trees, tuberoses, champahs, and oriental jessamines, wafted by gentle breezes over the lake: these scenes were truly delightful, especially when illumined by the lunar ray, or the emerald-light of the fire-fly, (Lampyris noctiluca) twinkling in immense numbers among the flowering shrubs.

These delightful evenings hardly compensated for our suffering during the heat of the day, when the hot winds blew from ten in the morning until sun-set, and were so dry and parching that our thirst was never quenched: in the soldiers' tents, composed only of single canvas, Farenheit's thermometer often rose to 116 degrees; it sometimes exceeded 114 in the officers' marquees, with a fly, or separate awning, rising some feet above the tent. This exceeded every thing I had before experienced, and had it continued long no European constitution could have supported it: the transition between health and fever, life and death, was so sudden that medicine had not time to operate,.and our men died rapidly; to all, respiration became difficult, and an oppressive languor and weariness were the general complaint.

The greatest luxury I enjoyed during this sultry season was a visit to the English factory, where the resident had one room dark and cool, set apart entirely for the porous earthen vessels containing the water for drinking; which were disposed with as much care and regularity as the milk-pans in an English dairy: on the surface of each water-jar were scattered a few leaves of the Damascus rose; not enough to communicate the flavour of the flower, but to convey an idea of fragrant coolness when entering this delightful receptacle: to me a draught of this water was far more grateful than the choicest wines of Schiraz, and the delicious sensations, from the sudden transition of heat, altogether indescribable.

Chardin mentions that the Persians use rose-water for cleansing the leather bottles which contain the water for drinking; they cause them to imbibe the rose-water, to take off the taste of the skin: roses are the delight of the orientals upon all occasions. When Doubdan was leaving the holy sepulchre at Jerusalem, the people presented his party with nosegays of flowers, and fresh-gathered roses, others sprinkled them from bottles of rose-water.

The nosegays of roses, mogrees, and jessamine, gathered in the cool of the morning, and brought in with a basket of fruit and vegetables to the English breakfast-table in India, are very pleasing and refreshing: so are the Japan roses, oleanders, and other richly-coloured flowers which ornament the gindey and ewer presented to each guest for ablution after dinner.

We continued in an inactive state at Narranseer until the 15th of April, when an express arrived with the interesting intelligence that Ragobah's generals had collected his scattered forces, and were then on their march to Cambay; but as the enemy were near them, in great force, they requested that Ragobah and the English detachment would proceed as soon as possible, as a speedy junction would be of infinite advantage.

On a confirmation of this news, we struck our tents on the sultry plains of Narranseer, and by short marches arrived at Darah, where the junction so ardently desired was effected on the 19th of April. Ragobah's army was said to consist of thirty thousand cavalry and infantry, with about twice as many camp-followers, women and children; but in reality, from this motley mass, there were not more than twelve thousand fighting men, commanded by four of Ragobah's principal generals; they narrowly escaped the ministerial army on the banks of the river Sabermally, who reached the pass too late to prevent their crossing, not expecting that so large a force could have proceeded with such rapidity; for, eluding the vigilance of the enemy, they marched sixty coss, or ninety English miles, without halting, followed by their elephants, camels, bazar, and baggage.

Govind Row Guykwar, an independent chieftain of Guzerat,

and one of Ragobah's principal allies, arrived soon afterwards with a body of eight thousand cavalry, but very few infantry in proportion; this being all the reinforcement expected, it was resolved to march without delay and attack the enemy, then encamped on the banks of the Sabermally.

On completing this junction with the Mahratta army, the allied forces might altogether amount to twenty-five thousand men in arms. The English detachment, under the command of colonel Keating, consisted of eighty European artillery, and one hundred and sixty artillery lascars, natives employed in that line; five hundred European infantry, and fourteen hundred sepoys, with a proportionate number of officers. Our field train of artillery contained two eighteen pounders, four twelve, and four six pounders; two eight-inch mortars, and howitzers of smaller caliber, with stores and ammunition in great abundance.

The encampment at Darah, on an arid plain, bare of trees, and exposed to the blasts of the hot winds, was intolerable: we looked back with regret to the lovely lake and shady groves of Narranseer. There was indeed a large tank at Darah, which accommodated us tolerably well before the arrival of Ragobah's forces: from that period the concourse of elephants, camels, horses, and bullocks, with thousands of men, women, and children, rushing into the water, soon destroyed its fluidity, by mingling it with the mud, from which with difficulty we strained off a most unpleasant beverage.

When our allies had sufficiently recovered from the fatigue of their forced march, we joyfully left our unpleasant encampment at Darah, and marched towards the enemy's ground on the banks of the Sabermatty, where we promised ourselves the unspeakable refreshment of a running stream. We now found by experience the beneficent character of the banian-tree, the ficus indica, so frequently mentioned for its picturesque beauty; we sometimes met with one of these umbrageous pavilions, sufficiently extensive to shelter a thousand men from the sultry rays of a meridian sun, and found no house so pleasant or cool as this magnificent bower. The shade of the tamarind tree, still cooler, is not so salutary, but when in blossom the fragrance is delicious: the atmosphere of the mango tree is impregnated with the heat and the smell of turpentine, which often communicates a disagreeable flavour to the fruit; this valuable production was every where attaining maturity when we commenced our march in Guzerat.

The deprivation of shade and water at Darah, and our early encampments, was a serious evil to the English soldiers, who suffered very materially from the intense heat. In the mild climates of Europe we calmly read of the march of an army over the arid plains of Asia, or a pilgrimage amidst the stillness and desolation of the Arabian deserts, but we must have experienced some of their difficulties before we can participate in the joy of the Israelites, when, after tasting the bitter waters at Marah, they came to Elim, and encamped near twelve wells of fine water, and threescore and ten palm-trees. The rich colouring in the pastoral psalms and prophetical writings, of rivers, groves, and pastures, was intended to depict the greatest blessings both in a literal and a figurative sense. Mahomet, a native of Arabia, promises his disciples, among the chief pleasures of his voluptuous paradise, beautiful groves and gardens, fountains of incorruptible water, rivers of milk, and brooks of honey; he well knew how such allurements would work upon the imagination of his Arabian converts. Often on the burning plains of Darah did this affecting soliloquy of Hassan the camel-driver occur to my memory, which I most feelingly introduced in a letter written on the spot.

"Ah! little thought I of the blasting wind,
"The thirst, or pinching hunger, that I find!
"Bethink thee, Hassan, where shall thirst assuage,
"When fails this cruse, its unrelenting rage?
"Here, where no springs in murmurs break away,
"Or moss-crown'd fountains mitigate the day;
"In vain I hope the green delight to know
"Which plains more blest, or verdant vales bestow:
"Here rocks alone, and tasteless sands are found,
"And faint and sickly winds for ever howl around!

COLLINS's *Oriental Eclogues.*

Engraved by J. Shury

SCULPTURE *in a Subterraneous* HINDOO TEMPLE *at* CAMBAY.

Published by Richard Bentley, 8, New Burlington St. 1834.

CHAPTER XVII.

ACCOUNT OF THE MAHRATTA ARMY; WITH THE MANNERS AND CUSTOMS OF THE VARIOUS NATIONS AND TRIBES OF WHICH IT WAS FORMED.

1775.

A various host they came—whose ranks display
  Each mode in which the warrior meets the fight;
The deep battalion locks its firm array,
  And meditates his aim the marksman light;
Far glance the line of sabres flashing bright,
  Where mounted squadrons shake the echoing mead;
Lacks not artillery, breathing flame and night,
  Nor the fleet ordnance whirl'd by rapid steed,
That rivals lightning's flash in ruin and in speed.
A various host—from diverse realms they come,
  Brethren in arms, the Indian chief to aid. W. SCOTT.

CONTENTS.

Account of a Mahratta army—composed of various tribes and nations —armour—jemidars—feudal system among the Mahrattas—irregularity of the army—encampment—standards—cavalry officers of distinction—rich caparison of the horses—chopdars and heralds—titles of honour—female names—distinguishing characteristic of the officers—character of Ragobah's chief officers—magnificence of the Indian tents—military character of the Indians—business in the durbar tent—superiority of English tactics—variety of warriors—Mahomedans from various countries—Nujèeb—Rajepoots—Husserat troops—different orders of cavalry—pindarees—bazar—brahmins —superiority of the lowest brahmin over a sovereign of another caste —particulars of a brahmin feast—Mahratta caste calculated for a military life—pleasures and amusements in camp—their wives and children—conduct of a family on a march—provender for cavalry —dancing-girls, plunderers, and marauders of various denominations—number of cattle—horses in great variety—elephants, for state and service—their docility, affection, and sagacity—extraordinary anecdote of Ragobah's elephants—camels, their use in an Indian army—general description—Mahratta wealth and state—behaviour in expectation of a battle—girdle of battle, for their jewels and papers—hermaphrodites in camp—their number—distinguishing characteristics and occupation—improvement in Mahratta tactics—method of besieging a city—war rockets.

CHAPTER XVII.

The junction of the English detachment with Ragobah's allies having been thus happily effected, before I proceed with an account of the campaign, I will endeavour to describe the heterogeneous mass called a Mahratta army, from the observations which I made during a long residence among these extraordinary people.

The Mahratta armies are generally composed of various nations and religions, who consequently form a very motley collection: they wear no regular uniform, are under very little discipline, and few in the same line, either of horse or foot, have similar weapons; some are armed with swords and targets, others with match-locks or muskets; some carry bows and arrows, others spears, lances, or war rockets; many are expert with the battle-axe, but the sabre is indispensable with all. The men in armour make a strange appearance; a helmet, covering the head, hangs over the ears, and falls on the shoulders; the body is cased with iron net-work, on a thick quilted vest; their swords are of the finest temper, and the horsemen are very expert at this weapon; they are not so fond of curved blades as the Turks and Persians, but prefer a straight two-edged sword, and will give a great price for those which they call Alleman, or German, though formerly brought from Damascus.

In the Mahratta army are no regular commanders by seniority or merit; the principal officers are called jemidars: some command five thousand horse, others, though equally dignified in title, only five hundred. The Mahratta government, in many instances, resembles the feudal system in Europe: the great chieftains, like the ancient barons, hold their lands by military tenure; they enjoyed their estates, on condition of furnishing a stipulated number of knights, esquires, and armed-men, in proportion to their territory; and thus in the Mahratta empire, the principal jaghiredars, or nobles, possessed of landed property, when summoned by the peshwa, appear in the field with the number of men expressed in their firmauns, or grants of land; and there they exercise every act of authority, without appeal, more fully than was claimed by the powerful barons in the Germanic bodies, when issuing from their northern forests, and emerging from Gothic barbarism, they marched against the degenerate Romans, and conquering their provinces, established that military system, which, under different modulations, so long prevailed in Europe.

Every rajah, prince, or leader among the Mahrattas, is in some degree responsible to the peshwa, or head of the empire, for his general conduct; he pays a tribute for his district, and attends, when summoned, with the stipulated body of men, according to its wealth and population: over this corps he has the entire command; to him and his fortune they are alone attached, and adhere to whatever party he joins. This variety of independent commanders destroys that authority and subordination which prevails in European armies, and may in some measure account for the want of discipline in so large a body; where every man beats a drum, blows a trumpet, or fires his match-lock when he pleases, and frequently when loaded with ball. It was with difficulty the British commanding officer suppressed this dangerous practice in Ragobah's army, where it was so prevalent, that it could only be prevented by cutting off the fingers of a delinquent.

The Indian camps display a variety of standards and ensigns; each chieftain has his own: red seems the prevailing colour, but they are seldom decorated with any thing like armorial bearings. The banner which was always carried before Ragobah was small, and swallow-tailed, of crimson and gold tissue, with gold fringes and tassels; called by the Mahrattas, zerree puttah: some of the flags are on very high poles, and larger than a ship's ensign: in the European armies, the knights banneret erected their own standard among their followers; the knights bachelors, or simple knights, did not: similar distinctions are observed among the Mahrattas; the most considerable chieftains display their own colours, have separate encampments, and their own bazar, or market; in which they collect duties, and make such regulations as they think proper, without control from the sovereign.

The Mahratta cavaliers of distinction frequently ornament their saddles with the bushy tails of the Thibet cows, as also the horse's head. On one side an attendant carries a rich umbrella, called an aftaphgere, generally of velvet, embroidered with gold; on the other, is a man with a large fan, or chouree, formed by the tail of the wild cow from Thibet, covered with long flowing hair, delicately white, and soft as silk: the handle is gold or silver, sometimes studded with jewels. The chouree is useful in keeping off the flies and other insects that swarm in hot climates, and also forms a part of oriental state. The cruppers, martingales, and bridles of the horses, are ornamented, according to the rank and wealth of the owner, with gold or silver plates, knobs, coins, and a variety of decorations: the tails of the grey horses are frequently dyed of a red and orange colour, and the manes plaited with silk and ribbands, interspersed with silver roses: the camp abounds with farriers, and every thing necessary for their profession.

The great men have also servants with gold and silver staves of rich workmanship running before them, called chopdars and assaburdars; a sort of heralds, who sing their praises, and proclaim their titles in the hyperbolic style of the east: in general, their lord levels the mountains, and exhausts the ocean; he awes the earth, subdues the nations, and makes the people tremble at his nod. The chaunters of Judea thus sang the exploits of the heroes of Israel when Saul had slain his thousands, and David his ten thousands. The generals are likewise distinguished by some title, exclusive of their family name; sometimes it is given at their birth; but oftener conferred by the prince for gallant behaviour, and a reward of military merit; as the valiant swordsman, the illustrious conqueror, the victorious hero, the ornament of the age, or some other honourable appellation. The women also have names expressive of their personal charms, or their lord's affection; choice of my heart, delight of my eyes, morning star, fragrant rose, coral lips, and a thousand similar fancies, distinguish the favourite ladies in the haram, from Taje Mahal, the crown of the seraglio at Agra, to the wife of the humblest peasant.

In the durbar tent, and at other courts in India, I frequently observed the officers to whom we were introduced, addressed, not by their family name, but by the appellation given them after some signal exploit, or analogous to some perfection in their character. A little history seemed to be attached to each warrior, similar to those we read of in the ancient poets, and the thirty-seven mighty men at the court of David: the chief among whom was Adino; he lifted up his spear against eight hundred, whom he slew at one time: after him was Eleazar the Ahothite, one of the three mighty men with David when they defied the Philistines, and smote them until his hand was weary and clave to his sword: and three of the thirty were there, who fulfilled the wish of David when the Philistines were in Bethlehem, and longing for water, he said, Oh! that one would give me drink out of the well of Bethlehem! and they brake through the host of the Philistines, and drew the water out of the well, and brought it to David. And Benaiah, the son of a valiant man of Kabzeel, who slew two lion-like men of Moab; and also slew a lion in the midst of a pit, in the time of snow; and he slew an Egyptian, a goodly man, and plucking the spear out of his hand, slew him therewith.

On the junction of Ragobah's army with the British forces, we were introduced to general officers, and mighty men of valour, whose prowess, according to their chopdar's account, far exceeded the exploits of those who fought with David in Hebron: they dwindle into insignificance when compared with the achievements of the Mahratta chieftains who joined Ragobah's standard in Guzerat. The sequel of the campaign will evince how well they deserved the encomium, and answered the proclamation of their hyperbolical heralds. I shall only observe at present, that they could not, like Scipio Africanus, Germanicus, and other Roman generals, claim an honorary title from the countries they conquered, or the martial exploits they performed.

The magnificence of the Indian tents, pavilions, and summinianas, or canopy, far exceeds any thing of the kind in Europe, especially among the Moguls: these accommodations are the more necessary where their women and children accompany them to the field. The Mahrattas seem to prefer their tents to houses, and enjoy more pleasure in a camp than a city. The martial tribes of Hindoos, and Mahommedans of distinction, in other professions, generally wish to shine in a military capacity. During the commonwealth of Rome, consuls, senators, and priests, headed her legions: the brahmin sovereigns of Poonah have engrafted the military spirit on the sacerdotal character; brahmins not only serve in the Hindoo armies, but there are many of that tribe among the sepoys, or native troops, belonging to the English. In general, whether a man is occupied in the political cabinet, or engages in the civil departments of Hindostan, he is not in such estimation as when he annexes to it the character of a soldier.

A military profession seldom interferes with other occupations: in the durbar tent, where Ragobah presided as peshwa of the Mahratta empire, business was conducted with the same facility as in the court at Poonah: every evening the principal officers and cabinet ministers attended his levee, and there, as secretary, I often accompanied the English commander: politics, war, and public business, were then discussed, and orders issued for the ensuing day; complaints were heard, grievances redressed, and the usual justice of oriental governments administered.

The native princes of India considered the English tactics as superior to their own; although, from national pride, and bigotry to ancient usages, they seldom allowed us a preeminence in other respects: they were then convinced, by experience, how often a small body of Europeans had decided the fate of kingdoms, where immense armies of Asiatics had long been fruitlessly contending for superiority; and trifling as the numbers of our detachment may appear to those unacquainted with the vulnerable irregularity of oriental troops, Ragobah ceded very valuable acquisitions, and stipulated to pay a large sum for such assistance. The different tribes and clans of warriors in the Indian armies have various degrees of merit, and differ as much in courage and discipline as they do in customs and dress. The common Hindoo and Mahratta infantry are inferior to those from the northern parts of India: Mahommedans from the southern provinces enlist in these armies; many of whom are descended from the Arabians; who coming from the countries bordering on the Red Sea and the Persian gulf, settled on the coasts of India, and from thence extended themselves by conquest and proselytism into the interior regions. The Affghans from Candahar, and the mountains between Persia and Hindostan, are commonly called Pathans; the Tartars from Samarcand and the adjacent provinces, Moguls. All these Mahommedan tribes have intermarried with each other, and the natives of India, and are now blended into a race of similar manners, features, and complexion, generally styled Mussulmans, or Moors.

A number of those adventurers are still pouring into India from Arabia and Tartary, who for a time preserve the hardy character and manly virtues of their country; but, from the enervating climate, and tender pampered education of the southern Moguls, their native character gradually subsides, and they blend into the common mass: these adventurers frequently bring with them a horse and arms, and enter into the service of the Indian princes, who prefer them according to their merit. There are some corps, styled *nujeeb*, or men of good family; originally formed by Sujah Dowlah, and subsequently introduced into the Mahratta armies: these are foot soldiers, invariably armed with a sabre and matchlock, and having adopted some semblance of European discipline, are much respected: as are also the rajepoots, poorbeas, or eastern-men, and many other soldiers of fortune, who enlist under their banners, and are highly esteemed for fidelity and regularity.

The rajepoots are all of a high caste, or clan; proud of being nobly born, and bred to arms, they display a magnanimity, courage, and virtue, uncommon in the Indian character: renowned for fidelity and attachment to the prince whose salt they eat, they are esteemed among the best soldiers of the east; these warlike tribes chiefly inhabit Ajmere, Chetere, and the provinces north of the Nerbudda, a country in many respects resembling the habitable mountainous tracts of Switzerland, and, like that once free and happy country, may be considered, more than any other oriental region, the nurse of liberty and independence. The rajepoot governments have never been entirely subdued by Mahommedan invaders; in the dreadful scenes which marked their conquests, the fastnesses and strong-holds, on mountains accessible only by difficult passes and narrow defiles, afforded an asylum to the rajepoots, who there preserved the Hindoo worship, manners, and customs in genuine purity. This country, chiefly situated in a delightful climate, between 24 and 28 degrees of north latitude, affords some of the grandest and most picturesque scenery in Asia.

The Mahratta cavalry are divided into several classes: the husserat, or household troops, called the *kassey-pagah*, are reckoned very superior to the ordinary horse, and belong entirely to the peshwa's government. Those of the second order are contracted for with government, either by their own commanders, or persons employed for the purpose: the third class are the Moguls, poor-beahs, and other soldiers of fortune, just mentioned, who with their own horse and arms enlist in the service of the oriental sovereigns on the best terms they can. Besides these, and the other cavalry corps which under various descriptions accompany the Mahratta jaghire-dars and chieftains, are a prodigious number of pindarees, or licensed marauders, who join the army in quest of plunder: these cruel wretches spread ruin indiscriminately on friends or foes, wherever they appear, and purchase the privilege for so doing by a moiety of the spoil to the commander of the corps to which they respectively attach themselves.

These pindarees, and various descriptions of unarmed followers of the camp, swell the Indian armies to an amazing number. When Ragobah's forces marched towards the ministerial army, after the junction, they consisted of an hundred thousand, including camp-followers of all sorts; the cattle exceeded two hundred thousand: the confederates were still more numerous.

Ragobah's encampment covered a space of many square miles;

the bazar, or market-place, belonging to his own division, and to the principal generals, contained many thousand tents, where every trade and profession was carried on with as much regularity as in a city. Goldsmiths, jewellers, bankers, drapers, druggists, confectioners, carpenters, taylors, tent-makers, corn-grinders, and farriers, found full employment; as did whole rows of silver, iron, and copper-smiths; but those in the greatest and most constant requisition, seemed to be cooks, confectioners, and farriers. However erroneous their tenets, I should be unpardonable to omit mentioning the veneration paid to public worship in the Mahratta camp: in the different divisions was a temporary dewal, or tent, consecrated to religious duties, where brahmins regularly officiated, and prayer and sacrifices are offered to the deities with the same ceremonies as in the Hindoo temples.

In the Mahratta camp, as in all the Hindoo governments, except that of the brahminical peshwa's at Poonah, there exists a class of people in many respects superior to the sovereign on the throne; this is the tribe of brahmins so often mentioned. Princes and governors, as also most persons employed in the political and military departments of state, belong generally to the second order of the four principal castes into which the Hindoos, as a people, are divided: those brahmins who are not engaged in public functions, or the administration of religious rites, from the superiority of caste alone, are treated with respect and deference by their respective sovereigns. So tenacious are they of their privileges, and so conscious of the preeminence to which the code of Menu entitles them, that among the officers in the Mahratta army, a brahmin in an inferior station would send part of his dinner ready dressed, as a mark of distinction to an officer of higher rank, and a much greater command, but of a lower caste; who accepted it respectfully, and ate it with pleasure: no such return could on his part be offered to the brahmin; who, in whatever outward condition, would be degraded and polluted by tasting, or even by touching the food from one of an inferior class.

As it is not common for Europeans to eat with a brahmin, or even to see them at their meals, I shall give a description of a brahmin dinner, not only from my own observation, but with the assistance of a medical friend, who lived much among them, and was sometimes invited to partake of their repast.

When the dinner is prepared, the brahmin first washes his body in warm water; during which operation he wears his *dotee*, or that cloth which, fastening round his loins, hangs down to his ancles: when washed, he hangs up the dotee to dry, and binds in its place a piece of silk, it not being allowable for a brahmin to wear any thing else when eating. If a person of another caste, or even a brahmin who is not washed, touches his dotee while drying, he cannot wear it without washing it again. After going through several forms of prayer and other ceremonies, he sits down to his food, which is spread on a table-cloth, or rather a table-cover, formed of fresh-gathered leaves, fastened together to the size wanted for the company. The dishes and plates are invariably composed of leaves; a brahmin may not eat out of any thing else: tin vessels, or copper tinned, may be used for cooking, but a brahmin cannot eat out of them.

The food, after being prepared in the kitchen, is placed in distinct portions, on dishes of different size, form, and depth, on the large verdant covering in a regular manner. The feast of a brahmin generally consists of seasoned bread, rice, curry, vegetables, pickles, and a dessert.

Their bread, in its simple state, is prepared from the flour of wheat, juarree, or bahjeree: besides which, they are very fond of a thin cake, or wafer, called *popper*, made from the flour of oord, or mash (phaseolus max.) highly seasoned with assa-fœtida; a salt called popper-khor; and a very hot massaula, composed of turmeric, black pepper, ginger, garlic, several kinds of warm seeds, and a quantity of the hottest Chili pepper. These ingredients are all kneaded with the oord flour and water into a tenacious paste, to form the popper, which is rolled into cakes not thicker than a wafer; these are first dried a little in the sun, and then baked by fire until crisp.

The curry of a brahmin is seldom more than heated butter-milk, with a little gram-flour, slightly seasoned; this they highly esteem. Something similar is wurrun, a dish composed of tuor, or doll, a sort of split-pea, boiled with salt and turmeric (curcuma); this they eat with ghee, or clarified butter, which they say destroys its flatulency.

In the centre of the cover is always a large pile of plain boiled rice, and at a feast there are generally two other heaps of white and yellow rice, seasoned with spices and salt; and two of sweet rice, to be eat with *chatna*, pickles, and stewed vegetables: the latter are chiefly berenjals, bendee, turoy, and different kinds of beans, all savourily dressed, and heated with chilies of every description. The *chatna* is usually made from a vegetable called cotemear, to the eye very much resembling parsley, but to those unused to it, of a disagreeable taste and smell: this is so strongly heated with chilies as to render the other ingredients less distinguishable. The chatna is sometimes made with cocoa-nut, lime-juice, garlic, and chilies, and, with the pickles, is placed in deep leaves round the large cover, to the number of thirty or forty, the Hindoos being very fond of this stimulus to their rice. These pickles are not prepared with vinegar, but preserved in oil and salt, seasoned with chilie and the acid of tamarinds, which in a salted state are much used in Hindostan. Brahmins, and many other Hindoos, reject the onion from their bill of fare. Ghee, which, in deep boats formed of leaves, seems to constitute the essence of the dinner, is plentifully dispensed. The dessert consists of mangos preserved with sugar, ginger, limes, and other sweetmeats; syrup of different fruits, and sometimes a little ripe fruit, but the dessert is not common. Such is the entertainment of a rich brahmin, who eats of no animal food.

In the extraordinary artificial distinction of castes amongst the Hindoos, the Mahrattas rank but little above the lowest; and therefore being universally educated in the labour and simplicity of rural and agricultural society, they are admirably prepared for the endurance, privations, and bodily exertions of a military life: this has been the origin of many other warlike nations. The brahmins and higher orders are prohibited the use of all animal food: that restriction lessens as it reaches the lower classes; amongst whom the Mahratta is placed in such a degree of assigned degradation, that the flesh of animals, except of the sacred ox and cow, is no pollution, affording a latitude more consistent with the exigencies and necessities of a soldier's life. It has been remarked, that there is an honesty, simplicity, and courtesy in the true Mahratta character, not common among the political brahmins at the peshwa's court, or in other public situations: their chicanery, duplicity, and cunning, are obvious to all who have been concerned with them in the diplomatique and revenue departments.

Fond of a wandering life, the Mahrattas seem most at home in the camp; the bazars being supplied with necessaries for the soldiers, and such luxuries as those in a higher station require, they know no wants, and are subject to few restraints: surrounded by their wives and their children, they enjoy the pleasures of domestic life; and many of the principal officers keep greyhounds, chetaus, and hawks, trained to hunting, for their amusement on a march, or when encamped in a sporting country.

Not only the officers and soldiers, but in general the followers of the camp, have their wives and families with them during the march: the women frequently ride astride with one or two children on a bullock, an ass, or a little tattoo horse, while the men walk by the side On reaching the encampment, the fatigued husband lies down on his mat, and the wife commences her duties: she first champoes her husband, and fans him to repose; she then champoes the horse, rubs him down, and gives him provender; takes some care of the ox which has carried their stores, and drives off the poor ass to provide for himself: she next lights a fire, dresses rice and curry, or kneads dough for cakes, which are prepared and baked in a simple manner. When the husband awakes, his repast is ready; and having also provided a meal for herself and children, the careful matron occupies the mat, and sleeps till daybreak, when all are in motion and ready for another march.

Of the Mahratta cavalry, those soldiers who have neither female companions nor servants to attend them, on finishing the march immediately champoe their own horses, by rubbing the limbs, and bending the joints; which not only refreshes the animals, but enables them to bear fatigue with a smaller quantity of food than would be otherwise necessary. It is generally difficult to provide provender for horses on these campaigns: hay is not common in India; the villagers fodder their horned-cattle, and the few horses they possess, with straw and a little grain. In the fair season, when there is no pasture, the horsemen and their attendant grass-cutters sally out of the camp to dig up the roots of grass, which are washed and given to their horses as more nutritive than the stems of dried reedy grass and other vegetables, which from their rapid growth in the rainy season, have even then very little nutritious juice: but, whatever may constitute the other food of the horses, they must have a daily quantity of grain, or some composition of heartening aliment, whether on war service, or kept for recreation at home.

Besides the married women, a number of dancing girls and tolerated courtezans attend the camp; some of the former officiate as choristers in the sacred tents dedicated to the Hindoo gods; many belong to the officers, and others form a common cyprian corps. Children of both sexes accompany the army in the severest marches; they know no home but the camp, and from habit prefer this wandering life.

Swarms of beyds, looties, and pindarees, all different classes of plunderers, follow the armies, and are far more destructive than the soldiers in the countries through which they pass. These marauders receive no pay, but prefer a life of spoil and rapine to any other profession: armed with spears and sabres, and provided with hatchets, iron crows, and implements of destruction, they enter villages already laid waste by the army, and deserted by the inhabitants: there, as if a general pillage of grain, furniture, and other moveables, had not been sufficiently distressing, the pindarees deprive the houses of locks, hinges, and every kind of iron-work, with such timber as they think proper; then digging up the floors in search of grain, and demolishing the walls in hopes of finding concealed treasure, they conclude by setting fire to what they cannot carry off: although there is scarcely any thing that does not turn to account in the camp-bazar, where a rusty nail is taken in exchange for some article of provision.

The number and variety of cattle necessarily attendant on an Asiatic army is astonishing; there were at least two hundred thousand in the Mahratta camp, of every description; the expense of feeding these animals, as also the difficulty of procuring provender, is very great; and their distress for water in a parched country and sultry climate, often fatal. Exclusive of the Mahratta cavalry trained to war, were many thousand horses belonging to the camp-followers; the bazar alone required twenty thousand bullocks to convey the commodities of the shop-keepers, besides a number of small horses and asses. Some thousand camels were employed to carry the tents and baggage; but the elephants, proud of their distinguished elevation, were appropriated to some honourable service, or covered with caparisons of embroidered velvets and scarlet cloth, decorated with gold and silver fringe, were destined to carry the houdahs of Ragobah and his chief officers with majestic pace to join the princely retinue on state occasions: the houdah sometimes contains two or three small apartments under a dome supported by gilded pillars, for the chieftain and his attendants. The elephant is extremely useful in other respects, and, notwithstanding his enormous bulk and surprising strength, is very docile and tractable.

The largest elephants are from ten to eleven feet in height, some are said to exceed it: the average is eight or nine feet. They are fifty or sixty years before they arrive at their full growth; the female goes with young eighteen months, and seldom produces more than one at a birth, which she suckles until it is five years old: its natural life is about an hundred and twenty years. The Indians are remarkably fond of these animals, especially when they have been long in their service. I have seen an elephant valued at twenty thousand rupees; the common price of a docile well-trained elephant is five or six thousand; and in the countries where they are indigenous, the Company contract for them at five hundred rupees each, when they must be seven feet high at the shoulders. The mode of catching and training the wild elephants is now well known: their price increases with their merit during a course of education. Some for their extrarordinary qualities become in a manner invaluable; when these are purchased, no compensation induces a wealthy owner to part with them.

The skin of the elephant is generally a dark grey, sometimes almost black; the face frequently painted with a variety of colours; and the abundance and splendour of his trappings add much to his consequence. The Mogul princes allowed five men and a boy to take care of each elephant; the chief of them, called the mahawut, rode upon his neck to guide him; another sat upon the rump, and assisted in battle; the rest supplied him with food and water, and performed the necessary services. Elephants bred to war, and well disciplined, will stand firm against a volley of musquetry, and never give way unless severely wounded. I have seen one of these animals, with upwards of thirty bullets in the fleshy parts of his body, perfectly recovered from his wounds. All are not equally docile, and when an enraged elephant retreats from battle, nothing can withstand his fury: the driver having no longer a command, friends and foes are involved in undistinguished ruin.

The elephants in the army of Antiochus were provoked to fight by shewing them the blood of grapes and mulberries. The history of the Maccabees informs us, that " to every elephant they appointed a thousand men, armed with coats of mail, and five hundred horsemen of the best; these were ready at every occasion: wherever the beast was, and whithersoever he went, they went also; and upon the elephants were strong towers of wood, filled with armed men, besides the Indian that ruled them."

Elephants in peace and war know their duty, and are more obedient to the word of command than many rational beings. It is said they can travel, on an emergency, two hundred miles in forty-eight hours; but will hold out for a month, at the rate of forty or fifty miles a day, with cheerfulness and alacrity. I performed many long journeys upon an elephant given by Ragobah to Colonel Keating; nothing could exceed the sagacity, docility, and affection of this noble quadruped: if I stopped to enjoy a prospect, he remained immoveable until my sketch was finished; if I wished for ripe mangos growing out of the common reach, he selected the most fruitful branch, and breaking it off with his trunk, offered it to the driver for the company in the houdah, accepting of any part given to himself with a respectful salam, by raising his trunk three times above his head, in the manner of the oriental obeisance, and as often did he express his thanks by a murmuring noise. When a bough obstructed the houdah, he twisted his trunk around it, and though of considerable magnitude, broke it off with ease, and often gathered a leafy branch, either to keep off the flies, or as a fan to agitate the air around him, by waving it with his trunk; he generally paid a visit at the tent-door during breakfast, to procure sugar-candy or fruit, and be cheered by the encomiums and caresses he deservedly met with: no spaniel could be more innocently playful, nor fonder of those who noticed him, than this docile animal, who on particular occasions appeared conscious of his exaltation above the brute creation.

The Ayeen-Akbery mentions elephants that were taught to shoot an arrow out of a bow, to learn the modes which can only be understood by those skilled in music, and to move their limbs in time: we there learn, that upon a signal given by his keeper, the elephant hides eatables in the corner of his mouth, and when they are alone together, takes them out again, and gives them to the man: that with his trunk he draws water out of his stomach which he has reserved there, to sprinkle himself in hot weather; from thence also he takes grass on the second day, without its having undergone any change, doubtless to appease his hunger in case of an emergency, which does not often happen to the tame elephants. The Mogul emperors allowed their favourites one maund and twenty seer of food a day, equal to fifty English pounds: they had besides five seers of sugar, four seers of ghee, and half a maund of rice, with pepper and spices, mixed with twenty quarts of milk; and in the season of sugar canes, each elephant had a daily allowance of two or three hundred canes, according to his size, for the space of three months.

I could mention many anecdotes of the elephant's sagacity and tractability, but will confine myself to one occurrence with Ragobah's elephants in camp; which, like those belonging to the Mogul emperors abovementioned, besides their daily provender of grass, fresh-gathered leaves, and vegetables, were fed with balls, called *mossaulla*, composed of flour, spices, sugar, and butter; ingredients generally expensive, especially in a camp where every thing was extravagantly dear. A vegetable diet, and about thirty pounds of grain, is the usual daily allowance for an elephant; the mossaulla is an indulgence on service, and was accordingly allowed to the peshwa's elephants and Arabian horses, in a country frequently laid waste, and affording little provender for cattle. In our Guzerat encampments, man and beast suffered many deprivations, and were often at a loss for food; notwithstanding this general deficiency, an ample supply of mossaulla was allotted to Ragobah's favourite elephants: yet they became gradually emaciated, and pined away without an apparent cause: the keepers were suspected of withholding their mossaulla, as those delicate balls were composed of the most expensive and savory parts of the pilau's, curries, and other dishes, too costly for persons in their situation: the fraud being proved, the keepers were punished; and the master of the elephants (who like the master of the horse in European courts is generally a man of high rank), appointed inspectors to see them fed, which for a time had the desired effect; the elephants regained their strength, and appeared in good condition. Some months afterwards they fell off again; the inspectors were astonished, as they daily saw them fed, examined the mossaulla, found its ingredients excellent, and the quantity not diminished. The cause, once more discovered, confirms Abul Fazel's account, and evinces the influence the keepers had attained over these extraordinary animals: they taught them to receive the balls with their trunk, and convey them to their mouth in the inspectors' presence, but to abstain from eating them; these docile creatures actually practised that self-denial; they received the food they were so fond of from their hands, put it into their mouth with their trunk, but never chewed it; the balls remained untouched until the inspectors withdrew, when they took them out, and presented them to the keepers with their trunks, accepting only of such a share as they thought proper to allow them.

> " 'Twixt this and *Reason*, what a nice barrier?
> " For ever separate, yet for ever near!
> " *Remembrance* and *Reflection* how ally'd;
> " What thin partitions sense from thought divide!

Elephants are a common present of honour among the Indian princes and generals; and choice camels, used for expresses, sometimes accompany other gifts at the durbar. The camel is a patient serviceable animal, but deficient in the rational qualities ascribed to the elephant: his diet requires no dainties; the leaves of almost every tree he meets with afford a meal; and from a peculiarity in his internal structure, he carries a reservoir of water, from which he draws a small supply for several days without replenishing. The camel will carry a heavy load, and patiently submit to the utmost his strength will bear, kneeling down for the convenience of his keeper; if he adds more than the accustomed burden, he will not rise, but, making a loud moaning, continues on his knees until the additional weight is removed; nor can any threatening or blows of the driver effect the contrary. The number of camels in the Mahratta camp occasioned a disagreeable smell; they were seldom free from sores, and their breath was generally offensive.

Few countries or climates agree so well with the camel as the Persian and Arabian deserts, where they are bred in great numbers; as also on the sandy shores of the Indus, in the domain of the prince of Scindy: many are brought from Malwa, Ajmeer, and Nagóre. This animal is fit for service at the age of three years; they seldom live more than twenty-five years in India, and do not often breed in the southern provinces. Moisture, either in soil or atmosphere, is not congenial with their constitution, which is formed for the arid tracts they traverse, laden with rich merchandize, content with the coarsest food, and a small portion of water. Were it not for this valuable animal, those immense plains of undulating sand would be an insurmountable barrier between the kingdoms on their borders; but the camel conveys both the merchant and his goods from one country to another, with astonishing facility, over deserts trackless as the ocean, which has occasioned the Arabians to name it emphatically, "the ship of the desert."

A camel's travelling load should not exceed five hundred pounds, some can carry from six to seven hundred; under a weight proportioned to his strength, he will perform the longest journey under great privations; when loaded his pace never exceeds three miles an hour, nor will severity make him quicken his pace any more than increase his load. The Mahratta chiefs keep a few light camels and dromedaries, called sadnies, to carry dispatches, which travel with great expedition. In the southern part of Hindostan the camel is of more show than service, and is seldom seen but with the army, or in state processions: but in the north-west provinces, intersected by few navigable rivers, and abounding with extensive deserts, trade is chiefly conducted by means of this valuable animal.

A Mahratta's state generally consists in elephants, horses, and camels: his wealth in jewels, particularly rows of pearls, valued at forty or fifty thousand rupees a necklace: their diamonds are seldom well cut, and usually table-diamonds; the rubies and emeralds are sometimes cut and polished, but oftener set as they come from the mines, in bracelets, rings, and an ornament for the turban, called serpech. A Mahratta is not ambitious to make a figure in his house, furniture, or apparel; his elephants, horses, and jewels, are what he most esteems; if possessed of the finest Persian and Arabian horses, he seldom rides them; preferring for service the fleet mares from his own country, of the Bhimra Tuttee breed.

When a Mahratta expects a battle where there is a chance of being defeated, he mounts a Bhimra mare, and girds himself with a broad belt round the loins, the better to enable him to bear the fatigue of a forced march: this girdle is generally made of strong leather, covered with velvet, and divided into small compartments, containing his most valuable papers and precious jewels: the selected companions of his flight, and a sure resource in adversity.

I have one of these girdles of battle, admirably suited to the purpose. In Pitts' Travels is an anecdote identifying the same kind of girdle among other nations; when a slave to a respectable Mahomedan, and journeying with his master on a pilgrimage to Mecca, the latter was taken extremely ill, and thinking he should die, he took off a girdle which was concealed under his sash, and gave it to Pitts, who had always been a great favourite; in it he found a considerable quantity of gold, and his own letter of freedom.

Among the followers of an oriental camp, at least of the Mahratta camp to which we were attached, I must not omit the hermaphrodites; there were a great number of them in the different bazars, and I believe all in the capacity of cooks. In mentioning these singular people, I am aware I tread on tender ground; I cannot solve doubts and difficulties, nor shall I enter into particulars repecting them. There were a considerable number of human beings called hermaphrodites in the camp, who were compelled, by way of distinguishing them from other castes, to wear the habit of a female, and the turban of a man. I was called into a private tent, to a meeting between the surgeon-major and several medical gentlemen of the army, to examine some of these people: my visit was short, and the objects disgusting. Thevenot, an author of great veracity, writes thus: "The first time I saw hermaphrodites "was at Surat; it was easy to distinguish them: for seeing there "is a great number in that town, I was informed beforehand, that "for a mark to know them by, they were obliged, under pain of "correction, to wear upon their heads a turban like men, though "they go in the habit of women."

There are doubtless many alterations and improvements of late

late years in the Mahratta tactics, which are foreign to this campaign: at that time when they intended to besiege a town, they generally encamped round the walls; and having by that measure deprived the garrison of all external means of assistance, the besieging army waited with patience until the garrison was starved into a capitulation: I have been informed, that when the Mahrattas took Ahmedabad, the capital of Guzerat, they had surrounded it in their desultory manner for several years, before the garrison surrendered. A few shot were sometimes exchanged, but seldom with effect: when I was with the Mahratta army they did not understand the use of mortars.

The war-rocket used by the Mahrattas, which very often annoyed us, is composed of an iron tube, eight or ten inches long, and near two inches in diameter; this destructive weapon is sometimes fixed to a rod of iron, sometimes to a straight two-edged sword, but most commonly to a strong bamboo cane, four or five feet long, with an iron spike projecting beyond the tube: to this rod, or staff, the tube filled with combustible materials is fastened, and on the lighted match setting fire to the fuze, is projected with great velocity; if well directed, which is an uncertain operation, it causes much confusion and dismay among the enemy, from the difficulty of avoiding its terrifying and destructive effects.

A FOOT SOLDIER *in the usual Costume of the Native* INDIANS.

Published by Richard Phillips, [illegible]

Engraved by T. Wageman.

A MAHRATTA HORSEMAN, Sketched in the Camp.

[illegible]

Published by [illegible] New Burlington St. [illegible]

CHAPTER XVIII.

CONTINUATION OF THE CAMPAIGN IN GUZERAT, FROM THE JUNCTION OF THE ENGLISH FORCE WITH RAGOBAH'S ARMY: THEIR ENGAGEMENTS WITH THE ENEMY BETWEEN THE SABERMATTY AND MYHI RIVERS; AND ENCAMPMENT NEAR BAROCHE.

1775.

But what most shews the vanity of life,
Is to behold the nations all on fire;
In cruel broils engag'd, and deadly strife:
Despotic kings, enflam'd by black desire,
With honourable ruffians in their hire,
Cause WAR to rage, and blood around to pour:
Of this sad work when each begins to tire,
They sit them down just where they were before;
Till for new scenes of woe peace shall their force restore.

THOMSON.

CONTENTS.

scenes on the field of battle—flying hospital—Ragobah's grant of thirty lacs of rupees, as a donation to the British army—names of Ragobah—the allied army cross the Myhi—pass of Fazal-poor—march to Baroche—beautiful and expensive well—beauty and fertility of the country—robbers and plunderers—Thevenot's remarks on that part of Guzerat.

CHAPTER XVIII.

SMALL parties of Ragobah's army that had been dispersed in different districts, or had not been able to keep up with the main body on their forced march to effect the junction, occasionally dropped in at Ginnich and Darah: some we had reason to suppose fell into the enemy's hands, and many were lost in fording the Sabermatty. So completely intimidated were his principal generals after their defeat on the plains of Arras, that they refused to make any movement towards joining our army unless the commander in chief sent an envoy personally to announce his arrival, and future intentions, and to assure them of the English friendship and protection. He accordingly dispatched a German gentleman, then a volunteer in our camp, with an intelligent native officer in the sepoy corps, of integrity and attachment to the defeated generals, at the Copperwange hills. Knowing we were surrounded by spies, and fearful of treachery, the envoys with only one attendant were secretly sent off at midnight, with a promise of promotion if they succeeded in the hazardous enterprize of passing the enemy's posts. After many extraordinary adventures and singular escapes, they succeeded in their mission, but the faithful German fell a sacrifice to the fatigue and hardship of the undertaking; he died a few hours after reaching his tent; the attendant was cut across the body with a sabre in passing an out-post, and the native officer was promoted.

Having at length collected all the scattered remnants we had reason to expect, we left our unpleasant encampment at Darah, and marched towards the enemy's post on the banks of the Sabermatty: the country was delightful, the land highly cultivated, and the villages populous, generally surrounded by mango and tamarind trees, overshadowing the wells and tanks which abound in Guzerat; but it being now the end of the dry season, we found all these reservoirs insufficient for our army, and we seldom remained a night without exhausting them all. The commencement of a morning march was pleasant, but by the time the Mahrattas were in motion, and the sun had gained an ascendancy, the heat and fatigue became excessive; a fierce glow impregnated the atmosphere; clouds of burning sand driven by hot winds continually overwhelmed us; and to complete the unpleasant combination, the *coup-de-soleil* frequently struck the European soldiers with instant death.

Heat and dust pervaded the camp, fetid smells and swarms of flies rendered it inconceivably offensive: I can easily suppose the plague of flies was not one of the smallest judgments inflicted on Egypt; few things, not venomous, could be more troublesome than these insects; they entirely covered our food, filled the drinking vessels, and made it difficult to distinguish the colour of a coat. Those who had read Gulliver's Travels, magnified these disagreeable effects by recollecting the loathsome slime and disgusting appearance of the flies in Brobdignag.

As we marched northward we found the villages burnt and abandoned; passing over extensive fields of wheat and other grain long ready for the sickle, our allies took away as much as they wanted, and, according to the general Mahratta system, destroyed all the remainder. We intended to halt one or two days at Versara, our next encampment, but in a single night all the wells and tanks in the neighbourhood were exhausted; we therefore proceeded the next morning towards the Sabermatty, finding that nothing less than a river could supply the necessity of such a multitude.

On our approaching the Sabermatty, a detachment of the ministerial army, posted on the southern bank, immediately crossed the river, and joined the main body, who soon commenced a disorderly retreat: the English troops forded where the water was rather shallow, and ascending the northern banks, pitched their tents without molestation. The bed of the Sabermatty was there two hundred yards broad, the stream much narrower, and seldom more than three feet deep, gliding gently over a silver sand, and abounding with carp and smaller fish: like most other rivers in India, it often overflows its banks during the rainy season, and floods the country.

The blessings of a well in the torrid zone I have endeavoured to appreciate; those of a river are inestimable: the Sabermatty was the first we saw in Guzerat; it afforded the harassed troops and cattle abundance to drink, and a delightful bath after a sultry march. The joy of our allies on encamping near the Sabermatty was extravagant: the pleasure of drinking it had long been anticipated, nor were we disappointed in the delicious beverage; the

Indians say it is both meat and drink, so nourishing and salutary that their cattle require less grain than when drinking other water. Their encomium and general delight reminded me of the water of the Nile, which Maillet, formerly French consul at Cairo, says is so delicious, that the Egyptians do not wish the heat diminished lest the sensation of thirst should subside: they eat salted things purposely to excite it anew, and when absent dwell upon the pleasure they shall enjoy in drinking it again: all foreigners who taste it, declare they never met with such water any where else, having something inexpressibly agreeable to the taste, though mingled with much sweetness. Herodotus says the Memphians filled large jars with the Nile water, and transported it to the Syrian deserts: Aristides adds that the Egpytians preserved it in earthen jars, three or four years; it never became impure; on the contrary, its value was enhanced by age, as is that of wine in other countries.

Finding the enemy were encamped within a few miles of us, we struck our tents early on the following morning, and, hoping to bring them to action, marched along the banks of the Sabermatty, to the village of Hossamlee; from whence we perceived the whole confederate army on the opposite side of the river, advancing in order of battle. The English line immediately formed, and a cannonade across the river commenced on both sides, which continued two hours; at length we silenced their guns, and compelled their left wing and centre to retire: the right kept their ground, and a strong body of cavalry crossing the river repeatedly charged a detachment under the command of captain Stewart, with two field-pieces directed by lieutenant Torriano, who repulsed them so gallantly as to be publicly thanked by the commander in chief: Ragobah presented the former with a diamond ring, the latter was promoted to the rank of captain of pioneers.

At noon the enemy retreated; they amounted to sixty thousand, chiefly cavalry: their artillery, consisting of fourteen field-pieces of different caliber, kept up a brisk fire for some time, but from being too much elevated, did little execution: they were served by Europeans, mostly French. The confederates lost two sirdars, or principal officers, several of inferior rank, and about four hundred men, besides three elephants, and a number of horses and camels; in the English line three Europeans and five sepoys were wounded, none killed; Ragobah's army seemed to be mere spectators.

The river dividing the armies, our fatigued troops were incapable of pursuing flying cavalry; we therefore marched a mile further, and encamped near Hossamlee, on ground lately occupied by the enemy; who in that expectation had cut down the trees, destroyed the village, and burnt all the corn and provender they could not carry off; the surrounding plain, deprived of its verdant ornaments, was covered with putrid carcases and burning ashes: the hot wind wafting from these, fetid odours, and dispersing the ashes among the tents, rendered our encampment extremely disagreeable. During the night hyænas, jackals, and wild beasts of various kinds, allured by the scent, prowled over the field with a horrid noise; and the next morning a multitude of vultures, kites, and birds of prey were seen asserting their claim to a share of the dead. It was to me a scene replete with horrid novelty, realizing the prophet's denunciation: "I will appoint over them four kinds, saith the Lord;

the sword to slay, and the dogs to tear, and the fowls of heaven and the beasts of the earth to devour and destroy."

We remained two days in this disgusting situation, and crossing the Sabermatty on the third morning, marched six miles, through a delightful country, to the village of Chonwar, where we encamped in a large mango grove on the banks of the Wartruc, or Bakruc; a small river which joins the Sabermatty at a little distance. The enemy appearing on the opposite side, our artillery commenced a brisk fire, and compelled them to retreat towards Kairah, a fortified town belonging to Futty Sihng, one of the confederate chieftains, a few miles to the northward.

We followed them early the next morning, and fording the Wartruc near the village of Mahter, four miles from our last ground, halted on the opposite banks, while the artillery and baggage crossed the river: this being effected, we marched towards Kairah, when a large body of the enemy suddenly appeared on our right flank, advancing at full charge. Captains Stewart and Torriano, now appointed brigade major, advancing with a small reconnoitering party, were nearly taken prisoners, having only time to unlimber an eight-inch howitzer, which stopped the enemy's career until the line was formed to receive them. A discharge of artillery soon checked their ardour, and turned their attention to the rear of our allies, where Ragobah was stationed on his state elephant: but finding an English detachment, with two field-pieces, posted there for his protection, they made a precipitate retreat.

In this action the confederates were reported to have lost twelve hundred men, killed and wounded. Ragobah's halcarras and spies, no doubt, thought to please him by a little exaggeration; half that amount was probably nearer the truth: their artillery was not so well served as formerly, but their cavalry made some desperate charges on the allies, who received them with intrepidity, and in general behaved well; several were killed, and many wounded: among the latter was Saccaram-Hurra, paymaster-general of Ragobah's forces and one of his prime ministers; the English detachment did not lose a man. One of the peshwa's elephant-drivers being wounded, the elephant escaped, and was taken by the enemy. I mention the loss of this animal because the Asiatics consider them a valuable and honourable spoil; as much so as Europeans estimate cannon and standards.

Before the engagement a spy was detected in the camp of the allies, and carried into Ragobah's presence, who ordered his tongue to be cut out previous to his being returned to the enemy. As the poor wretch could neither write nor read, this might be intended as a figurative oriental language, and the measure, however cruel to the individual, was perhaps necessary. The miseries of war are manifold; but from a wish to condense the events of the campaign, I suppress reflections which naturally occur to every feeling mind. It was sometimes deemed necessary to hang a person suspected as a spy, and to finish the execution; at others, when neither threats nor half-hanging could extort a confession, it was thought proper to lower the struggling wretch, slacken the cord, and restore suspended animation to a harmless villager who had unfortunately strayed too near the line.

Necessity alone compels Britons to adopt these stern decrees: a different spirit rules the Asiatics: the Mogul history is replete with blood, nor is the Hindoo character free from cruelty and revenge. It has been remarked that the sway of a despotic government has taught the Hindoos patience, and the coldness of their imagination enables them to practise it better than any people in the world; they conceive a contemptible opinion of a man's capacity who betrays any impetuosity in his temper: they are the acutest buyers and sellers in the world, and preserve through all their bargains a degree of calmness which baffles all the arts that can be opposed against it. This will be allowed by those most conversant with their general character, but they also know that the patient Hindoo who shudders at the death of an insect, and preserves the tranquillity of temper just mentioned, can as calmly meditate on the most cruel tortures prepared for an enemy, or one he deems to be so: the love of money is in general his ruling passion; throughout Hindostan cruelty and oppression are the servants of avarice.

We encamped, after the action, on the field of battle, a hot sandy plain, without a tree, or any kind of shade; yet being on the banks of the Wartruc, it was preferable to a cooler situation without that advantage. After remaining there three days, we marched towards Kairah: before the vanguard had proceeded half a mile, the enemy suddenly appeared, advancing rapidly towards us; the British line immediately formed, and on firing a few shot, they retreated to Kairah; this detained us some time, and the day becoming intensely hot, we encamped on the spot; early the next morning we marched under the walls of Kairah without molestation, and found the confederate army had retired to some distance.

Kairah, a large town, situated at the confluence of the Serry and Wartruc rivers, is fortified in the Indian manner with a brick wall flanked by irregular towers, mounting forty-seven guns; the buildings were almost concealed by trees. Leaving Kairah unmolested, we marched to Coomlah, and pitched our tents in a delightful spot near the village, on the banks of the Serry, a small deep river, abounding with fish; the surrounding country was covered with wild fruit trees, and berries of a beautiful hue and pleasant flavour, which we found refreshing during a sultry march; these indigenous fruits and some tasteless figs were all that remained, the enemy having robbed the country of all the ripening mangos, tamarinds, and other valuable productions.

Happy would it have been for the delightful province of Guzerat, had their depredations been confined to such devastation; but alas! all was laid waste and destroyed. The peaceable Hindoos, by whom Guzerat is mostly inhabited, are greatly to be pitied, from its being so often the seat of war; for notwithstanding the frequent changes of their oppressors, from a Mogul nabob to a Mahratta chief, the lower classes take very little concern in such revolutions. They seldom quit the village where their fathers were born and died; there they plough the fields, reap the harvest, and tend the cattle to the groves and lakes which surround their humble dwellings, built of mud and straw, where their wives and daughters spin cotton, grind corn, and prepare their simple repast of pulse, milk, and vegetables. It must be allowed that too large a share of the produce is collected for the government, and its subordinate despots; yet in general a sufficiency is left for the peasantry, whose wants are few, to encourage them to remain at home, and renew the annual cultivation.

Thus peaceably they pass their lives with the monkeys, squirrels, and peacocks attached to every village, which, although in a manner wild, and perfectly independent, seem fondly to associate with man, and are universally fostered and protected. The peacocks find sustenance in the cullies, or threshing floors, where the corn is trod out by oxen, and divided among the villagers; there the playful squirrels claim a little share, while the cunning monkeys, concealed in the overhanging branches, watch a favourable opportunity to jump down, and carry off a considerable portion. The trees are also enlivened by a variety of small birds, never molested, who repay their benefactors in a wild melody. I made many additions to my oriental ornithology in Guzerat, especially among the muscicapæ, or fly-catchers.

The villagers, who seldom visit cities, preserve an innocent simplicity of manners; the women are modest and delicate; their drapery, however coarse, is rendered becoming by an elegant carelessness of the folds, and their attitudes are peculiarly graceful. Greatly resembling the pastoral manners of the Mesopotamian damsels in the patriarchal days, the young women of Guzerat daily draw water from the public wells, and sometimes carry two or three earthen jars, placed over each other, upon the head; which requiring perfect steadiness, gives them an erect and stately air. An English lady in India, whose great delight was to illustrate the sacred volume by a comparison with the modern manners and customs of the Hindoos, reading the interesting interview between

Abraham's servant and Rebecca at the gate of Nahor to an intelligent native, when she came to that passage where the virgin went down to the well with her pitcher *upon her shoulder*, her attentive friend exclaimed, " Madam, that woman was of high caste:" this he implied from the circumstance of carrying the pitcher upon her shoulder, and not on her head. Some of the highest classes among the brahmins do the same.

The Guzerat villagers are not without their amusements, being often visited by travelling comedians, who exhibit puppet-shows and act historical plays by these miniature performers with laughable effect. Musicians, dancing-girls, singing men and women, occasionally beguile an idle hour; jugglers and wrestlers perform extraordinary feats of agility and sleight of hand; dancing-bears, trickish goats and monkeys, are also carried about for amusement.

Such was the peaceful state of Guzerat. During the war this pleasing picture was sadly reversed; the villages were deserted and destroyed, the harvests reaped by lawless marauders, and not a passenger to be seen on the public roads: the cattle that had escaped the armies, were driven for protection under the walls of cities, where the peasants were promiscuously huddled together in famine and wretchedness of every description. The melancholy situation of the Guzerat peasants is pathetically pictured in the song of Deborah. " The enemy came up with their cattle and " their tents, and they came as locusts for multitude, for both " them and their camels were without number, and they entered " into the land to destroy it. The highways were unoccupied, and " the travellers walked through by-ways; the inhabitants of the "villages ceased; the noise of archers drove them from the places "of drawing water: they betook themselves to the dens in the "mountains, and to caves and strong holds. When they had "sown, the enemy came up, even the children of the east came "up against them; and encamped, and destroyed the increase "of the earth, and left no substance, neither sheep, nor ox, "nor ass."

We marched next to Hyderabad, where we were once more suddenly interrupted by the confederate army, who had taken the advantage of a commanding situation to renew the attack; in about two hours we again repulsed them with great loss, few in the English line were killed or wounded, but our allies suffered considerably, the enemy directing their principal fire to that quarter where Ragobah, on a state elephant, displayed the imperial standard. At the commencement of the action I happened to be within a few yards of the peshwa, and finding myself in the immediate line of fire, took shelter under a large mango-tree, with a great number of his troops who ought to have been better employed. The shot falling thick among us, I endeavoured to save my head by standing under a large arm of the tree, my body being perfectly secured by the pressure of the crowd. I had not long enjoyed its protection when a cannon ball struck the branch, and shivered it over us. Nothing could exceed the panic of the motley group by which I was surrounded; Ragobah at the same instant alighting from his elephant increased their consternation, and caused them to bear away like a flood, by which I was carried a considerable distance, without touching the ground, among wounded horses, elephants, camels, and oxen, all running off in an indescribable confusion of dreadful yells, furious hot blasts, and clouds of burning sand. The enemy now advanced so near the British line that our grape-shot and musquetry did great execution, and some shells bursting among their cavalry compelled them to make a hasty and confused retreat; a deep narrow river dividing the armies saved their guns.

Exclusive of those who fell in action, the battle of Hyderabad was attended by many catastrophes on the part of our allies. While I was under the mango-tree a cannon-ball tore off the horns of an ox, and another, in passing a young woman suckling her infant within a few yards of me, carried it from her breast. During the engagement at Hossamlee, sitting with the surgeon-major under a banian-tree, at the portico of a Hindoo temple, anxious to know the proceedings on the field of battle, we desired one of the palanquin-bearers to mount on a high branch, and give us information: he did so, and while making his report a cannon-ball took off his head; the body falling at our feet occasioned a precipitate retreat within the walls of the temple.

The brigade major, who had frequently led Ragobah's cavalry to the charge, was present at an extraordinary scene during the action at Hyderabad. A detachment of cavalry advanced from each of the Mahratta armies, one headed by three brothers, the other by two more who had espoused a different cause: each party endeavoured to convince the other they were acting wrong, and during the parley both sides remained inactive. Had there been a prospect of accommodation, it would have been rendered ineffectual by one of the brothers who had joined the ministers tauntingly observing that Ragobah was more indebted to the English artillery for his late successes, than to the prowess of his generals: this irritated the peshwa's friends; from high words they proceeded to a furious combat, in which one of the opposite party lost his life, and another left his hand and broken scimitar on the field.

Finding the enemy retreated after every engagement, and yet continued near enough to molest us and cut off our supplies, knowing also that harassed European infantry were incapable of pursuing flying cavalry, and that our Mahratta allies would never advance half a mile from the British line, Ragobah assembled his principal generals and the English commander to a council of war in the durbar tent, when it was determined no longer to follow the enemy in the northern parts of Guzerat, but to penetrate into the Deccan without delay, and endeavour by quick marches to reach Poonah, the Mahratta capital, before the setting in of the rains.

Many of us regretted the intended march to the southern districts without seeing the imperial city of Ahmedabad, the metropolis of Guzerat, celebrated in oriental history as the occasional residence of the Mogul emperors, and still indicating many splendid remains of ancient grandeur. Deprived of this gratification, we commenced our march southwards, towards Neriad: detached parties of the enemies cavalry hovered near us, and endeavoured to retard our progress, but were always repulsed with little loss on our side. They had not yet encamped in the country through which our route now lay, we therefore found its natural beauties undiminished; and although deficient in picturesque inequality of hill and dale, it was covered with enclosures highly cultivated, rich groves, and extensive lakes, abounding with game, hares and partridges being often taken close to the tents. On finding us taking a southern route, the enemy sent detachments to burn the villages and provender, and to drain the wells and lakes; so that all the cottages around us were in flames, and the smoke of distant towns and hamlets indicated their further ravages.

To see this beautiful and fertile country destroyed, and its wretched inhabitants compelled to fly to foreign states for protection, added a poignancy to other distresses. The calamities of war fall heavily on the Indian peasantry: the collectors in those despotic governments make no abatements of rent nor attend to any remonstrance: nothing remains for the wretched farmer but the cruel alternative of flight or punishment.

> " O! think to these depopulated realms
> " What dreadful mischiefs from ambition flow;
> " But heroes, whirl'd in victory's thundering car,
> " Nor hear the widow's cry, nor orphan's woe!"

Aurungzebe, marching through Hindostan, set an example worthy the imitation of other princes, by observing the most exact discipline, and permitting no ravages nor injustice by his troops: when he encamped among corn lands, he either paid the estimated value to the owners, or ordered a receipt to be given for it, as part of the revenue due to the crown; saying, " Although I am compelled into a war by the machinations of my brother, I cannot consider myself as in an enemy's country." Ragobah was now in a similar situation, but neither himself nor the army he commanded paid any attention to such humane considerations.

We marched to Neriad through a continuation of the lovely country just mentioned. This city was the capital of Conda Row, uncle to Govind Row, one of Ragobah's principal partizans, then with his army at the head of eight thousand cavalry; Conda Row had also promised to join his standard with a considerable force; but uniting with his other nephew, Futty Sihng, one of the most powerful chieftains in Guzerat, they went over to the opposite party, and fought for them during the whole campaign.

These princes were all styled Guickwar, in addition to their family name, as Futty Sihng Row Guickwar, Govind Row Guickwar, and Conda Row Guickwar; the word literally means a cow-keeper, which, although a low employment in general, has, in this noble family among the Hindoos, who venerate that animal, become a title of great importance. As they possess a large domain in Guzerat contiguous to the British provinces, and as their history is blended with the Mahrattas, and in the political and territorial arrangements with the English in that part of India, I shall detail the accounts I collected with some difficulty on our march and subsequent encampments in the Guickwar dominions.

By the conquests obtained over the Moguls in Guzerat, the beginning of the eighteenth century, the Mahrattas annexed the greater part of this rich country to their rising empire: these conquests were gained entirely by Pilajee, and his son Damajee, two renowned generals of the Guickwar family, who thereby possessed so much power, wealth, and influence in Guzerat, that the Poonah government, fearful of their adopting the system of the Mogul nabobs, and becoming totally independent, gave them a jaghire, or grant, of their large possessions, including some of the richest purgunnas and principal cities in the province.

The revenue, as well as the government, of these districts was assigned over to them and their heirs for ever, on condition of paying the Mahratta government an annual tribute of eight lacs of rupees, and furnishing three thousand horsemen armed and accoutred for the public service, to be maintained at the expense of the Guickwar family, agreeably to the feudal tenure already mentioned. It was further stipulated, that on urgent occasions the Guickwar princes should furnish the state with a troop of two thousand cavalry extraordinary, to be paid for from the public treasury at Poonah, and by this treaty one of the family was always to be stationed at the Mahratta capital in command of the Guzerat troops.

Damajee succeeded his father Pilajee in the sole command of the Guickwar domain, and died only a few years before the commencement of the civil wars which carried us into this noble principality. Damajee left five sons, Siajee Row, Govind Row, Futty Sihng, Monackjee, and an infant prince, with Guickwar added to each name. Damajee having been married some years, and his wife proving barren, he took a second, in conformity to the Hindoo law, which in such cases admits of polygamy; by her he had two sons, Siajee and Futty Sihng. A few months after the birth of the latter, his first wife, so long childless, bore a son, named Govind Row. After this Damajee had several children; Siajee, the eldest, being a lunatic, was set aside from the inheritance, and when we were in Guzerat resided at Songhur, a southern fortress. Govind Row, although in fact a few months younger than Futty

Sihng, was by the Hindoo law entitled to inherit his father's possessions, from being the eldest son of his first wife, in preference to Futty Sihng, the fruit of a second marriage: this was the cause of the disputes then subsisting in the Guickwar family.

At the time of Damajee's death Futty Sihng was at Brodera, the capital of the Guickwar domain, Govind Row commanded the Guzerat troops at Poonah: Futty Sihng immediately seized the patrimony, and being of good capacity, endowed with a large share of that cunning which constitutes a Mahratta politician, and well acquainted with the venality of the peshwa's court, when he remitted the stipulated tribute to the Poonah treasury, always accompanied it by a valuable present from himself to the peshwa and nobles, that they might detain Govind Row in the Deccan; there being nothing he so much dreaded as his brother coming in person to claim his paternal inheritance. The character of these brothers was very different, and so much in favour of Govind Row, that Futty Sihng apprehended a revolt should he appear in Guzerat: his bribery to a corrupt ministry overbalanced the merit and just pretensions of Govind Row, until the massacre of Narron Row in 1773.

Govind Row, long stationed at Poonah, had been always a a firm friend to Ragobah, and on his accession to the Mahratta government he obtained leave to proceed with his troops to Guzerat, and claim his patrimony: he accordingly appeared at the head of a considerable force before the walls of Brodera, which Futty Sihng, with a strong garrison, resolved to defend to the last extremity. At this time the civil war breaking out in the empire, Ragobah left Poonah for Guzerat, while Govind Row and ten thousand men were investing Brodera. Ragobah, then in reversed circumstances, claimed his friendship and personal attendance with all his men. Gratitude for past favours from his unfortunate prince, with the prospect of seeing himself in possession of his legal patrimony, induced him to comply with Ragobah's request; relinquishing his own cause, he cheerfully enlisted under Ragobah's standard, and was from that time a faithful friend in all his adverse fortune, though strongly solicited to join the confederate generals.

On effecting the junction between Ragobah's army and the English detachment near Cambay, Futty Sihng, fearful of our proceeding against Brodera, commenced a correspondence with Ragobah, and sent a vackeel, or envoy, to the British commander, who concluded a treaty in which he promised to desert the enemy and join us on the first favourable opportunity. An English gentleman was sent to him, at his express desire, for the ratification, which he most craftily eluded by pretending that the confederate generals, among whom he was encamped, had got intelligence of the negociation, that he was surrounded by spies, and would not answer for his personal safety unless the treaty was instantly destroyed, not by tearing it in pieces, but by mastication, that not a particle of it might be visible, and no fire could be procured to burn it without suspicion. The gentleman complied in part, and was glad to be escorted safely to the British lines. The whole was discovered to be an artful contrivance of Futty Sihng, who had made better terms with the confederates than the English, and afterwards openly fought against us in every action.

Neriad being the principal town belonging to Conda Row, who had joined in all Futty Sihng's machinations against Ragobah, he determined to give it up to pillage, or levy a contribution from the inhabitants. This city is one of the prettiest in Guzerat, nearly three miles in circumference, fortified in the eastern manner with a slight wall flanked by round towers at irregular distances; it has nine strong gates, and a dry ditch round the walls: in the seventeenth century it was a place of great trade, frequented by the English and Dutch merchants, and now contained about twelve thousand families, chiefly employed in fabricating the finest baftas, and other cotton manufactures: they also cut and polish the sprig stones from Copperwange, in a beautiful manner.

On approaching Neriad, Conda Row's Subahdar sent the keys of the garrison to Ragobah, accompanied by every token of respect and submission, in hopes of preventing the intended hostilities: he offered terms, and British troops took possession of the gates until they were settled. The confederate army only left Neriad the day before our arrival, and were then encamped within ten miles, waiting our movements. We pitched our tents near the walls among rich groves of mangos and tamarinds, and copses of an inferior kind of sandal-wood, with a profusion of good wells and an extensive lake.

Ragobah, considering Conda Row's delinquency, was thought to have been very moderate in levying a contribution of only sixty thousand rupees on the inhabitants of Neriad; which, as usual, they refused to pay until the threats of immediate pillage effected a compliance. Each caste was assessed according to its wealth and number; but some sects of Brahmins, and a very peculiar tribe of people called Bhauts, claimed an established privilege of being exempted from every kind of tax and imposition.

The Bhauts reside chiefly in the province of Guzerat, but are not unknown in other parts of India; like the troubadors and minstrels in Europe in the days of chivalry, they seem chiefly occupied in repeating verses of their own composition, or selections from the mythological legends of the Hindoos; they chant their verses in a style peculiar to themselves, not unpleasing to a stranger, as the modulation of the voice, and an energetic graceful action give effect to the poetry; which, like the old ballads in Europe, is either to praise some renowned warrior, commemorate a victory, record a tragical event, or panegyrise a present object. The Hindoo rajahs and Mahratta chieftains have generally a Bhaut in their family, who attends them on public occasions, and visits of ceremony; during these processions he loudly sounds their praise, and proclaims their titles in hyperbolical and figurative language. Tacitus mentions the historic songs and traditions of the German bards: the Greeks and other ancient nations encouraged them; perhaps Homer himself may be included in a class which like him repeat their legendary tales, and are the oral historians of the country.

Although this is the usual occupation of the Bhauts, many of them have another mode of living; they offer themselves as security to the different governments for payment of their revenue, and the good behaviour of the Zemindars, Patels, and public farmers; they also become guarantees for treaties between rival princes, and the performance of bonds by individuals. No security is esteemed so binding or sacred as that of a Bhaut, because, on failure of the obligation, he proceeds to the house of the offending party, and in his presence destroys either himself or one of his family, imprecating the most dreadful vengeance of the gods on the head of him who had compelled them to shed their blood. This is deemed a dire catastrophe; as the Hindoos are taught to believe that the Bhaut's life, to which a superstitious veneration is attached, over and above their common horror of bloodshed, will be demanded from the aggressor by an offended deity; it is therefore very uncommon for an obligation to be broken where a Bhaut stands security.

For this responsibility the Bhauts receive an annual stipend from the district, village, or individual they guarantee: they sign their name and place of abode to the agreement, but instead of affixing their seal, as customary among the other tribes, they draw the figure of the catarra, or dagger, their usual instrument of death.

This custom of the Bhauts shedding their own blood, or that of their family, has some analogy with many passages in ancient history, especially among those nations who ratified their solemn covenants by a bloody sacrifice. One method was to kill an ox, and after many religious rites, to distribute it in pieces among their friends; all who eat of it were from that moment connected by a sacred tie, and bound to perform their part of the covenant, whether to revenge an injury, or for any other purpose. Lucian says, " When any one of the ancient Scythians received an injury, and had not the means of avenging himself, he sacrificed an ox, and cut it in pieces, which he caused to be dressed, and publicly exposed; he then spread out the skin of the victim, and sat upon it with his hands tied behind him. All who chose to take a part in the injury which had been done, took up a piece of the ox, and swore to revenge him according to their respective ability." Herodotus mentions a circumstance of the same people still more resembling the public engagements of the Bhauts, on the occasion where the contracting parties cut their arms with a knife, and let the blood run into a bowl of wine: of which all who were present drank, with the most dreadful impecations against him who should violate the treaty.

The Ayeen Akbery mentions Charuns and Bhauts, both employed in singing hymns of celebration, and reciting genealogies; in repeating martial feats during a battle to animate the troops, and in discovering parables and secret things: every great man in those days had several in his service, both Bhauts and Charuns; the former equalled the latter in poetical talent, and excelled them in chronology.

Although the Bhauts possess landed property, and cultivate it by the tribes employed in agriculture, as a privileged order they are exempted from taxes, and every attempt to levy an assessment is succeeded by the *Tarakaw*, a most horrid mode of murdering themselves and each other: this, from invariable custom, it is absolutely incumbent upon them to do; for were they voluntarily to submit to any imposition, those of their own tribe in other places would refuse to eat with them, or to intermarry with their family; they therefore prefer a voluntary death to this state of ignominy and excommunication.

Many families of this tribe resided in Neriad, from whence

they travelled when wanted officially, and were always considered as a most respectable part of the community. As this city had been twice assessed and plundered in the three preceding months, Ragobah's imposition reduced the inhabitants to the greatest distress. The most melancholy scenes occurred in every quarter, of families delivering up their last mite, and houses robbed of every moveable to answer their proportion of the tax: if insufficient, the wretched owners, stripped of clothes and necessaries, were left in nakedness and poverty; or, under pretence of secreting valuables they never possessed, tortures were inflicted with merciless rigour. So common are these executions among the Mahrattas, that our allies thought nothing of the cruelties in Neriad. Britons were not so unconcerned, their generous bosoms glowed with indignation against such wanton oppression: but all remonstrances were vain; Ragobah and his officers, like Gallio of Achaia, "cared for none of those things."

When these cruelties and the refusal of the Bhauts to pay the tax were reported in the English camp, the commanding officer sent the brigade-major privately into the town, to convene the principal Bhauts, and assure them if they discharged their quota quietly, they might rely upon protection, sincerely lamenting the necessity of the measure. The heads of the tribe informed the officer they were able to pay more than was demanded in any other mode, but if Ragobah persisted in compulsory assessment, they should prefer death to submission.

These humane remonstrances and persuasions proving ineffectual, and Ragobah continuing inexorable, the whole tribe of Bhauts, men, women, and children, repaired to an open space in the city, armed with daggers, and with a loud voice proclaimed a dreadful sacrifice: they once more prayed for an exemption, which being refused, they rushed furiously upon each other, and a considerable number perished before our astonished troops could disarm them. One man, more cool and deliberate than the rest, brought his family to the area before the durbar: it consisted of two younger brothers, and a beautiful sister, all under eighteen years of age; he first stabbed the unresisting damsel to the heart, instantly plunged the dagger into the breast of one brother, and desperately wounded the other before he could be prevented; indeed the whole horrid deed was in a manner instantaneous. I afterwards heard this man boast of having sacrificed his father a few months before in the glorious cause for which he had now become a fratricide.

A particular sect of brahmins claimed the same privilege of exemption: on being refused, they likewise vowed revenge; but acting more wisely than the Bhauts, they purchased two aged matrons of the same caste, who having performed the duties of life, were now past the enjoyment of its pleasures, and quietly submitted to the sacrifice. These ancient ladies were sold by their daughters for forty rupees each, to enable them to defray the expense incurred by the funeral ceremonies, on which the Indians all lay a great stress. The victims were then conducted to the market-place, where the brahmins, calling aloud for vengeance, dispatched them to another state of transmigration. After these sacrifices neither brahmins nor Bhauts thought it any disgrace to pay their share of the imposition. What an anomaly is sometimes found in the human character, and what a deviation from the general system does the conduct of these people exhibit!

> "Our depths who fathoms, or our shallows finds,
> "Quick whirls, and shifting eddies of our minds?
> "On human actions, reason though you can,
> "It may be REASON, but it is not MAN;
> "'Tis education forms the common mind,
> "Just as the twig is bent, the tree's inclined."
>
> POPE.

The Neriad assessment being at length collected, on the 14th of May we left that ill-fated city, and marched towards the river Myhi. During our progress the enemy's advanced cavalry burnt every village on the road, destroyed the forage, and as far as possible exhausted the tanks and wells; their whole army came twice unexpectedly upon us, but were repulsed with loss. It was sometimes reported that they poisoned the wells and tanks, as well as burnt the villages and corn-ricks: the latter we daily witnessed, but I do not recollect an instance of the former more than once, and then it appeared doubtful. To our numerous army and camp-followers that step would have been of little consequence, unless they could have produced deleterious effects on an extensive lake; since, as already observed, nothing less could satisfy us for more than one night; brooks at this late season were dried up, and we never allowed them time to alter the course of a river, as is sometimes practised. Hezekiah, on the approach of the Assyrian army to Jerusalem, took counsel with his princes and mighty men to stop the waters of the fountains which were without the city, and the brook that ran though the midst of the land; Babylon was taken by turning the course of the Euphrates: and many modern oriental cities would easily fall by the same means.

On the 18th we reached the plains of Arras, the spot which had been so fatal to Ragobah in his last battle with the ministerial army, before the English junction: there, in conformity to the Hindoo superstition of omens, astrological calculations, and Brahminical predictions, the enemy resolved once more to try their fortune in a general action. Most of the Indians firmly believe in omens, whether from cows, birds, or accidental circumstances; ignorant and superstitious, the brahmins and Mullahs encourage such a disposition, and make their advantage of it. The practice of astrology has prevailed in a greater or less degree among most nations unenlightened by Christianity. Suetonius mentions the army of Vitellius to have been directed by the flight of an eagle in the way they were to march. "Præmisso agmini lœtum evenit auspicium; siquidem a parte dextra repente aquila advolavit: lustratisque signis, ingressos viam sensim antecessit." Homer abounds in omens; the Jews were continually requiring signs and tokens, and positively ordered to place no confidence in diviners, nor to hearken to dreamers.

Ragobah and the superstitious brahmins who surrounded him were aware of the prevailing opinion in the enemy's camp; they doubtless performed many prayers and ceremonies to avert the fatal consequences, but we had reason to suppose they placed greater confidence in British valour, superior tactics, and formidable artillery: still it was unpleasant as well as inconvenient to act under such a superstitious prince. A few days before our arrival at Neriad, the enemy on a particular occasion sent a herald under a flag of truce to Ragobah, and at the same time the officer who accompanied him informed the colonel, that if we (the English) would quit their guns, they would be more upon a par with each other, and it would shew a more generous courage; or, if we selected a champion from our forces, they would appoint another from theirs to meet him, and decide the event of the war by single combat; but that the effects of our grape-shot and shells were unfair and cruel.

On entering the plains of Arras we perceived the enemy advancing in two divisions, who soon commenced a cannonade on the rear, where Ragobah was seated on his state elephant: his body guard, at his particular request, had been this day strongly reinforced from the English detachment. Our line immediately formed, and a further reinforcement of infantry was ordered to Ragobah's assistance, but no artillery; the field pieces remained with the line, and kept up a heavy fire till the enemy's cannon were silenced, and their cavalry dispersed with considerable loss. The colonel having frequently told Ragobah that he would attack the enemy's guns whenever they brought them on a plain without the separation of a river, now gave orders for a strong party to advance and take them. The detachment was immediately formed, and advanced with captains Myers and Serle at the head of their companies of European infantry, and a strong party of sepoys. The enemy on observing our intention returned at full speed with their artillery, and threw in a large body of cavalry between our advanced party and their guns, who twice charged the British detachment with great impetuosity: they were repulsed and fled. At this time another large body of cavalry, with several war elephants, penetrated between our advanced party and the British line, who declaring themselves Ragobah's partizans, were permitted to approach unmolested; especially as their assertions were confirmed by Hurra Punt, an officer of rank in his army. Here we were fatally deceived, and Hurra Punt proved a traitor! Several among our allies overheard this infamous man calling on the enemy to seize the opportunity of striking a decisive blow, by cutting off the advanced division; in consequence they commenced a vigorous attack, and nearly surrounded them by their elephants and cavalry. Our brave fellows repulsed them gallantly in front and rear; many were cut to pieces, among them captains Myers and Serle: when by some unaccountable mistake of the officer who then took the command, the grenadiers facing to the right about, to change their ground, commenced a retreat; the other Europeans and sepoys followed their example. Unfortunately at this time a tumbril of shells belonging to the howitzer, pierced by a rocket, blew up, and added to the general confusion. Although our men retired with precipitation, they preserved some order until they reached an impenetrable hedge of the thorny milk-bush; here they entirely broke their ranks, and leaving a field-piece in the hands of the enemy, endeavoured to push through the formidable barrier, though repeatedly ordered by the surviving officers to form. Another body now advanced against this devoted detachment; their officers in vain endeavoured to rally them, and fell a sacrifice. The enemy pursued the fugitives to the advancing British line, which now recommenced a brisk fire; our grape-shot and shells at length drove off the whole confederate army, and we remained masters of the field. The brigade major with a company of grenadiers had previously retaken the field-piece; the tumbril of ammunition was lost in the explosion.

The engagement lasted near four hours. Situated as we were in respect to Europeans, the victory was dearly purchased: out of fifteen British officers in the advanced division, seven were killed and four wounded, besides a great many native officers and two hundred sepoys; we also had to lament eighty Europeans killed and missing, mostly grenadiers. The officers at that unfortunate crisis separated from the line, and, deserted by their soldiers, bravely fell in the bed of honour. I had been conversing with most of them during the morning march, and in the evening was called to bury them in a large pit with their unfortunate comrades. A field of battle is indeed a scene of horror!

> "For then does DEATH line his dead chaps with steel,
> "The swords of soldiers are his teeth, his fangs;
> "And now he feasts, mouthing the flesh of men,
> "In undetermin'd differences of kings!" SHAKESPEARE.

During the retreat of our advanced division a Mahratta officer of cavalry came upon ensign Tureen, a gallant youth of sixteen, who lay upon the ground severely wounded: he ordered him to mount behind on horseback immediately; the young officer declared it to be impossible, from loss of blood, and the nature of his wounds; the Mahratta then ordered him to deliver his sash as a token to his commanding officer that he had done his duty; which having complied with, he was instantly ran over by a troop of cavalry, and almost trampled to death. He was again severely wounded in colonel Bailie's memorable action in the Carnatic, and finished his short career of glory in a subsequent engagement with the sultan of Mysore.

In the battle of Arras the confederates lost several principal officers, and upwards of a thousand men, with a number of horses and elephants; many of the Mahrattas fell in attempting to carry off the killed and wounded, an act of humanity to which they pay the greatest attention. They seldom leave a body on the field, and venture almost to the cannon's mouth, rather than suffer the remains of a friend to be exposed: out of the number killed in this action only seven bodies were found after their retreat.

The dreadful scenes on the field of battle before the sepulture of our dead, and the removal of the wounded, together with the groans of elephants, camels, horses and oxen, expiring by hundreds, united to the noise of vultures, and screams of other ravenous birds hovering over them, realized the sublime invitation in sacred writ for the birds of prey to come to the feast of death. "Come, and gather yourselves together, that ye may eat the flesh of kings, and the flesh of captains, and the flesh of mighty men, and the flesh of horses, and of them that sat thereon, both small and great."

The traitor Hurra Punt, who betrayed our unfortunate detachment into the enemy's hands, was punished as his infamous conduct deserved; a grenadier sepoy of the British line pulled him from his horse, and Ragobah's Arabs, who had suffered severely by his treachery, cut him to pieces.

We continued several hours on the field of battle, assisting the wounded, and burying the dead: the heat was intense, and the plains of Arras not affording a drop of water, we proceeded towards the banks of the Myhi; but, unable to reach that noble river, we encamped at Bettassee, a good village, where providentially meeting with some large wells, and a tank not quite exhausted, we remained the next day to perform the necessary amputations, and administer such comfort as we could to the sick and wounded; our flying hospital now consisting of more than four hundred patients, most of them in violent fevers in consequence of the extreme heat, and the wounds received in the battle of Arras.

About this time Ragobah, or rather Ragonath Row, peshwa of the Mahratta empire, signed a phirmaun, or grant, by which he engaged himself to pay the English detachment under colonel Keating employed in his service, the sum of thirty lacs of rupees on his arrival at Poonah, and re-establishment in the government of the Mahratta empire; specifying that this donation is intended in lieu of plunder, prize-money, and all demands of that kind. This is a usual method of recompensing European troops for their services to the Indian princes.

I have already mentioned the inconvenience and confusion occasioned by calling the same person by different names. In this instrument of royalty, Ragobah styles himself Ragonauth Row, Ballajee Peshwa, Pundit Purdun, of the Mahratta empire. This was his title as sovereign. Ragonauth Row was his name of respect; Ragobah that by which he was generally addressed, and called by the army; and Dadah-Saheb, the familiar and endeared name used by his family.

The following morning we crossed the Myhi at the pass of Fazal-poor: on approaching the banks, we found the ground full of hollow ways, and ravines two or three hundred feet deep; the steep banks were bare of trees, but covered with prickly bushes. The celebrated pass at Fazal-poor is a deep narrow defile, where only one of our baggage carts, exceeding four hundred in number, could proceed at a time, on a very indifferent road; here the enemy might have annoyed us, but we were suffered to pass unmolested. The bed of the river is there about four hundred yards broad, but the pellucid stream, running over a silver sand and shells, does not exceed fifty at that advanced season.

We fully expected to have encountered the enemy at Fazal-poor. On the preceding evening the brigade major volunteered to proceed from Bettassee, and reconnoitre the pass and fortress on the banks of the Myhi, where, from the natural strength of the position, we supposed the confederates would make a stand. Ragobah ordered a select troop of cavalry to accompany the major on this service, and provided a fleet, to facilitate his retreat, if necessary. They returned at midnight, with the pleasing intelligence that the enemy had crossed the Myhi after the battle of Arras, and leaving a garrison in Fazal-poor, the main-body proceeded in full speed towards the Nerbudda, and left the pass of the Myhi free. On the brigade major's report, captain Stuart offered to march immediately to Fazal-poor with his battalion of sepoys, and drive the enemy from the fort, but the commanding officer thought the risk too great for the proposed object.

At sun-set the English detachment, artillery and stores, had all safely crossed the Myhi; we encamped on the southern banks, and early in next morning marched towards Baroche, where it was intended to halt a few days, to obtain a supply of money, ammunition and stores, and to send the sick and wounded to the hospital. On leaving Fazal-poor, we proceeded through a continuation of deep defiles, and almost subterraneous passes, for two miles; from whence we entered a cultivated plain, in the Brodera Purgunna, which having hitherto escaped the ravages of war, presented a perfect garden.

Near a village called Sevasee Contra, I left the line of march, to sketch a remarkable building, which formed an oblong square of two hundred feet by fifty; the walls were low, and a small dome at each corner gave it the appearance of a Mahomedan mausoleum. On a nearer approach, I discovered it to be a well of very superior workmanship; of that kind which the natives call *Bhouree*, or *Bhoulee:* the portal was elegant, the roof supported by pillars, each a single stone, twelve feet high; this led to a flight of an hundred and twenty steps, of hewn stone, terminating at a reservoir of fine water; the space from the fountain to the portal, the perpendicular height of these noble stairs, was ornamented with six tiers of pillars, of an elegant order, each tier supporting large stones across the breadth; these columns were of a single stone twelve feet high, the base, shaft and capital well proportioned. These two rows of pillars, and two of pilasters corresponding on the side walls, formed three magnificent avenues to the fountain at the bottom, and produced a good effect from the different resting places, which were adorned with niches, and a profusion of carved-work; the cross stone on the uppermost tier was richly sculptured, and contained an inscription, which I did not stay to copy, as several detached parties from the fortress of Fazal-poor hovered near us, in the rear.

A Mahratta general assured me this reservoir cost fifteen lacs of rupees, or one hundred and eighty thousand pounds sterling; which is not improbable, when it is known that in the Guzerat province, in the space of several hundred square miles together, not a stone is to be met with; we must also recollect the former wealth of Guzerat, and the execution of the work, when the price of labour was comparatively trifling. I have already mentioned the encomium lavished on such public benefactors by sacred and profane writers: to construct a Bhouree of this kind establishes the founder's fame throughout Hindostan.

About two o'clock we encamped near Padrah, a large town in the Brodera Purgunna, defended by a brick wall and irregular towers; the houses are well built, the town populous, and the surrounding country highly cultivated. The Brodera district is one of the richest in Guzerat; the land divided into extensive enclosures, the hedges adorned with mango and tamarind trees: the latter, then in fresh verdure and full bloom, diffused a fragrant odour, and afforded a refreshing shade. The banian trees near Padrah, from their amazing size, appeared coeval with the deluge, and formed a canopy for our troops impervious to the meridian sun: they were filled with monkeys, squirrels and peacocks, all favoured and protected by the Hindoos. The country abounded with antelopes, deer, hares, porcupines, partridges and quails; the lakes and rivers were covered with water-fowl; few encampments could be more delicious.

The following morning we marched ten miles to the banks of

the Dahder. Crossing the river at the pass of Maun-poor, we pitched our tents in a shady spot on the south side of the river, and found the plains adorned by a beautiful species of the mimosa, covered with fragrant blossoms of rose-colour and yellow; also a thorn, bearing a red flower, succeeded by a small plum varying in tints of green, pink, blooming lilac, and dark purple.

On the 25th we marched towards Baroche, through the Ahmood districts, generally a rich black earth, favourable to cotton, juarree, and many valuable productions; the Brodera Purgunna was mostly a light reddish soil, very productive. The next day we entered the Baroche Purgunna, belonging to the English: it is extensive and productive: the soil in different parts partaking of the Ahmood and Brodera districts, resembles them in crops.

No enemy having been there, we found the country in the highest style of cultivation, the inhabitants peaceable and happy, the villages, seldom more than two miles from each other, contained from fifty to a hundred cottages, with a tank, and one or two public wells; the white dome of a Hindoo temple, or a Mahomedan minaret rising among the mango and tamarind trees, added to the general beauty. They are usually planted when the village is built, and in a few years form a useful and ornamental grove; where the women spin, and the weavers fabricate cotton cloth of every texture, from coarse canvas to delicate muslin. Many other occupations are carried on under this verdant canopy.

We encamped for the night at Sourban, one of the best villages in the Baroche Purgunna. In our march thither we passed through the country described by Thevenot in the seventeenth century, as a wild tract, once inhabited by anthropophagi; that I suppose admits of a doubt; not so that many parts are still infested by tribes of wild men, and most audacious robbers, under the names of Gracias, Bheels, Coolies, Cotties, and other plunderers; who, either in gangs or individually, way-lay the traveller. During our sojourning on the banks of the Myhi, Sabermatty, and other Guzerat rivers, not a night passed in which our camp was not robbed and plundered by these banditti. Thevenot's Merdi-Coura certainly no longer remain, but as the existence of such a people is a curious circumstance, which probably will be proved hereafter, it may not be uninteresting to mention his remarks on the country near Sourban, where we were now encamped, and from whence we marched the following morning to Baroche.

"On leaving Baroche," this intelligent writer observes, "I journeyed to Sourban, and having crossed the brook Dader, I arrived at Debca, which lies on the side of a wood; the inhabitants thereof were formerly called Merdi-Coura, or Anthropophagi, man-eaters; and it is not very many years since man's flesh was there publicly sold in the markets. It seems to be a nest of robbers; the inhabitants, who are for the most part armed with swords, are a most impudent sort of people: passengers are always upon their guard; nay, they are obliged to carry a lance with them whenever they go only to the water-side. When my friends found I was to travel through this country, they advised me, for my security, to take a Tcheron (I suppose one of the Charuns mentioned with the Bhauts at Neriad) with a woman of his caste or tribe, to wait upon me until I were out of danger. These Tcherons are a caste of Gentiles, who are highly esteemed amongst the idolaters; if a traveller have any of these with him he thinks himself safe, because the Tcheron acquaints the robbers they meet, that the stranger is under his guard, and that if they come near him, he will cut his own throat, and the woman threatens them that she will cut off one of her breasts with a razor, which she shows them; and all the heathen look upon it to be a great misfortune to be the cause of the death of a Tcheron, because ever after the guilty person is an eyesore to his whole tribe, from which he is turned out. From Pitlad, we came to Sousentra (most probably Sevasee-contra,) where I saw a very lovely well, and met upon the road an infinite number of apes of all sorts, not only upon the trees in the fields, but also by the way-side, which were not in the least afraid of any body. I several times endeavoured to make them fly with my arms, but they stirred not, and cried their pou-pou like mad; which is, as I think, the houp-houp of which Monsieur de la Boulaye speaks."

CHAPTER XIX.

EVENTS OF THE CAMPAIGN IN GUZERAT; THE MARCH OF THE ARMY FROM BAROCHE, SETTING IN OF THE MONSOON, WINTER-QUARTERS IN DHUBOY, AND PROCEEDINGS IN THE MAHRATTA CAMP TO THE CONCLUSION OF THE WAR.

1775.

He travels and expatiates, as the bee
From flow'r to flow'r, so he from land to land;
The manners, customs, policy of all
Pay contribution to the store he gleans;
He sucks intelligence in every clime,
And spreads the honey of his deep research,
At his return—a rich repast for me.
He travels, and I too. I tread his deck,
Ascend his topmast, through his peering eyes
Discover countries; with a kindred heart
Suffer his woes, and share in his escapes.

COWPER.

CONTENTS.

palanquin-bearers, on that subject—anecdote of Narrain Doss—water for drinking—scruples concerning it—vessels for cooling it—mangos—Mahratta tents—illness of the writer—conclusion of the war—subsequent fate of Ragobah.

Memorial relative to a Mahratta army, by Sir Charles Malet.

CHAPTER XIX.

On the 27th of May, the English detachment encamped near the walls of Baroche, and continued there until the 8th of June: this city then belonged to the English, and having many friends there in the Company's service, I resided among them during our stay, and doubly enjoyed the comforts of domestic life, after a fatiguing campaign in the hottest season of the year; when, except to change them, I had seldom taken off my clothes, or slept out of a palanquin.

Baroche is situated on an eminence, on the north banks of the Nerbudda, in the twenty-second degree of north latitude; about forty miles from Surat, sixty from Cambay, and twenty-six from the entrance of the river; it is two miles and a half in circumference, fortified in the oriental manner with high walls, perforated for musketry, and flanked by towers, mounted with cannon; there are two principal gates, and several smaller outlets: the suburbs are extensive and populous, and the surrounding country fertile and pleasant. Baroche, from its natural situation and strength of the works, may, for an Asiatic city, be deemed a formidable fortress, and cost the English some loss and much trouble to take it from the nabob in 1772; from which time until 1783 it remained in the Company's possession.

The ancient history of Baroche is of little consequence, nor can I trace its origin; it is with great reason supposed to have been the Barygaza of Ptolemy. It formerly belonged to the Hindoos, but when the Mahomedans conquered Guzerat, and subdued Ahmedabad, Cambay, and Surat, Baroche shared a similar fate. From that period, until taken by the English, it was governed by a nabob; first as a delegate from the Great Mogul, and then by usurped authority as an independent prince: although the Mahratta chieftains of Brodera compelled the nabobs at different times to assign over six tenths of the Baroche revenue; which were then paid by the Company to Futty Sihng, the chief of Brodera: the whole revenue amounted to six lacs of rupees, upwards of seventy-five thousand pounds.

The houses in Baroche are built like those at Surat and Cambay; the streets are generally narrow and dirty: the durbar, or palace of the late nabob, occupies a large range of buildings, commanding a view of the river, and a rich country beyond the southern banks. There were formerly several musjids at Baroche, especially one, called by way of eminence the silver mosque, situated in the centre of a large area containing several marble tombs, under a handsome cupola; on the west side is the musjid, or house of prayer; on the south, a small temple enclosed with a lattice, covered with thin plates of silver, has obtained this dignified appellation. There, under velvet canopies, are deposited the remains of the former nabobs of Baroche; the last, after the loss of his capital, fled to a distant country, and fell a sacrifice to his misfortunes.

General Wedderburne, Commander in Chief of the Bombay forces, was killed during the siege; a tomb is erected to his memory near the flag-staff tower. In the vicinity of Baroche are several other dilapidated mosques and mausoleums, particularly one called Bawhran, on an extensive scale. The nabob's gardens without the walls, nearly a mile in circumference, are laid out with some taste; they contain several summer pavilions, fountains, and canals, with abundance of oriental fruits and flowers.

Situated in a fertile province, this city is well supplied with provision: fine beef, mutton, kid, and poultry, at very reasonable rates; with venison, game, wild-fowl, and plenty of fruits and vegetables; the river Nerbudda, which washes the southern walls, abounds with carp and other fish.

Baroche has always been a place of considerable trade; very extensive cotton manufactures are carried on there; and large consignments of raw cotton from the adjoining districts are exported in boats to Surat and Bombay, to be shipped for China and different parts of India; as, from the dangerous navigation in the gulf of Cambay, few large vessels venture up higher than Surat.

The Nerbudda rises in the mountains far to the north-east: it is esteemed one of the sacred streams of the Hindoos, and throughout the whole day the women of Baröche are bathing in the river, without being at all abashed by spectators, though no females are more modest than the Hindoos; they shift their garments, consisting of a single drapery, elegantly folded, in the most expeditious manner, without the least offence to decency. Custom reconciles every thing; and not a spark of jealousy enters the breast of a brahmin or banian husband, when he sees his wife bathing in the same stream with a hundred of the opposite sex. Besides the flowery sacrifices daily offered to the gods of the Nerbuddah, there are solemn rites at stated periods; about once in forty years, as regulated by astrological calculations in the brahminical calendar, a grand jatterah, or festival, is celebrated on its banks, to which pilgrims resort from all parts of Hindostan; every Hindoo who can accomplish the journey, is desirous once in his life to assist at this solemnity, and anticipates it with as much enthusiasm as the zealous mussulmaun does his pilgrimage to the sacred shrines in Mecca and Medina.

During our stay at Baroche, great discontent prevailed in Ragobah's army, which at length produced murmurs and remonstrances, occasioned by long arrears of pay, and other disappointments. Govind Row Guykwar, one of the peshwa's principal adherents, declared he would not accompany him to Poonah, unless he was put into the possession of Brodera, his paternal inheritance. The Arab and Scindian infantry insisted on receiving their arrears before they crossed the Nerbudda; a thousand of the former, under arms, marched out of the camp with music playing and colours flying, and never returned. These seditions caused a change of measures in Ragobah's council: it was now finally resolved to remain in Guzerat during the rainy months, and proceed to Poonah at the commencement of the fair season. Dhuboy, a fortified city about fifty miles from Baroche, was the place destined for our winter quarters; accordingly on the eighth of June we marched from Baroche, along the banks of the Nerbudda, towards that place, which was then in possession of the enemy.

In our route thither we passed near the celebrated banian-tree, called Cubbeer-burr, eighteen hundred feet in circumference, as fully described in another place. Proceeding from thence by Coral, Ranghur, and Zinore, all situated on the lofty banks of the Nerbudda, the army encamped two nights in a delightful spot not far from the water-side, from whence the country in every direction presented a charming picture: to the north and west an extensive cultivated plain, abounding with mango groves and villages, on the east and south the river meandered boldly through a fertile and populous champaign, bounded by the woody hills and lofty mountains of Rajpipley. This hilly tract belongs to an independent rajah, whose wild domain is situated in the midst of the Mahratta empire. By paying an annual tribute, he remained unmolested.

Our march on the tenth was very fatiguing; in hopes of surprising the enemy, we had not pursued the direct road to Dhuboy, but followed them towards the pass of Bowa-Peer, where we were informed they had encamped. The heat this day was dreadful; a European serjeant was killed instantaneously by a coup de soleil, and several in the ranks were recovered with difficulty. The country was still beautiful, but the hot winds and burning dust which continually overwhelmed us, were an alloy to every pleasure; the immense clouds of the latter, occasioned by the motion of three hundred thousand men and animals, in a light soil, which for eight months had not been moistened by a single shower, is inconceivable, nor have I language to describe the rage of the hot winds. Bernier, in his excursion with Aurungzebe from Delhi to Cachemire, truly characterises our situation, as well as my sensations for having exposed myself to such an ordeal; it is written in the style of the seventeenth century.

" C'est trop de curiosité, il y a de la folie, ou du moins de la " temerité á un Européen de s'exposer à de telles chaleurs, et à " de si facheuses et dangereuses marches; c'est se mettre en evi- " dens peril de la vie: mon corps est devenu un vray crible, sec " et aride, et je ne me suis pas plûtost jetté une pinte d'eau dans " l'estomac, (car on n'y va point à moins) que je la voy en mesme " temps sortir de tous mes membres comme une rosée jusques " aux bouts des doigts; je crois en avoir aujourd'huy beu plus de " dix pintes; encore est-ce une grande consolation qu'on en peut " quasi boire autant qu'on veut sans quélle fasse de mal, pourveu " qu'elle soit bonne.

" Le soleil ne fait que de se lever, cependant il est insupport- " able, il n'y a pas un nuage; pas un souffle de vent; mes chevaux " n'en peuvent plus; ils n'ont pas veu une herbe verte depuis " Lahor; mes Indiens avec toute leur peau noire, seche et dure se " rendent, tout mon visage, mes mains et mes pieds sont pelez, et " mon corps est tout couvert de petites pustules rouges, qui me " piquent comme des aiguilles; hier un de nos pauvres cavaliers " qui n'avoit point de tente, fut trouvé mort au pied d'un petit " arbre dont il s'estoit saisi. Adieu, l'ancre se seche au bout de " ma plume, et la plume me tombe de la main! adieu!"

This sultry and fatiguing march brought us in the evening to Serulah, a village in the Zinore Purgunna, the residence of several respectable families in the tribe of Bhauts. After halting until midnight we renewed our march to beat up the enemy's quarters at the pass of Bowa Peer; where, notwithstanding their usual vigilance, we understood from our Halcarras and spies, they were lulled in security, from a supposition of our having crossed the Nerbudda, at one of the western fords. We marched in tolerable order by moonlight for two hours, when becoming extremely dark, Ragobah's cavalry continually broke through our line, and obliged us to halt until day-break; we then proceeded to the heights of Ranghur, from whence at sun-rise we discerned the enemy's camp, with their tents and colours all standing, at three miles distance. The sight of our advanced guard threw them into the greatest confusion; they struck their tents with precipitation, and filled the bed of the river with elephants, camels, and fugitives of every description: their bazar, escorted by seven thousand cavalry, had already crossed; the rest of the army now followed them in all directions. The British troops, disregarding heat and fatigue, marched with alacrity, but were retarded by the deep fissures and defiles on the banks of the Nerbudda. Instead of forming, as usual, and marching towards us when we approached their camp, the enemy fled in the utmost disorder, and our round and grape had but little effect.

The halt after midnight prevented our completely surprising their camp at day-break, otherwise we should have made many prisoners, and found considerable plunder; but this delay afforded an opportunity to carry off their valuables, and leave us little more than some grain and provender. It was impossible for harassed European infantry and sepoys to pursue flying cavalry, nor could we stimulate Ragobah's horse to follow them, or indeed to advance in a body beyond our guns: a few independent parties took an advantage of still smaller troops of the enemy, to bring off an elephant, twenty camels, two hundred horses, and a great number of pack oxen: a detachment under their own leader crossed the river without orders, and plundered the rear of the enemy's bazar; but none attempted to pursue the main body. The only article of booty obtained by the British troops fell to the lot of the brigade major, who observing a sepoy with a bundle under his arm, pursued by a native officer, who seemed resolved to share the spoil, he rode up just as they opened the parcel, which to their surprize and disappointment contained a new-born infant, which some unfortunate mother had most probably dropped in her flight. Both parties most willingly consigned their treasure to the humanity of my friend, who immediately procured a wet nurse for the little foundling, the only want in a climate where infants wear no drapery.

At eleven o'clock we encamped on the enemy's ground, on the banks of the Nerbudda, near the pass of Bowa-peer, which takes its name from a celebrated Mahomedan saint, buried there eight hundred years before; his tomb, covered with silk and embroidery, is daily strewed with flowers, and nightly illuminated by small lamps; his character is so highly estimated, that Hindoos and Mahomedans approach his shrine with equal reverence. The Fakeer who resides in a sacred grove near the tomb, and performs the stated religious ceremonies, informed us that when the enemy first discerned our approach, they threw several of their cannon, and a great deal of ammunition into the river; some of them were taken up by our pioneers.

Early on the 12th of June we marched from Bowa-peer towards Dhuboy, twenty miles distant; the day was cloudy: a few showers had cooled the air, and rendered the country delightful. On leaving the river, we passed several large villages, embosomed in groves, and abounding with wells, but found the tanks exhausted until we reached Thain-telow; which takes its name from a large reservoir of water, enclosed with a wall of hewn stone and surrounded by a noble flight of steps, the labour and expense of former ages. This village being only six miles from Dhuboy, we pitched our light tents for the night, with the intention of marching into Dhuboy the following morning, to take possession of winter quarters.

The shades of evening approached as we reached the ground, and just as the encampment was completed the atmosphere grew suddenly dark, the heat became oppressive, and an unusual stillness presaged the immediate setting in of the monsoon. The whole appearance of nature resembled those solemn preludes to earthquakes and hurricanes in the West Indies, from which the east in general is providentially free. We were allowed very little time for conjecture; in a few minutes the heavy clouds burst over us

> " With the big stores of steaming oceans charg'd;
> " There thunder held his black tremendous throne;
> " From cloud to cloud the rending lightning rag'd;
> " Till in the furious elemental war
> " Dissolv'd, the whole precipitated mass
> " Unbroken floods, and solid torrents pour'd."

Thomson's high-coloured picture is no exaggerated description of this unexpected tempest. I witnessed seventeen monsoons in India, but this exceeded them all, in its awful appearance and dreadful effects. Encamped in a low situation, on the borders of a lake formed to collect the surrounding water, we found ourselves in a few hours in a liquid plain. The tent-pins giving way, in a loose soil, the tents fell down and left the whole army exposed to the contending elements. It requires a lively imagination to conceive the situation of an hundred thousand human beings of every description, with more than two hundred thousand elephants, camels, horses, and oxen, suddenly overwhelmed by this dreadful storm, in a strange country, without any knowledge of high or low ground; the whole being covered by an immense lake, and surrounded by thick darkness, which prevented our distinguishing a single object, except such as the vivid glare of lightning displayed in horrible forms. No language can describe the wreck of a large encampment thus instantaneously destroyed, and covered with water; amid the cries of old men and helpless women, terrified by the piercing shrieks of their expiring children, unable to afford them relief. During this dreadful night more than two hundred persons and three thousand cattle perished, and the morning dawn exhibited a shocking spectacle. Among those who fell a sacrifice was the little foundling from the enemy's camp.

Such was the general situation of the army, such the conclusion of the campaign. As secretary to the commanding officer, I was always one of his family, and generally slept in his tent. At this time he was ill with a violent fever, and on the commencement of the storm had been removed in his palanquin to the village: I endeavoured to follow him; but up to my knees in water, and often plunging into holes much deeper, I was compelled to return to the tent; there being left alone, and perceiving the water gradually rising, I stood upon a chair, to keep me above its surface: by midnight it had risen above three feet. The shrieks of the surrounding women and children, and the moaning of cattle, especially of dying camels, were horrible. To increase my distress, the pins gave way, and the tent fell upon me, when no calls for assistance could be heard. Providentially it was a small Indian tent, with a centre pole, round which it clung; had it been the colonel's usual marquee, of English canvas, I must have been smothered. At last, finding myself nearly exhausted, I determined to make one effort more for my deliverance, in which I happily succeeded. Guided through the lake by tremendous flashes of lightning, after many difficulties, I reached the hut whither they had conveyed the colonel, and there found the surgeon-general, and several other gentlemen, drying their clothes round a large fire in the centre: with them I passed the remainder of this miserable night, among serpents, scorpions, and centipedes, which the fire within and the heavy rain without had driven from their hiding places. Several of our men were stung by the scorpions, and bit by snakes and centipedes; none fatally. The scorpion, though less dangerous than the malignant serpents, inflicts a wound which, like that of the centipedes, is attended with inflammation and fever; his sting at the end of the tail he darts with great force at the object of his fury; the latter bites by means of strong forceps at the mouth: this reptile is more common than the scorpion, and more easily concealed. If the scorpion is surrounded by flaming spirits or burning embers, and can find no egress, he stings himself to death.

Such was our night: the next morning the camp exhibited a

scene of woe; the train of artillery was sunk several feet into the earth, and covered by the water. To convey them and the heavy stores to Dhuboy required the utmost exertion, and, with the assistance of elephants, could not be accomplished in less than seven days, although only a distance of six miles.

On the 15th we made our first attempt, and proceeded one mile from Thain-Thelow to Vurrage, the next village. The plain, covered with carcases of horses, camels, and oxen, some at their last gasp, suffocated in the mud, others in a state of putrefaction, presented a shocking spectacle. The groans of a dying camel are dreadful; but the mind of feeling was more distressed by the sight of infirm men and expiring women; of parents, unable to support their helpless offspring, or in agonizing grief carrying them dead in their arms for sepulture or cremation.

Had I attempted to walk over this Golgotha, I might have shared their fate: my bearers could not carry me in a palanquin. With some difficulty I effected it on horseback, for no road could be traced through the waters, and the ravines were dangerous. We remained at Vurrage until the artillery and ammunition were transported from Thain-Thelow, which, although only the distance of one mile, was a work of five days. This being accomplished, we employed two more in finishing our journey of five miles to Dhuboy, occasioned by the Herculean labour of dragging the artillery. I made this second attempt on an elephant, and from such an eminence had an extensive view of the country, which presented a boundless sheet of water, encompassing the rising grounds, covered with trees and villages, like so many islands.

The officers and privates in the English detachment were soon provided with comfortable quarters in the ancient city of Dhuboy. The remains of its fortifications, gates, and temples, indicate great magnificence. The temple near the east gate, called the Gate of Diamonds, a work of immense labour and expense, must have employed a number of artificers many years. The city is nearly quadrangular, exceeding two miles in circumference: such parts of the fortifications as remain entire are of large hewn stones, and the interior colonnade is a beautiful and useful work: within the walls is a large tank, surrounded by strong masonry, with a grand flight of steps, the whole extent descending to the water, from the Hindoo temples, choultries, and solemn groves, which generally border this beautiful reservoir.

Dhuboy, with the other Hindoo cities in Guzerat, became an early part of the Mahomedan conquests, and remained in their possession until the Mahrattas took it on the decline of the Mogul power, in the eighteenth century; it is now chiefly inhabited by Hindoos: a few Mahomedan families are permitted to reside there, on condition of not eating beef. The pundit, or governor, appointed by the ministers at Poonah, submitted to Ragobah, and on our approach acknowledged him as peshwa of the Mahratta empire; the latter immediately levied a contribution of three lacs of rupees from the inhabitants, which they were unwilling and almost unable to pay; for, although some cotton manufactures are carried on there, Dhuboy and its dependencies are poor.

The durbar and some of the principal houses were well built, and the streets generally broad and airy: many acres within the walls were cultivated, and produced abundant crops of corn and vegetables: the city contained about forty thousand inhabitants, and nearly as many monkeys, which occupied the roofs of the houses, or enjoyed the shade of the mango and tamarind trees with the peacocks, squirrels, and green pigeons, that lived there as unmolested by the Hindoos as if in the midst of a forest. Pelicans, wild-ducks, adjutant-birds, and a variety of water-fowl, animate the beautiful lake, adorned by the nymphea and many aquatic plants.

The adjutant-bird, or argali, a large bird of the crane species, is sometimes near six feet high, and from twelve to fifteen from the extremity of each wing. The adjutant, one of the ugliest in the Indian ornithology, is as useful as the stork in Holland, or the ibis in Egypt, and equally venerated by the Hindoos; it not only destroys serpents and noxious reptiles, but eats up the carrion and offal in towns and villages, which in that climate are extremely offensive. I know not why this bird is called the adjutant; the name of sentinel would perhaps be more appropriate; for, when not in quest of food, they stand motionless, in a pensive attitude, like so many statues. Their pendent red craw, and coarse breast, bare of feathers, but protruding some long dark hairs, have a forbidding appearance.

Soon after the English troops were settled at Dhuboy, Ragobah encamped with his army at Bellapoor, a pass on the river Dahder, at ten miles distance. The commander in chief residing there more than in Dhuboy, my time was divided between the Mahratta camp and the city; especially during a negociation between Ragobah and Futty Sihng, the Guykwar chieftain of Brodera, when all correspondence with Bombay was in cipher. My journeys to Bellapoor were frequent, and in favourable weather not unpleasant. After the first heavy falls of rain, the face of nature was soon adorned with beauty: the hedges enriched with a variety of climbing plants perfumed the air, from blossoms of mingled hues and fragrance, springing cotton, crops of various grain, plants for oil, with large fields of cucumbers, gourds and melons, gave the country the appearance of a well-cultivated garden; but the sudden transition in the rainy season from a bright serenity to an overwhelming tempest, was an alloy to these delights, especially to one so much exposed to their inclemency.

My journey from Dhuboy to Bellapoor, a distance of only ten miles, frequently occupied as many hours, notwithstanding I was mounted on a strong elephant, whose sagacity generally guided me in safety through a continued sheet of water which entirely covered the roads. Once, when important business required my attendance at Ballapoor, I arrived at the pass of the Dahder, and found the stream, seldom more than three feet deep, suddenly risen to forty, and running with astonishing velocity. The mountain torrents had joined the overflowing lakes and rivulets; whose united streams rushing furiously to the river, swept away corn-ricks, cottages, trees, and cattle, and then hurried them to the ocean; together with some feeble inhabitants of the plains, and several of Ragobah's camp-followers, who lost their lives in attempting to get the trees and rafters for fire-wood; for although the Indians are generally expert swimmers, the current was too rapid for their exertions.

While detained on the banks of the Dahder I witnessed several of these catastrophes; and in view of a comfortable encampment on the opposite side, at only a few yards distance, but separated by this impassable flood, I found the evening approach, when I had neither food, fire, nor hovel to afford me shelter. A volume of Pope's Homer had beguiled the journey. We doubly enjoy the similes of the Grecian bard when read in a country of similar manners and customs. While contemplating the scene just described on the banks of the Dahder, the following passage was truly impressive,

> " Thus when in autumn, Jove his fury pours,
> " And earth is loaden with incessant showers,
> " From their deep beds he bids the rivers rise,
> " And opens all the flood-gates of the skies:
> " Th' impetuous torrents from their hills obey;
> " Whole fields are drown'd, and mountains swept away:
> " Loud roars the deluge 'till it meets the main,
> " And trembling man sees all his labours vain!"

While sitting on the elephant's houdah, waiting for the fall of the river, or for some means of crossing it, this scene ceased to be ideal: at sun-set, a darkness resembling that at the setting in of the monsoon covered the horizon, and a deluge of rain fell the whole night. The houdah, or covered throne, which at first served for my habitation, being soon broken by the tempest, and filled with water, I sheltered myself to the leeward of the elephant, and remained until day-break, with the faithful animal and his driver; the wet sod our bed, the watery clouds our only canopy. When the morning dawned I beheld the river rising still higher, and, being unable to hold any communication with the camp, I returned to Dhuboy through a continued flood, impassable by any other conveyance than a boat or an elephant.

During my next visit at Ragobah's camp, a circumstance occurred which affords another trait of Asiatic manners and despotic power, under the influence of jealousy and revenge. I have mentioned the ladies of Ragobah's zenana, on our departure from Surat: they accompanied him throughout the campaign, and generally rode on horseback. As the Hindoos do not wear veils, they were frequently more exposed on the line of march than is usual for the eastern ladies. But in camp their tents were always surrounded by high canvas walls; where, concealed from view, they passed their lives in solitude, apathy, and disgust. Anandabhye, the only wife of Ragobah, was not with him on this campaign. Of his seven concubines, one only attracted attention; a pretty lively girl, who rode gracefully, and seemed pleased with observation: many of our officers admired her, but her charms made a deeper impression on the heart of Esswant Row, a young soldier of fortune and distinction in the Mahratta army.

It is unnecessary to detail the particulars of an amour: however modified by education, the passions in the eastern and western hemispheres are much the same; love, perhaps, burns with a fiercer flame in the torrid zone, and an intrigue is carried on with more difficulty in an oriental zenana than in the fashionable circles of Europe. These lovers cherished a mutual attachment, and by means of a confidant baffled for a time the Argus-eyes of Asiatic jealousy. The eunuchs and duennas at length suspecting the intrigue, gave information to Ragobah. On the rumour of a discovery, Esswant Row absconded, leaving his tent, armour, and horses in camp; and had not his attachment to an Arabian horse got the better of his prudence, he would have effectually escaped; but in hopes of carrying off this favourite animal, he returned the following night to his tent: on approaching the tree where the horse was picketed, he was made a prisoner. Ragobah ordered him to be instantly beheaded, by torch-light, at the extremity of the camp, and his remains exposed as a public spectacle throughout the next day. While the ministers of death dispatched the unfortunate lover, his ill-fated mistress was sowed up in a sack, and thrown alive into the river; the confidant was condemned to have her nose cut off, and thus remain an example to the other slaves in the haram.

Midnight is generally the time for oriental executions; sometimes the criminal is put to death with the utmost privacy, at others an alarm-gun from the imperial tent, at that silent hour proclaims the exit of the devoted victim.

> " Let barbarous nations, whose inhuman love
> " Is wild desire, fierce as the suns they feel;
> " Let eastern tyrants, from the light of heaven
> " Seclude their bosom-slaves, meanly possess'd
> " Of a mere lifeless violated form;
> " While those whom love cements, in holy faith,
> " And equal transport, free as nature live,
> " Disdaining fear." THOMSON.

Niebuhr mentioned a circumstance at Bussora, of a rich merchant who had been received into the powerful body of janizaries, and a pilgrimage to Mecca had stamped a still higher value on his character; but the governor being his enemy, he was strangled privately, and his dead body thrown into the market place. After this public spectacle, like that of Esswant Row, the friends were permitted to take away his remains; but in a history of Morocco, we read of a man being sawed asunder, and after this cruel death, his body would have remained to be eaten by the dogs, if the emperor had not pardoned him. It appears extraordinary to pardon a dead man; but unless the despotic tyrant had extended this clemency to the deceased, no person would have dared to bury him.

About this time, from being so much exposed to the violence of the weather, and sleeping in a wet camp, I was seized with a fever; which, resisting all the power of medicine, constantly returned every springtide, and left me in a weak and languid condition; but having much to do, in my official capacity, with Futty Sihng, the Brodera chieftain, which occasioned several inclement journeys to his capital, I resisted its effects as long as possible, and continued with the colonel at Bellapoor. A summer campaign in India is generally pleasant, but an encampment in the rainy season far otherwise; the soft and muddy quality of the soil, the humidity of the atmosphere, and the rank grass which springs round the tents, united with the fetid odours in every quarter, render it a disagreeable residence: it is with difficulty that the pins and ropes keep the tents upright in the soft earth, and it is still more difficult to preserve them dry during the long and heavy falls of rain.

These are perhaps the only inconveniences attending the rich soil of Guzerat, but they are compensated by its fertility and beauty. In happier times this province was styled the paradise of nations, and it deserved the appellation; for when conversing with oriental travellers, and comparing it with other countries, I have heard them in the very words of Moses, call it " a land flowing with milk and honey:" and when the Hindoos and Moguls at this day are describing a pleasant and well-cultivated district they distinguish it as, in scripture language, " a land of brooks of water, of fountains and springs; a land of wheat and barley, of vines, fig-trees and pomegranates, a land of oil olive and honey."

Our own army, both Europeans and sepoys, had comfortable winter-quarters at Dhuboy; the public buildings and largest houses were appropriated for their accommodations: and the principal caravansary, situated on the border of the tank, was converted into an hospital. These reservoirs were seldom thought complete without a caravansary for the convenience of travellers, and a temple for the worship of the deity. Some of them are very extensive. Dr. Buchanan mentions a dilapidated tank in the Mysore, so large, that in a country where labour is extremely cheap it would cost more than three thousand guineas to remove the mud collected in the bottom, and to put it into order.

However unhealthy may be a winter encampment in Guzerat, I think it far preferable to the extreme heat which I have so often mentioned; we had not indeed the simoom of Arabia, nor the sirocco of Italy, but we experienced the mingled effects of the scorching heat of the former, and the languor occasioned by the latter. A scarcity of water in such situations was a dreadful evil, which we frequently encountered; I remember almost dying of thirst, when I had emptied my own cantine for some wounded soldiers, and entreated a friend to give me a few drops without effect; his was almost exhausted, and when there is but little water in a leather cantine, the hot wind soon dries it up. Often, during a short slumber in my palanquin, have I realized the affecting description of "the thirsty man dreaming; and behold, he drinketh! but he awaketh; and behold he is faint, and his soul hath appetite!" How exquisite is the truth and beauty in Park's description of such a slumber. "No sooner had I shut my eyes, than "fancy would convey me to the streams and rivers of my native "land; there, as I wandered along the verdant bank, I surveyed "the clear stream with transport, and hastened to swallow the de-"lightful draught; but, alas! disappointment awakened me, and "I found myself a lonely captive, perishing of thirst amidst the "wilds of Africa."

The Mahrattas do not seem to mind heat or cold, wet or dry encampments, nor any other inconvenience; fond of a rambling life, predatory excursions are their great delight. The followers of the camp, so often alluded to, are generally a singular set of people. I do not mean the regular shop-keepers, or persons who hold situations in the army, but those who attach themselves to it with their wives and children, to pick up what they can find; who have no other place of abode, nor mode of obtaining a living: each man possesses a poor half-starved ox, or an ass, which is laden with the wealth of the family, perfectly corresponding with an ancient picture of the wily Gibeonites in their pretended embassy to Joshua, who "worked wilily, and went and made as if they came from a very far country, and took old sacks upon their asses, and leather bottles, old and rent, and bound up; and old and clouted shoes upon their feet, and old garments upon them; and all the bread of their provision was dry and mouldy."

Asses are common in many parts of Hindostan, and are used as beasts of burden. This humble animal seems to be ill-treated in all parts of the world, and seldom meets with a due reward for his patience and resignation. But the Hindoos carry their aversion to a greater length than is customary elsewhere. Dr. Buchanan mentions a dispute among the Hindoos, near Seringapatam, which was not likely to be terminated without killing a jack-ass in the street of the town where they lived. "This," he says, "may be considered as a very slight matter, but it is not so; for it would be attended by the immediate desolation of the place: there is not a Hindoo in Karnata that would remain another night in it, unless by compulsion: even the adversaries of the party who killed the ass, would think themselves bound in honour to fly."

The camp-followers are a very independent set of people; and only remain with the army to which they attach themselves as long as it suits their convenience; nor are they subject to that oppression which is so generally prevalent in Hindostan. The Hindoos, as Craufurd justly observes, "are great observers of decorum; their manners are unaffected, they possess much natural politeness, and are cautious never to say or do any thing which they imagine may give offence:" but, in my opinion, there is not that urbanity and benevolence so generally prevailing as we might expect among a people so closely connected by caste and religion.

From long observation among the Mahratta chieftains, and principal officers in the camp, they seemed more or less influenced by a jealousy of each other, and trying which should gain the ascendency by duplicity, chicanery, and intrigue. In my attendance, as secretary to the British commander, at the durbar tent, where Ragobah generally held a cabinet council every evening, I had excellent opportunities of seeing the higher ranks; from the brahmins, who under the peshwa administration held secular situations, to all the principal military officers and ministers of state. Dissimulation seems to be the predominant trait in the Asiatic character; very few Europeans are a match for them. In my visits to Brodera during the negociation with Futty Sihng I witnessed such dissimulation, treachery, and meanness in the prince and his ministers, as would with difficulty be believed by a generous Englishman unused to these people. On one occasion his naib, or vizier, thought proper to deprive me of my sword, and detain me a prisoner for some hours in a close room in the palace: a circumstance to a person then in a public character, which his master could not be ignorant of, though he afterwards thought proper to assert it was done without his knowledge. Nothing could exceed the insolence of the men in office when they obeyed the vizier's commands; nor the mean apologies of himself and all concerned, when they repented of their error, and honourably dismissed me to Ragobah's camp.

The proceedings of the great men in Ragobah's councils, Futty Sihng's palace, and most of the pundits and zemindars with whom I had any transactions, would have classed them high in the school of Tiberius, who reckoned dissimulation among the cardinal virtues. "Nullum æquè Tiberius, ut rebatur, ex virtutibus suis, quam dissimulationem diligebat. Eò œgrius accepit, recludi quæ premeret."—Tacitus Ann.

I am aware of what has been generally advanced in favour of the innocent and harmless Hindoos, and of the impressions made in Europe, a few years ago, by the imaginary system of cruelty in

British India, most pathetically detailed, by senatorial eloquence, to establish facts which had no foundation, except in the warm imaginations of a party under the influence of prejudice and misinformation. During my residence in India I constantly witnessed the reverse of those assertions; I beheld English generosity and clemency stretch forth the hand of mercy and protection, and endeavouring to rescue the peasantry from the oppressions of the zemindars and merciless officers in the revenue departments. The devastations by the Mahratta armies, and the cruelties committed by the Gracias, Bheels, and other banditti, are notorious deviations from the national character of peaceful innocence. An accurate writer, in describing the march of the Mahratta forces under Purseram Bhou through the Mysore, a march marked as usual by devastation, famine, and murder, says that "After two days, the Mahratta general took Shiva-mogay, a town in Canara, which then contained six thousand houses; the whole of them were destroyed, the women ravished, and the handsomest carried away. Such of the men as fell into the hands of the Mahrattas were killed, and of those who escaped the sword, a large proportion perished by hunger; every eatable thing having been swept away by those whom the people in Europe are pleased to call the gentle Hindoos. These ruffians did not even spare the guroo, or head priest of all the Mahratta brahmins of the Smartal sect, and who is by them considered as an actual incarnation of the deity. His college was plundered and burnt; but this cost the peshwa dear, as the enraged guroo held out threats of instant excommunication, and was only to be pacified by a present of four hundred thousand rupees."

That the brahmins themselves, with all their professions of mildness, benevolence, and sanctity, can be guilty of deliberate revenge and murder, is evident not only from Ragobah's conduct on the massacre of his nephew Narrain Row, as particularly mentioned in the Mahratta history, but still more so from the following account of the Telinga brahmins at Poonah, communicated to me by Sir Charles Malet, as a most extraordinary event, which happened during his embassy at the Mahratta court, in 1791.

On the 29th of August, thirty-four men of the caste of Telinga brahmins having been confined in a chokey, or close room, by the officers of the cutwal, the head magistrate of the police at Poonah, twenty-one were taken out dead the next morning, and the remaining thirteen were with difficulty restored to life. In the evening the popular clamour became violent against the cutwal, who was a gour brahmin, named Gaunseram, a native of Aurungabad, and whose office, in a city where the most rigorous police is established, necessarily rendered him an obnoxious character. The peshwa improperly yielding to the furious mob, delivered up the cutwal, who was tied backward on an elephant, and in that manner conveyed to a prison without the town, amidst the scoffs and insults of the populace, while guards were sent to seize his family, dependants, and property. The day following the clamour grew more violent, being encouraged by many persons desirous of mortifying the ruling minister, through the ignominy of the cutwal, his dependant. The unhappy man was tied backward on a camel, and in that disgraceful manner reconducted into the city, amidst the reproaches of the people: here he was made to alight, and his head having been publicly shaved, he was again placed in the same manner on the camel; and having been carried through the principal streets of Poonah, escorted by a strong guard, he was for the last time led to a spot about a mile from the city, and there ordered to dismount: one of his hands was then strongly fastened to the end of a turban between twenty and thirty feet long, and the other end committed to some Hallalcores, the lowest outcasts of the Hindoo tribes, who contaminate all other castes by their touch. It was then made known to the Telinga brahmins that the cutwal was delivered up entirely to their disposal, either as a sacrifice to their vengeance, or an object for their mercy; on which twelve brahmins of that tribe, in the most savage manner, immediately attacked the fallen magistrate with large stones. The Hallalcores who held the turban, by straitening it, kept him at full length running in a circle, pursued by his relentless murderers; who at length, by repeated blows on the head and breast, brought him to the ground; and there, with an eagerness disgraceful to humanity, though merciful to the prostrate object of their cruelty, these brahminical murderers dispatched him by a succession of large stones thrown violently on his head and breast.

Such is the weakness of human nature, that on his murderers approaching the degraded cutwal with huge stones in their uplifted hands, this unfortunate man, who, when overwhelmed with misery and disgrace, had incessantly called for immediate death, now rose up, and as far as his cruel liberty in the length of the extended turban permitted, attempted in vain to avoid the deadly blows inflicted by his executioners.

Thus fell a brahmin, a foreigner, who for many years had been invested with the whole criminal jurisprudence of the capital of the Mahratta empire! who had spent the emoluments of his office, in building an elegant tank or reservoir for the ornament and convenience of the city, and bringing its supply of water from a great distance, with a spirit of generosity and expense so far above the ability of the rich native brahmins, as to subject him to their envy, and to the cruel sufferings of an ignominious death.

Instances of cruelty are not confined to the brahmins of Telinga, they appear among the Jaina, Smartal brahmins, and other sects among that elevated caste. I shall not again enter into those artificial distinctions in the Hindoo tribes: the subdivisions of caste are innumerable; in the Ayeen Akbery, the tribe of *Bania*, or, as generally styled by the English, the *Banian-caste*, is divided into eighty-four sects, each having their distinguishing characteristic. There also exists some essential difference between the Concan and Deccan brahmins, and those of Malabar, the Bengal provinces, and other parts of Hindostan. From the latest and best authorities we find that many of the Bengal brahmins eat fish, and several sorts of animal food; they are not only allowed them, but at some particular ceremonies they are enjoined so to do. They certainly are different in Guzerat, and those who held political situations under Ragobah appeared to confine their diet to grain, fruit, and vegetables, variously modified. They sometimes sent pilaus and curries to the British commander from their own dinner; which, like the supplies from Ragobah's table, were entirely composed of rice and vegetables, flavoured with spices, and light of digestion: but they never contained any animal substance, except milk and clarified butter.

The Mahrattas, though all Hindoos, are by no means rigid

in their penances, ablutions, or food. The lower classes, especially, eat of almost every thing that comes in their way; as mutton, goat, wild-hog, game and fish. Major Moor mentions two places by name where the Mahrattas eat beef, and permit cattle to be killed, and publicly exposed to sale. I should rather have supposed it was intended for the food of Mahomedans, had not this discriminating writer been so very particular.

The lower tribes of Hindoos are not so scrupulous as the higher about what they eat, or what they touch; especially if they are not observed by others. When at a distance from their families, and out of sight of their priests, many divest themselves of these nice ideas of purity. Those domesticated with Europeans generally affect to be very scrupulous: an English table, covered with a variety of food, is necessarily surrounded by a number of servants of different castes to attend the guests. At Baroche, Surat and Bombay, a Hindoo will not remove a dish that has been defiled with beef, a Mahomedan cannot touch a plate polluted by pork, nor will a Parsee take one away on which is hare or rabbit. I never knew more than one Parsee servant who would snuff a candle, from a fear of extinguishing the symbol of the deity he worships; nor would this man ever do it in presence of another Parsee.

The palanquin-bearers, although in general a pleasant set of people, are sometimes on a journey extremely tenacious of their privileges of caste, and carry their prejudices to a ridiculous length. I knew a gentleman, who having formed a party for a little excursion into the country, provided a round of beef, as a principal dish in the cold collation: as he was going on horseback, he desired the beef might be covered with a cloth, and put into his palanquin to keep it cool; the bearers refused to carry a vehicle which contained such a pollution. The gentleman, on finding that neither remonstrances, entreaties, or threatenings, were of any avail, cut off a slice of the meat, and eating it in their presence, desired them to carry him to the place of rendezvous. This produced the desired effect; the bearers were the first to laugh at their folly, and exclaimed " Master come wise-man, with two eyes; while poor black-man come very foolish, with only one:" and taking up the palanquin with the beef, set off towards the tents in great good humour.

Such scruples are not confined to any particular caste; they more or less pervade every tribe in India, and are cherished by the active soldier, as well as the pious brahmin. In the Ayeen Akbery we read of Narrain Doss, a principal chief in the Rahtore tribe, in command of five hundred cavalry and two thousand infantry, who lived with such austerity, that his only food was grain which had passed through oxen, and been separated from their dung: an aliment considered by the brahmins as the purest of all food.

The Indians are also very scrupulous about the water they drink, and the vessels which contain it. The rich generally have the water of the Ganges carried with them on a journey. Most of the Mogul emperors travelled with it for their own beverage; and Akber, who never drank any other, called it, when cooled with saltpetre, " the water of life."

In cities, in the armies, and with Europeans on country excursions, the water for drinking is usually carried in large leather bags, called *pacaulies*, formed by the entire skin of an ox, sewed up, except at one corner left open for filling them: these are hung on each side of a bullock, or tame buffalo, and poured into guglets of a porous earth, brought from Persia, Goa, and different parts of India; in these the water soon becomes cool, and, as a great luxury, is sometimes iced with salt-petre. Often during this campaign, when suffering from thirst, and panting under the extreme heat, have I envied the village buffaloes, who in such weather seem the happiest beings in the country: they either get under water, or conceal themselves in the thin slimy mud on the margin of the lakes and rivers; there they remain during the sultry hours without any part of them appearing above the surface.

Good water and ripe mangos were the greatest luxuries I aspired after in this campaign: the latter are extremely fine in most parts of Guzerat, though inferior in size to the mangos of Agra, which sometimes weigh two pounds each. A basket of high-flavoured mangos, accompanied by a wreath of mogrees or champachs, were a frequent present from the Mahratta officers to the English gentlemen, and from the peshwa to the commander in chief.

The mango topes, tamarind groves, and springing crops in the extensive plains round the Mahratta camp, were very delightful during the fair intervals of the rainy season. Few countries equal the Brodera Purgunna in fertility and beauty; but the heat, added to the moisture and fetid smells of the camp, were intolerable, and attended with pernicious effects. Fortunately there were seldom any Europeans there besides the colonel and myself; he was often ill with an intermittent fever; and I soon experienced the bad effects of sleeping in a damp tent, on my palanquin, raised only a few inches from the ground, covered only by a cotton carpet; for, notwithstanding all the trenches, the heavy rains pervaded every thing. Few European constitutions can resist the combinations of heat and moisture; mine was gradually undermined, and at length fell a sacrifice to a severe relapse of fever at the return of every new and full moon.

The Mahratta generals had excellent tents for the rainy season, formed of many folds of quilted cotton, purposely to resist the elements. When Ragobah resolved to form his winter encampment at Bellapoor, all his tents were pitched, and those separately appropriated to worship, eating, sleeping, the zenana, and attendants, occupied a very large site, at some distance from the rest of the army, and guarded by a select body of troops. The durbar-tent, where the peshwa gave audience and administered justice, was placed near the dhall-flag, or royal standard, distinguished from all others, like the prætorium of the Roman generals, so called from the ancient Latins, who styled their commanders prætors. Scipio Africanus first formed the prætorian cohort, stationed near his tent, and ready to attend him on all emergencies: such are the husserat, or household troops of the Mahratta peshwa, and the life-guards of the British sovereign.

My manuscript volumes contain the transactions, during the winter quarters at Dhuboy and Bellapoor camp, for some time longer;

but those events have ceased to be interesting. My fever increasing, attended by many symptoms of the liver complaint, I was obliged, not only to leave the army in Guzerat, but to return to Bombay, and embark in the first vessel for England, in hopes of re-establishing my health.

I shall therefore only add, that in consequence of orders from the newly appointed governor-general in council at Bengal, an embassy was sent from thence to the ministers at Poonah, by which means a peace was concluded between the Mahrattas and the English, the Bombay detachment withdrawn, and Ragobah compelled to resign the peshwa sovereignty to the posthumous child of Narrain Row. As a compensation for this sacrifice, he was to be allowed a jaghire from the Mahratta government, and some other privileges: but becoming discontented with a private station, he again asserted his claim to the sovereignty; was once more assisted by the Bombay government in an expedition sent from thence in 1779, which proved unsuccessful: and Ragobah's death happening soon afterwards, terminated the civil wars in the Mahratta empire.

I shall close the subject of the campaign in Guzerat with an account of the Mahratta army in 1795, communicated to me by Sir Charles Malet, at that time the British ambassador at the court of Poonah; in which character he accompanied the peshwa in an expedition against the Nizam. This information, derived from such a source, I consider a most valuable acquisition to the preceding narrative; especially as it elucidates many points which I had no opportunity of investigating.

Memoranda relative to a Mahratta army,
by Sir CHARLES MALET.

I shall here endeavour to prevent the treachery of memory, by committing to writing a few leading traits in the construction, organization, and movement of a Mahratta army, which so essentially differs from the arrangement of European troops. The computed number now assembled under the peshwa, as executive head, and all the other great chiefs of the empire, amounts to upwards of one hundred and twenty seven thousand cavalry and infantry, exclusive of the troops belonging to the Guikwar, and the sons of Govind Bundela, Ballajee and Gungudur, now employed in concert with Ally Bhadur in subduing the country of Bundelcund to the peshwa's obedience.

Peshwa's own force, as head of the empire, under their respective generals	70,665
Dowlat Row Sindia	25,000
Tookajee Holcar	10,000
Ragojee Bhosla	15,000
Purseram Bhou	7,000
Horse and foot, total	127,665

Organization.

The foregoing bodies of troops are either under the command of feudatory chieftains, whose authority over their own troops is absolute, and without appeal, as the four last chieftains, and many other leaders of corps paid by government, either in money or land, denominated *nukdee* or *tankaw*, which are assignments of land resumable at pleasure. In the same manner as the mass of the force of the Mahratta empire is thus composed, so the force of the various chieftains is, in like manner, composed in a smaller or greater degree of the same materials. Thus, for instance, the general Mahratta force is composed of jaghiredars, like Sindia and Holcar; of nugdee, or ready-money corps, as Shah Meer Khan, and Buchaba Serolkar; or of Tankadars, as Bugwant Sihng and other paugheas. Now all these different descriptions are again detailed in the composition of the Sindian, or other jaghiredar's force; that is to say, it contains every species of service: but the number is generally far short of the quota stipulated by the original feudal tenure. Although the nugdee or ready-money corps are not looked upon in so respectable a light as those paid in land, yet are the commanders absolute in the management of them, and in the disposal of the sums they receive for their payment; which generally runs at a certain rate per man, and a fixed sum for the commander. And, as in the management of these corps the payment by government is usually very tardy, the commanders have recourse to every trick, to elude, if possible, the checks by which government attempts to insure faithful service: such as the appointment of a duan, furnavees, and other officers to each corps, who are themselves guilty of the most scandalous venality, in conjunction with the commanders; by which means it happens, especially in the peshwa's service, that a corps of one hundred men has seldom more than fifty effective, while the allowance of government is reduced to one half before it reaches the sepoy.

The corps of the paugheas, that is, commanders of cavalry, paid either in ready-money or land assignments, are smaller or greater, according to the interest of the paughea: thus one has a paughea of fifty, another of five hundred, reckoning the whole at a certain sum per head, with a distinct allowance for the chief, who again distributes that allowance at his pleasure, giving to one twenty, to another two hundred rupees per month. Properly speaking, the paugheas should be composed of the horses belonging to the government, or the chief, mounted by *bargheers* or hired troopers: but this is not always the case, because *silladars*, (literally armiger, bearer of arms), or horsemen with their own horses, often compose a large portion of a paughea; and although every horseman, throughout a Mahratta army, looks upon himself as company for his chieftain, and always sits down with him, yet is the silladar considered as rather superior to the bargheer.

To the paugheas, as to the nugdee corps, there is an establishment of civil officers to enforce justice between government and its servants; but the multiplication of checks seems to have had no other end than the increase of corruption; for not only is half the grain and forage allowed to the horses embezzled, but horses are changed, reported dead, and every species of the most flagitious peculation practised with impunity, arising from the general interest and participation therein; insomuch that I have sometimes been inclined to think that the government must have some mode of reimbursement for these palpable defalcations, by withholding the pay due to its troops; for, although they sometimes clamour, yet from the ample profits of peculation the chief is generally wise enough to keep his complaints within bounds, since his illicit profits are secure; and his tardy receipt of payment from government furnishes a specious pretext for not paying the poor sepoy, who through poverty is often forced to take another service, with the loss of all his arrears, which his chief collects as he can; or to compound the whole for a part, which is generally anticipated by loans taken up of his jummadar, or the *karkuns*, who are the civil officers of his corps, at an exorbitant interest.

Besides bargheers and silladars, there is another description of horsemen, known in the Mahratta armies by the denomination of *yekandia*, which signifies single: these are generally men of family, who, with a few attendants, go in quest of service, and are frequently entertained on the footing of companions by the great chiefs, on most ample allowances, from one hundred to one thousand rupees per month, with one or two horses from the chief's stable at their command.

The arms of the Mahratta cavalry are swords, spears, matchlocks, and a few bows and arrows; the sword is universal and indispensable, the matchlock very frequent in the paugheas, and seems to be daily gaining ground of the long spear, formerly a very favourite weapon with the Mahrattas: but many of the silladars, yekandias, and those who claim, or affect superiority of birth and rank, seldom encumber themselves with any thing but two swords; one of a hard temper, consequently brittle and very sharp, called *serye;* the other, more tough and less sharp, named *asseel.* It must be understood that the arms, accoutrements, and clothing of the horseman being his own property, there is not the smallest uniformity, every individual equipping himself conformably to his taste or circumstances.

Few paugheas have more than one large *routy*, the most common kind of tent; and perhaps a shameana, or canopy, belonging to the paughea, pitched at one end of a street, formed by the horses of the troop, picketed in two lines, fronting each other. The routy serves to shelter the troopers and their furniture in bad weather, and as a place of assembly for the corps morning and evening. At other times the trooper generally posts himself, with his saddle and arms, in front of his horse; there he also sleeps, having nothing more than what he can conveniently carry to any distance upon his horse. There are generally a number of tattoos, small horses, attached to each paughea; which, while the army is under march, are dispatched with the syses, or grooms, to forage; by which means they generally get to the ground as soon as the main body of the army, laden with provender for the paughea horses; or they sally forth in quest of it as soon as they have disposed of their burthen on the new ground; though the failure of this reliance would not distress the Mahrattas, who are not yet sufficiently pampered by wealth to despise that necessary part of military duty, or to affect being above providing provender for the noble animal who administers so effectually to their ease and advantage.

Over and above the foregoing constituent parts of a Mahratta army, it is to be observed that they have now introduced large trains of artillery, and formidable bodies of regular infantry; the organization of which being copies of our own, needs no particular explanation: I shall therefore proceed to the orders for marching.

These orders, abstracted from emergencies, are signified by

notes to the chieftains, and promulgated by a crier to the army the preceding night. About four o'clock on the ensuing morning, the signal for moving is given by the great nabut, or drum; on the second beating, the beenee walla, an officer corresponding in some measure with our quarter-master-general, sets out with the peshwa's, or principal chieftain's flag, escorted by his own corps, occasionally strengthened, as circumstances may require. With him, or a little before, proceed parties from all the different chieftains, with their respective flags, bazars, followers, infantry and artillery, forming a mass called *beheer* or *boongha:* these proceed promiscuously in vast multitudes, and without the smallest order, until they see the peshwa's dhall-flag, which is erected at the option of the beenee walla, always in a spot in which the convenience of water is the principal consideration, without regard to rough or even ground, defensible situation or otherwise. By this flag the erection of all others in the army (and every chief has one) is regulated: for although, except in the line of the bazar, which generally forms a fine street in front of the chief's tents, there is not the smallest internal regularity in the pitching of a Mahratta camp, yet, with respect to head-quarters, all the chiefs have their relative stations to the right and left, from which a deviation is by no means allowable. If a particular chief is stationed next to head-quarters, no other officer must come between them, nor must this general arrangement be infringed upon. Although this has the semblance of a regular line, yet as no distances are marked out, and no chief's numbers are definitively known, the whole exhibits an appearance of utter confusion: for if the camp is on a fordable river, both banks are constantly occupied; nor do they care how far they advance in front or rear, their only object being to preserve their right and left vicinity.

The head-quarters being ascertained, as above mentioned, by the erection of the dhall-flag, all the flags of the other chieftains are pitched as fast as they arrive, and also their tents; their followers dispose of themselves as they can, with their numerous herds of cattle, women, children, and retainers, in their repective stations. The chief or chiefs, in the mean time, remain on the former ground, reserving a small tent, or shameana, for the purpose of eating their first meal; which, except on great emergency, is an indispensable custom, and going through their religious ceremonies, called poojah; whereas the bulk of the army, having dispatched their tents and equipage with the beenee walla, remain unsheltered, with their horses in their hands. These avocations, pooja, ashman, rooswae, devotion, ablution, and eating, which are more indispensable with the brahmins than the Mahrattas, being discharged, the chieftain, if a brahmin, is generally ready to proceed by nine or ten o'clock; if a Mahratta, a little earlier. He generally sets out on an elephant, in great state, as far as number can supply the want of order, accompanied by all the cavalry, except the corps advanced with the flags, and reaches his new ground according to the distance of the march, where he finds his tents and equipage ready. This mode of proceeding suits very well with the convenience of the chiefs and principal brahmins in their morning meals and religious ceremonies, especially as they are generally provided with baggage sufficient to reserve a small covering for that purpose, and with elephants and palanquins for the march; but it is much complained of by the bulk of the army, who are deprived of shelter during great part of the day, and obliged to march at the hottest time; which, if through an open arid country, frequently causes a great loss in men and cattle.

Encampment of a Mahratta Army.

The dhall, or standard, of the chief being erected, as mentioned in the preceding acount of the march, the flags of all the other chiefs and leaders of corps are pitched as fast as possible, by their respective beenee wallas, or quarter-masters; and all the inferior commanders dispatch proper people with the flags of their respective chief, to secure quarters as well as they can in the general scramble. On this occasion severe affrays frequently happen. The only part of the camp which carries the appearance of regularity is the bazar; which generally forms a long and broad street to the tent of the great chieftain, and to that of each chief of any consequence; whereas the rest of the camp is so straggling and destitute of order, that it is extremely difficult to penetrate through the crowd of camels, horses, and bullocks, to the interior; which subjects them to the utmost confusion in case of an alarm: and so totally is all regard to situation and disposition neglected, that I have seen the artillery-park so stationed, as to be rendered entirely useless, except by sacrificing their own people which surrounded it.

As soon as the camp is pitched, the baggage tattoos, attached in great numbers to the paugheas, gallop off with wonderful activity in quest of forage, if an opportunity has not offered of picking up any thing on the march; nor are the camels far behind them in these occupations, so that they generally return laden by the time the souarrce, or equipage, of the chief reaches the ground. These foraging parties are more destructive to a country than locusts, and so bold and active, as often to overwhelm large villages: nor are territories of friend or foe exempt from their depredations, fire-wood and forage being allowed to be collected even from their own villages; insomuch that I suppose there was scarcely a piece of wood, or blade of grass or hay left in the villages, for the space of twelve miles round the peshwa's camp, after two days continuance, and a great number of villages were totally demolished.

The safety which the Mahratta armies enjoy as to their communications, from the multiplicity of their cavalry, insures them such ample supplies from vast companies of banjarahs, or grain-merchants, who hover near, or march with them, with immense droves of oxen laden with grain, that they seem to be totally indifferent to every other circumstance of encampment, except water; and as to magazines of provision, or a dependence on the protection or supply of fortified cities, they seem unacquainted with those grand objects of consideration to an European army. This security gives a peculiar character to their camp and armies; for so little danger seems to be apprehended from following their camps, that shop-keepers, mechanics, and people of every profession, carry on their respective callings apparently as much at their ease as in their towns. This gives a convenience and facility to a military life perhaps not to be met with among any other people; which, added to the simplicity of manners, and absence of wants with the Mahrattas, accounts for their spending their lives as happily in the field as other nations do in cities: hence also they have a vast advantage over other armies, who, while in the field, are in a constant state of exertion and hostility with their convenience. This is a point of view in which the military character of this nation merits a particular comparison with the indulgence and luxury of European armies in India.

The safety of the Mahratta camp is to be attributed to the number of their cavalry, hovering round in every direction, rather than to any of the precautionary measures of trenches, posts, and guards, systematically used in European armies; they have indeed at night patrols of horse, called *shabeena,* sent out in different directions, but their ample equipment, at least of the host with which I marched, and of which I now write, enabled them always to keep a large army, under the denomination of *harole*, or van-guard, in advance; and when they approached the enemy, to divide that again by an advance named *toage jereede,* which signifies the unincumbered army; and it is literally so, having seldom a tent belonging to it, every thing, except the immediate apparatus for service, being left at a convenient distance, and under a very slender guard, on what they call *beheer*, or *boonga*, the baggage-camp; so that, at the time of battle with the Nizam, the Mahratta army consisted of three camps, the peshwa's, or head-quarters, being upwards of twenty miles in the rear of the toage jereede, whose beheer was between both.

It will be readily understood, that while this division of force, both in marching and encamping, opens a field of great advantage to an active enemy, provided with cavalry, an army of infantry ,or one much inferior in cavalry, can avail themselves of it very little; as their camp must be, in a manner, constantly blockaded by the numerous troops of the enemy, so as to prevent the smallest movement without discovery; for, exclusive of these hosts of cavalry serving for pay, there are always a great number of pindarees, or looties, a set of predatory horsemen, who march with the Mahratta armies; and, instead of receiving pay, actually purchase of the chief the privilege of plunder at their own risk and charge; a predicament which gives a singular edge to their appetite for depredation, and renders them infinitely more active and destructive than those who, by receiving pay, have not an equal stimulus to rapacity. But though bold and active plunderers, little dependence is to be placed on their military prowess, since, being only desirous of acquiring their booty with tolerable safety, they carefully avoid all situations of danger not pregnant with the grand object of their rapacious spirit.

These pindarees have their distinct quarters, and encamp with the chiefs to whom they are attached: those which fell under my observation were generally Mahomedans; but, as may be supposed, not very rigid observers of any religious tenets. But although generally Mahomedans, all tribes are to be found among them, since nothing seems wanting but a will to join in depradation, so that this corps is generally composed of men whose minds and bodies are best suited to their practice. They reside principally in Malwa, and usually follow the armies of Holkar and Scindia. As those who acquire wealth seldom expose themselves while it lasts, these people are generally poor. Their horses are small and hardy, and their equipment mean, so that they are by no means a match for any cavalry tolerably appointed. The depredations of the pindarees are so dreaded throughout Hindostan, that in those countries most exposed to their ravages, the villages are generally walled, and have a little *gurry*, or citadel, in the centre.

Battle of the Mahrattas.

I have heard but of two instances in which the forces of the Mahratta empire may be said to have engaged in pitched battles; one was at Panniput, where, being previously reduced to a strait by the superior activity of the Patan and Mogul cavalry cutting off their supplies, they were forced into a desperate attempt to extricate themselves, and failing, were subjected to one of the most bloody defeats recorded in history. The other was the battle in which Trimbuck Mamma defeated Hyder Ally, not far from Seringapatam; but I am unacquainted with the order of battle on these occasions. It is reasonable to suppose that the introduction of infantry and artillery, forming so large a part as they now do in the Mahratta armies, must cause a material alteration, if not a total change, in this part of their military service; while, by giving to their army a kind of base, or centre of union, it alters their former predatory and desultory style of warfare: and while on the one hand it makes their invasions infinitely more formidable to states unprovided with the means of opposing them with that increase of strength, I am not without an idea, that as such an alteration is necessarily attended with increasing incumbrances, hostile to rapidity, that an increase of that description of strength may be disserviceable to their operations against a state like ours, in the degree that the increase of strength is effectually inferior to the decrease of the effect of the former desultory velocity. The decision of this point, in which I suppose our infantry and artillery to be as light and rapid as the Mahrattas', will, whenever the contest happens, form an epoch of the most critical interest to the welfare, if not to the existence of the British empire in the East: and I confess, when I view the different manners of the rivals, and the advantages which these people possess in the most unexampled simplicity, absence of wants in food and clothing, absolute submission to the will of their superiors, and constant inurement to the most laborious field service; when I observe these things, and contrast them with the opposite traits in our manners and customs, and add thereto the immeasurable difference and disproportion of our numbers, I confess I cannot help feeling some anxiety for the issue; but, without anticipating the event of so great a struggle, let me revert to the order of battle observed by the Mahrattas in their late action with the Nizam, when, with so little lost or gained on either side, such immense advantages accrued to this empire by the Nizam's pusillanimity. From concurring testimony it appears, that on the news of that prince marching, the Mahratta light army advanced in the order in which it was encamped, about six miles off, to hang on and embarrass his line of march. The movement of such an immense line, so great a distance, over broken and difficult ground, must necessarily have been extremely irregular, in point of distance of the different bodies from each other, and the time of their approaching the Nizam's army: but this does not appear to have precluded an ultimate and effectual cooperation. For it seems that Purseram Bhou being entirely unincumbered with infantry or artillery, having advanced too near the enemy, was forced back with considerable precipitation: but this untoward event, instead of evil, appears to have produced good; for in this interval of time, it seems all the other bodies, both of horse and foot, had advanced so far, as on Purseram Bhou's retreat to present an insurmountable obstacle to the advance of the pursuers, who indeed were not very numerous. It also appears, that although doubtless the whole mass of the Mahratta cavalry might have overwhelmed that small part of the Mogul army which had advanced, yet, so far from taking that advantage, it is certain the cavalry did not advance after Purseram Bhou's retreat; and that the falling back of the corps advanced from the Mogul army, was caused entirely by the cannon with Sindia's infantry on the left, and the effect of the Bhosla's rockets on the right. At all events there does not appear to have been a concerted plan of action, or order of battle; but, except in the act of general advance, every chief acted as circumstances and inclination prompted. In like manner I have no reason to think that, except the small parties left at the different baggage camps, and the body with the peshwa, upwards of twenty miles off, there was any corps allotted for a reserve, any plan fixed for a retreat, or place appointed for a rendezvous, in case of defeat.

Although there appears to be a total deficiency in the common measures used by armies on such occasions, I am assured that the particular division consisting of Sindia's quota, Perron's brigade of infantry, and the corps of Michael and John with their guns, preserved a tolerable degree of order, both in their march, and during the action, being supported by their cavalry, drawn up in the rear, and extending far enough to cover and protect both their flanks.

From my observation of the manners of the Mahrattas, and their extreme looseness of particular discipline and general arrangement, I am strongly of opinion they would afford a very easy conquest to an army of a more vigorous composition, which could bring a sufficient number of cavalry to prevent their making a sport of war, and retreating when they are no longer disposed to maintain the contest, in safety and at leisure.

C. W. MALET.

British Embassy, Mahratta camp,
March 1795.

CONTENTS.

Departure from Bombay to England—regret on leaving India—sail for the Cape of Good Hope in the Betsey schooner—Cape Bassos and the coast of Africa—mermaids at Mosambique and Mombaz; various accounts of those creatures—Melinda—calms and unpleasant weather near the equator—Cape St. Sebastian—currents; storms near the Cape of Good Hope—whales—Bay False—Simmons' harbour—Isthmus between Table Bay and Bay False—Dutch settlement at Simmons' harbour—journey from thence to Cape-town—carriages—roads—general aspect of the country—protea—account of the Cape—climate, variation of the compass, and weather—Table mountain—contiguous mountains—Cape-town—public and private buildings—gardens; fruits, flowers, trees—menagerie—inhabitants of Cape-town—character of the men, inferior to that of the women—disproportion of the sexes—boarding houses—cheapness of living—fraud of the washerwomen—price of different articles—scarcity of timber—beauty and variety of the plants—distant farms—character of the Dutch farmers; their cruelty and savage traits; some causes assigned for their degeneracy—great stock of those farms—vineyards—Dutch government of the colony—first establishment there—character of the Hottentots—Boshmen—Caffraria—wild animals at the Cape—hippopotamus—rhinoceros—camelo-pardalis—zebra—monkeys—orang-outang—mongoose—mocock—birds in southern Africa—ostrich—cassowary—Java pigeon

—secretary-bird—penguins—African lions—villas, gardens, and farms near Cape-town—variety and excellence of the fruits—tent wine—flowers and vegetables—myrtle hedges—Constantia and its vineyards—grand mountain scenery near the Cape.

Voyage from thence to St. Helena—beauties at sea—St. Helena pigeons—general appearance and geographical description of the island—volcanic eruption—fortifications—town—public and private buildings—romantic appearance of the country, beauty of the interior vallies—climate—inhabitants—first establishment of the English—government—cattle—provisions, fruits and vegetables—birds—rose-linnets, Java-sparrows—trees and plants, indigenous and exotic—fish—sail for England—unpleasant weather near the line—anchor on the coast of Guinea—unfortunate detention there—sultry weather—apathy of the crew—meet a French vessel—variety of fish on the gold coast—Medusa—sharks—favourable winds—Cape de Verd Islands—Fogo—Azores—sudden tempest—St. Mary's island—arrival at Corke—Cove of Corke—departure from Ireland—rapture on landing in England—conclusion.

CHAPTER XX.

Pursuant to the resolution mentioned in the last chapter, I sailed from Bombay for Europe, on the 1st of December 1775. With regret I left a spot, where I had spent several happy years, in a delightful society; heightened by the charms of friendship, and animated by the hope of acquiring that independence which first led me to its distant shores. Although illness frustrated the enjoyment of these pursuits, I endeavoured to encourage the pleasing anticipation of seeing parents, friends, and my native country, and returning to India with renewed health and an advantageous appointment.

The ships of that season had been all dispatched to Europe previous to my determination of leaving India; I was therefore under the necessity of embarking for the Cape of Good in the Betsey schooner, a vessel built on an Indiaman's long-boat, and perhaps the smallest ever sent on such a voyage, having only four European sailors besides the captain and two officers; the rest of the crew were Lascars, or Indian mariners.

Soon after leaving Bombay we fell in with the north-east trade-wind, which in thirteen days carried us off Cape Bassos on the coast of Africa, which we saw at a few leagues distance. The next day we crossed the equator, and passed a range of sandy hills and lofty mountains. A steady wind befriended us to the sixth degree of southern latitude, when it was succeeded by variable breezes, calms, thunder, lightning and heavy rain. The sea was enlivened by a variety of birds, uniting with dolphins, albacores and bonitos, in hostility against the unfortunate flying-fish.

Near the coast we saw many other sorts of fish, but did not meet with any of the mermaids so often mentioned in these seas; and especially by Mr. Matcham, a gentleman of great respectability, and at that time superintendant of the company's marine at Bombay. I have heard him declare, that when in command of a trading vessel at Mozambique, Mombaz, and Melinda, three of the principal sea-ports on the east coast of Africa, he frequently saw these extraordinary animals from six to twelve feet long; the head and face resembling the human, except about the nose and mouth, which were rather more like a hog's snout; the skin fair and smooth; the head covered with dark glossy hair of considerable length; the neck, breasts, and body of the female, as low as the hips, appeared like a well-formed woman; from thence to the extremity of the tail they were perfect fish. The shoulders and arms were in good proportion, but from the elbow tapered to a fin, like the turtle or penguin. These animals were daily cut up, and sold by weight in the fish markets of Mombaz; nor was the flesh easily distinguished from the fishy pork which those who have resided at Calicut or Anjengo are well acquainted with.

Although the existence of mermen and mermaids is doubted by many, the history of England, Holland, Portugal and other countries, proves the reality of these creatures. In the fifteenth century, after a dreadful tempest on the coast of Holland, one of them was found struggling in the mud, near Edam in West Friesland; from whence it was carried to Haarlem, where it lived some years; was clothed in female apparel, and it is said was taught to spin. In 1531 another, caught in the Baltic, was sent as a present to Sigismund, king of Poland; it lived some days, and was seen by all his court. In 1560, the fishermen of Ceylon caught seven of both sexes, which were seen by several Portugueze gentlemen then at Menar, and among the rest, by Dimas Bosquez, physician to the Viceroy of Goa, who minutely examined them, made dissections, and asserted that the principal parts, internal and external, were conformable to those of the human species.

Our small vessel approached much nearer the African coast than is customary for India ships homeward bound. We were not far from Melinda, that hospitable port which received Vasco de Gama and his brave comrades after encountering the storms of the Cape, and escaping the treachery of the Moors at Mombaz and Quiloa. Here they met with a friendly monarch to supply their wants, and found a number of merchants from various parts of India, who opened a scene of glory and profit to Gama's aspiring mind, and furnished him with pilots to navigate the first ships from Europe across the Indian ocean to Calicut, then the grand emporium of commerce in the oriental world.

From Melinda our voyage was protracted by light winds and calms, and sometimes by strong southerly gales. A favourable current generally carried us twenty or thirty miles a day; and more than once, when we had no advantage of wind, on taking an observation we found the current had advanced us upwards of fifty miles on our course. Nicholson remarks, that in these latitudes a wind prevails from south-east to south-west; which, blowing strong, with squalls and rain, meets the north-east winds, and these repelling each other with great fury, occasion terrible storms and tempests. These winds fly about like a whirlwind; the sky is dark and gloomy, and the clouds pour forth deluges of rain, succeeded by calms, a sultry atmosphere, and oppressive languor.

> For there the line its torrid influence throws,
> The sky turns gloomy, and the ocean glows;
> Along the heavens th' incumbent vapours brood,
> Eclipse the day, and darken all the flood;
> No gentle air allays the smother'd heat,
> While nature sickens with the sultry weight;
> The breath grows short, the heart but feebly plays,
> And the dim orb of light forgets to gaze;
> At length the slumbering combination breaks,
> The lightning kindles, and the storm awakes;
> Th' assembled winds from every quarter roar,
> The weeping skies a liquid deluge pour.

Continuing our course along the eastern shores of Africa, on the 2d of January we saw Cape St. Sebastian, at ten leagues distance; the currents, which had hitherto ran to the south, now changed their direction, and carried us westward of our reckoning. On leaving St. Sebastian we encountered rough seas, and having run down the thirty-third degree of latitude, considered our voyage as nearly terminated. While anticipating the pleasure of shortly landing and enjoying the summer refreshments at the Cape, a storm suddenly burst upon us from the south-east, and continued with unabated fury six and thirty hours. The sea was dreadful; and the situation of our little bark, elevated on its foaming mountains, or plunged into a dark abyss, filled every soul with horror.

We saw a number of whales and grampuses in those southern latitudes, which we sometimes wished at a greater distance, from an apprehension of mischief from their enormous bulk. "There go the ships, and there is that leviathan, whom thou hast made to take his pastime therein." But the sports of these immense animals, emerging and diving, often cause a concussion in the waters which proves fatal to small vessels.

On the 13th of January, sounding on the great sand-bank at the extremity of Africa, we found ground at ninety fathoms, and soon afterwards saw the land. Unfavourable gales again prevented our entering Bay False until the 20th, when a fair wind carried us up that noble bay, and we anchored at noon in a small cove, called Simmons' Harbour, where fifteen ships may lie secure in the most stormy weather; situated on the western side of False-bay it is at all times more commodious than Table-bay, the summer harbour near Cape-town. The two bays are separated by an isthmus, covered with sand and small shells, most probably once under water. The Cape mountains, rocky hills, sandy plains and cultivated tracts on the peninsula, contiguous to Cape-town, form a territory upwards of thirty miles long, and eight broad.

The Dutch settlement at False-bay then consisted of only a few houses, gardens, and store-houses, scattered at the bottom of the mountains which form Simmons' cove; with a pier and crane for the landing of goods, great conveniencc for watering the ships, abundant supplies of fresh provisions, fruit, and vegetables, and tolerable accommodation for passengers at the boarding houses. Having no inducement to remain there, I proceeded to Cape-town, about twenty miles distant, in a light waggon drawn by eight horses. The coachmen, or waggoners, who are generally slaves, drive these eight in hand with wonderful dexterity, making the hills resound with the smack of their long whip, and continual vociferation to the horses. The vehicle contains six or eight persons sitting on benches before each other, which is the usual mode of travelling in this part of the world.

The road for the first six miles, to a place called Muisenburg, was over a sandy beach, or the acclivities of the mountains, sometimes on dangerous precipices, under rocks loosened from the mountains, and apparently threatening destruction. The pass at Muisenburg, defended by a fortress, is deemed impregnable. From thence we entered a sandy plain, little cultivated; but presenting a succession of natural beauties in the variety of heaths and other plants indigenous to its sterile surface, the ornament of European conservatories. The country was not otherwise interesting until within a few miles of the capital, when it became suddenly enriched with farms, villas, plantations, vineyards, and gardens; embellished by groves and avenues of oaks, elms, and protea-argentea, a most elegant tree: it does not attain a large size, from growing extremely close, and is thickly covered with leaves soft and glossy as satin, glittering like a forest of silver undulated by the breeze. The golden protea, more gaudy than its modest rival, arrayed in foliage of yellow-green edged with scarlet, appears in the sunbeams like waves of fire; they form a lovely contrast. These novelties beguiled a rough heavy road, until our arrival at Cape-town, situated at the foot of the Table-mountain; near a large bay full of ships, opening to the ocean and several rocky islands.

The Cape of Good Hope forms the western part of Bay Falso, and terminates the south point of the African continent. It was formerly called Cabo dos Tormentos, the Cape of Storms, a name expressive of its situation amidst contending elements. John king of Portugal changed it to Boa Esperanza, when De Gama, after conquering all difficulties, doubled this formidable barrier, and opened the passage to India. It is situated in the latitude of 34° 24′ south, and 18° 30′ east longitude. The variation of the compass was then 19° west; mariners pay great attention to this variation, it being the surest guide for the longitude in the voyage from India. The north-west winds generally prevail from May until the beginning of September; the south-east during the other months. The latter are cold, dry, and unpleasant, but the atmosphere clear and healthy. The climate may be called temperate, the heats seldom last long, and it rarely freezes in winter, although the summits of the interior mountains are frequently covered with snow. The barometer varies from 27 to 28 inches chiefly in the winter; in which season the thermometer at sunrise is from 40 to 50 degrees, and at noon from 65 to 70; in summer it rises from 70 to 90 degrees, and sometimes approaches 100.

The view of this stupendous promontory from the sea presents a scene of massy rocks and barren mountains: that, from its flat surface, called the Table-land is most conspicuous, and seen from a great distance. The fatigue and difficulty of its ascent are amply repaid by the extensive prospects from the summit; where the eye, as on a map, stretches over an immense space of sea and land; comprising the boundless ocean, rocky isles, majestic mountains, softer hills, a large town, crowded harbour, and scenes of cultivation. The Table mountain is said to be covered with its table-cloth when mantled with white clouds, falling in a striking manner on its sides. Half concealed by these immense volumes rolling over its surface, it makes a very grand appearance, but in height is inferior to many others of less note, being only three thousand six hundred feet above the level of the sea. On the summit is a lake of fresh water, which supplies the town and shipping; the stream in its descent falling over grotesque rocks, forms beautiful cascades. At each end of the Table-land, is a lofty mountain connected with it; one called the Lion's Rump, the other the Devil's Mountain. They are all composed of rocky strata, but are said not to be volcanic. Their inhabitants are chiefly hyenas, wolves, monkeys, vultures, and sometimes run-away slaves.

Cape-town is large, and regularly built; the principal streets, leading to the great square, intersect each other at right angles: in 1776 it contained six or seven hundred houses, and about eight thousand inhabitants, including slaves. The houses, built in the European style from one to three stories high, have uniformly that neat appearance which characterizes the best towns in Holland. The square, and most of the wide streets, are planted with avenues of oaks and poplars, on each side of a narrow canal, before the houses. There were then only two churches, one Calvinist, the other Lutheran. The principal public buildings were the stadt-house, library, hospital and prison. The fort at the south end of the

Engraved by W. Angus

TABLE LAND, and distant View of Cape Town at the CAPE of GOOD HOPE.

town was not deemed a place of strength; there were several other batteries in different situations.

The public gardens, adjoining the town, were much frequented by the inhabitants, and formed a delightful resort for strangers. They contained five walks, half a mile long, shaded by oaks, and perfumed by hedges of myrtle on each side; which separated them from square orchards and gardens, divided by formal narrow walks and hedges; but richly stored with standard peaches, apricots, figs, apples, pears, and other European and Indian fruits, planted amidst a profusion of roots and vegetables for the use of the hospital, and ships belonging to the Dutch East India company. Two enclosures before the governor's house, are appropriated to flowers, and curious plants. The garden was terminated by a large menagerie, containing the most remarkable beasts and birds indigenous to Africa, or brought from other parts of the world.

The inhabitants of Cape-town have generally a good complexion, and some of the young women are pretty; but they soon incline to corpulency, and lose the elegant symmetry so attractive in the female form. The men are perhaps less phlegmatic than the Hollanders in Europe. Descended from an heterogeneous mixture of Dutch, Germans, French, and other emigrants, they have, in some measure, lost the peculiar traits of national character, and by a constant intercourse with foreigners, have acquired more affability aud courtesy than we usually meet with. The colonists had mostly large families, matrimony was encouraged, luxury and dissipation discountenanced; there were then no theatres, casinos, nor public exhibitions of any kind. The morning was dedicated to business, the evening to family meetings: frequently enlivened by music and dancing. On the arrival of any distinguished strangers the governor gave a public ball to the principal inhabitants and passengers from the ships.

Such is the pleasing side of the picture; for it must be confessed, that, when compared with the refinements of Europe, or the political, military, and commercial pursuits in India, the inhabitants of the Cape appear to pass a dull, monotonous, indolent life. With little employment in commerce or agriculture, no taste for intellectual pleasures, or mental improvement, the gratifications of animal appetite usurp a primary consideration, and the important concerns of eating, drinking, and smoking, engross a large portion of time which might be dedicated to nobler pursuits. The women merit a more amiable character; the girls were educated for domestic life, the mother instructed them in needle-work, and the various branches of household economy. The father, assisted by such masters as were procurable, taught them the French and English languages, writing and arithmetic; nor were the elegant accomplishments of music, drawing, dancing, and works of ingenuity neglected in the higher classes of society.

I was informed there were, at least, eight women to one man among the white inhabitants at Cape-town. Naturalists have observed that a larger proportion of females are born there than elsewhere: but another cause may be ascribed for this deficiency; all the girls remain at the colony, while the boys are generally sent to Europe and the East Indies, to enter a more ample field for fame and fortune.

When I first visited the Cape there was no respectable tavern or hotel; but many of the best families accommodated strangers for a Spanish dollar a day. Mr. de Witt's was then esteemed the genteelest boarding-house; where, for this sum, I was provided with a neat bed-chamber, the use of the parlours and drawing-room; and four meals a day, besides tea and coffee. At dinner we always sat down with his well-regulated family to a table plentifully covered with fish, meat, poultry, and game; a dessert of choice fruit, and every sort of Cape-wine, except constantia.

Some articles, notwithstanding, were very expensive, especially fuel and washing; strangers often found the latter peculiarly so; for however honest the washerwomen might appear in returning clean linen corresponding in tale with the articles delivered, they generally deferred bringing in the last assortment until the passengers were just going on board their ship, who seeing the number correct, suspected no other fraud; but I have known more than one lady much mortified, when, far from any reparation on the distant main, she has found a muslin gown deprived of a breadth, and her cambric handkerchiefs reduced a few inches in size; nor were the gentlemen less annoyed on beholding their shirts and cravats equally curtailed.

Coach-hire was thought extravagant; they charged eight dollars a day for a country excursion, and four for an evening ride. Bread was always at fixed a price; that made of the best wheat flour one penny per pound, which the bakers were allowed to charge after the most plentiful harvests, but not permitted to advance in a season of scarcity. The common Cape-wines then sold for ten, twelve, and fifteen dollars the pipe; so that the lower classes amply enjoyed the two great blessings of bread and wine;

the earth supplied abundance of fruit and vegetables, and the extensive sand bank, at the end of their promontory, a variety of fish.

Some of the interior districts are said to contain inexhaustible forests of timber, but from a want of means to convey it to the Cape, the Dutch company preferred sending timber and plank from Holland and Batavia. It could probably be transported by sea from Mussul-bay and other places at less expense. From this cause timber and plank were at an immoderate price; firewood was procured with difficulty: to gather it in small quantities was the sole occupation of numerous slaves; and a small cart-load of roots and brush-wood could not be purchased for less than three or four dollars, consequently all manufactures requiring the operation of fire were extravagantly dear.

Although there is so great a deficiency of timber, and useful trees, near the Cape, no country can boast of more curious and beautiful plants than this part of Africa. The variety of erica, geranium, ixia, and other elegant tribes, lately brought to Europe, is astonishing, and the number is continually increasing. Were I master of the subject, it would be too copious to enter on a Linnæan description of the lovely plants which "waste their sweetness on the desert air" of Africa, but become the pride and delight of the English collections. In the season of spring, between the months of September and December, the infinite variety and beauty of these plants springing up on the sandy plains, covering the sides of the mountains, and adorning their rugged summits, is astonishing; their colours are brilliant, and many are extremely odoriferous.

Exclusive of the plantations and villas in the Cape territory, many gentlemen had estates at a great distance in the interior districts, particularly round Mussul-bay, four hundred miles on the eastern shore, where their planters cultivate corn, wine, fruit, aloes, and other drugs; but I believe there were no manufactories at the capital, or throughout the colony. Some of the principal farmers, we were told, employed two hundred slaves and Hottentots in agriculture and breeding cattle: the former were either born in slavery at the Cape, or brought from India, Madagascar, and the Comorro isles; the latter, whether they in reality enjoy their liberty or not, are considered to be a free people.

I heard of many farms situated a month's journey from Cape-town, among the friendly Hottentots. Those farmers are mostly descended from the Dutch, French, and German protestants, who, on various occasions, rather chose to encounter the dangers of a foreign country than endure the cruelty they experienced in their own. They generally speak the Dutch language, and retain the European complexion. Scattered throughout those extensive wilds, they have little communication with each other, but many of them accompany their wives and children once a year to Cape-town, in large waggons, loaded with wine, grain, butter, dried fruits, hides, and other articles. With the produce they purchase wearing-apparel, furniture, utensils, and necessaries for a family. Some of those planters are men of amiable manners; honest, industrious, and hospitable, but ignorant of every thing beyond the extent of their farm: the want of books and social intercourse renders them credulous and inquisitive, characteristics usual among people thus situated, especially so in the remote districts of the United States in America.

Such were the better sort of farmers in the Dutch colony when I made my inquiries; I am sorry to add that another, and I fear a much larger class, bore a different character; and perhaps a more unprincipled, unlettered, and cruel race of people nowhere existed. I do not make this assertion from my own experience; I travelled but little into the interior, and only occasionally saw the farmers who brought their commodities to town; but from reports of its inhabitants, confirmed by the accounts of Barrow, Percival, and other intelligent travellers, who made long journies among them, we know these colonists are, in many respects, no better than savages, and in clemency, urbanity, and other social virtues, far inferior to the Hottentots among whom they dwell. The latter are a mild, amiable, gentle race, compared with the Dutch boors and yeomanry of the Cape, composed of the lowest classes of Dutch, French, and German emigrants, and their descendants. Their cruelty to their slaves, cattle, and Hottentots, has become proverbial, and has been fully detailed. Many of these colonists have served in the ranks of the Dutch and German regiments, from whence they became servants and overseers in the farms, and marrying the farmers' daughters, have in time purchased landed property for themselves; and without retaining the virtues of a soldier, have introduced the vices of the army into a different order of society.

Thus, far distant from the civilized manners and refinements of the capital, deprived of the blessings of public worship, and the social delights of a returning sabbath, the generality of these people had descended, or rather degenerated, into an almost savage state, and were given up to ignorance, cruelty, and animal gratification. The moral and political laws of Holland, and even the by-laws of the colony, had little influence in regions so remote from the seat of government; every head of a family found himself at liberty to act without control; and his conduct generally evinced, that unrestrained power, whether exercised in the durbar of an Asiatic sovereign, or usurped by a Dutch boor in the wilds of Africa, has always a fatal tendency.

In the colonial farms it is not uncommon to have a hundred oxen for the plough, thirty or forty milch-cows, eighty horses, and a thousand sheep: I was told of some that fed ten or twelve thousand sheep, with horses, oxen, slaves, and Hottentots in proportion; the oxen are particularly serviceable in drawing large waggons over the indifferent roads in those extensive regions.

Many vineyards in advantageous situations produce a hundred pipes of wine at a vintage. The vines were originally brought from France and Germany; but, except from the two vineyards at Constantia, the Cape wines are not much esteemed. The principal inhabitants drink those imported from Madeira and Bourdeaux, and prefer Dutch ale and English porter to the best malt liquor brewed at the Cape. As the duties were not exorbitant, the Teneriffe and Madeira wines were drank at a moderate expense; nor was there any want of brandy, rum, or Batavia arrack.

On every account, the Cape of Good Hope is one of the finest places in the world for ships to refresh at. Advantageously situated midway between Europe and Asia, they here meet with most of the fruits and vegetables of the torrid and temperate zones, with plenty of excellent mutton, beef, and lamb; all of which, when I was there, sold for a halfpenny per pound; I believe the foreign ships paid something more. The medium price of wheat was about two shillings and fourpence the bushel. The settlement of the English at the Cape, and the consequence of a large garrison established there, have caused many alterations of which I am not competent to judge.

The governor was then appointed by the Dutch East India company, and had the rank of an *edele heer*, equal to one of the council of regency at Batavia. Under him was a council, consisting of eight members, including the fiscal, and the major who commanded the garrison; these gentlemen held the principal posts in the settlement, and were assisted by junior servants. The colonists had nothing to do with the police or government, but seemed to enjoy much comfort and tranquillity under their administration.

The Dutch had been in possession of this colony ever since the middle of the seventeenth century; the Hottentots, who, were easily captivated by presents of tobacco, brandy, and cutlery, permitted them to extend their territory, establish farms, and, for these trifling considerations, to become masters of their flocks and herds, far distant from the southern rocks where they first settled. In a short time, when under the pernicious effects of brandy and tobacco, they in a manner pawned themselves and children to the Dutch. Although it may not amount to direct slavery, they have ever since performed all the hard services of agriculture for the colonists.

Those Hottentots who preferred the blessings of liberty and a pastoral life to such debasing gratifications, drove their cattle into the interior parts of the country, among extensive forests and high mountains, far from the European settlements; there they still continue in separate hordes, and fix their kraals at pleasure, where pasture, water and shade most invite. They appear to be an innocent people, in what may be called a savage state; for they certainly have made no progress towards refinement, though the christian missionaries have been rather successful in converting them.

In stature they are seldom above the middle size; their complexion is dark brown, with short black curling hair, like the negroes, whom they also resemble in features; the young women are not unpleasing in their form, and soft and feminine in their manners.. The different tribes vary something in their dress, which generally consists of the skins of wild beasts; and both sexes wear a skin cloak, called a kross, which ties over the shoulders: the women have also a little apron, sometimes covered with beads, and an ornament on their head, composed of the same materials. Both sexes are fond of painting themselves, and rubbing their bodies with the fat of animals; which, as they go almost naked, prevents the bad effects of the sun in the summer heats. Their usual arms are bows and arrows, spears and lances; which they use with great dexterity against their enemies, and the wild beasts that infest the kraals, and carry off their cattle. They sometimes shoot with poisoned arrows, especially at the latter; for which purpose they have many vegetable poisons in the inland parts of Africa, but the most fatal is said to be the venom of serpents.

The Hottentots subsist chiefly upon animals caught in the

chace, and the milk of their cattle, with a few roots peculiar to the country, and sometimes a sheep from the flocks; but I believe they nowhere cultivate corn, nor have any idea of gardening. Cheerful, harmless, and hospitable, they are perhaps happier in ignorance, than some other nations with their boasted refinements. They are fond of music, singing, and dancing; but nothing can be more simple than their musical instruments, more monotonous than their songs, nor more ungraceful than their dances.

The boshmen, or wood-men Hottentots, are a set of people who live by plundering their neighbours, whether Hottentots, Caffrees, or Dutch farmers, at places the most remote from protection; they shoot with poisoned arrows, and their appearance always spreads alarm among the planters. I believe they are not of any particular tribe of Hottentots, but form a community of banditti, composed of the vilest wretches from the other hordes; as also from negro and mulatto slaves, who desert from the Cape, and unite with these people in devoting themselves to a life of plunder, devastation, and cruelty, throughout the Dutch colony, and the peaceful tribes of Hottentots.

Of Caffraria, which joins the Hottentots' country on the north, and other distant parts of this vast continent, the inhabitants of the Cape, when I was there, seemed to have but very little knowledge, except from the prejudiced relations and improbable stories propagated by the ignorant planters who were settled nearest to their districts.

In the menagerie at the Cape I had an opportunity of making drawings of most of the wild animals and curious birds from the interior parts of Africa. Lions, tigers, elephants, hyenas, jackals, and smaller quadrupeds abound in the rocky wilds and forests. The hippopotamus, rhinoceros, zebra, and camelo-pardalis, animate the distant solitudes. I not only delineated all these animals, but endeavoured to obtain the best information I could respecting their natural history and local habits, from the farmers who visited the Cape-town, from the inland provinces; but so many excellent accounts have been since published by English travellers, who had still better means of obtaining information, that I need not introduce my own remarks; indeed the farmers and planters seemed to deal so much in the marvellous, not only respecting the savage race, but the Hottentots and their brother farmers in the remote districts, that it is necessary to be very cautious in crediting their narrations; I shall therefore confine myself to a very few particulars.

The hippopotamus, although in size next to the elephant, is a a mild and gentle animal, heavy and slow in its motions by land, but more active in the water; and, when irritated by the huntsmen, it sometimes does mischief in that element: it feeds principally on grass, and is caught in pits which the Hottentots dig on the banks of the rivers, where it comes to graze. These pits are ten or twelve feet deep, concealed by green turf and boughs, from whence this ponderous animal can never extricate himself. Its flesh is esteemed a delicacy, and the ivory of the tusks preferable to that of the elephant; the planters obtain much oil from the hippopotamus, the rhinoceros, and the elephant, both for medicinal and domestic use. The feet and trunk of these animals are thought excellent by the Hottentots and colonists, who make them into a rich stew; the rest of their flesh, which is seldom all devoured while fresh, is cut up into long thongs, and dried in the sun for future provision. Had we known in the Guzerat campaign that an elephant's foot was esteemed a luxury, we might often have been regaled when so many were left on the field of battle.

What a beautiful description does the book of Job give us of the hippopotamus, under the name of Behemoth. "Behold now be-
"hemoth which I have made, he eateth grass as an ox; his strength
"is in his loins, and his bones are like bars of iron; he moveth
"his tail like a cedar, and his sinews are wrapped together: the
"mountains bring him forth food; he lieth under the shady trees,
"in the covert of the reeds and the fens: the shady trees cover
"him with their shadow, and the willows of the brook compass
"him about; behold, he drinketh up a river, and hasteth not;
"he trusteth that he can draw up Jordan into his mouth!"

As the hippopotamus is undoubtedly the behemoth, so the rhinoceros is supposed to be the unicorn of scripture: these animals attain a prodigious size in Africa, and are said to be the most powerful of the savage tribe; it is not naturally ferocious, but its coat of mail affords a complete defensive armour, and its horn is so formidable a weapon of offence, that he generally remains unmolested by the lions, tigers, and other beasts of prey. Here, as well as in Hindostan, I found many extraordinary virtues attributed to the horn of the rhinoceros, especially in drinking out of it as an antidote to poison. It feeds upon grass, sugar-canes, and esculent plants found in its haunts.

Many improbable stories are circulated at the Cape of the camelo-pardalis, or giraffe, which is certainly one of the most singular animals we are acquainted with; its height is often magnified, but I believe none have yet been met with that measured more than sixteen feet, from the hoof to the tip of the horns, or short bony excrescences on the top of the head, which are eight or nine inches in length; the neck is very long in proportion to the body, which is only seven feet; the length of the shoulder-bone makes the fore-legs appear much longer than those behind, and gives the animal an inclining posture: the male is richly spotted with a dark brown on a grey ground, the female of lighter hue. I did not see one alive, but made my drawing from a stuffed specimen then ready for Europe. The camel-leopard is an innocent peaceable animal, and feeds chiefly on the leaves of the mimosa trees, which adorn the interior forests.

The zebra, another native of the African deserts, is a beautiful animal: in form, colour, and graceful motion, it has the comeliness of the horse, the swiftness of the deer, and the independence of the lion. It is larger than the common ass, and although sometimes taken alive, I believe not one has been completely tamed, or converted to any use.

The adjacent country abounds with monkeys of various kinds; many of them are domesticated by the inhabitants. Among others, I often visited an oran-outang, which had been brought from Java; in many instances it approached very near the human species, and seems to be the uniting link in the grand chain of creation between man and beast. At the Cape they have playful mongooses and mococks, from Madagascar and the Comorro isles, some of them beautifully marked.

Africa abounds with a variety of birds, but their rural haunts were at so great a distance from the Cape, that I could only draw those I met with in cages, or in the public menagerie. In South America, where the loveliest vallies skirt the city of St. Sebastian, every walk presented beautiful subjects for the pencil; not so the country near the Cape. The African deserts nourish thousands of ostriches; some were kept in the menagerie, with the secretary bird, and others from the same wilds; together with the cassowary, the columba-coronata, and many curious birds from the Dutch settlements in the East Indies.

The ostrich is so well known in the African ornithology, that it would be needless to describe it. Among other peculiarities, it is said to digest stones and iron. I am ignorant of their digestive powers, but they certainly voraciously devour pieces of glass, iron, and similar substances, when thrown into the menagerie. The ostrich is the largest of the feathered tribes, and is called in Arabia the camel-bird, from its resemblance to that animal; it runs swiftly over the desert, by means of its long legs and expanded wings, which are not formed for an aerial flight. The Arabians, Caffrees, and Hottentots, hunt them for their feathers, and eat the flesh of the young ones; their eggs, fifteen inches in circumference, also afford a plentiful meal. Among the luxuries of the Roman emperors we read of Heliogabalus having destroyed six hundred ostriches to furnish one dish of brains. The large thick shell of this bird is frequently carved with subjects from scripture history and other ornaments. Not rivalling the sculpture of an Italian basso-relievo, they are sold for a trifle to the passing stranger by the slaves who carve them; as are also other of these egg-shells cut into longitudinal bars, like a bird cage; in which some poor canary-bird, or other unfortunate songster is perched, and sold with his singular prison, for a couple of dollars.

The cassowary, more formidable in appearance, and more savage in disposition than the ostrich, is generally his companion in the Cape menagerie: not much inferior in size, and stronger made, he is capable of doing much mischief, and sometimes evinces his power, as our party one day experienced. The cassowary then exhibited had it seems an invincible aversion to the fair-sex, which the keeper had not informed us of: a young lady approaching, he instantly struck her down with his foot, and got the better of two gentlemen who attempted to rescue her, before the keeper, with an immense whip, put an end to the combat. He was altogether a very formidable adversary; the head, instead of a crest or soft plumage, being armed with a hard bony excrescence, like a helmet; his large black eyes are encircled with hairs, which sparingly cover the head and neck instead of feathers.

Among other curious birds was the Columba-coronata, or Java pigeon, a bird nearly as large as a turkey, with a plumage of dusky blue, and a beautiful tuft on the head. Also the secretary-bird, a native of the southern parts of Africa; about three feet high, chiefly arrayed in purple, with some long feathers elegantly falling from the head; it destroys serpents, rats and vermin, and is on that account much esteemed, for the Cape abounds with venomous snakes, scorpions, scolopendræ, and noxious reptiles, as do many situations between the tropics; also with lizards of many descriptions, the land tortoise, and gryllæ, or locusts, in variety, abundance, and depredation, equalling their destructive hosts in other countries. The penguins, seals, sea otters, and other animals in the amphibious parts of the Cape zoology, found among the rocks and islands near this southern promontory, open an ample field to the naturalist.

The lions, hyenas, and wild beasts in the interior of the colony are very formidable and destructive. The wonderful stories of these animals, related by farmers from the more distant regions, require no common degree of faith; some of their narrations would have staggered Vaillant himself. There appears to be very little difference in the habits of the African lion, and the royal tiger of Hindostan; both are equally crafty, ferocious, and cruel. We read of the noble behaviour and generous conduct of the sovereign of the forest, in ancient history, and cherish the pleasing ideas early imbibed of his attachment and friendship to man. Modern lions have certainly the same propensities as all of the feline genus in other countries; and the Cape farmers now complain as loudly, if not as elegantly, as Virgil's shepherds.

> " Impastus ceu plena leo per ovilia turbans,
> " Suadet enim vesana fames, manditque trahitque
> " Molle pecus." Æn. 9.

> " The famish'd lion, thus, with hunger bold,
> " O'erleaps the fences of the nightly fold,
> " And tears the peaceful flocks." Dryden.

I had no time for distant excursions, but joined several parties to the villas and plantations beyond the sandy plains, three or four miles from Cape-town; where the governor had a country house, and most of the principal citizens, plantations, farms, and vineyards, surrounding a rural habitation. The gardens and orchards were extremely pleasant, and very productive, mingling the peach, apricot, and apple of Europe, with the guava, banana, and pomegranate of tropical climes. There were mango trees in the company's garden, which had not then produced fruit. The peaches, apricots, and plums were all standards, and in January, the commencement of the Cape autumn, were bending under their grateful produce; nectarines had not succeeded, and cherries were uncommon: strawberries abound earlier in the season, with a few gooseberries and currants; oranges, lemons, figs, and mulberries are as prolific as the apples and pears, every where in great profusion. Nothing can exceed the plenty and variety of the grapes; one of the most delicious, produces the tent-wine, a black grape, with a rich crimson juice like blood; which may have caused it to be selected for the sacramental wine.

The avenues are generally planted with almond, chesnut, and walnut trees, which attain a large growth, and protect the flowers, vegetables, and tenderer fruit trees, from the high tempestuous winds, which so powerfully prevail in that part of the globe. The kitchen gardens abound with cabbages, cauliflowers, artichokes, asparagus, pease, beans, french-beans, beet-root, turnips, carrots, potatoes, salads, and most of the European vegetables; many of them much improved by the climate. They seem to be more attentive to these productive and useful crops, than to the cultivation of flowers, for which the Dutch are generally famous. Yet a variety of European flowers seemed to flourish among the aloes, geraniums, and elegant heaths indigenous to Africa. A chief beauty of the Cape gardens, are the luxuriant myrtle hedges, which surround every enclosure, to a great height; their bloming branches waving over the head of the passenger, unite in fragrance with the odoriferous exhalations from the orange and lemon trees, abounding in these enclosures.

I shall take leave of this pleasing subject with a few lines from a manuscript poem, descriptive of the gardens and orchards at the Cape, written among their delightful variety.

On flowers, in Europe yet unseen, I tread,
And trees of stranger form embrace my head;
The product here of every clime is known;
This generous soil adopts them all her own:
Arrang'd the vegetable tribes appear,
And plants, like nations, grow familiar here:
Around her soft perfume the citron throws,
There, through the gloom, the rich pomegranate glows;
The brightening orange next attracts the view,
The paler lime succeeds, with fainter hue;
There the blue fig the purple grape entwines,
Here with the rose the Persian-jasmine joins;
Here towers, with native grace, the tender palm
Beneath the weeping shrub distils with balm;
There the fair aloe rears its flow'ry head,
Here the dark cypress forms its equal shade.
A thousand birds, of various form and sound,
Diffuse luxurious harmony around;
Not brighter colours paint the heavenly bow,
Than grace their wings, and o'er their plumage glow.

We spent one day at Constantia, the celebrated vineyard, twelve miles from Cape-town. We travelled, in coaches drawn by eight horses, over the sandy plains already mentioned in the journey from False-bay, until we approached the mountains, and entered a country abounding with farms and young woods of oak. Much trouble and expense have been bestowed to produce this effect in a wide waste of barren mountains, rocky precipices, and sandy hills. On a rising ground, in this once dreary region, are situated the house and vineyard of Constantia: the former is a plain comfortable mansion, sheltered by plantations, and approached by an avenue of venerable oaks. The vineyards are in the best aspect, whither after visiting the cellars and tasting the choicest wine, we were conducted. In general, we were invited, not only to eat as many grapes as we pleased, but to carry them away with us. At Constantia the vine-dresser requested us to pick only a little fruit from the trees, but not to gather a bunch; the wine is too precious for this indulgence: it must ever be deemed a rare, as well as a delicious cordial, because the peculiar soil of Upper Constantia gives the muscadel grape a value there, which cannot be imparted to the same vine when planted elsewhere, and treated exactly in the same manner; it always produces a different grape, and wine of inferior flavour. The experiment has been repeatedly tried in the adjoining vineyards of Lower Constantia, without success.

We dined at an adjacent villa, delightfully situated among citron, orange and lemon groves, and all the pleasing variety just mentioned, contrasted also by the rough scenery of rocks and mountains which surround it. The vineyard seldom yielded less than forty pipes of wine each vintage, inferior in strength and richness to Constantia, but resembling it in flavour; it was then sold in casks containing twenty gallons, at twelve dollars the cask. The hospitable proprietor had lately purchased this estate, with a good house, excellent wine-vaults, gardens, vineyard, oak-plantations, and an extensive tract of contiguous waste land, for six thousand rix-dollars.

I do not particularize the aquatic excursions we made to Penguin island, and other rocks near the Cape, inhabited by penguins, seals, and sea-fowl. We sometimes extended them to a greater distance, to have a better view of the Table-land and its contiguous mountains, which I had only seen before through the medium of a dreadful tempest. The scenery around Bay Falso, and that of Table-bay is singularly striking. Captain Percival's animated description shall conclude my first visit to this grand boundary of southern Africa.

" The immense masses which rise in many places almost perpendicularly from the sea, and are lost among the clouds; the vast gullies and caverns, which seem to sink to an immeasurable depth amidst these stupendous mountains; the long-extended ledges of rock, over which, in a few places, are scattered some tufts of stunted trees and withered shrubs; the successive ridges of white sandy hills, each of which appears like a valley to the one by which it is surmounted; the terrible surf which is continually raging on the beach, along which these ridges are stretched; with the spray, which is thrown to an immense height by the waves recoiling from the more rocky parts; all these objects rushing at once upon the eye of those who approach the Cape, produce an effect which can be but faintly conveyed by description.

" This surf which is driven to the land with such fury, produces a phenomenon in the sandy deserts, even far removed from the sea. In the time of the violent south-east winds it is carried to a great distance into the country, presenting the appearance of a thick mist. It gradually quits the atmosphere, lighting on the trees and herbs, and lining the surface of the sands. On the commencement of the rainy season it is again dissolved; and being carried off by the streams which are then formed, it is lodged in a number of small lakes; which, by a natural process, in time become absolute salt-pans, and thence it is that the Dutch colonists collect the salt which supplies their consumption. A person walking on the sandy beach during the continuance of the south-east winds, so as to be exposed to its influence, soon finds his clothes covered and encrusted with saline particles; while his skin is quite parched up, and his lips begin to feel their effects very sensibly."

As the small vessel which brought me from Bombay to the Cape was not permitted to proceed to Europe, I embarked on board the Calcutta Indiaman, commanded by captain William Thomson, from whom I received the kindest attentions, and joined a party of friends, who were passengers for England, and had sailed from Bombay ten weeks before my departure. As I had no intention of leaving India at that time they were astonished to find me at the Cape, and that my voyage thither was completed in seven weeks, while theirs exceeded seventeen.

After a pleasant passage of fourteen days from the Cape, we arrived at St. Helena. A constant succession of fair winds, smooth water, and fine weather, however delightful to the voyager, presents but little to amuse the reader: the continued prospect of sky and water affords no topic for a descriptive pen; although the glorious spectacle of the rising and setting sun is perhaps no where beheld with such grand effect as on the boundless ocean: a scene to which neither the language of Milton, nor the pencil of Claude can do justice.

Before we discovered the island, we saw several of the St. Helena pigeons, a sea-bird which has obtained that name, although it bears no resemblance to the genus. These birds are always seen to the windward of the island, but never to the leeward; thus directing the wanderers on the ocean to this haven of repose and refreshment, after a long voyage, although it is little more than a volcanic eruption, rising in the vast Atlantic, and but a speck in a map of this terraqueous globe. There is every appearance of volcanic agency throughout the island, which is situated in the latitude of 16 degrees south, and 5° 44′ of west longitude, from London. It is twenty seven miles in circumference, consisting chiefly of high rocky mountains, and deep vallies; composed of lava, scoria, ashes, and marine shells, similar to the strata of Etna, Vesuvius, and other volcanoes. The highest hill is called Diana's Peak, and its summit is 2696 feet above the level of the sea. The stupendous cliffs on the coast are so extremely steep, that a ship sailing under them appears from their lofty summits no bigger than her buoy; and we could but just distinguish the islanders surveying us, as we passed close under their perpendicular sides sixteen hundred feet high.

St. Helena affords neither anchorage nor soundings, except at Sandy-bay, and the bank on the north-west side of the island, where the vessels ride in safety, about half a mile from the shore; the different hills and vallies near it are fortified with batteries and redoubts. From hence St. Helena appears to the greatest advantage, presenting a prospect of St. James's valley, the landing-place, governor's house, and the only town on the island; it consists chiefly of a long narrow street, with houses ranged at the foot of the mountains, built in the English style, and furnished from Europe or India. The church is neat; the government house convenient, and pleasantly situated; in front commanding a view of the ships, and opening behind into the Company's garden; which, after those at the Cape, appeared rather insignificant. This valley is fortified towards the sea; and on the sides of the mountains are winding roads, leading to the country. These roads are only intended for horses, wheeled carriages would be useless. The ladies are bold riders, and gallop up and down the most formidable precipices.

Notwithstanding the dreary appearance of St. Helena towards the sea, many of the inland vales are sweetly rural, bounded by magnificent scenery. From some of the least tremendous heights the stranger beholds a bold crater, in the centre of steep rocky hills, accessible only to wild goats, but the gentler acclivities are dotted with neat farm-houses, shaded by trees, and surrounded by verdant meadows or enclosures of yams, potatoes, and such productions as the soil and climate admit of. These farms are animated by herds of cattle and flocks of sheep, while many a murmuring rill falling from the mountains gives a fine effect to the sublime and beautiful landscape. This, although written at first under the impression of novelty, appeared to me equally true after a second visit, and since I have enjoyed the beauties of Switzerland and other alpine scenery on the continent and in Great Britain.

A short walk from these picturesque views leads to immense cliffs and craggy precipices, opening on the unbounded ocean, bringing to a stranger's mind the unenviable situation of the islanders, secluded from the rest of the world, and entirely dependant on foreign supplies for the necessaries of life; for though the valleys and acclivities of the mountains are covered with a thin surface of mould, which by cultivation would produce a variety of grain, in consequence of the rats and mice, that have escaped from the ships, and infest the island, not an ear of it could attain maturity.

The monotony of the town and its local anecdotes present few attractions to the inquisitive traveller. In so confined a spot the refinements and elegancies of society are not to be expected; but nature is always new, always delightful, and as I anticipated another long confinement on the realms of Neptune, I spent as much time as possible in the country, and have sometimes been so enveloped in clouds, on the summit of the hills, that I could hardly see my horse's head. These vapours penetrate through the thickest coat, but are not often of long continuance. Leaving the tops of the mountains clear, they roll in immense volumes over the valleys, and sometimes present a picture half lighted by the sun, and half concealed in an impenetrable mist.

> " Nature there
> " Wantons, as in her prime, and plays at will
> " Her virgin fancies, wild above rule or art." MILTON.

When no ships are at St. Helena the town is forsaken; most of the inhabitants reside at their farms during great part of the year; as the valley, which is the general name for the town, is, from its situation, very warm, and the prospects confined: there the thermometer rises to 78 or 80 degrees, but seldom exceeds 67 or 68 on the hills. The whole island, considering its situation so near the equator, is remarkably cool, the air mild and salubrious; few disorders are known, and the small-pox is particularly guarded against. The ladies have fine complexions, for natives of a warm climate; which is generally unfavourable to the roses of my fair countrywomen in India, where the blushing flower of love soon decays, and the jonquil subdues the snowy tint of the lily. At St. Helena health and pleasure sparkle in the countenances of the young islanders; who are in general lively, smart, and agreeable, although superficially endowed with those accomplishments and refinements which are only to be acquired by education.

The English took this island from the Dutch in 1673; it had been first discovered by the Portugueze in 1508, on St. Helen's day: they thought it too barren for a settlement, but left poultry and goats to run wild, and afford refreshment to such vessels as might occasionally touch there for water. The number of inhabitants in 1776 did not exceed two thousand; more than half of those were slaves and black servants from Asia and Africa, the rest were Europeans and their descendants, including four hundred soldiers, and officers; the other inhabitants capable of bearing arms, both black and white, are formed into a militia, regularly disciplined. The government was vested in a governor, lieutenant governor, and two members of council, under whom were a few junior servants; no foreign trade was permitted. The governor's table was kept at the Company's expence, but his salary and emoluments did not then exceed seven hundred pounds a year, the lieutenant governor was allowed five hundred, and the other servants proportionably less.

The island at that time contained about two thousand head of cattle, which were not deemed sufficient to supply the ships, and keep up a stock. The mutton is good, but not abundant: geese, turkeys, and smaller poultry were dear; pheasants, partridges, and Guinea-fowls, scarce, though often seen wild upon the hills. The gardens and plantations produced a variety of fruit; the plantain was most attended to, from forming with the yam the chief food of the slaves. Apples, peaches, mulberries, figs and melons were good; the peaches large, coloured like an apricot, and highly flavoured, but grapes were scarce. In some of the best gardens were pine-apples, mango and tamarind trees, several oriental shrubs and flowers lately introduced; they had also begun to cultivate the tuar, or doll, of Hindostan, which if it succeeds will be a valuable acquisition.

The apple-trees are deservedly esteemed at St. Helena, for when the summer fruit is ripe the winter crop on the same tree begins to blossom; but this valuable fruit only succeeds in particular situations: oranges, limes and citrons grow well; the custard-apple, papah, and pompelmoos had been lately introduced from India; all seemed to flourish; and it must afford delight to every voyager, to contribute to the improvement of this interesting spot; where the British oak and banian-tree of Hindostan unite their friendly shade with the indigenous ebony and Caledonian fir-tree: where the African aloe and prickly pear, the Indian bamboo, and Arabian coffee, grow luxuriantly in the same border with the apple, the peach, and the mulberry from Europe.

The ficus indica, or banian-tree, thrives at St. Helena; still more so the ficus religiosa, or pepal. The string-wood I have only seen on this island; its long strings of red blossoms give this tree a beautiful appearance; its drooping branches, and the thick foliage of the standard peaches, shelter the rose linnets, which now abound in St. Helena, perhaps brought from South America, where their rosy bosoms form a beautiful contrast to the snowy blossoms of the orange groves. This is the passerculus orientalis, a small bird of delicate brown plumage, varied by rose-colour and white, the eyes encircled with feathers of a bright red. They build two nests, one above the other; in the largest below, the hen lays her eggs, and, like the interesting baya of India, the cock watches in the upper apartment, and sings to his mate during her incubation. The Jâva sparrows are more common; they were first brought from China and Batavia for their beauty, but from their wonderful increase, are become a great annoyance to the farmers.

The cotton plant had not been long introduced at St. Helena; with what success it may be cultivated time must determine. The Gŭm-wood, (solidago-leucadendron,) seems the most thriving tree on the St. Helena hills, it produces a resinous substance like gum-benjamin. They also abound with ferns in great variety and beauty, particularly the dicksonia, or tree-fern, which grows to the height of twenty feet; the seed of the furze brought from England, and scattered about the hills, clothes them with beauty and fragrance.

The variety of fish daily brought to market, is a source of

entertainment to a stranger, as well as a luxury at his meals. Many are curious and finely coloured, but I am no adept in icthyology, and only sketched the most beautiful; the mackarel are inferior to those in Europe; the little fish called the bull's-eye is delicious, equally so the cunning-fish, thus called from its stealing the bait, and eluding the hook. The hog-fish is curious, and the green-fish vies with the dolphin in alternate changes of purple, crimson, green, and gold.

We left St. Helena on the last day of February, and favoured by the south-east trade-wind crossed the line on the 12th of March; there it forsook us, and was succeeded by variable breezes, squalls, calms, thunder, lightning, and heavy rain, with a hot condensed atmosphere. This unpleasant weather continued until the 23d, when being in the latitude of 7° 12′ north, we flattered ourselves with the hope of meeting the north-east trade wind, and soon terminating our voyage; but different scenes awaited us: after a moderate breeze all that day, followed by a mild evening, we retired to rest as usual about ten o'clock. At midnight the officer upon deck was alarmed by the noise of a swelling surf, and very soon distinctly heard the hollow surges successively rolling upon a near shore. The captain was instantly called, and a general alarm succeeded: on sounding we found only ten fathoms water, when we imagined ourselves on the Atlantic ocean,,some hundred miles from land. As the wind blew fresh on the land, there was no time for deliberation; we therefore anchored immediately, and at day-break beheld within a mile of the ship a sandy beach, shaded by groves of cocoa-nut and tamarind trees, but could not distinguish any hills or mountains. We now knew it to be a part of the coast of Guinea, near St. Ann's, generally called the Gold coast, from its producing gold, ivory, and slaves; but as none of the natives came off, and we sent no boat on shore, I had not an opportunity of making further observations.

Although it was deemed imprudent to have any communication with the natives, or partake of nature's bounty on shore, we unfortunately continued near it a long time. We weighed anchor the next morning, but could neither get out of soundings, nor lose sight of the coast. The land-winds were too faint to assist us, and the sea breezes always contrary; to render our situation still more distressing, an unfavourable southern current set so strong that frequently when we had sailed several miles to the northward, the observation convinced us we were far south of our last reckoning; and thus, after a fortnight had elapsed, we were further from England than when we first saw the land. The wind seldom varied more than two points from the north-west, which was the very course we wanted to steer; we crossed the line several degrees more to the eastward than is customary for the homeward-bound ships from India.

The days were sultry, and the nightly dews unwholesome; the pressure of the atmosphere caused a lassitude both of body and mind. Nothing can be more uncertain than the weather on the coast of Guinea: from a sky perfectly clear and serene, in a moment bursts a storm of thunder, lightning, rain, and wind; the sea instantly becomes confused and tumultuous, its lovely tints of azure and aqua-marina, assume the sable hue of the overspreading gloom; this as suddenly subsiding leaves the air more sultry than before, producing all the enervating effects of the Italian Sirocco.

Thus we continued in a state of listless apathy for some weeks, when after stealing gently on with a faint land breeze during the night, we were agreeably surprized one morning at day-break with the appearance of a vessel at a few miles distance. Pleased with the novelty, we dispatched a boat, and found her to be a French ship from Mauritius, bound to l'Orient, which had already been a month in these latitudes, amid calms, contrary winds, and southerly currents. We kept company many days, and frequently dining with each other, diverted our ennui; for, notwithstanding their misfortunes, the French captain and passengers were cheerful and volatile.

Among a variety of fish on the coast of Guinea, the most beautiful is the Medusa, or Portugueze man-of-war, which enlivened the surface of the ocean, sailing by thousands before the wind. It appears individually like a large bubble or inflated bladder, perfectly transparent, and varying with the most lovely tints of blue, pink, and violet; it is generally of an oval shape, two or three inches long, with a protuberance at each end, something like a bird's head and beak. I could never discover eyes, nose, or mouth, yet it certainly belongs to the tribe of fishes, with a cartilaginous body, assuming different shapes as it is more or less inflated. On the top of the body it spreads a pink transparent sail, supported by delicate fibres, which enable it to raise or lower the sail at pleasure; with this they scud away before the light breezes, but are seldom seen in a boisterous sea; under the body are suspended several filaments of the most beautiful blue, of unequal length, and always in the water. These appendages are of a pungent caustic quality, and wherever they touch the skin it rises in blisters like a burn, followed by acute pain.

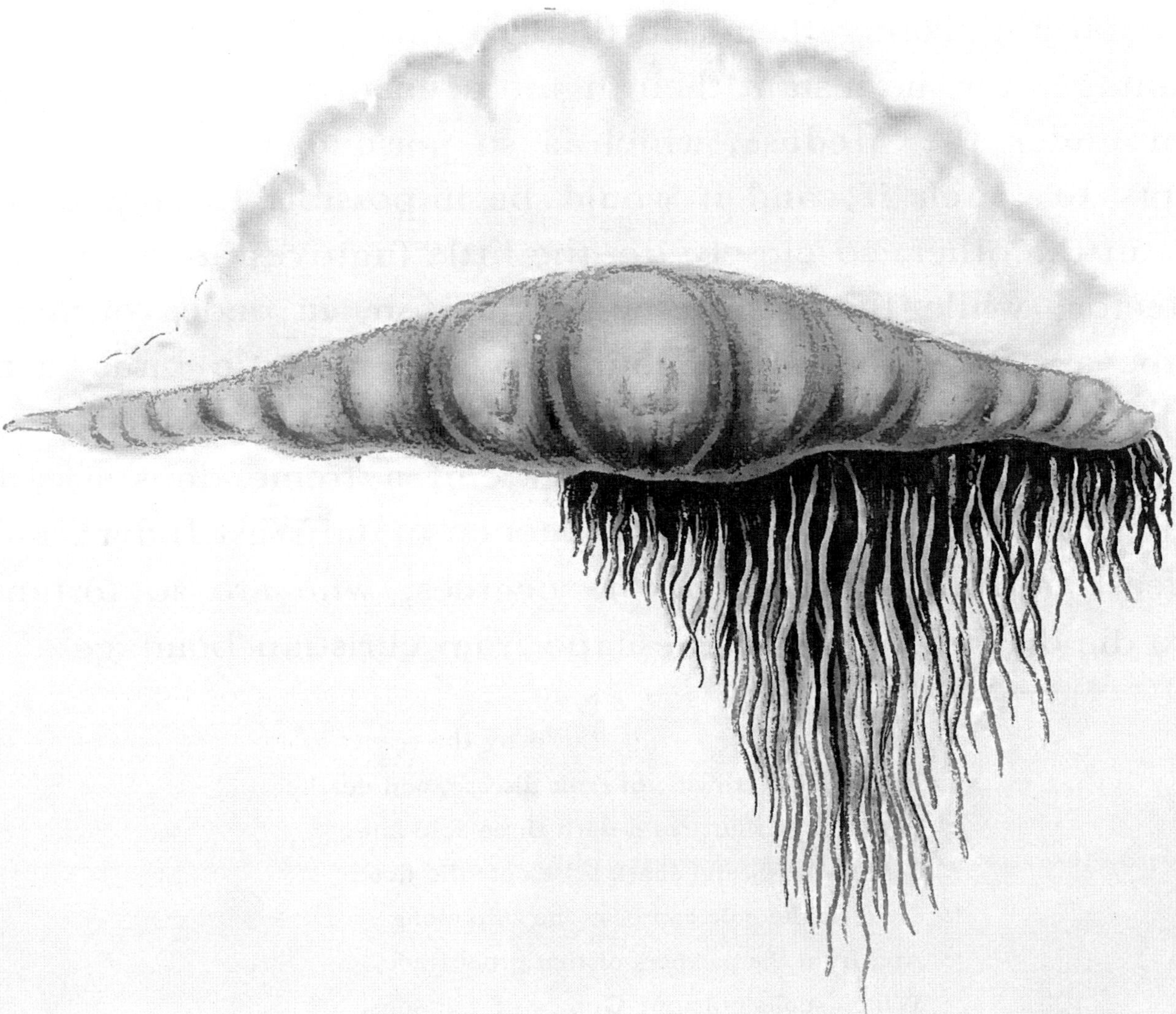

THE MEDUSA,

or Portuguese Man of War.

These curious animals are attended by a train of beautiful fish, six or seven inches long, marked with dark stripes over the pale hues of the iris, like the pilot fish, which always accompany the shark, and like them I never saw these little fish but under the Medusa; whose protection they seem instinctively to claim from the bonitos, albacores, and other voracious fish, which are continually pursuing them and the flying-fish; but these have the advantage, for the instant their gigantic enemy approaches, they swim under the Medusa, which is so poisonous that no fish attempts to touch it; and it would be impossible to snap up one without the other, so closely do the little fugitives adhere to their protector; while the unfortunate flying-fish, in endeavouring to escape a watery foe, are devoured by the aquatic birds continually hovering over them.

The sharks on the Guinea coast are of a tremendous size, and often follow the slave vessels from thence to the West India islands; to feast upon the bodies of the negroes, who are so fortunate as to die on the voyage, and escape from christian bondage.

> " Lur'd by the scent
> " Of steaming crowds, of rank disease, and death,
> " His jaws-terrific arm'd with three-fold fate,
> " Behold the direful shark! he cuts the flood
> " Swift as the gale can bear the ship along;
> " And from the partners of that cruel trade,
> " Which spoils unhappy Guinea of her sons,
> " Demands his share of prey: their mangled limbs
> " Crashing at once, he dyes the purple seas
> " With gore, and riots in the vengeful meal."
>
> THOMSON.

On the 17th of April, having proceeded considerably to the westward of the coast of Guinea, we had the happiness to find the wind veering gradually from west, and at length it settled in the regular north-east trade. We soon forgot all our late misfortunes; the anticipation of pleasures in our native isle again seasoned our repast, and we sailed gaily on. In three days we saw St. Jago, Brava, and several of the Cape de Verd Islands, and were detained by a calm close to Fogo, a barren mountainous island, only ten miles in circumference, which takes its name from a burning mountain, that frequently sends forth liquid lava and other volcanic matter, like the more sublime alembics of Etna and Vesuvius. Brava, situated between Fogo and St. Jago, seems to be an uninhabited mountain, three or four miles long. I have already described St. Jago in my voyage to India; very few of the homeward-bound ships ever fall in with the Cape de Verd Islands.

From thence pleasant gales and fair weather carried us to the Azores, or Western Islands, which we saw on the 13th of May; I must except one half-hour, when we were suddenly assailed by a violent storm, with thunder, lightning, and rain. It came on so instantaneously that we had no time to prepare against it before all our sails were split to pieces: it commenced from the south-east, and in a moment shifted to the north. I shall not attempt to describe this dreadful scene; its horrors exceeded every thing I could have conceived, and the oldest seamen declared they had never met with any thing to equal it. Fully indeed did we realize the description of my favorite bard.

> " Amid the heavens
> " Falsely serene, the tempest brooding dwells:
> " Fiery and foul, the small prognostic hangs!
> " ———————— then down at once
> " Precipitant descends a mingled mass
> " Of roaring winds, and flame, and rushing floods!" THOMSON.

Sailing eastward of the Azores, a pleasant breeze wafted us along the coast of St. Mary's, within sight of its orange-groves, villas, hamlets, and corn-fields, scattered among craggy precipices and foaming cascades. We passed between St. Mary's and a chain of rocks called the Homugas, on which the waves beat violently; and after coasting along St. Michael's, famous for its oranges, we saw several other islands belonging to Portugal, situated about three hundred leagues to the westward of that kingdom. The climate of the Azores, though subject to earthquakes, is mild and salubrious; they afford the inhabitants all the necessaries of life, and abound with corn, wine, and fruits. Angra, in the island of Tercera, is the seat of government, and the residence of the governor-general, the bishop, and principal officers; this capital contains a cathedral, and several other churches; there is a good harbour, and generally a brisk trade.

After leaving the Azores, the Atlantic presented a lively scene of vessels sailing in all directions: we spoke with several, and exchanged presents of tea, arrack and Indian delicacies, for the grateful return of English porter, butter and cheese, on which we regaled for the remainder of the voyage; which, notwithstanding it was now the beginning of summer, was not concluded without fresh gales, boisterous seas, and cold weather; so late as the 30th of May, the decks were covered with snow. At that time our water and provisions running low, and the sails being in a shattered condition, we steered for the Cove of Cork in Ireland; where we arrived the next day, after a voyage, by the log, of twelve thousand nine hundred miles from Bombay.

The prospects on the coast of Ireland were very pleasant, especially in the Cove of Cork, which presented a continued succession of villas, parks, and farms, with the ruins of castles and religious edifices. The Cove is spacious, and reckoned one of the most commodious harbours in Europe. We found it crowded with vessels, and anchored near the small town of Cove, about nine miles from Cork, from whence, early the next morming, the Calcutta was filled with company, from the principal nobility to the lowest shopkeepers, flocking on board for India bargains. All the beauty and fashion from the city and the nearer villas were constantly arriving. Longing to be on shore, I accompanied the captain and passengers to Cork; sailing up the river in an open boat, we had beautiful views of several noblemen's and gentlemen's seats on the acclivities of hills sloping to the water's edge, covered with groves, gardens and farms; while the busy sons of industry and commerce in the different vessels enlivened the picture.

We were treated with the greatest kindness and hospitality by many of the principal families at Cork, which ranks next to Dublin in magnitude and wealth, and carries on a more extensive commerce. It contains about fifty thousand inhabitants. As the Calcutta was likely to be detained there for some weeks, and I ardently longed to reach home, I left Ireland on the 6th of June, with several of our passengers, in the Pitt yacht.

We sailed with a fair wind, and next evening saw the lights on

Scilly; on the third morning we were off the Land's-end in Cornwall, and swiftly passing the romantic coasts of Devon, on the fourth evening we were near the Isle of Wight; the wind then becoming contrary, we landed on the 10th of June at Hastings in Sussex, with feelings which I cannot express; the thrillings of joy were too powerful, and produced a sickness of the heart well known to minds of sensibility.

" Bliss goes but to a certain bound—
" Beyond 'tis agony!"

We ordered supper, but I could not taste it, nor did I sleep the whole night; which indeed was very short; for at three the next morning we set off in a post-chaise and four for London. It was indeed an interesting journey, and most delightful did every thing appear in this lovely month; orchards and hawthorn hedges in full bloom and fragrance, verdant meadows and springing corn-fields, all united to endear my native land, from which I had been absent eleven years. My happiness was complete on reaching my father's house and finding my family well.

" How are thy servants bless'd, O Lord!
" How sure is their defence!
" Eternal wisdom is their guide,
" Their help, Omnipotence!

" In foreign lands, and realms remote,
Supported by thy care,
" Through burning climes I pass'd unhurt,
" And breath'd in tainted air.

" Thy mercy sweeten'd every soil,
" Made every region please;
" The torrid clime of Asia cheer'd,
" And smooth'd the raging seas.

" In midst of dangers, fears, and death,
" Thy goodness I'll adore;
" I'll praise thee for thy mercies past,
" And humbly hope for more!"

CHAPTER XXI.

A DESCRIPTION OF BAROCHE,

AND THE ADJACENT DISTRICTS, IN THE PROVINCE OF GUZERAT,

UNDER THE GOVERNMENT OF THE ENGLISH.

1778.

But not alike to every mortal eye
Is the great scene unveil'd: some in finer mould
Are wrought, and temper'd with a purer flame.
To these the SIRE omnipotent unfolds
The world's harmonious volume, there to read
The transcript of himself. On every part
They trace the bright impressions of his hand.

AKENSIDE.

CONTENTS.

of Baba-Rahan—history of that saint—illustration of scripture respecting idols cast to the bats—comparison between modern Hindoos and Mahomedans—bigotry of the latter—letter from Tipoo Sultaun—dress of an oriental female—rajhpoots—origin of that high caste—anecdotes concerning them—their noble character—extraordinary circumstance relating to a rajhpoot family in the Baroche Purgunna—singular exit of a Hindoo family at Bombay—trial and execution of the superstitious Hindoo which occasioned it—anecdotes from Lord Teignmouth.

CHAPTER XXI.

The voyage to Europe, and a residence of nine months in England restored my health; when having obtained from the Court of Directors an appointment to the first vacancy at Baroche, a settlement in the province of Guzerat, subordinate to Bombay, I embarked a second time for India in 1777, with a beloved sister, and several agreeable passengers.

After a pleasant voyage, without an hour's bad weather, losing a man by sickness, or meeting with accident or adventure, we arrived at Bombay in little more than four months from leaving Portsmouth. We stopped a few days at the Cape for water and refreshments; I renewed my visit to the different objects mentioned in the last chapter, but saw nothing new. Thus circumstanced, a voyage of twelve thousand miles affords no subject for communication; numerous passengers, like myself, have probably traversed the expanse of rolling oceans between Europe and Asia, without once reflecting on the situation which afforded Sir William Jones enthusiastic delight; it requires a mind enlightened and expanded as his own to enjoy the sensations which he describes in his preliminary discourse to the Asiatic Society at Bengal. I confess it is a passage I never read without envying his feelings, and distantly participating in his pleasure.

"When I was at sea last August," says our great Orientalist, "on my voyage to this country, which I had long and ardently desired to visit, I found one evening, on inspecting the observations of the day, that India lay before us, and Persia on our left; whilst a breeze from Arabia, blew nearly on our stern. A situation so pleasing in itself, and to me so new, could not fail to awaken a train of reflections in a mind, which had early been accustomed to contemplate with delight, the eventful histories and agreeable fictions of the eastern world. It gave me inexpressible pleasure to find myself in the midst of so noble an amphitheatre, almost encircled by the vast regions of Asia, which has ever been esteemed the nurse of sciences, the inventress of delightful and useful arts, the scene of glorious actions, fertile in the productions of human genius, abounding in natural wonders, and infinitely diversified in the forms of religion and government, in the laws, manners, customs, and languages, as well as in the features and complexions of men!"

Justly does Lord Teignmouth, his worthy successor, as president of the Asiatic Society, thus speak of his departed friend. "The faculties of his mind, by nature vigorous, were improved by constant exercise; and his memory, by habitual practice, had acquired a capacity of retaining whatever had once been impressed upon it. To an unextinguished ardour for universal knowledge, he joined a perseverance in the pursuit of it, which subdued all obstacles; his studies began with the dawn, and during the intermission of professional duties, were continued throughout the day. Reflection and meditation strengthened and confirmed what industry and investigation had accumulated. It was a fixed principle with him, from which he never voluntarily deviated, not to be deterred by any difficulties that were surmountable, from prosecuting to a successful termination what he had once deliberately undertaken."

To spread thy fame two rival worlds contend,
To worth, to learning, and to genius just;
And Love's and Friendship's mingling tears descend,
To embalm thy memory, and bedew thy dust.

'Twas thine, with daring wing and eagle eye,
To pierce antiquity's profoundest gloom;
To search the dazzling records of the sky,
And bid the stars the sacred page illume.

Nor did th' instructive orbs of heaven alone
Absorb thy soul 'mid yon ethereal fields;
To thee the vegetable world was known,
And all the blooming tribes the garden yields.

From the tall cedar, on the mountain's brow,
Which the fierce tropic-storm in vain assails,
Down to the humblest shrubs that beauteous blow,
And scent the air of Asia's fragrant vales.

But talents, fancy—ardent, bold, sublime,
Unbounded science,—form'd thy meanest fame;
Beyond the grasp of death, the bound of time,
On wings of fire RELIGION wafts thy name.

And, long as stars shall shine or planets roll,
To kindred virtue shall that name be dear;
Still shall thy genius charm th' aspiring soul,
And distant ages kindle at thy bier!

After residing six months at Bombay, a vacancy happened at Baroche, and I took the first opportunity of succeeding to my appointment. I went by sea to Surat, and from thence across the country to Baroche. Surat I have already described; it afforded no further novelty; and the voyage thither is too short and unvaried to interest a distant reader. A land-wind every night, and a sea-breeze throughout the day, equally assisted us; the morning presented a splendid sun, rising over the eastern mountains, and the western sky and curling waves were tinged by his evening beams. The pleasure of the voyage was heightened by a serene atmosphere and regular winds; we felt their salubrious influence, and were amused by the sportive inhabitants of the deep, and interested in the commercial intercourse with different sea-ports which we passed.

The little journey of thirty-six miles from Surat to Baroche is delightful. Soon after leaving the former, I crossed the Tappee, and travelled through a fertile country to *Kimcatodrah Chowkey*, a caravansary on the banks of the river Kim, about half way to Baroche: situated in so great a thoroughfare it is much frequented by merchants, and travellers of all descriptions; especially by senassees, yogees, and other religious pilgrims. I have there met with Hindoo mendicants, who had made the tour of Hindostan, extended their journey to Persia, and some of them had even penetrated into Russia, and reached Moscow.

Mr. Stewart remarks, that " the Indians have an admirable method of rendering their religion lucrative; it being usual for the fakeers to carry with them in their pilgrimages from the sea-coasts to the interior parts, pearls, corals, spices, and other precious articles, of small bulk; which they exchange, on their return, for gold-dust, musk, and other things of a similar nature; concealing them easily in their hair, and in the cloths round their middle; carrying on, in proportion to their numbers, no inconsiderable traffic by these means."

These people were often brought to me secretly, to know if I would purchase ottah of roses, pearls, or other concealed commodities: I had frequently some trouble with them as custom-master at Baroche.

Kimcatodrah, being near the river, is amply supplied with water. Most villages in this tract of country have public wells and tanks, where the pilgrim and his cattle are sure of finding abundance, except in dry seasons; and then some charitable individual generally alleviates the failure, by placing a person to dispense water gratis from a temporary receptacle. On our Saviour's words, "Whosoever shall give you a cup of water to drink, in my name, verily I say unto you he shall not lose his reward." Harmer justly remarks, that "the general thought is plain to every reader; that no service performed to a disciple of CHRIST, out of love to his master, though comparatively small, should pass away unrewarded: but those in more temperate climates, are sometimes ready to think that the instance our LORD mentions, is of so very trifling a nature, that it appears almost ludicrous. It certainly would not be so now to an inhabitant of the east; nor did it then, we have reason to believe, appear in that light to them, to whom he immediately made that declaration; a cup of cold water is to them a refreshment not unworthy of acceptance." To this, Dr. Clarke adds a further illustration, that "it appears from the most authentic information, the Hindoos go sometimes a great way to fetch water; and then boil it, that it may not be hurtful to travellers who are hot; after this they stand from morning till night in some great road, where there is neither pit nor rivulet; and offer it, *in honour of their gods*, to be drunk by the passengers. This necessary work of charity in those countries, seems to have been practised among the more pious and humane Jews; and our Lord assures them, that if they do this *in his name*, they shall not lose their reward. This one circumstance of the Hindoos offering the water to the fatigued passengers *in honour of their gods*, is a better illustration of our Lord's words, than all the collections of Harmer upon the subject."

I spent the heat of the day at Kimeatodrah, and passed the night at Occlaseer, a pleasant Hindoo town, the capital of a small purgunna in the Baroche districts, then belonging to the English. Occlaseer is not many miles from the south bank of the Nerbudda, where I arrived the next morning, and crossed the river to Baroche.

As my trip proved barren of incident, I shall add Dr. Fryer's entertaining account of the same journey, a century before. "Going out of Surat by the Baroche-gate, we fell into a notable beaten way; and found the roads pestered with cophales of oxen, camels, and buffaloes; with heavy waggons drawn by teams of oxen, yoked eight, sometimes a dozen or sixteen times double, bringing and carrying goods of all sorts; there with guides, here with guards, for fear of thieves descending from the mountains, or lying in ambuscade among the thickets. Here are no caravansaries nor inns to shut them in a-nights, for then is their time of travelling; and when they rest, if they have no tents, they must shelter themselves under shady trees, or sometimes great tombs on the high-way; and where rivers are deficient, they want not great tanks, or deep stately wells."

" We passed pleasant enclosures and flourishing fields of corn, and plantations of tobacco, baiting when it grew hot, under groves of palm or toddy-trees: when the crows came to roost there we departed, and at midnight arrived at Occlaseer. We slept at the broker's house, and at sun-rise proceeded over delicate meadows to Baroche river, round about which is all champaign. We met more than five hundred oxen, laden with salt for the inland countries. We then crossed the river in a boat; it is broad, swift, and deep; but on account of the sands, forced down by the rains, good pilots are required to steer clear of them; by whose directions good lusty vessels are brought up to the city walls, where they are laden with salt and corn; and also excellent wheat, and good cottons, the growth of the country; it is likewise the great thoroughfare to Lahor, Delhi, Agra, and Ahmedabad."

Such as the journey then was, such I found it a hundred years afterwards; for in India we are not to expect much variety or novelty either in the manners and customs of the inhabitants, or in the general aspect of the country. It is difficult to persuade a Hindoo to adopt any improvement; and it is astonishing what inconveniences and deprivations he will submit to, rather than do any thing out of the usual way to prevent it. " My father and grandfather never did so," is a sufficient reason for the refusal; and what is not the business of any one particular caste, is never done at all. I am not at present alluding to religious tenets or moral duties. It is observed by Sir William Jones, that "whoever travels in Asia, especially if he be conversant with the literature of the countries through which he passes, must naturally remark the superiority of European talents. The observation is as old as Alexander; and though we cannot agree with the sage preceptor of that prince, that the Asiatics are born to be slaves, yet the Athenian poet seems perfectly in the right when he represents Europe as a sovereign princess, and Asia as her handmaid; but, if the mistress be transcendently majestic, it cannot be denied that the attendant has many beauties, and some advantages peculiar to herself."

I have already mentioned the establishment of the English factory at Surat in 1615. The Company were soon afterwards permitted to have factors at Ahmedabad, and other cities in Guzerat, where they carried on a considerable trade. Sir Thomas Roe, in the progress of his embassay from James the First to the Emperor Shah Jehan, stayed some days at Brampore, where Sultan Currum, the emperor's second son, was encamped with his army. During that visit, Sir Thomas Roe, by his negociation with Mahobet Caun, received a phirmaun, granting him permission to establish a factory at Baroche, with several valuable immunities. The words of Sir Thomas Roe will best describe his opinion of these privileges; they also contain some curious particulars in that early period of our oriental commerce.

"On the two and twentieth of July 1616, I received letters from Brampore, in answer of those to Mahobet Caun; who at first request granted my desire; making his phirmaun to Baroche most effectual to receive our nation, and to give them them a house near the governor; strictly commanding no man to molest them, by sea or land, or to take any custom of them, or any way trouble them under colour thereof. Finally, that they might buy, sell, and transport any commodity at their pleasure, without any molestation; concluding that they should expect to hear no other from him, and therefore they should be careful in the execution. I received with it a letter from himself, which was more civility than all the Indies yielded me, full of courtesy and humanity, and great respect, protesting his desire to give me content, and that what I had demanded I should make no doubt of performance; and if I had any other occasion to use him, he desired me to write, and it should be performed. The copies are worthy the seeing, for the rareness of the phrase. The phirmaun I caused to be sent to Surat, in order to be forwarded by the agency there to Baroche: so that Baroche is provided for a good retreat for the prince's injuries, and the custom given; whereby fifteen hundred pounds per annum will be saved, besides all manner of searches and extortions. For the performance of this no man maketh any doubt; for that all men confess, that he careth not for the prince, and so feareth not, nor needeth any man; being the only beloved man of the king, and second person in his dominions; and in all his life so liberal of his purse, and honourable of his word, that he hath ingrossed good reports from all others: and concerning custom, the king takes none; the governors make it their profit, which he professeth to scorn, that he should abuse the liberty of the king's ports."

The trade of the ancients with India, as recorded by Ptolemy, Arrian, and other writers having been mentioned at Surat and Mirjee,

I shall now only particularize their commerce with Baroche, the BARYGAZA of the Greeks: on which subject the publications of Dr. Robertson and Dr. Vincent have thrown considerable light.

Dr. Robertson's account of the ancient commerce of this city is taken from Arrian's treatise of the navigation of the Erythrean sea. After describing the trade of Pattala on the Indus, he says "a far more considerable emporium on the same coast was Barygaza; and on that account the author, whom I follow here, describes its situation, and the mode of approaching it, with great minuteness and accuracy. It situation corresponds entirely with that of Baroche, on the great river Nerbudda; down the stream of which, or by land carriage, from the great city of Tagara across high mountains, all the productions of the interior country were conveyed to it. The articles of importation and exportation in this great mart were extensive and various. Among the former, our author enumerates Italian, Greek, and Arabian wines, brass, tin, lead, girdles or sashes of curious texture, melilot, white glass, red arsenic, black lead, gold and silver coin. Among the exports he mentions the onyx, and other gems, ivory, myrrh, various fabrics of cotton, both plain and ornamented with flowers, and long pepper."

The modern imports and exports of Baroche are similar to those mentioned by Dr. Robertson; wines indeed are not included, except for the consumption of Europeans, and the trade in onyxes, cornelians, and agates, from the Sardonyx mountain of Ptolemy, not many miles from Baroche, has been transferred from thence to Cambay, where these stones are exclusively cut and polished.

Engraved by J. Shury

BAROCHE on the Banks of the NERBUDDA in Guzerat

Jam Forbes 1778

Dr. Vincent's Periplus of the Erythrean sea gives an exact account of the trade in India from the Arabian gulf. The articles imported from thence at Barbarike, a mart situated in the middle channel of the Indus, are similar to those mentioned by the former historian: clothing, plain, and in considerable quantities; clothing, mixed; cloth, larger in the warp than the woof; topazes, coral, storax, frankincense, glass vessels, plate, specie, and wine. The exports from India to Europe by the same channel were emeralds, sapphires, spikenard, the spice costus, the gum bdellium, yellow dye, cotton, indigo, silk, and hides from China. Most of these articles are still exported from Baroche and Cambay.

The unknown author of the Periplus, generally minute and accurate in his descriptions, is in none more so than his account of the tides in the gulf of Cambay, which I particularly mentioned when sailing with the British detachment to the assistance of Ragobah. It is pleasant and satisfactory to see them described by an accurate voyager two thousand years ago. "At Barygaza the violence of the flux and reflux of the tides is so remarkable, that without warning, you see the bottom laid bare, and the sides next the coast, where vessels were sailing but just before, left dry as it were in an instant; again, upon the access of the flood tide, the whole body of the sea is driven with such violence, that the stream is impelled upwards for a great number of miles, with a force that is irresistible. This makes the navigation very unsafe for those that are unacquainted with the gulf, or enter it for the first time. No anchors are a security; for when the vehemence of the tide commences, there is no intermission, no retreat: large vessels caught in it are hurried away by the impetuosity of the current, and thrown on their sides, or wrecked upon the shoals; while the smaller ones are completely overset. Many also that have taken refuge in the creeks, unless they have fortunately changed their place in due time (which it is very difficult to do on account of the instantaneous fall of the water) upon the return of the tide are filled with the very first head of the flood and sunk. But all these circumstances united concur more especially if the new moon falls in conjunction with the night tide; for then, if you have been prepared to enter upon the first flood, and when the sea appeared perfectly calm, you shall hear, in a moment, a rushing sound like the tumult of battle, and the water driving forward with the utmost impetuosity, covers the whole of the bare shoals in an instant."

Upon this passage Dr. Vincent remarks, "it will immediately appear, that the description relates to that sort of tide which is called the bore; and is common to many places in Europe as well as India. On the coast of Egypt, or in the Red Sea, the author could have seen nothing that resembled it; and he dwells upon it, therefore, with more minuteness than a modern observer would employ; but from this very cause it is that we have a picture which cannot deceive us; and a conviction that the author relates what he had himself experienced."

Three years had elapsed since my last visit to Baroche, with Ragobah's army; I found it much improved in buildings, population, and commerce. The cotton trade was very considerable; and the manufactures of this valuable plant, from the finest muslin to the coarsest sail-cloth, employed thousands of men, women, and children, in the metropolis and adjacent villages. The cottonclearers and spinners generally reside in the suburbs, or *poorahs* of Baroche, which are very extensive. The weavers' houses are mostly near the shade of tamarind and mango-tees; under which at sun-rise they fix their looms, and weave a variety of cotton-cloth, with very fine baftas and muslins; Surat is more famous for its coloured chintzes and piece-goods. The Baroche muslins are inferior to those of Bengal and Madrass; nor do the painted chintzes of Guzerat equal those of the Coromandel coast.

Nothing can exceed the simplicity of the oriental manufacturers and mechanics. In Surat and Baroche, the silver-smith, if convenient to his employer, brings his apparatus to the house, and there makes such things as are required; in a style of strength and neatness that answers every useful purpose; and in some parts of India, especially at Sumatra and Anjengo, the work of the natives in gold and silver filigree executed with only an iron nail, is beautiful. The carpenters and cabinet-makers generally came to our own houses, and made up our furniture; I have had a chariot, in the English style, begun and finished, under my own roof, except the heavy parts of the iron-work.

Besides the numerous cotton manufactures at Baroche, both for home consumption and exportation, during my residence there, more than twenty thousand bales of raw cotton were annually sent from thence to China and Bengal; which at the medium price of thirty-five rupees a bale, amounted to eighty thousand pounds. Exclusive of that valuable article, the Baroche districts abound with wheat, juarree, rice, and a variety of grains and pulse; nuts and seeds for oil; also shrubs and plants for dying the cottons.

The Baroche purgunna, which then belonged to the East India company, contained one hundred and sixty-four villages; and its revenues amounted to six lacs of rupees, or something more than seventy thousand pounds a year, which was six tenths of the whole produce; the remainder belonged to the cultivators. In the reign of Akbar, at the end of the fifteenth century, the circar of Baroche, or Bheroatch, to which the Purgunnas of Occlaseer, Hansoot, and some others, were then annexed, contained fourteen mahls, three hundred and forty nine thousand seven hundred beegahs of land, and yielded a noble revenue.

Sir Thomas Herbert, who was here in 1626, says "in quondam times the royalties of Baroche were spacious, sovereignizing over many towns and provinces of note, a great way distant: each of which now enjoys peculiar podestates; howbeit, the Mogul has received hereout, as an annual tax or tribute, no less than one million two hundred and threescore thousand *mamooders*, or shillings, which revenue, from one province, shews what a vast exchequer all his empire yearly contributeth."

The Baroche villages are rural and pleasant; each is embosomed in its own mango and tamarind grove, and the surrounding country resembles a luxuriant garden; the rich crops of grain are contrasted by extensive fields of capsicums, or chilies, glowing with scarlet; large tracts of yellow cossumba, (carthamus) which makes a valuable red dye, and acres of tobacco, crowned with flowers of a pale rose-colour. Several villages cultivate the sugar-cane, as also the turmeric, amomum curcuma, Lin.; fenugreek or meti; meti trigonella, fœnum-grœcum, Lin.: benda, hibiscus esculentus, Lin.; fulsi, ocymum, and many other useful plants and vege-

Engraved by Bale

GARDEN-HOUSE *in a Village near* BAROCHE, *in* GUZERAT,

Jas. Forbes. 1778

Published by White Cochrane & Co. Fleet Street June 1st 1812

tables, peculiar to the country; it is almost unnecessary to mention that turmeric, ginger, and capsicums, are planted, wherever they will grow, throughout Hindostan; they form a principal ingredient in most of the oriental dishes; spices, savoury herbs, and hot seeds, are particularly used in the vegetable curries of the Hindoos.

The cultivated tracts abound with hares, antelopes, foxes, and jackals; also partridges, quails, and other game; and every village has its monkeys and pea-fowl; the wood-lands, and wilder parts towards the eastern hills, shelter tigers, leopards, hyenas, and hogs; the lakes and rivers are covered with flamingos, pelicans, ducks, and water-fowl in great variety. The partridges frequently roost on high trees; and several sorts of wild ducks settle on the lofty branches of the palmira, borassus flabelliformis, Lin. The bamboo, bambusa, grows in many of the wilds; it is also cultivated near some of the villages. In Guzerat the natives are seldom distressed for grain; but in many parts of India the poor eat the seed of the bamboo. The bamboo forms an impenetrable hedge round the villages, when thickly planted for that purpose; and the branches uniting at the top, produce a shady walk, with the effect of a gothic cloister.

The water-melons at Baroche are esteemed the best in India, especially those which grow on a sandy island in the Nerbudda, near the city. I think the water-melon, (anguria citrullus, Lin.) one of the pleasantest and most refreshing of the tropical fruits; I have found them extremely good in the south parts of Europe, particularly at Venice and Naples, where they are very abundant. An eminent physician observes, that “ the water-melon, is providentially calculated for the southern countries, as it affords a cool refreshing juice, assuages thirst, mitigates feverish disorders, and compensates thereby, in no small degree, for the excessive heats of those climates." Melons of every kind abound in their season in most parts of India, and the best musk-melons are often sent as presents from a great distance. Chardin mentions having eat melons at Surat which grew in Agra, a journey exceeding thirty days; they were carried by a man on foot in baskets, hung on a pole, one at each end, the pole being laid over one of his shoulders, from whence, for ease, he shifted it to the other from time to time, and travelled seven leagues a day with his load.

The Indian pomegranates, although sometimes tolerable, are by no means equal to those brought from Arabia by the Muscat Dingeys: these are a very fine fruit; large, and full of juice, highly flavoured; some are red, others white. The most luxurious method of eating them is to have the juice expressed from the seeds and interior film, by which means the harsh seeds and bitter flavour are avoided. It is a delicate beverage, and one of those pomegranates will sometimes fill a small bason. They make a pleasant wine from this fruit in Persia and Arabia, to which there is probably some allusion in the Song of Solomon, where they are mentioned as growing in orchards. "I will cause thee to drink of spiced wine of the juice of my pomegranates." I have never tasted this, nor any other Persian wine, except that of Schiraz, which, although much extolled by poets, I think inferior to many wines in Europe.

Wine is so little publicly drunk in India by any of the castes, that I can say nothing of it, whether spiced, or iced. But there are various methods of cooling sherbet and water-melons: in that state I always considered the latter a great luxury, although seldom introduced at the English tables: they are then like the iced-fruits in Europe, and dissolve in the mouth like snow. I never met with ice during my residence in India: it is now I believe generally used by all who can afford it, especially in Bengal, where it is procured without much difficulty or expense. How Alexander the Great at the siege of Petra, a city of India, procured a sufficient quantity of this luxury to fill thirty ditches, is difficult to account for. Chares, the Mytelenean, is cited by Athenæus for this anecdote, and adds that it was preserved for a long time by covering it with boughs of trees.

As perfumed and spiced sherbets are much esteemed in the east for the palate, so are perfumed oils and spicy unguents for the person. A variety of fragrant oils are made in Persia and India, by putting blossoms of mogrees, jasmine, and other highly scented flowers into the most delicate oil; which after a certain time imbibes the flavour, and is poured off into small bottles, stopped with cotton and wax, to be dispersed throughout the provinces by borahs, gosannees, and yogees, who carry the most costly of these oils, with ottah of roses, pearls, and other valuables that take up little room.

The borahs are not only considerable traders in commercial towns, but are the chief travelling merchants in Guzerat and the western parts of India; going about like the Jews in Europe with boxes of different commodities; particularly perfumes and jewels.

These fragrant oils are not only used by all descriptions of Indian females, but the venerable Mahomedan is fond of perfuming his beard; which, when grey, is often died black, or a dark brown, with a composition of al'hinna, and other herbs; especially among the Turks and Persians who reside in Hindostan; where they have also introduced the custom of perfuming their beards by holding them over salvers of smoking incense, which are also offered to their guests. They likewise unloose the shawls and open their vests, to receive as much as possible of this favourite delicacy. The use of perfumes has been immemorially practised in the east. Moses gives particular directions for the preparation of oils and fragrant ointments for the sanctuary. Domestic happiness and brotherly union is beautifully compared by the Psalmist to "the precious ointment upon the head, that ran down unto the beard, even unto Aaron's beard, and went down to the skirts of his garments,"*

In Persia, Cashmere, and the northern parts of India, they make very delicate conserves, and syrups of roses, violets and jasmine, which on particular occasions are presented to visitors, with sherbets of falsee, lemons, and acrid fruits, mingled with odoriferous waters, or a few drops of these rich syrups.

The tribe of Mahomedans, called Borahs, are settled in Baroche, Surat, Bombay, and other parts of Hindostan: they appear to be very distinct from the Moguls and other sects of Mussulmans in India. The English at Bombay consider them as a sort of Mussulman Jews; on what foundation I know not. The only mention made

* It having been objected that the words—going down to the *skirts* of the garment, imply a needless profusion of precious ointment, it has been suggested that the Hebrew word translated the *skirt* signifies more properly the *opening* (or *mouth)* of the *garment,* where it is fastened round the neck, immediately under the beard.

The Mausoleum of BAWA RAHAN near Baroche

of them to my knowledge is by Mr. Hunter at Oujein, where he says, "they distinguish their own sect by the title of *Ismaeeliah;* deriving their origin from one of the followers of the prophet, named Ismaeel, who flourished in the age immediately succeeding that of Mahomed. This singular class of people forms a very large society, spread over all the countries of the Deccan, particularly the large towns. Surat contains six thousand families; and the number in Oujein amounts to fifteen hundred. But the head-quarters of the tribe is at Burhanpoor, where their mullah, or priest, resides. The society carries on a very extensive and multifarious commerce in all those countries over which its members are dispersed; and a certain proportion of all their gains is appropriated to the maintenance of the mullah, whose revenue is consequently ample. He is paramount in all ecclesiastical matters, and holds the keys of Paradise; it being an established article of faith, that no man can enter the regions of bliss without a passport from the high priest, who receives a handsome gratuity for every one he signs. He also exercises a temporal jurisdiction over his tribe, wherever dispersed; and this authority is admitted by the various governments under whose dominion they reside, as an encouragement to these people, who form the most industrious and useful class of the inhabitants. A younger brother of the mullah resides at Oujein; and, with that same title, exercises over the borahs resident there the authority, spiritual and temporal, annexed to the office. Five mohillas of the city are inhabited by them, and subject to his jurisdiction."

The tomb of Baba Rahan, and other sacred places belonging to the Mahomedans, are visited at stated seasons by pilgrims;

and often resorted to by fakeers and pretended saints of that religion; who, like their religious brethren among the Hindoos, are guilty of those various extravagancies, indecencies, and immoral practices so well described by Dr. Fryer: " These fakeers, or holy men, profess to be abstracted from the world, and resigned to God. On this pretence they commit many extravagancies, and put themselves on voluntary penances. Here is one that has vowed to hang by the heels until he get money enough to build a mosque to Mahomed, that he may be held a saint: another shall travel the country with an horn blowed before him, and an ox it may be to carry him and his baggage, besides one to wait on him with a peacock's tail; whilst he rattles a great iron chain fettered to his foot, as big as those elephants are foot-locked with, some two yards in length, every link thicker than a man's thumb, and a palm in length; his shaking this speaks his necessity, which the poor Gentiles dare not deny to relieve; for if they do, he accuses them to the cazy, who desires no better opportunity to fleece them; for they will not stick to swear they blasphemed Mahomed, for which there is no evasion but to deposit, or be made a Moor.

" Most of these are vagabonds, and are the pest of the nation they live in. Some of them dwell in gardens, and retired places in the fields, in the same manner as the *Seers* of old, and the children of the prophets did; their habit is the main thing that signalizes them more than their virtue: they profess poverty, but make all things their own, wherever they come; all the heat of the day they idle it under some shady tree, at night they come in troops, armed with a great pole, a *mirchal,* or peacock's tail, and a wallet, more like plunderers than beggars: they go into the market, or to the shopkeepers, and force an alms, none of them returning without his share: some of them pass the bounds of a modest request, and bawl out in the open streets for an hundred rupees, and nothing less will satisfy them.

"They are clothed with a ragged mantle, which serves them also for a mattress, for which purpose some have lion's, tiger's, or leopard's skins to lay under them. The most civilized of them wear flesh-coloured vests, somewhat like our brick-makers' frocks, and almost of that colour. The merchants, as their adventures return, are bountiful towards them, by which means some of them thrive upon it. These field-conventiclers, at the hours of devotion, beat a drum, from them called the fakeer's drum. There are of these strollers about Surat enough to make an army, so that they are almost become formidable to the citizens, nor is the governor powerful enough to correct their insolence; for lately setting on a nobleman of the Moors, when his kindred came to demand justice, they unanimously rose in defence of the aggressor, and rescued him from his deserved punishment."

The above is an excellent description of the Indian fanatics, who go even greater lengths than is there mentioned, as many injured husbands and deluded females can testify: but I imagine Dr. Fryer has in some measure confounded the Hindoo Gosanness and similar tribes with these Mahomedan saints; especially as to numbers. I never saw or heard of such a multitude either at Surat or Baroche, where they most abound: it is easy for a stranger to mistake appearances from their general pursuits being the same. The Hindoo austerities far exceed any which the followers of the Arabian prophet have attempted; many are almost incredible. In my journey from Surat to Baroche, I saw some which, as I was then just returned from Europe, much astonished me; they, however, bore so near a resemblance to those formerly described that I shall not enter into particulars; but it may be interesting to mention the parent stock from which the Hindoo devotees seem to have derived their severest penances; which Mr. Halhed traces to *Tarakee*, a devotee in the wood Midhoo, on the confines of the kingdoms of Brege, who there performed incredible penances. This ingenious writer enumerates their variety, and the length of time he allotted to each; which I omit as fabulous, and foreign to the subject, but the penances themselves seem to have formed a model for his misguided disciples; and as such, I select a few from the number there mentioned.

For many years Tarakee held up his arms and one foot towards heaven, and fixed his eyes upon the sun. For a considerable length of time he remained standing on tiptoe, nourishing himself with water; sometimes he stood and made his adorations in the river, at others buried up to his neck in the earth, and frequently enveloped with fire. He often stood upon his head, with his feet towards heaven; or upon the palm of one hand resting upon the ground; and then varied the penance by hanging from a tree by one hand, or suspending himself from a branch with his head downwards.

These I believe to be the principal penances of the Hindoo enthusiasts, and I have seen most of them performed. Cui bono? necessarily occurs on the perusal of such things. The monastic institutions in the church of Rome, although in some respects liable to censure, and perverted from their original intention, had many advantages; they afforded an asylum to learning and science in the dark ages, and, before the art of printing, were the depository of the manuscripts that escaped the wreck of the Roman empire. They were the hospitals and places of refreshment for travellers at a time when inns and houses of entertainment were unknown in Europe. I can gratefully acknowledge, with many other travellers, the hospitality and kindness of the monks of Grand St. Bernard, after a long and fatiguing ascent up the Alps to the well-named Hospice of that benevolent society. There, on the loftiest site of any human habitation in Europe, Asia, or Africa, these good fathers exercise the noblest charities to every weary stranger, without a question as to religion or country; it is sufficient that he is "a man and a brother." Not only do they leave their convent in the darkness of the most tempestuous nights, to seek the bewildered pilgrim, but train dogs to search out the wretched traveller lost in the snowy tracts of those dreary regions:

> Stung with the thoughts of home! the thoughts of home
> Rush on his nerves; and call their vigour forth,
> In many a vain attempt. How sinks his soul!
> What black despair, what horror fills his heart!
> He plunges deep amid the drifted heaps,
> Far from the tract, and blest abode of man!
> While round him night resistless closes fast;
> And every tempest, howling o'er his head,
> Renders the savage wilderness more wild! THOMSON.

We contemplate the Hindoo colleges and brahminical seminaries, at Benares and different parts of Hindostan, with pleasure;

they are useful institutions; and, however limited in their benefits to particular castes and descriptions of people, they are the nurseries of literature, medicine, and science, as far as is deemed necessary among the Hindoos. But I cannot praise a religion which encourages thousands, perhaps millions, of idle vagabonds, who practise no virtue; but under the mask of piety, with a sort of stoical apathy and pharisaical zeal, undergo these needless austerities and penances near their celebrated temples, or pervade the provinces of Hindostan, singly, and in large bodies, to make depredations on the hard-earned property of the poor villagers, and violate the chastity of their wives and daughters, under a cloak of sanctity and religious perfection.

The number of these medicants who assemble at the festivals and jattaras held in the vicinity of Baroche, and especially under the embowering fane at Cubbeer-Burr, is astonishing. The island covered by that sacred tree, the banks of the Nerbudda, and the river itself, are thronged beyond conception from the adjacent districts, and distant parts of Hindostan: especially the holy precincts of Succulterah, a large village on the banks of the Nerbudda, a few miles from Baroche, much celebrated for the sanctity of its temples. In the *Sacred Isles of the West*, Captain Wilford mentions this as a place of great antiquity, under the name of Sucla-Tirtha; and relates a curious anecdote which occurred there about three hundred and fifteen years before the Christian æra, taken from the Cumarica-chanda.

" About the time of Alexander's invasion of India, Chanacya, a wicked and revengeful priest, that he might establish the base-born Chandra-gupta on the imperial throne, caused his eight royal brothers, the legitimate sons of his father, to be murdered. After this paroxysm of revengeful rage was over, Chanacya was exceedingly troubled in his mind, and so much stung with remorse for his crime, and the effusion of human blood which took place in consequence of it, that he withdrew to Sucla-Tertha, a famous place of worship on the bank of the Nerbudda, to get himself purified. There, having gone through a most severe course of religious austerities, and expiatory sacrifices, he was directed to sail upon the river in a boat with white sails; which, if they turned black, would be to him a sure sign of the remission of his sins, the blackness of which would attach itself to the sails: thus it happened, and he joyfully sent the boat adrift, with his sins, into the sea. This ceremony, or another very similar to it (for the expense of a boat would be too great) is performed to this day at Sucla-Tirtha; but instead of a boat, they use a common earthen pot, in which they light a lamp, and send it adrift with the accumulated load of their sins."

In the Agni-purana this expiation is mentioned differently by the Carshagni: it there consists in covering the whole body with a thick coat of cow-dung; which, when dry, is set on fire. This mode of expiation, in desperate cases, was unknown before; but occasionally performed afterwards. Chandra-gupta, when firmly established on the imperial throne, accompanied Chanacya to Sucla-Tirtha, in order to get himself purified also. Chanacya's crimes, repentance, and atonement, are the subject of many legendary tales in verse current in Guzerat.

I have mentioned the Hindoo jattaras, and some of their principal festivals, in another place; they are solemnized with great delight at Baroche, and the sacred spots in its vicinity. But as it had been a Mahomedan principality before the English conquest, and was still inhabited by numerous Mussulmans, their fasts and festivals, although celebrated with less pomp and expense than formerly, were strictly observed by all the followers of the prophet. Their two grand festivals are those of the Ramazan and Beiram, when the princes and great men repair in state to the mosques. I have described the procession of the nabob of Surat on this occasion. The Mogul splendour is mostly subsided at Baroche; few families of eminence now remain there; their religious ceremonies therefore were by no means expensive: but on the feast of Beiram they all made the best appearance they could, and generally contrived to procure a new dress for the occasion. D'Herbelot mentions a curious anecdote of Mostanser Billah, caliph of Bagdad, on the approach of the Beiram. This monarch going one day to the highest part of his palace, saw many of the flat roofs around him "spread with clothes of different kinds, and being told by his vizier, upon his asking the reason of it, that the inhabitants of Bagdat were drying their clothes, which they had newly washed on the account of the approach of the Beiram, which is a very solemn Mahomedan festival, Mostanser was so concerned, that they were so poor as to be obliged to wash their old clothes, for want of new ones with which to celebrate this festival, that he ordered a great quantity of gold to be instantly made into bullets, proper to be shot out of cross-bows, which he and his courtiers threw, by this means, upon every terrace upon the city where he saw their garments laid a drying."

The anniversary of the death of Houssain, the grandson of

Mahomed, is celebrated with great parade by all the Mussulmans in Hindostan of the sect of Ali. They call it the death of Houssain and Hussen, two imans or successors to Mahomed in his religious and civil government. Houssain was murdered on the plains of Kerbela, by an officer of the usurper Yezid, on the 10th of the month Mohurrum, in the 61st year of the Hejira. Houssain was grandson to Mahomed, by his daughter Fatima, who was married to Ali; and this murder was the cause of the enmity which subsists to this day between the Ommiades and Abassides. On the anniversary of that catastrophe the Mahomedans at Baroche, and other large towns in India, of the sect of Ali, go in procession through the streets, making the most dismal howlings and lamentations, and often inflict severe wounds on each other, in the mock combat, in memory of the attack on the plains of Kerbela, where Houssain, with seventy-two of his family, were cut to pieces. They were surrounded by ten thousand of Yezid's cavalry, and after fighting desperately, himself, his children, and the whole party were destroyed.

This combat is rather the termination of the tragedy; for the spectacle commences with solemn processions, plaintive music, and religious ceremonies. According to Chardin the Persians annually solemnize this massacre to the fullest extent. They continue the mourning for ten days, during which they suspend all appearances of joy and pleasure, and appear as mourners in their dress; affecting discourses relating to the murder are pronounced in numerous assemblies; mournful cries of Houssain unite with melancholy music; numbers personate Houssain, at the time of his death, when fainting with thirst, and covered with blood gushing from his wounds. They daub themselves with black paint, to represent the first, supposing that extreme thirst produced this effect on the prince; others use a red powder to resemble him when covered with blood. Hymns are sung in the royal palace in honour of the race of Ali, in presence of the prince, as well as the funeral dirges among the populace.

In the Tanzea, or Lamentations, composed for this occasion, and annually recited at the commemoration of this martyrdom, are the following stanzas, which I have selected from the affectionate dirge supposed to have been uttered by the Lady Zineb, sister to the murdered prince, Sekeena, his daughter, and the youth Zeen-ul-Abedeen his son, upon the horse of Houssain, called Zu-al-Jinnah, returning to the tents, covered with blood, without his master.

ZINEB.

O! Zu-al-Jinnah! where is the son of Ali?
Where is the martyr of Kerbela?
Whither is fled my comfort, my support?
The favoured of God, whither is he fled?

ZEEN-UL-ABEDEEN.

O! Zu-al-Jinnah! what hast thou done with the prince of religion? What is become of the fragrant flowers of the garden of Kheen-ul-Nissa, the most excellent of women? Of Fatima, the daughter of the prophet, the wife of Ali, and the mother of Houssain? Alas! alas! O misfortune, and distress!

SEKEENA.

O Zu-ul-Jinnah, stained with blood!
What hast thou done with my father?
Where lieth the crown of my delight?
My companion, my morning, my evening!
Where is the iman beloved of God?
Where is the father of Sekeena?
Where is the bright taper of Sekeena's nights,
Where is the support, the comfort of thy daughter?
Alas! I am now an unfortunate orphan!
My father, my protector, is no more!

Soon after my arrival at Baroche, I purchased a small house and some land in the village of Vezel-poor, about a mile from the city, situated between two English gardens bounded on the north by a ruined mosque and sacred grove, the occasional retirement of an English gentleman from Baroche, and on the south by the Nerbuddah, there near a mile broad. My garden occupied about six acres; I formed it as much as possible after the English taste, and spared no pains to procure plants and flowers from different parts of India and China: it contained several large mango, tamarind, and burr-trees, which formed a delightful shade; besides a variety of smaller fruit-trees and flowering-shrubs. At the southern extremity a bower, elevated on a mount overlooking the river, commanded an extensive view of the plains of Occlaseer, and a rich tract of country bounded by the Raje-Pipley hills. Shade and water were my grand objects; without them there can be no enjoyment in an Indian garden; even with those advantages, the time of enjoyment is short, especially during the hot winds. One great desideratum is the verdant lawn almost peculiar to the English gardens; a tropical sun would not admit of it in the fair season, and during the rainy months the rank luxuriant grass more resembles reeds and rushes than the soft carpet bordered by an English shrubbery.

Beautiful as are the British gardens and pleasure grounds, insomuch as to have become proverbial on the continent, I do not think their charms can be fully appreciated by those who have not travelled in the torrid zone; the deprivation of shady groves and living streams has taught them to know their value. We can form some idea of the traveller's joy from the sensations they have expressed on leaving the burning deserts of Syria and Arabia, and approaching the groves of Yemen, or the gardens of Damascus. The beauty and value of a garden thus refreshed by shade and water, is perhaps no where more highly estimated than by the prophet Jeremiah; who, in foretelling the return of the Jews from the Babylonish captivity, uses a variety of customary images to express their joy. " I will build thee, and thou shall be built, O virgin of Israel! thou shalt again be adorned with thy tabrets, and shalt go forth in the dances of them that make merry. Thou shalt plant vines upon the mountain, upon my mountain in the field: I will cause thee to walk by the rivers of waters, and keep thee as a shepherd keepeth his flock. They shall flow together for the goodness of the Lord, for wheat, and for wine, for oil, and for the young of the flock; their soul shall be a *watered garden*: they shall sorrow no more!"

I have mentioned various modes of irrigating the oriental gar-

SCENE *in the* GARDEN *at* YEZELPOOR, *near* BAROCHE;

dens and orchards; a practice in constant use in our garden at Baroche, which generally employed three men and a boy eight hours every day. This custom seems to illustrate a passage in scripture respecting the gardens of Egypt, which were probably watered by small streams, conducted from a reservoir filled at the annual overflowing of the Nile. "The land whither thou goest to possess it, is not as the land of Egypt; where thou sowedst thy seed, and *wateredst it with thy foot* (or by an instrument worked by the foot) *as a garden of herbs*; but it is a land of hills and valleys, and drinketh water of the rain of heaven." Two under gardeners raise the water from the well to the reservoir by a yoke of oxen, working on an inclined plane, extended according to the depth of the well; the head man attended by a boy conducts it from thence, by artificial channels, to each bed of herbs, and every favourite flower. These little conduits being made in the mould, near the borders, require constant attention to remove obstructions, and give a free circulation to the rill, which seldom exceeds a few inches in breadth. This the gardeners sometimes do in a stooping posture with their hands, oftener in an upright position with their feet, and by practice become very expert.

My favourite seat was under a tamarind tree, near the well just mentioned; the adjoining shrubberies were generally enlivened by squirrels, parrots, and bulbuls; vines and creeping plants were trained to conceal two pillars of rude construction, that supported the beam over the well, to which the large water bucket was suspended: one of these I entirely covered with the lively ipomea, and every variety of clematis; the other I modernized a little in the European taste, and placed an urn on the summit, dedicated to the naiad. One sultry morning, when enjoying the luxury of shade, and listening to the falls of water, under this umbrageous canopy, a few lines occurred, which I addressed to the nymph of the fountain, and inscribed on the pedestal supporting the urn. It requires an apology for introducing my first poetical essay to the public eye, now transcribed from the manuscript letter; and which my partial friends will not allow to be suppressed.

Lines inscribed under an Urn in a Garden at Baroche, near a Spring overshadowed by a Burr, or Banian-tree, surrounded by flowering Shrubs.

To Medhumad'ha,[a] lovely nymph,
The guardian of my spring;
To thee, this votive urn I raise,
Where bulbuls[b] sweetly sing.

Thy gurgling, cool, pellucid stream
Fair naiad, gently pour;
And murmuring softly from thy font,
Awake each opening flower.

Let spicy groves luxuriant rise
Around this blest retreat,
And Indra[c] balmy zephyrs breathe
On every peaceful seat.

Let lofty champa's[d] graceful boughs
Diffuse their fragrance far;
Al'hinna,[e] tulsee,[f] mogree,[g] sweet,
Perfume the ambient air.

Bright Mahadavi's[h] crimson stars
On pensile tendrils stray
Around the mango's[i] stately trunk,
And with the breezes play.

Then, gentle naiad, kindly pour
Thy vivifying dew;
And tint the flowers that kiss thy stream
With beauty's loveliest hue!

But the lov'd burr's[k] entwining trunk
Claims most thy fostering care;
Emblem of God! its out-stretch'd arms
Beneficence declare!

When Mitra[l] throws his powerful rays
On every distant tree,
My favor'd plants shall gaily bloom,
And owe that bloom to thee.

---

[a] Medhumadha, a water nymph in the Hindoo mythology.

[b] Bulbul, the Indian nightingale.

[c] Indra, god of the seasons.

[d] Champa, a flower of great fragrance, growing on a large tree, similar to the magnolia glauca.

[e] A favorite shrub with the oriental ladies, who use the flowers for dying their nails and fingers of a lively red.

[f] Tulsee, a plant held sacred by the Hindoos.

[g] Mogree, a beautiful species of Arabian jessamine.

[h] Mahadavi, a most elegant crimson creeper; ipomea; often mentioned in the drama of Sacontala, and universally admired.

[i] Mango; esteemed the best fruit in Hindostan.

[k] Burr or banian-tree. Ficus bengalensis; a sacred tree of the Hindoos; considered as emblematical of the Deity, from its out-stretching arms, and overshadowing beneficence.

[l] Mitra, the sun, or solar deity of the Hindoos.

I shall not enter on a description of the various birds, insects, and plants, which accompanied my drawings from Baroche, as in general they varied but little from those at Bombay and on the Malabar coast. The serpents in Guzerat were more numerous, and in greater variety; many were of a large size, and especially a species which seemed peculiarly partial to the shrubs and creeping plants which overshadowed the large well in my gardens; these the gardeners would neither destroy, nor suffer to be molested, as they looked upon them to be the genii, or guardian-angels of the garden, and often invoked them under the endearing appellations of father, mother, and other respectful and affectionate epithets. This veneration for serpents is confined to Hindostan; the ancients thought there was something divine in these reptiles. Esculapius, and several of the heathen deities are supposed to have appeared in this form; their statues were often adorned with serpents, and the cobra de capello makes a conspicuous appearance among the Hindoo sculpture in the temples of Elora, Salsette, and the Elephanta.

Whether our hortensial snakes were evil genii, or guardian-angels, I shall not determine; Harrabhy, the head gardener, considered them as the latter, and paid them religious veneration: on that account I never disturbed them until I had erected a cold bath in an orange and lemon grove for an English lady, who retired thither at sun-rise, with her sable nymphs, to enjoy one of the greatest luxuries in the torrid zone. This bath, perfectly concealed from view, was more useful than ornamental, and very unlike the lake of Diana, or any of the modern hummums in oriental cities; it was indeed nothing more than a humble shed, thatched with the leaves of the palmyra; and although as sacred to chastity as the speculum Dianæ, or the gardens of Susanna, it neither attracted an Acteon, nor an elder of Babylon. It certainly did attract another visitor, equally unexpected and disagreeable; for one morning the young lady, in the state of Musidora, was alarmed by a rustling among the palmyra leaves which covered the bath; and looking up, beheld one of the garden genii, with brilliant eyes under the expanded hood of a large cobra de capello, pushing through the thatch, and ready to dart on the fountain. Pure and unadorned as Eve when her reflected beauties first met her eye, the lady and her hand-maids made a precipitate retreat through the grove, and gained her chamber, heedless of gazers, whether in the form of gardeners, snakes, or monkeys.

I have mentioned the ordeal trials, and the practices of diviners in India: whatever may be our opinion of such things, we are often, from various motives, under the necessity of acquiescing in them. Residing in a family at Surat with the same English lady, she lost a gold watch on which she set a particular value. Several modes of divination were practised to discover the thief; one was similar to that used among the ancient Chaldeans and Egyptians, and perhaps not unlike the cup of divination belonging to the viceroy of Egypt found among the shepherds of Canaan. On this occasion the name of every person in the house was placed in a separate ball of paste or wax, and thrown into a vessel of water: one only swam on the surface; the rest fell to the bottom, and there remained. On opening the floating ball, it contained the name of an unsuspected female, who immediately confessed she had stolen and secreted the watch. Supposing this to be like other

Asiatic juggles, I gave it very little attention; but afterwards at Baroche I attended minutely to an ordeal in which myself and Harrabhy were more immediately concerned.

On removing from our country house at Baroche to Surat, we packed up most of our things, and placed them in the front veranda, where the peons slept on their moveable beds. An iron plate-chest was for greater security deposited in an inner room near that where the family slept: we saw it there when we retired to rest, and in the morning it was missing. The contents being valuable, and the time of our departure near, we used every means to discover so extraordinary a robbery, in which, from the weight of the chest, three or four persons must have been concerned. Promises and threatenings were of no avail, the delinquents were concealed. I suspected an individual, but not knowing how he could have accomplished the robbery, I was silent. The public officers belonging to the court of Adawlet not being able to discover the robber, at the earnest solicitations of all our servants, Hindoos, Mahomedans, and Parsees, we had recourse to divination by balls in the water; our own names were included with the rest. On forming a circle round the vase, I observed the man I suspected to change colour, and become a little agitated: no other person remarked it until on the balls being immersed in water one only rose to the surface; his confusion was then evident; still more so, when on opening the ball it contained the name of Harrabhy. He had lived with us several years as head gardener, without our having any reason to suspect his honesty: he positively denied the robbery, and we had no other proof than the ordeal, which, although fully satisfactory to all the Indians, was not so to us. They requested that neither Harrabhy nor any other person might leave the spot until we had gone through the rice ordeal; to this we submitted, though by no means palatable to Harrabhy. He reluctantly complied, and with all the rest of us put a few grains of unboiled rice into his mouth: it was previously intimated that from the mouth of the innocent after mastication it would come out a milky liquid, from the guilty a dry powder. We were all of the milky party except Harrabhy: mingling with the saliva it became a white fluid; with him it remained a dry powder, notwithstanding a number of fruitless efforts to liquefy it. He was compelled thus to spit it out: his complexion changed from a rich brown to a sort of livid blue, his lips quivered, and his altered countenance plainly indicated guilt; he would make no confession, and on this evidence we could only put him in confinement under the court of Adawlet, until we obtained further proof. The next day a little slave-boy, whom I afterwards brought to England, discovered the bent iron hasp of the plate-chest just appearing out of the steep bank of the Nerbudda, at the end of our garden, about twenty feet above the river, and as much below the summit of the cliff; there we found the chest, buried in the earth. The robbers had attempted to wrench it open, and the clasps fastened by padlocks had given way; but the lock occasioning greater difficulty, they waited for a more favorable opportunity. When the culprit found the chest had been discovered and restored to the owners, and had no prospect of benefiting by its contents, he confessed that in concert with three other men he had carried it off in the night, while our people were asleep, and was in hopes we should have departed without finding it. Profane history abounds with ordeals; the bitter water of chastity, and many similar trials in the sacred page, prove their prevalence among the Jews.

As his guardian genii the snakes could not protect Harrabhy from the hands of justice, so neither could they always save their mortal form from destruction: for the greatest enemy the serpents have to encounter is the little mongoose, (viverra Ichneumon Lin.) an animal of the weasel kind, in all respects the same as the ichneumon of Egypt; they destroy rats, mice, and other vermin, but seem most inimical to serpents; on which they dart with an inconceivable agility. I was informed at Anjengo, by many eye-witnesses of the fact, that on the mongoose being wounded by the serpent, he immediately retired, and ate of a certain herb, which proved an antidote to the poison; after which he returned to his antagonist, renewed the combat, and generally gained a victory. The ichneumon destroys the eggs of the serpents, and providentially has the same propensity for those of the crocodile, which the female deposits on the banks of the Nile; for which reason this little animal, with more reason than can be assigned for the bean or onion, was worshipped among the deities of the ancient Egyptians.

My garden at Baroche was not only frequented by Harrabhy's genii, but by a variety of other serpents, green, blue, scarlet, and black, and by one shaded with every varied hue in a Turkey-carpet; for that reason called the carpet-snake. They never molested us, nor did I ever hear of an accident there; indeed I believe very few of them are venomous.

Our gardens produced abundance of fruit and vegetables; and

few places are better supplied with provisions than Baroche; meat of all kinds is excellent and cheap; there is no want of poultry: the bazars are stocked with indigenous fruits and vegetables, and the Nerbudda supplies a variety of fish, exclusive of that brought in by the fishing boats from the sea. The carp in the Nerbudda are uncommonly large; they sometimes weigh fifty pounds; these, when stuffed and baked in a plantain leaf, are much esteemed; it is most probably the same as the rooee and cutlah of the Ganges, which often weigh forty pounds. Long after my arrival in England, I accidentally met with an official report, sent to me by the clerk of the market when I was acting for the chief of Baroche, then absent in the Purgunna. It contains an authentic account of the principal commodities publicly sold there, at the price in Indian money, and their own weights and measures, which I have brought as near as possible to the English standard. It should be remarked, that at Baroche most articles for the table are about one third of the price for which they can be purchased at Bombay. Grain is not much dearer in general; it being imported there from the northern settlements, the prices at Surat are much the same as in the Baroche markets.

To JAMES FORBES, Esq. &c. &c.

Report of the Markets at Baroche, 7th January, 1782.

PRICES OF GRAIN IN THE WAREHOUSES.

		£.	s.	d.
Wheat	12 rupees per culsey, about 600 lbs. English,	1	10	0
Juarree	8 . . ditto	1	0	0
Mutt	8 . . ditto	1	0	0
Tuar. dohl	13 . . ditto	1	12	6
Gram	13 . . ditto	1	12	6
Bahjeree	9 . . ditto	1	2	6
Rice	11 . . ditto	1	7	6
Oored	11 . . ditto	1	7	6
Moong	8 . . ditto	1	0	0

PRICES OF SUNDRY ARTICLES IN THE SHOPS.

Ghee	7 rupees per maund, 28 lbs. English .	0	17	6
Gingely oil	$2\frac{3}{4}$. ditto	0	7	0
Erinda oil	$2\frac{1}{2}$. ditto	0	6	3
Jaggaree	$3\frac{1}{4}$. ditto	0	8	3
Foreign sugar	7 . ditto	0	17	6
Sugar-candy	13 . ditto	1	12	6
Pepper	13 . ditto	1	12	6
Cloves	6 rupees per seer, a weight rather less than 1 lb.	0	15	0

		£. s. d.
Nutmegs	5½ rupees per seer, a weight rather less than 1 lb.	0 13 9
Cardamoms	5 . ditto	0 12 6

PRICE OF PROVISIONS IN THE MARKETS.

Beef	2	pice per seer, about one penny per lb.	
Mutton	4	. . ditto . . .	two-pence ditto
Veal	3	. . ditto . . .	three halfpence
Lamb	18	. . quarter . .	nine-pence
Kid	18	. . ditto . . .	nine-pence
Fish	3	pice per seer, . .	three halfpence

Bombalos, dried fish, ten for 1 pice, one penny

Bajee spinach 3½ seer for 1 pice

Beans 1½ seer for 1 pice

Cucumbers 3 seer for 1 pice

Bendey 1½ seer for 1 pice

Bringals 1½ seer for 1 pice

Onions 2 seer for 1 pice

Garlick 1½ seer for 4 pice

Limes one hundred 12 pice

Plantains and bananas, 4 for 1 pice

Guavas 5 for 1 pice

Radishes 12 for 1 pice

(Signed) J. Rigo, *Clerk of the Market.*

The price of labour, at Baroche and the neighbouring districts, is from two to four rupees per month. The labourers in my garden received three rupees and a half each man, the boy who attended the water-rills only two; with this they were perfectly contented, and it was probably more than they would have got from a wealthy native in a similar situation. The price of labour, servants' wages, and many other expenses appear small when compared with the same classes in England; but the number of persons necessarily employed in every department of domestic economy in India, brings the expense of an English family, in each country, more upon a level than may at first be imagined.

In most parts of Guzerat, a small native family of the low castes may live comfortably in their humble cottage for forty and fifty rupees a year; perhaps for less. When the wants of a people are so few, and those few so easily supplied, the same quantity of land must be able to support a much greater number of inhabitants than the same quantity in England; it has been calculated at three, and in some places at four to one.

For petty offences committed by the inhabitants of the Baroche districts, the court of Adawlet established in the city, and the power of the English chief as a magistrate, seemed adequate; in cases of a more criminal nature the prisoners were tried by the quarter sessions at Bombay, and civil suits of importance were decided there by the Mayor's court, and court of appeals, agreeably to the laws of England and the charter of the East India company.

Among the works of art at Baroche, is the Jumma Musseid, the silver mosque, and a few other remains of Mahomedan buildings; but the most interesting is a mausoleum called Baba-Rahan, or Bawrhan, which is built on an eminence, a mile from the city, near a spacious tank and shady groves, where are many Mahomedan tombs of less importance. But the grand mausoleum is in the Saracenic, or Moorish style of architecture; where columns and arches form corridores, and support several large domes and smaller cupolas, richly ornamented, which cover the marble tombs. This monument of Mahomedan splendour was erected seven hundred years ago, and is still held in great veneration: its lofty terrace, which was one of my usual evening excursions, commands an extensive prospect.

In the year 1078 of the Christian æra, and 492 of the Mahomedan hejira, while the government of the Hindoo rajahs remained undisturbed in this part of Hindostan, a mussulman saint, called Baba-Rahan, came into the Baroche country from Bagdad, accompanied by a number of fakeers and dervises, to convert the Hindoos to Islamism; but the saint, like many other Mahomedan champions, after a successful mission, no longer trusting to the persuasive powers of eloquence, drew the sword of intolerant zeal to increase the number of true believers, and caused such disturbances in the province, that the rajah of Baroche sent his son, Roy-Currun, to oppose him with a considerable force. Baba-Rahan not thinking it prudent to contend with so powerful an antagonist, entered into a treaty with the young prince, and in a few days converted him to the tenets of the Koran, and gave him the name of Mullick Mahomed. By their united endeavours the princess Bhaga, the rajah's daughter, embraced the new religion; and many other Hindoos, following the example of the royal converts, left the shrines of Brahma, and became disciples of Baba-Rahan. But as the most pure and peaceable of all religions has been too often perverted to the most cruel purposes, as ambition, interest, or misguided zeal, have spread their pernicious effects, so it was with these Mahomedans; for the prince of Baroche, forgetting every moral and filial duty, took up arms against his father, and was killed in an engagement near Bawrhan, where the bodies of himself, his sister, and a number of converts who fell in the action were interred. Soon after this catastrophe Baba-Rahan made his peace with the rajah, and at his death was buried on this sacred mount.

When this country was settled under the Mogul government a prince named Jengis Shah erected a mausoleum over the graves of the saint and his disciples; future nabobs added to the embellishments, and ordered their remains to be interred in this holy spot, at the same time endowing lands to keep the buildings in repair; but during the lapse of time these bequests have been converted to other purposes, and the whole is in a state of decay.

An evening walk to Bawhran was one of my favourite excursions; the prospect from the upper terrace was delightful; the breeze over the lake refreshing; and the scene altogether formed for meditation. Monkeys, squirrels, doves, and pea-fowl, animated the groves; the decayed parts of the building were occupied by bats, owls, and noxious reptiles, the usual inhabitants of desolation. Some of the dark sepulchral chambers contained fragments of sculpture, and other decorations, rudely heaped together from the mouldering tombs; but the stench of the bats was so intolerable, that it was impossible to remain many seconds to examine them. These bats were of very large size, and their gloomy retreats illustrated the prophetical language—" Thou hast forsaken thy people, because they be replenished from the east, and are soothsayers like the Philistines; their land also is full of idols; to whom the mean man boweth down, and the great man humbleth himself; but in that day the lofty look shall be humbled, and the haughtiness of man shall be bowed down; and the Lord alone shall be exalted: in that day, shall a man cast his idols of silver, and his idols of gold, which they had made, each one for himself to worship, to the moles and to the bats."

Whatever might have been the animosities between the Hindoos and Mahomedans in the time of Baba-Rahan, or during subsequent periods, it is certain, as an intelligent writer observes, that now "the professors of both religions have acquired a habit of looking on each other with an eye of indulgence unusual in other countries between those who maintain such opposite tenets. Thus the Hindoo is often seen to vie with the disciple of Ali in his demonstrations of grief for the fate of the two martyred sons of that apostle; and in the splendour of the pageant annually exhibited in their commemoration, he pays a respect to the holidays prescribed by the Koran, or set apart for the remembrance of remarkable events in the life of the prophet or his apostles. This degree of complaisance is perhaps not surprizing in the disciple of BRAHMA, whose maxim is, that the various modes of worship practised by the different nations of the earth, spring alike from the Deity, and are equally acceptable to him; but even they who follow the intolerant doctrines of the Koran are no longer those furious and sanguinary zealots, who, in the name of GOD and his prophet, marked their course with desolation and slaughter, demolishing the Hindoo temples, and erecting mosques on their ruins. They found the patient constancy of the Hindoo superior to their violence; that the fear of torments and of death was unable to make him desert the tenets which his ancestors had handed down to him from an unfathomable antiquity; but that, if left in the quiet possession of these, he was a peaceable, industrious, and valuable subject. Accordingly, we observe among the Mussulmauns of Hindostan a great deference for the prejudices of their neighbours or dependants of the Hindoo persuasion, particularly in the *hooly*, or *saturnalia* of India, when liberty of speech and action towards superiors are allowed to as great an extent as among the ancient Romans; the Mussulmauns are seen to enter into the diversion with as much alacrity as the Hindoos themselves."

These remarks are very just; they establish the liberality of sentiment which now generally prevails in the mingled society of commercial cities. We had no invidious distinction between Mahomedan and Hindoo at Baroche; but a very unpleasant schism existed among the Parsees, who formed a considerable part of its inhabitants.

However delightful it is to cherish the idea of such liberal opinions among the Hindoos and Mahomedans in the British settlements, it is well known there exist under the Turkish and Persian governments thousands of intolerant bigots, who act diametrically opposite to those philanthropical sentiments, and pervert certain passages of the Koran to the most cruel and diabolical purposes. In this number, few have been more active, determined, and powerful than the late Tippoo Sultaun, whose misguided zeal led him to commit the most atrocious cruelties. In the curious history found in the palace at Seringapatam, mentioned by colonel Wilks to have been written by himself and his secretary, among other diabolical suggestions and false aspersions on the Christians, is this sanguinary passage from a letter written by the Sultaun to general Macleod at Mangulore, which stamps the character of the tyrant of Mysore.

"It is admitted by the concurring testimony of all religions, that no apostle, excepting the seal of the apostles, has been invested with the power of the sword; and that the text of "slay them wheresoever thou canst find them" has descended from the Almighty avenger to no other. That holy personage did, in conformity to the command of the great Creator, let loose the infidel-destroying sword, without distinction, on the Jews, the Nazarenes, the Sabians, and other idolaters. And Ali, the victorious lion of the Lord, who was the rightful Imaun, and the absolute vicegerent of the seal of the prophets, removed the darkness of infidelity and association (that is the doctrine of assigning to God associates in power) and sent abundance of associators on the road to the abode of misery. Therefore God, and the apostle of God, and all his elect, abominate and abhor you, and you have incurred the wrath of the throne of God. Wherefore, all sects being bound by the laws and precepts of their respective apostles, it follows, that killing and slaying, and bravery, and heroism, and holy war, and the destruction of infidels, and the arts which belong to the gallant and the brave, have descended as an hereditary right to us from our apostle."

I need not particularize the inhabitants of Baroche; the Hindoos are much the same every where. The high Moguls and other

Mahomedans at Baroche and Surat are a dignified, polite, and respectable people; the manners and dress of the females are delineated in the prophet Ezekiel's portrait of an oriental lady: "I clothed thee with broidered work, I girded thee with fine linen, and covered thee with silk: I decked thee with ornaments; I put bracelets upon thine hands, and a chain on thy neck; I put a jewel on thy forehead, and ear-rings in thine ears, and a beautiful crown upon thine head. Thus wast thou decked with gold and silver; and thy raiment was of fine linen, and silk, and broidered work; thou didst eat fine flour, and honey, and oil; and thou wast exceeding beautiful."

In the Baroche purgunna were many families of the *Rajhpoots*, or *Rajhputs*, a noble race of Hindoos, divided into distinct tribes, and settled in various districts, chiefly in the northern parts of Hindostan. Some of the highest distinction trace their origin to the *suryabans*, or children of the sun, and in that respect vie with the incas of Peru. This celestial descent is confined to few families; but the Rajhpoots all pride themselves on their noble ancestry, and seldom disgrace their pedigree by an ignoble action. I became acquainted with several in Guzerat who confirmed these sentiments, and I knew some of their females, who considered themselves very superior to the surrounding Hindoos. The Rajhpoots make the best soldiers in the country; imbued with a noble spirit, great energy, and generally of an athletic form, they have the grand essentials of a military character, and are highly respected by all the other castes.

Some of the Rajhpoot tribes can furnish from twenty to thirty thousand fighting-men. In Mr. Hunter's journey from Agra to Oujein, we find the descendants of one of their princes at this time able to raise forty-one thousand troops, which he particularly specifies as to number and family. It is unnecessary to mention these, but some peculiar characteristics of the tribe to which they belong are interesting: it is named *Cuchwa'ha*, and is of the *surybans*, or children of the sun, already noticed, being descended from RAMA, the celebrated rajah of Ayodhya. RAMA had two sons, one named LOH, the other CUSH; the descendants of LOH are named *Bud-Gujer*, and the descendants of CUSH, *Cuchwa'ha.* From CUSH, the Jayanagar chronologers reckon two hundred and ten rajahs, in succession, to Prit hi Raj, who succeeded to the musnud of *Ambh'er* in Sumbut, 1559, or A. D. 1502; and died in Sumbut 1584, in the twenty-fifth year of his reign.

PRIT'HI RAJ had eighteen sons; BHA'RAMUL, the eldest, succeeded him on the throne; BHIM, the second, was established the *Raj*, or *Nirwir*; four died without children. To the remaining twelve sons, PRIT'HI RAJ, to avoid the contention which he foresaw was likely to happen after his death, assigned, in his lifetime, portions of territory, which descended to their offspring, and are called *Cut'hri*, or the twelve chambers of the house of *Cuchwa'ha.* Of these twelve sons the descendants of eight can now furnish a corps of forty-one thousand horse and foot in the northern districts; of the other four sons no descendants are now remaining; but to complete the number of chambers, four other tribes have been adopted in their room. The whole families descended from the rajahs of *Ambh'er* are fifty-three in number, under their respective chieftains; and these, including the above forty-one thousand, can raise a corps of cavalry and infantry amounting together to one hundred and forty-seven thousand.

I shall not pursue the subject further; but so noble and distinct a race of people, more or less dispersed throughout the northern provinces, deserves our notice. The character they every where preserve of a dignified martial spirit, throws light on the following anecdote, and shows the insufficiency of the English laws among such a people.

About four years before my appointment to Baroche, some Mahomedans, walking through a village where a family of *Rajhpoots* resided, approached their house, and accidentally looked into a room where an elderly woman was eating. They intended no insult; they saw her at her meal, and immediately retired: but this accident occasioned a disgrace on the Rajhpoot lady for which, on her part, there could be no expiation. She at that time lived with her grandson, a fine young man, who was absent when the Mahomedans committed their trespass: on his return home she related the circumstance, and her determination not to survive it; she therefore entreated him instantly to put her to death, a step which she had only deferred that she might fall by his hand. The youth's affection and good sense induced him to remonstrate with his venerable parent, whom he endeavoured to dissuade from her purpose by alleging that none but her own family knew of the disgrace, the very men who were the innocent cause of it being unconscious of the offence. Persevering however in her resolution, but unable to persuade either her grandson, or any other person, to perform the sacrifice, she calmly waited until he next went from home, and then beat her head against the wall, with dreadful violence. On his return he found his venerable parent in this agonizing and shocking state! She again entreated he would finish the sacrifice, and release her from misery: he then stabbed her to the heart. By the English laws he was secured as a murderer, sent to Bombay for trial, and confined in the common prison until the ensuing sessions. The grand-jury found a bill for murder; the petty-jury, composed half of Europeans and half of natives, found him guilty; and the judges condemned him to death. The Rajhpoots in general have a noble mien and dignified character; their high caste is stamped in their countenance: this young man possessed them all. I saw him receive his sentence, not only with composure, but with a mingled look of disdain and delight not easy to describe. Unconscious of the *crime* laid to his charge, he said he had nothing to accuse himself of, but disobedience to his parent, by permitting humanity and filial affection to supersede his duty, and the honour of his caste: that life was no longer desirable; nor, if acquitted by the English laws, would he survive the ignominy of having been confined with European culprits, and criminals of the lowest castes, with whom he had been compelled to eat, and associate in a common prison; acts so contrary to every thing which he esteemed right and honourable, that the sooner he was transferred to another state of existence, the better. However inclined the government might be to clemency, it would evidently have been fruitless; the noble Rajhpoot would not survive the disgrace, and the sentence of the law was executed, in the hope it might prevent others from following his example.

The same motive operated in another instance which happened at Bombay about ten years before; and this, as well as the preceding trial of the Rajhpoot, is entered in the proceedings of the Court of Sessions. One of those Hindoo visionaries, whom I have frequently described, lived in the cocoa-nut woods at Bombay, in the neighbourhood of several Hindoo and Mahomedan families: he was a man of an amiable character, in the prime of life, married, and the father of four young children. Although the Christian sabbath is not held sacred by the Indians, yet in compliance with the English laws no shops are opened, and no business transacted among the natives; becoming consequently a leisure day, they consider it a holiday, and generally retire to their country-houses and gardens; or walk on a sandy beach near the sea, called Back-bay, a pleasant spot two or three miles in extent, bounded on one side by the sea, on the other by the cocoa-nut woods where this Hindoo resided. One Sunday afternoon he desired his wife to prepare herself and the children for a walk on the beach; from whence he intended to accompany them on a longer journey: on inquiring whither, he informed her he had received an invitation from the deity to go to heaven, and take his family with him; that they were to proceed by water, and depart from Back-bay. Thither the parents repaired with the children; the two eldest walked before them to the sea-side, and each carried an infant: in this manner they walked into the water. Hitherto there was nothing extraordinary in their conduct had there been strangers on the beach, because the Hindoos are more or less in the water throughout the day in their usual attire, performing ablutions and religious ceremonies, especially the females. What arguments or influence this Hindoo used to induce his wife to comply with his singular desire, is foreign to the subject; it is certain the infatuated parents drove their two eldest children into the sea, and saw them carried off by the waves. After plunging the helpless infants into the same abyss, the wife voluntarily followed: the husband was deliberately drowning himself, when he suddenly recollected, that, living under the English government, the disappearance of a family without any apparent cause, might involve his neighbours in trouble; he therefore determined to return once more to his habitation before his final departure, and inform them of the truth: he accordingly did so. The Hindoos received the intelligence very calmly, and some of them, probably, applauded his conduct; but a Mahomedan, among the number of his auditors, said the communication was so extraordinary, that as they *did* live under the English government, whose laws and customs so essentially differed from the Hindoo system, it might be difficult to convince them of the truth, and therefore the enthusiast must accompany him before a magistrate, and relate the story himself. With this he reluctantly complied, and they repaired together to the acting magistrate in the town of Bombay; who thought it an affair of such importance, that he placed the man under a guard, and the next morning convened a bench of justices, who committed him for trial at the ensuing sessions, where he was found guilty of murder, condemned, and executed. The only circumstance which caused him distress, was the procrastination of his change in the metempsychosis, and not being permitted to accomplish his exit in the manner he had intended.

I will not introduce any further anecdotes of this kind from my own knowledge: but in confirmation of such extraordinary facts, and at the same time to shew the cruelty which the brahmins frequently commit, I shall insert two or three instances communicated by Lord Teignmouth to the Asiatic Society, which throw further light on their manners and customs.

In 1791, SOODISHTER MIER, a *brahmin*, the farmer of land paying revenue, and tenant of tax free land, in the province of Benares, was summoned to appear before a native officer, the deputy collector of the district where he resided. He positively refused to obey the summons, which was repeated without effect; and after some time several people were deputed to enforce the process by compelling his attendance. On their approaching the house he cut off the head of his deceased son's widow, and threw it out. His first intention was to destroy his own wife; but it was proved in evidence, that, upon his indication of it, his son's widow requested him to decapitate her, which he instantly did. In this case the process against Soodishter was regular, his disobedience contemptuous; his situation in life entitled him to no particular exemption, he had nothing to apprehend from obeying the requisition, and he was certain of redress if injury or injustice were practised upon him.

Another *brahmin*, named BALOO PAUNDEH, in 1793, was convicted of the murder of his daughter. His own account of the transaction will best explain it, and his motives; I give it in abstract. That about twelve years before the period of the murder, he, BALOO, and another man were joint tenants and cultivators of a spot of ground, when his partner BALOO relinquished his share. In 1793 this partner again brought forward a claim to a share in the ground: the claim was referred to arbitration, and a decision was pronounced in favour of BALOO. He consequently repaired to the land, and was ploughing it, when he was interrupted by his opponent. The words of BALOO are as follows: "I became angry "and enraged at his forbidding me; and, bringing my own little "daughter APMUNYA, who was only a year and a half old, to the "said field, I killed her with my sword."

The last instance is an act of matricide, perpetrated by BEECHUK and ADHER, two brothers, *brahmins*, and zemindars, or proprietors of landed estates, the extent of which did not exceed eight acres. There had been a dispute among the zemindars respecting the revenues of the village, particularly with a person named GOWRY, and the immediate cause which instigated the brahmins to murder their mother, was an act of violence said to have been committed by the emissaries of GOWRY in entering their house during their absence at night, and carrying off forty rupees, the property of BEECHUK and ADHER, from the apartments of their women. BEECHUK first returned to his house; where his mother, his wife, and his sister-in-law, related what had happened. He immediately conducted his mother to an adjoining rivulet; where, being joined in the grey of the morning by his brother ADHER, they called out aloud to the people of the village, that although they would overlook the assault as an act which could not be remedied, the forty rupees must be returned. To this exclamation no answer was received, nor is there a certainty that it was even heard by any person. BEECHUK, without further hesitation, drew his scimitar, and at one stroke severed his mother's head from her body; with the professed view, as entertained and avowed both by parent and son, that the mother's spirit, excited by the beating of a large drum during forty days, might for ever haunt, torment, and pursue to death GOWRY and the others concerned with him. The last words which the mother pronounced were, that she would "blast the said GOWRY and those connected with him."

The Society will observe, with some surprize, that the perpetrators of the several acts which I have related, were *brahmins*."

CHAPTER XXII.

AN EXCURSION INTO THE WILDS OF TURCASEER; AND NATURAL HISTORY OF THE COUNTRY, NEAR THE RAJEPIPLEY HILLS, IN GUZERAT.

1779.

O Nature! Fille du ciel! tes œuvres annoncent ton origine! sainteté parfaite, science supréme, sagesse inexprimable! permets moi, qui ne suis qu'une atóme faconnée de la matiere animée, de desirer une connoissance suffisante pour pouvoir expliquer tes ouvrages merveilleux!

Each moss,
Each shell, each crawling insect, holds a rank
Important in the plan of HIM, who form'd
This scale of beings; holds a rank, which lost
Would break the chain, and leave behind a gap,
Which NATURE's self would rue. STILLINGFLEET.

CONTENTS.

Excursion of a shooting party in Turcaseer, its uninhabited and savage forests—wild beasts—monkeys—bheels—serpents—locusts, their appearance and astonishing depredations—locusts in Egypt—whether quails or locusts the food of the Israelites in the desert—feathered game of Guzerat—Florican—Culleim and Sahras—anecdote of a Sahras—beauty of the baubul, or acacia—curious instinct and sagacity in the baubul caterpillar—further description of the baya, or bottle-nested sparrow—instinct of various animals—Addison's remarks thereon—Rajc-pipley hills—Tiger mountain—number of wild animals in those unfrequented regions—size of the royal tiger—various habits of tigers—of hyenas and other beasts of prey—rhinoceros, the unicorn of scripture—wild hogs—bears—anecdote of their dreadful brutality.

CHAPTER XXII.

During my residence at Baroche I frequently joined the English chief on hunting and shooting parties in the neighbouring districts: not that I had any pleasure in those diversions, but his tents being often pitched in unfrequented forests, and savage tracts, little known to Europeans, I had an opportunity of exploring scenes of nature, which, on account of wild beasts and wilder men, it would have been impossible to have traversed without a strong and expensive guard.

The most interesting of these excursions occurred the year after my arrival at Baroche, when the sporting camp was formed in the environs of Turcaseer, a small Mahratta town which gives name to ruined districts once populous and cultivated, then containing only two inhabited villages, and the shabby capital. A scene so contrasted to the fertile plains in the Baroche purgunna, afforded me a fund of novelty and amusement; the woods and forests abounded with tigers, hyenas, wolves, jackals, elks, antelopes, spotted-deer, and a variety of smaller game.

We continued some time at Turcaseer, and then moved on, in the patriarchal style, from place to place, as shade, water, and game attracted us. The different quadrupeds just mentioned were occasionally seen; peacocks, doves, and squirrels, unaccustomed to molestation, approached our tents with familiarity; while monkeys in great number diverted us with their playfulness, and cunning devices to purloin the bottled-beer, fruit, or any delicacy that suited their taste. The gentleman who shot the female monkey formerly mentioned, was generally on these parties; they were from that time a privileged race with him and his friends. The Chinese are said to eat monkeys; but I never heard of any caste, tribe, or individual in Hindostan using them for food; not even the Pariahs and Chandalas, who eat carrion, and offal of every description.

The surrounding districts were nearly as wild and uncultivated as Turcaseer: the wildness increased as we approached the Rajepipley hills, and there every trace of agriculture and population ceased. The only human inhabitants are a set of cruel robbers called Bheels, more barbarous than the beasts among whom they dwell.

The serpents, reptiles and insects in these wilds were varied and beautiful, particularly some of the cicadæ and locusts; that called the creeping leaf was to be seen in great variety; they are not easily distinguished from the plants on which they feed. Guanas, cameleons, and lizards of every description; some of the latter, basking in the sun, appeared in alternate stripes of blue and gold; and a large kind of locust was arrayed in the same splendid hues.

Many of these insects, when separately viewed, are extremely curious, and very pleasing; but, considered collectively, as instruments of divine vengeance, and destroyers of a country, they appear in an awful light. Desolation and famine mark their progress; all the expectations of the husbandman vanish; his fields, which the rising sun beheld covered with luxuriance, are before evening, a desert; the produce of his garden and orchards is equally destroyed; for, where these destructive swarms alight, not a leaf is left upon the trees, a blade of grass in the pasture, nor an ear of corn in the field: all wears the marks of dreadful devastation; to be renewed no more until the next rainy season. The locusts not only cause a famine, by destroying the produce of the country, but in districts near the sea, where they had been drowned, they have occasioned a pestilence, from the putrid effluvia of immense numbers blown upon the coast, or thrown up by the tides.

It is not a few fields, or only two or three villages, that are ruined by these voracious creatures; the face of the country is covered with them for many miles; yet in India they are not near so pernicious as in Arabia, and many parts of Africa, where they prove a scourge of the severest kind. Soon after my arrival at Baroche I saw a flight of locusts extending above a mile in length, and half as much in breadth; they appeared, as the sun was in the meridian, like a black cloud at a distance; as they approached the density of the host obscured the solar rays, cast an awful gloom, like that of an eclipse, over the garden, and caused a noise like the rushing of a torrent. They were near an hour in passing over our little territory; I need not say with what an anxious eye we marked their progress, fearful lest the delicacies of our garden should allure them to a repast. We picked up a few stragglers, but the main body took a western direction, and without settling in the country, most probably perished in the gulph of Cambay. A few months afterwards a much larger army alighted on the opposite side of the Nerbudda, destroyed every vegetable production throughout the Occlaseer purgunna, and gave the whole country the appearance of having been burnt. Each of these flights were brought by an east wind, from whence I cannot say: they completely realized the picture so affectingly recorded in holy writ. "The Lord brought an east wind all night upon the land of Egypt; and when it was morning the locusts were brought, and went over all the land, and rested in all the coasts of Egypt; very grievous were they; for they covered the face of the whole earth, so that the land was darkened, and they did eat every herb of the land, and all the fruit of the trees, and there remained not any green thing on the trees, or on the herbs of the field throughout all the land of Egypt."

It has been a matter of dispute between learned commentators on the scriptures, whether the animals mentioned by Moses in the miraculous supply of food for the Israelites in the wilderness, were quails or locusts. Our translators render them the former; but, from the description given by the sacred historian, and from what I have observed of locusts, I rather incline to the opinion of Ludolphus, and the late bishop of Clogher, that they were locusts, and not quails, which the children of Israel ate in the desert. Moses says, "There went forth a wind from the Lord, and brought quails from the sea, and let them fall by the camp, as it were a day's journey on this side, and as it were a day's journey on the other side, round about the camp, and as it were two cubits high upon the face of the earth. And the people stood up all that day,

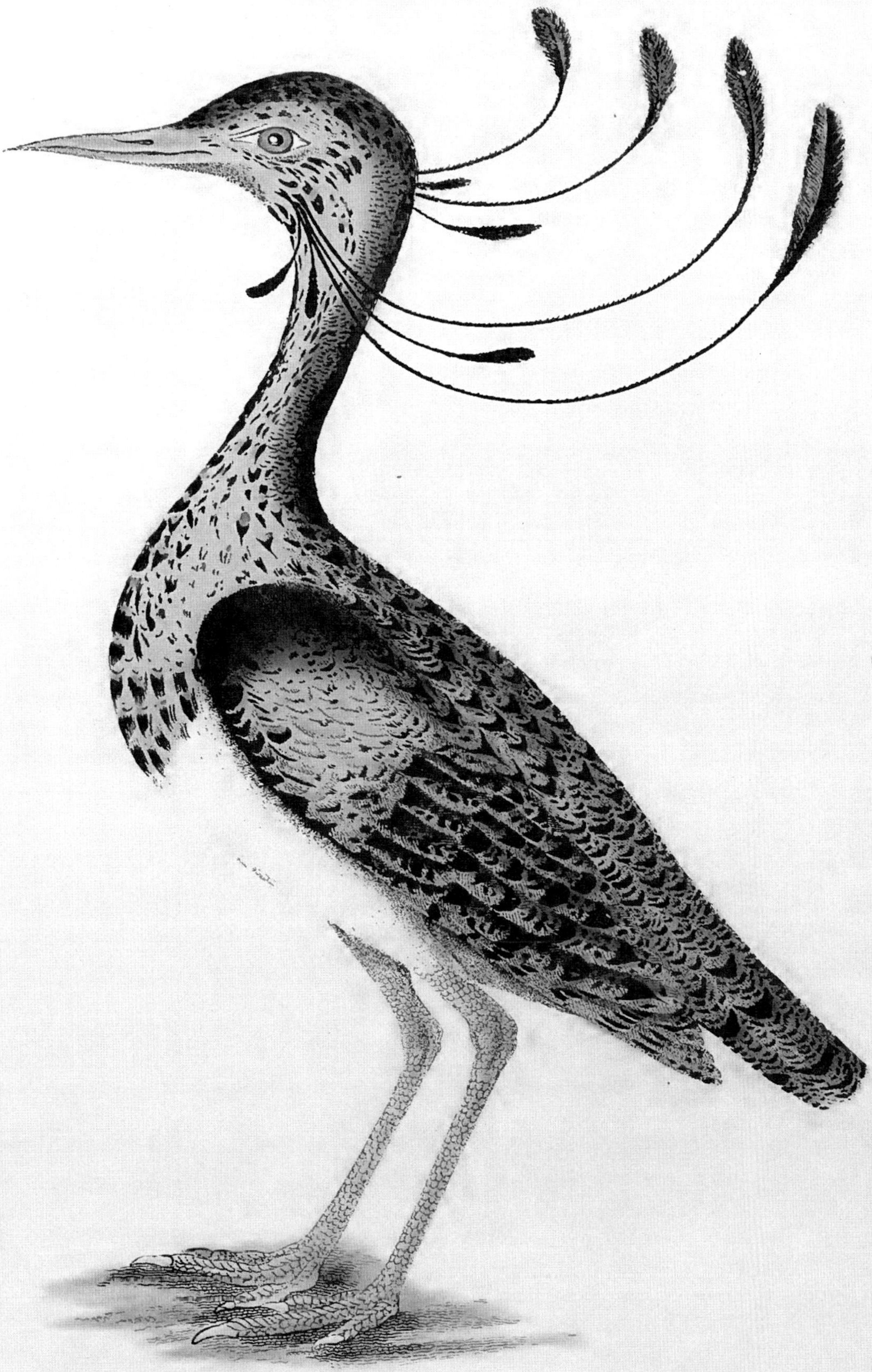

The CURMOOR *or* FLORICAN,

one of the highest flavoured Birds in India

about half the na[illegible] size

GREEN PIGEON *and* CUR CHAMPHAH *of the* CONCAN.

Jam. Forbes Ert Vict.

and all that night, and all the next day, and they gathered up the quails; he that gathered least gathered ten homers; and they spread them all abroad for themselves round about the camp."

These discussions are of little consequence in regard to the sacred truths of scripture, but they are 'pleasant and profitable investigations; and in the present instance, as the supply of food to the Israelites in the desert was altogether miraculous, and tended to illustrate the power and goodness of the theocracy, the only government under which they then lived, it is not of much importance whether the supply was of quails or locusts, since both are eatable; and the latter are an article of food among the Arabians, who inhabit the same desert, at this day.

The Nerbudda is enlivened by fourteen different kinds of wild-ducks; some are extremely beautiful in their plumage, and many roost on trees. Pelicans, spoon-bills, white and rose-coloured flamingos, storks, cranes, and a variety of aquatic birds frequent the lakes and marshes; woodcocks are sometimes seen in the cool season; snipes are more common, and immense flocks of wheat-ears and ortolans emigrate from distant countries during the harvest. The common partridge in shape and plumage is very like that in England; the feathers of that called the black-partridge are peculiarly rich; the quails are excellent. The florican, or Curmoor, (otis houbara, Lin.) exceeds all the Indian wild-fowl in delicacy of flavour; its varied plumage, lofty carriage, and tuft of black feathers, falling gracefully from its head, make him one of the most elegant birds in India; it is of the bustard species, but much smaller than the English otis. Green-pigeons, doves, and the usual variety of songsters, animated the woods of Turcaseer.

The cullum, or large crane, similar to the demoiselle of Numidia (ardea virgo, Lin.) is a majestic bird; some when erect are near six feet high; the sahras or cyrus, a bird of the same genus, equals it in stature, and excels it in the beauty of its plumage, generally of an azure hue, with a crimson head. The mention of these birds induces me to transcribe a circumstance from my memoranda, which, if not otherwise interesting, affords an additional instance of the instinct and memory of birds, to those related by Buffon, Goldsmith, and other naturalists.

Riding out one evening in the Dhuboy district, I left my hackery and attendants at a village, and taking my book retired as usual, with only one peon, to walk in the corn-fields; where, amidst a crop of juarree (holcus sorghum, Lin.) I saw a large flock of cullums and sahrases, devouring their share of the harvest. On our approach they all flew away, except one young sahras, who, being too weak to escape, was caught by the peon. He very contentedly ate some juarree out of my hand, and we carried him to Dhuboy, where he became quite domesticated. At Baroche he was equally beloved and caressed by all the family. Our garden-house was about a mile from the west gate of that city; the sahras generally walked thither at the dinner hour of the garrison; he was always a welcome guest, both with the Europeans and sepoys, and ate as much of their rice and cutcheree as he chose. This bird, when he attained his full growth, was near six feet high; with beautiful plumage, an elegant form, and stately air, blended with a pleasant familiarity. We were then preparing to leave India, and, however agreeable the sahras might be in the extensive precincts of a villa, I was fearful his size and appetite might cause

The SAHRAS *or* DEMOISELLE *of Guzerat*
from four to six feet in height.

him to be considered in a less favourable light as a passenger on board a crowded Indiaman: therefore, on embarking for England, I gave him to a friend, who went in another ship with fewer incumbrances. On our arrival the gentleman informed me the bird had made a pleasant voyage, was welcomed to every mess by the good-natured sailors, and soon after landing had been given to a friend, to oblige a nobleman from whom he had received particular favours.

Nine years afterwards I went with a party to Park-place, near Henley, then belonging to general Conway. After we had been delighted with the pleasing variety of those lovely scenes, we visited the menagerie; among other birds, a sahras, in a state of confinement, immediately brought my former friend to my recollection; nor could I help remarking, with some emphasis, the resemblance between them. On hearing my voice, the bird flapped his wings, pushed his head through the bars of the enclosure, and shewed signs of joy and impatience, which surprized us all, especially the gardener, who declared he had never seen him in such a transport. On telling him I believed the sahras was an old acquaintance, he thought it impossible, as his lady had possessed it several years, and had been assured it was the only living bird of his species in England. The more I noticed it, the more affectionate and violent were its gestures; until a sentiment of feeling, a mutual sympathy, or mutual instinct, convinced me it was my sahras. Upon further investigation I found this bird had been given to the lady by the nobleman to whom it was presented on its arrival. This anecdote being related at Park-place, procured us the kindest attentions from the hospitable owners, and gave rise to a correspondence between the general and myself. The bird died in the following winter. I had drawn its portrait in India; a recollection of its affectionate attachment induces me to offer it among those selected for engraving; for which, and the prolixity of the anecdote, I trust I shall be excused by every heart of sensibility.

A number of curious trees, shrubs, and aromatic plants, adorn the wilds of Turcaseer; among them are extensive forests of the baubul tree, the acacia, or Egyptian thorn, much esteemed in the materia-medica of the ancients for its gum, which it produces in great abundance, with every property of gum-arabic. The leaves, like all of the mimosa tribe, are pinnated, the branches covered with sharp white thorns, adorned with clusters of fragrant globular blossoms, in great profusion; pink, yellow, or white; the most beautiful is an oblong flower, the lower part nearest the stalk of a delicate rose-colour, the other half a bright yellow: the gum oozes from the bark on the trunk, and larger branches. The flowers are not converted to any purpose that I have known in India, but it is said the Chinese extract from them a valuable yellow dye.

The baubul tree afforded a curious specimen of insect sagacity in the caterpillars' nests, suspended by thousands to the branches. This little animal, conscious of its approaching change, and the necessity of security in its helpless state as a chrysalis, instinctively provides itself a strong mansion during that metamorphosis. As a caterpillar it is furnished with very strong teeth; with them it saws off a number of thorns, the shortest about an inch long, and glues them together in a conical form, the points all tending to one direction, the extremity terminating with the longest and sharpest. This singular habitation is composed of about twenty thorns, for the exterior, lined with a coat of silk, similar to the cone of the silk-worm, suspended to the tree by a strong ligament of the same material. In this asylum the baubul caterpillar retires to its long repose; and, armed with such formidable weapons, bids defiance to birds, beasts, and serpents, which might otherwise devour it. When the season of emancipation arrives, and the chrysalis is to assume a new character in the papilis tribe, the insect emerges from the fortress, expands its beautiful wings, and with thousands of fluttering companions, released at the same season from captivity, sallies forth to enjoy its shorted-lived pleasures. Paley has happily defined instinct to be a propensity prior to experience, and independent of instruction.

> "Whether with reason, or with instinct blest,
> "Know all enjoy that power which suits them best;
> "And reason raise o'er instinct as you can,
> "In this 'tis God directs, in that 'tis man.
> "Who taught the nations of the field and wood
> "To shun their poison, and to choose their food?
> "Prescient, the tides or tempests to withstand,
> "Build on the wave, or arch beneath the sand?
> "Who made the spider parallels design,
> "Sure as de Moivre, without rule or line?
> "God in the nature of each being founds
> "Its proper bliss, and sets its proper bounds."
>
> POPE.

The baubul trees are also covered by pensile nests of the baya, or bottle-nested sparrow, which I have formerly described. These birds seem to have formed immense colonies in the wilds of Turcaseer, and most of the Acacia forests in Guzerat; from fifty to an hundred nests are often suspended from one tree, each containing a numerous family. The noise of these sociable birds is wonderful, and their golden plumage glitters in the sun with great splendour. The baya, under the name of the toddy-bird, was not overlooked by a member of the Royal Society travelling in Guzerat in the seventeenth century. " Nature," says this intelligent writer, " affords us a pleasant spectacle, as well as matter for admiration, in the toddy-bird; whereby I know not why we should deny reason wholly to animals, unless it be, that man having so much, they seem comparatively to have none. This bird is not only exquisitely curious in the artificial composure of its nests with hay, but furnished with devices and stratagems to secure itself and young ones from its deadly enemy the squirrel; as likewise from the injury of the weather; which, being unable to oppose, it eludes with this artifice, contriving the nest like a steeple-hive, with winding meanders; before which hangs a penthouse for the rain to pass; tying it by so slender a thread to the bough of the tree that the squirrel dare not venture his body, though his mouth waters at the eggs and prey within; yet it is strong enough to bear the hanging habitation of the ingenious contriver from all the assaults of its antagonist, and all the accidents of gusts and storms. Hundreds of these pendalous nests may be seen on these trees.

The bottle-nested sparrow, taylor-bird, and sea-swallow, afford a source of amusement and wonder in the construction of their nests. Every bird's nest is indeed a matter of wonder when attentively considered. Addison pertinently and beautifully asks, " What can we call that principle which directs every different kind of bird to observe a particular plan in the structure of its nest, and directs all of the same species to work after the same model? It cannot be *imitation;* for though you hatch a crow under a hen, and never let it see any of the works of its own kind, the nest it makes shall be the same, to the laying of a stick, with all the other nests of the same species. It cannot be *reason;* for were animals endued with it to as great a degree as man, their buildings would be as different as ours, according to the different conveniences that they would propose to themselves. Animals in their generation are wiser than the children of men; but their wisdom is confined to a few particulars, and lies in a very narrow compass. Take a brute out of his instinct, and you find him wholly deprived of understanding."

Few situations afford more variety than the forests of Turcaseer; I only laid aside my pencil to traverse those solitary wilds, and procure new subjects, while my attentive friends brought every thing curious from their distant excursions. One of our keenest sportsmen left the party for a few days, with some expert Indian marksmen, to explore the Raje-pipley hills, and shoot on *Bhaug-Doongur*, the "*Tiger-mountain*," a spot abounding with tigers, leopards, hyenas, and wild beasts of various description. There, for the first time, he saw the mountain-goat (capra ibex Lin.) an animal resembling the steinbock, or bouquetin of Switzerland. In a narrow defile, where they were stationed for the destruction of tigers, a male elk, (cervus alces, Lin.) of noble appearance, followed by twenty-two females, passed majestically under their platform, each as large as a common-sized horse. They shot one, but being obliged to leave it, in pursuit of royal game, on their return next morning they found it nearly devoured by beasts of prey.

They saw many other herds of elks, and a great variety of deer, but never met with the niel ghou, or blue ox, though they seem to partake much more of the deer than the ox. These animals were frequently brought to Baroche and Surat as a curiosity from other parts of India.

There were no lions in that part of India; the royal tiger was considered as the lord of the forest, and a more powerful animal cannot easily be conceived. The adventures and escapes of our sportsmen from these ferocious beasts, and their encounter with boars, hyenas, and other savage monsters, highly entertained us in the tents. Distance of time, and the death of three fourths of the party, deprive them of interest; I shall therefore suppress them, and the observations I occasionally made on the animals in those wilds; except as they coincide with a few general remarks by the author of the Oriental Sports.

Some tigers in Turcaseer were nearly as large and ferocious as those in the *Sunderbunds* of Bengal, and were said to equal the largest ever killed there, which measured fourteen feet from the tip of the nose to the extremity of the tail, was four feet high at the shoulder, and the circumference of his foot near the paw twenty-six inches. Every action of the tiger confirms captain Williamson's idea, that it so closely resembles the cat, that the latter may be deemed a tiger in miniature. Their motions, tempers, habits, are all precisely similar; and, except in the number of young usually borne at a litter, it would perhaps be difficult to point out any distinguishing trait. They have two, three, and sometimes five cubs at a litter, seldom so many; they attain their full growth at two years of age.

"Those who are accustomed to see tigers only in a state of confinement, would imagine, from their wildness and apparent ferocity, that, were one to get loose, it would not rest until it had destroyed every living object within its view. But most probably its first act, when liberated from its cell, would be to gain some shelter, where it might be hidden from the eyes of man; for, notwithstanding the extreme boldness with which tigers act on some occasions, and which no doubt results either from extreme hunger, or from reiterated success, they are, generally speaking, very pusilanimous. It happens but rarely that they act openly, even in situations where persons may unhappily be exposed completely to their assaults. They delight in concealing themselves, especially when intent on making a prey, and should they adventitiously be discovered, or be defeated in their first attack, they ordinarily retreat with precipitation.

"The opinion entertained that a tiger will not at any time approach fire, is carried much too far: it is true that they are extremely averse to it; but when hungry, nothing will deter them from their object. The *dawks*, or posts, throughout India travel on foot, one man carrying the mail over his shoulder, and accompanied at night, as also through all suspicious places in the daytime, by one or more men with small drums, and eventually a *teereudaur*, or archer. Yet this precaution does not suffice to intimidate the ravenous animal during the day, however great his antipathy to noise, any more than two strong flambeaux which the postman has at night. An instance is well known of a tiger occupying a spot in Goomeah-pass for near a fortnight, during which time he daily carried away a man; generally one of the postmen. At one time he was disappointed of his meal, as he by mistake carried off the leather bag instead of its bearer; but the following night he seized one of the torchmen, and soon disappeared with him.

"A melancholy proof exists of the little respect a tiger pays to fire when hard put to for a meal, in the well-known fact of a young gentleman of a respectable family, and of the most amiable qualifications, having been taken away by one when benighted on Sanger's island, at the entrance of the Hooghly river, as a party were sitting by a fire which had been kindled for the purpose of security: the tiger sprung through the flames, and carried off the unfortunate victim in spite of the efforts of his companions, who were well provided with fire arms.

"The number of stragglers taken by tigers from a line of march, when troops are proceeding through a close country, would surprize persons unaccustomed to such events; three sentries have been carried off in one night, besides several camp-followers, who fell victims to their impatience in their attempts to get a-head of the line, by taking short cuts through the jungles. These become extremely dangerous on such occasions, owing to the great noise and concourse of persons preceding the troops, which move at an early hour in the morning, perhaps at two or three o'clock, and forming a constant chain of disturbance to all animals near the route, so as to occasion their retiring to some small distance from its verge; for, as has been already observed, the tiger will not, unless impelled by hunger, attack in an open or frequented situation, but quickly avails himself of the opportunity afforded by the deviating traveller, to secure a prey."

The tiger will eat nothing but what he destroys himself. The hyena, sya-gush, and even the leopard, will, on emergencies, act otherwise. The lion, with respect to eating, has the same propensity as the tiger, and in many instances they seem to blend something noble with their ferocity. These animals generally seem to have their own walks in the solitary regions which they inhabit, and are seldom seen more than two together. For several miles in extent, the Turcaseer forests, in the dry season, are destitute of water. There was a pool in a wild part, whither the natives informed us the savage race nightly resorted to drink; which they could only approach by one narrow pass. One of our eager sportsmen had a platform fixed among the branches of a lofty tree overhanging this path, where he passed two moon-light nights, and was highly gratified with his success. Among the variety of animals which went to the water, he saw five royal tigers marching together, which the Indians reckon a very extraordinary circumstance.

I mentioned the rhinoceros in the menagerie at the Cape of Good Hope; it is not uncommon in some of the Bengal provinces, and other parts of Hindostan frequented by the wild elephant, with whom it often has a desperate engagement: but as these animals are seldom seen to the westward of the Ganges, I shall here only add, that the skin of the rhinoceros is very valuable, forming shields said to be impenetrable to a musket ball: the foot is also highly esteemed by the Indians for medicinal purposes; and, exclusive of other useful properties, a cup turned from the horn of this animal is reputed to be an effectual antidote to poison. I have one of the largest and most beautiful I ever met with, being thirteen inches in circumference, though not turned from the thickest part of the horn. There can be little doubt of the rhinoceros being the unicorn of scripture; the questions in the book of Job perfectly correspond with his habits. "Will the unicorn be willing to serve thee, will he abide by thy crib? canst thou bind the unicorn with his band in the furrow, or will he harrow the valleys after thee? wilt thou trust him because his strength is great, or wilt thou leave thy labour to him? wilt thou believe him that he will bring home thy seeds, and gather it into thy barn?"

Next to the rhinoceros and buffalo, the wild boar is perhaps one of the most ferocious animals in India; and not only fierce, but so swift, that few of the savage tribes afford more variety of diversion to sportsmen. Their chief abode is in the jungles and forests; but when the grain is nearly ripe they do great mischief in the corn-fields, especially in sugar plantations, as they are extremely fond of the sugar-cane. The sows have very large litters of pigs, which are soon able to shift for themselves. There is a great variety in the form and colour of the wild hogs: the former varies according to the season. When the sugar-cane is full of juice, and the corn ripe, the hog is large and heavy; during a scarcity of food, he becomes meagre, light, and grim. When hunted in the proper season, we frequently had a young boar barbacued, or roasted with spices and madeira wine, in a sylvan style of cookery, which afforded a sumptuous feast. The largest boars are from three to four feet high at the shoulder; their tusks are five or six inches from the sockets; these render them a formidable adversary.

Not only the wild hogs, but bears, porcupines, and many other animals are particularly fond of the sugar cane, which supplies them with food and beverage of a delicious kind; and as they also afford a cool retreat in hot weather, their incursions are attended with incalculable mischief. Bears abound in many mountainous tracts of Hindostan: its natural history is too well known to need a description; but captain Williamson mentions some traits in their character of less publicity. This gentleman says it has often been in his way to see the operation of bears, and he is confident that no animals are more cruel, more fierce, nor more implacable. Such as have suffered under their brutality have, in all instances within his knowledge, borne the proofs of having undergone the most dilatory torments, some having their bones macerated with little breaking of the skin, with others the flesh was sucked away into long fibrous remnants, and in one instance the most horrid brutality was displayed.

Whilst stationed at Dacca, captain Williamson went with a party several times to Tergong, about five miles from thence. They had on many occasions seen bears among the wild mango tops, and did not consider them so dangerous, until one day returning with another gentleman from hunting some hog-deer, they heard a most lamentable outcry in the cover through which they had to pass. Being provided with guns and spears they alighted, not doubting but a leopard was attacking some poor wood-cutter. They met a poor woman, whose fears had deprived her of speech, and whose senses were just flitting; she however collected herself sufficiently to pronounce the word *bauloo*, which signifies a bear. She led them with caution to a spot not more than fifty yards distant, where they found her husband extended on the ground, his hands and feet sucked, and chewed into a perfect pulp; the teguments of the limbs in general drawn from under the skin, and the skull mostly laid bare; the skin of it hanging down in long strips, obviously effected by the talons. What was most wonderful, the unhappy man retained his senses sufficiently to describe that he had been attacked by several bears, the woman said seven; one of which had embraced him while the others clawed him about the head and bit at his arms and legs, seemingly in competition for the booty. The gentlemen conveyed the wretched object to the house; where, in a few hours, death released him from a state in which no human being could afford the smallest assistance!

Hector MASTER*ton* OIL PLANT *of Guzerat*.

CHAPTER XXIII.

DESCRIPTION OF DHUBOY,

AND THE SURROUNDING COUNTRY IN THE PROVINCE OF GUZERAT:

AN ACCOUNT OF THE RELIGIOUS BRAHMINS IN THOSE SACRED DISTRICTS;

WITH REFLECTIONS ON THEIR EXTRAORDINARY CHARACTER AND GENERAL CONDUCT.

1781.

"Travellers are often censured for enumerating what are called trifling occurrences: the censure appears to be unjust; trifling occurrences are often very amusing, and lead to important speculations. Every man of sense and observation must see, as he passes through a foreign country, some characteristic and singular circumstances, which cannot fail to please in the recital. Truth only is required: and truth, told with judgment and delicacy, will sufficiently recommend the narrative."

VICESIMUS KNOX.

CONTENTS.

man—lines on a celebrated picture by Guercino—Serpents at Dhuboy—guardians to Nero—story of the origin and magnificence of Dhuboy—its destruction by the Mahomedans, and subsequent history—custom of giving a new name to oriental cities—Dhuboy surrounded by the Mahratta army—official information relating to the purgunna of Dhuboy, Zinore, and Bhaderpoor—their revenues, commerce and agriculture briefly stated—the principal towns in those districts—reason for inserting the preceding documents.

Engraved by W. Angus

The DURBAR and adjacent Scenery at DHUBOY.

Jam. Forbes 1781

Publ. ... Richard Bentley 8 New Burlington St 1834

CHAPTER XXIII.

WHEN Dhuboy was made winter quarters for the Bombay army, during the Mahratta campaign in 1775, I little thought it would so soon belong to the East India Company, and that I should be entrusted with its government; a situation to which I was appointed in 1780, on its being surrendered to general Goddard, in command of the detachment from the Bengal army.

Dhuboy is the capital of a purgunna, or district, of the same name, in the province of Guzerat which contains eighty-four villages, and yields a revenue of four lacs of rupees, about fifty thousand pounds sterling per annum. The peninsula of Guzerat, two hundred miles long, and an hundred and forty broad, is formed by the Arabian sea on one side, and the gulph of Cambay on the other, extending inland in a north and east direction. From its numerous ports and commercial advantages, the sea-coast contains as great a variety of castes and religions as any part of Hindostan. The revenues of this soubah, or province, in the reign of Aurungzebe, at the beginning of the eighteenth century, amounted annually to one hundred and fifty lacs of rupees, or one million eight hundred thousand pounds sterling. Akber, the greatest of the Mogul emperors, divided Hindostan into eleven soubahs, or grand divisions; subdivided into smaller provinces, called circars; each circar contained a number of districts, or purgunnas; three of those purgunnas, in the soubah of Guzerat, Dhuboy, Zinore, and Bhaderpoor, with the little district of Chandode, were placed under my management as collector of the revenues for the India company.

The city of Dhuboy, upwards of two miles in extent, forms nearly a square; fortified in the Indian manner, with a high wall and fifty-two irregular towers. At each angle is a round tower, surmounted by a cavalier bastion. In the centre of each face is a double gate of hewn stone, richly ornamented, with a spacious area between them. Dhuboy at that time contained only forty thousand inhabitants: the magnificent remains of public buildings, and the site of numerous houses in a ruinous state, indicate it to have been, at a former period, a place of great importance, and much more populous.

Within the walls is a tank lined with hewn stone, and a flight of steps all around, three quarters of a mile in circumference; part of it was then much out of repair: its first cost exceeded five lacs of rupees, or sixty thousand pounds. This magnificent reservoir is supplied with water, not only by the periodical rains, but also from receptacles without the walls, by means of a stone aqueduct communicating with the tank; which it enters under a small temple in the hallowed groves of the brahmins, forming a cascade with a picturesque effect.

The opening this aqueduct at the commencement of the rainy season, affords a festival to the inhabitant for several days: like the Egyptians at the annual rising of the Nile, they make religious processions to the temples, and perform their flowery sacrifices in the surrounding groves. The elders look on with complacency, younger females dance on the banks, while the boys rush into the foaming cataract, and swim about the lake. This annual supply of water is far more beneficial than the gifts of Bacchus in other countries; the peasants and their cattle here assuage their thirst in seasons of drought, when the surrounding reservoirs fail, and the small rivers are generally exhausted.

These dances were less formal, and more active than any I had seen in India, unlike those of the dancing-girls, and little resembling the English country-dance; the tune and figure seemed both unstudied; and the songs which accompanied them, like the rhapsodies of the Italian improvisatore, or those of their own Bhauts and minstrels, were all extemporaneous effusions. The dances on this occasion reminded me of those mentioned in scripture, when "Miriam the prophetess, the sister of Aaron, took a timbrel in her hand, and the women went out after her, with timbrels and dances:" or perhaps they were more like those which Lady Wortley Montague describes among the modern Greeks; "whose manner of dancing is certainly the same that Diana is said to have danced on the banks of Eurotas. The great lady still leads the dance; and is followed by a troop of young girls, who imitate her steps, and if she sings, make up the chorus. The tunes are extremely gay and lively, yet with something in them wonderfully soft. The steps are varied, according to the pleasure of her who leads the dance, but always in exact time; and infinitely more agreeable than any of our dances."

During these festive rites the brahmins offer sacrifices, in the temples and adjoining groves, to their different deities; especially to ISA the god of nature, and INDRA, who presides over the seasons.

> In whose sweet garden tower'd a giant tree;
> Rock-rooted, on a mountain-top, it grew,
> Reared its unrivall'd head on high,
> And stretch'd a thousand branches o'er the sky,
> Drinking with all its leaves celestial dew.
> Lo! where from thence, as from a living well,
> A thousand torrents flow!
> For still in one perpetual shower,
> Like diamond-drops, ethereal waters fell
> From every leaf of all its ample bower.

> There Indra sat upon his throne reclin'd,
> Where Devetas adore him;
> The lute of Nared, warbling on the wind,
> All tones of magic harmony combin'd,
> To please his heav'nly mind,
> While the dark-eyed Asparas danc'd before him."
>
> KEHAMA.

The durbar, or governor's mansion at Dhuboy, where I resided, with its courts and garden, occupied seven acres; it was almost surrounded by the lake, except near the principal gate, communicating with the town; a pavement of large flat stones admirably united, formed a dry walk at all seasons, above the steps of the tank, shaded in most parts by lofty trees, and adorned with fragrant shrubs; through which only a few houses and towers on the walls were visible; so that from the windows of the durbar, overlooking the lake, every thing had more the appearance of a rural village, than a fortified city. Near the Durbar was a small woody island affording a nightly roost for cranes, kites and crows; and shelter for a number of those immense bats, not improperly called flying-foxes. To finish this picturesque scene a ruined Hindoo temple, nearly covered with moss, and the clematis in great variety, terminated the terrace walk in the garden, where the animal creation had hitherto been so unmolested, that my orange and lime trees were filled by peacocks, doves, and bulbuls; monkeys and squirrels feasted on my pomegranates and custard-apples; while pelicans, spoon-bills, and other aquatic birds occupied the lake.

The intrusion of the monkeys I could have dispensed with; their numbers were often formidable, and their depredations serious. I believe there were as many monkeys as human inhabitants in Dhuboy; the roofs and upper part of the houses seemed entirely appropriated to their accommodation. While the durbar was repairing, on my first arrival, I resided a short time in one of the public streets; the back of the house was separated by a narrow court from that of a principal Hindoo. It being the shady side, I generally retired during the heat of the afternoon to a veranda, and reposed on a sofa, with my book; small pieces of mortar and tiles frequently fell about me, to which, supposing them to be occasioned by an eddy of wind, I paid no attention; until one day, when I was so much annoyed by their repetition, accompanied by an uncommon noise, and a blow from a larger piece of tile than usual, that I arose to discover the cause; and, to my astonishment, saw the opposite roof covered with monkeys, employed in assaulting the white stranger, who had unwittingly offended by intruding so near their domain. Although my new situation invested me with considerable power, and made me the first man in the city, yet as

I knew I could neither make reprisals nor expect quarter from the enemy, I judged it most prudent to abandon my lodging, and secure a retreat.

I do not imagine the inhabitants of Dhuboy protect the monkeys from any other motive than humanity to the brute creation, and their general belief in the metempsychosis; but in Malabar, and several other parts of India, Dr. Fryer's assertion is very true, that "to kill one of these apes the natives hold piacular; calling "them half men; and saying they once were men, but for their "laziness had tails given them, and hair to cover them. Towards "Ceylon they are deified; and at the straits of Balagat they pay "them tribute."

I cannot omit mentioning one singular employment in which the monkeys of Dhuboy are engaged. I believe among the higher castes of the Hindoos duelling is every where unknown, and the lower classes are equally ignorant of the art of boxing; but as even Hindoos *do* quarrel, though they do not often lose their temper, one principal mode of offence is that of abuse; not by calling a man a rascal or a villain, for that would neither lessen him in his own opinion, nor in that of society; but to abuse his mother, his wife, his sister, or his daughter, would be esteemed the grossest insult, and only to be reconciled by a more abusive retaliation. If that is not accomplished, it remains a subject for future revenge, which brings me to the point in question respecting the Dhuboy monkeys, who are the innocent agents of this revenge.

Previous to the commencement of the periodical rains, about the middle of June, it is customary to turn the tiles on the roofs of all the houses in the towns and villages in Hindostan, both of

Europeans and natives. These tiles are not fixed with mortar, but are regularly laid one over the other, and by being adjusted immediately before the setting in of the rains, they keep the roof dry during that period; after which their being misplaced is of little consequence, in a climate where not a shower falls for eight months together. At this critical juncture, when the tiles have just been turned, and the first heavy rain is hourly expected, the injured person, who has secretly vowed revenge against his adversary, repairs by night to his house, and contrives to strew over the roof a quantity of rice, or other grain; this is early discovered by the monkeys, who assemble in a large body to pick up this favourite food: when, finding much of it fallen between the tiles, they make no ceremony of nearly unroofing the house, when no turners of tiles are procurable; nor can any remedy be applied to prevent the torrents of rain from soaking through the cow-dung floors, and ruining the furniture and depositories of grain, which are generally formed of unbaked earth, dried and rubbed over with cow-dung.

I have formerly described the severity of the setting in of the south-west moonsoon, when I was with the Mahratta army, a few miles from Dhuboy. I afterwards resided there several years during the rainy season; although in those months there were many delightful intervals of fair weather, yet the commencement and breaking up of the moonsoon was generally very severe: it was then I understood the force and beauty of Elihu's speech to Job, which is not so easily conceived in Europe. "Behold God is great, and we know him not! he thundereth with the voice of his excellency, and sendeth his lightning to the ends of the earth:

great things doth he, which we cannot comprehend, for he saith to the snow, be thou upon the earth: likewise to the small rain and *the great rain of his strength.*"

The upper terrace of the durbar overlooked the garden, the lake, and all its surrounding embellishments; consisting of rich groves, embowering Hindoo temples, Mahomedan mosques, and costly tombs of the principal Mussulmans. Beyond the city walls was seen a landscape replete with populous villages, luxuriant corn-fields, herds of oxen, flocks of sheep and goats, and a numerous peasantry, employed in agriculture: this charming plain was terminated on the north-east by the mountain of Powa-Gur, one of the strong-holds of the Mahratta empire; of a stupendous height, difficult ascent, and completely fortified at the summit. This majestic eminence is connected with a chain of hills, stretching eastward, until they join the mountains beyond the Nerbudda; that fertilizing stream which begins its course many hundred miles off, in a mountainous region on the confines of the Bengal provinces; and flowing from thence in a narrow channel to the falls near Chandode, there expands into a noble river, still increasing in size until it washes the walls of Baroche, and becomes navigable for large vessels to the gulph of Cambay.

Powa-gur is with great reason supposed to be the Tiagur, or Tiagura, of Ptolemy: though he there mistakes the river Narmada, or Nerbudda, for the D'had'hara, or Dahder, a contiguous stream often mentioned in these volumes. The Nerbudda, the Narmada of the Greeks, takes its rise in the mountains of Pindara, a wild and barbarous country. Near its source, the Hindoos erected a temple called Omercuntuc, which at stated times is much resorted to by pilgrims. In 1795 captain Blunt was sent to explore a route through that part of Hindostan, which lies between Berar, Orissa, and the northern Circars: he then approached within a few miles of the source of this celebrated river, but the cruel and savage manners of the mountaineers prevented him from proceeding nearer. He however obtained the most satisfactory information that the Nerbudda and Soane rivers take their rise at a little distance from each other, near the temple of Omercuntuc, where the Hindoos worship the consort of Siva, whom Sir William Jones, in his treatise on the gods of Greece, Italy, and India, mentions as being distinguished by the names of PARVATI, or the mountain-born goddess; DURGA, or difficult of access; and BHAVANI, or the goddess of fecundity; which latter is her leading name at Omercuntuc. The temple which contains the *moorat*, or image of BHAVANI, was built by one of the ancient rajahs of Rutturpoor, the principal place in that country.

"The spring from which the Nerbudda takes its source, is said to be enclosed by a circular wall, which was built by a man of the name of Rewah, and on that account the river is called Maht Rewah, from its source all through Mundilla, until it reaches the confines of Bhopaul."

From the classical streams of ancient Greece, to Pope's Lodona, rivers, fountains, and naiads, have afforded a copious subject for poetical fiction; the Nerbudda and the Soane, with poor Johilla, have in like manner enriched the Hindoo mythology: for the same intelligent writer informs us, that the images at *Omercuntuc* are said to represent BHAVANI, (who is there worshipped under the symbol of Nermada, or the Nerbudda river) much enraged at her slave Johilla, and a great variety of attendants preparing a nuptial banquet; to which a romantic fable is attached. Soane, a demi-god, being enamoured with the extreme beauty of Narmada, after a tedious courtship presumed to approach the goddess, in hopes of accomplishing the object of his wishes by espousing her. Narmada sent her slave Johilla to observe in what state he was coming; and, if arrayed in jewels, of lovely form and dignity, or worthy to become her consort, to conduct him to Omercuntuc. Johilla departed, met with Soane, and was so dazzled with the splendor of his ornaments and extreme beauty, that she fell passionately in love with him, and so far forgot her duty, as to attempt to personate her mistress; in which succeeding, Narmada was so enraged at the deceit, that, upon their arrival at Omercuntuc, she severely chastised Johilla, and disfigured her face in the manner said to be represented on the image. She then precipitated Soane from the top of the mountain to the bottom, whence that river rises; disappeared herself in the very spot where the Nerbudda issues; and from the tears of Johilla a little river of that name springs at the foot of Omercuntuc.

Such is the fabulous source of the Nerbudda, on whose banks I had a beautiful villa, and extensive gardens; in whose rural villages, shady groves, and holy island, I have enjoyed many delightful parties; and by a residence of seven years, generally within view of its bold meanders, have occasion to recollect many local circumstances with peculiar pleasure. The fate of Nerbudda is in many respects similar to that of Lodona, the chaste nymph of Diana, who, with her virgins, had for a season forsaken the haunts of mount Cynthus for the shades of Windsor: the metamorphosis of the former was the effect of enraged jealousy, that of the latter was exerted for the protection of chastity. Oriental and occidental poets are allowed the same privilege, and the man of taste enjoys their pleasing fictions. Narmada graces the Hindoo mythology, Pope has immortalized Lodona.

I shall, for the present, take leave of the Nerbudda with Beas Muni's address to her in the character of the goddess Narmada, extracted from the Vayer Purana, and presented by the pundits of Ruttonpoor to captain Blunt. "O Narmada! glorious as the sun and moon are thine eyes; but the eye in thy forehead blazes like fire: bearing in thy hand a spear like the tresul, and resting on the breast of Byroe. The blood of Anduk is dried up in thy presence; thy weuson (a sort of snow) is the dispeller of dread from the human race: Brahma and Siva resound thy praises; mortals adore thee. The Munis reverence thee; dewas (demi-gods) and hindras (angels) are thy progeny: thou art united with the ocean; thou art descended from Surya. By thee are mortals sanctified. Thou dispeller of want, thou increasest the prosperity of those who perform their devotions to thee. By thee are mortals directed to the blissful regions, and taught to avoid the mansions of punishment: thou art also Reba, a child of Hemala, the mountain of snow! Narmada answered, O Muni! thy words are perfect, and thy heart is pure: be thou chief of Munis! By reading this a man's life will be lengthened, his happiness and fame increased, and his progeny multiplied."

The affection of the Hindoos for lakes and rivers has been mentioned; in no part of Hindostan are they more venerated than at Dhuboy, Zinore, and Chandode; where I so often resided, encircled by the sacred groves and temples of the brahmins. The ablutions, strongly enforced in the Hindoo religion, are wise injunctions. Bathing is not only one of the most refreshing pleasures in a hot climate, but purity of body is supposed to be nearly connected with purity of soul: thus thought many of the ancient sages and philosophers; and in the sacrament of Christian baptism the one is typical of the other. I am willing to believe that acceptable prayers and praises ascend to heaven from the ablutions of the innocent Musnavi brahmin, who rising with the early dawn, washes himself in the holy stream of the Ganges, the Indus, or the Nerbudda; waiting for the appearance of the celestial luminary over the eastern hills, to worship OM, the GREAT INVISIBLE, who through this agency gives light, and life, and joy to his creation: but emotions of pity and of blame are mingled with our approbation when we behold these eastern philosophers worshipping GOD themselves in his UNITY, and at the same time sanctioning and teaching polytheism among all the other tribes of Hindoos; and saying to the poor Soodra and Chandala, "stand off, for I am holier than thou."

I know not whether these humiliated castes are permitted to worship any of the higher order of the Hindoo deities: Mariatalee, peculiarly styled the goddess of the Poor, is said to be composed of two distinct properties, the virtues of a goddess, and the vices of a criminal, from a monstrous union of impurity and virtue having accidentally happened by mistake, as particularly recorded in the Hindoo legends. Sonnerat says, Mariatalee is the great goddess of the Parias; to honour her they have a custom of dancing with several pots of water on their heads, placed one above another:

these pots are adorned with the leaves of the margosies, a tree consecrated to her. Southey in the "*Curse of Kehama*," has happily availed himself of this circumstance in saving the interesting Kailyal.

> Near to the holy river's verdant brink,
> The sculptur'd form of Mariatalee stood;
> It was an idol roughly hewn of wood,
> Artless, and poor, and rude.
> The goddess of the poor was she;
> None else regarded her with piety.
> But when that holy image Kailyal view'd,
> To that she sprung, to that she clung,
> On her own goddess, with close-clasping arms,
> For life the maiden hung.

Dhuboy was chiefly inhabited by brahmins of different orders; some of them were actively employed among the other castes of Hindoos; numbers seemed to pass their lives in a state of religious indolence, and an apparent abstraction from sublunary objects, like the devotees at Seringham, described by the elegant Orme, "living in a subordination which knows no resistance, and slumbering in a voluptuousness which knows no wants." The brahmins of Dhuboy repose from morning till night under the trees which border their sacred lake, meditating on the Institutes of Menu, or bewildering themselves with the AVATARS of Vishnu; nine incarnations of that deity, which form an interesting part of the Hindoo mythology.

In the inner court of the durbar at Dhuboy, into which my front veranda opened, an altar had been erected under a shady pepal-tree (ficus religiosa) which I carefully preserved; a hollow cavity on the top contained the tulsee, or tulsi, (ocymum) a sacred plant of the Hindoos, to which they frequently resorted; as also to a few of their dii penates, which were left in the surrounding niches; it was a scene nearly resembling that of Priam's palace in Troy.

"Ædibus in mediis, nudoque sub ætheris axe,
"Ingens ara fuit, juxtaque veterrima laurus
"Incumbens aræ, atque umbrâ complexa penates. VIRG. ÆN.

"In the centre of the court, and under the naked canopy of heaven, stood a large altar; "and near it an aged laurel, overhanging the altar, and encircling the household gods with "its shade."

I sometimes almost envied these peaceful Hindoos the pleasure they enjoyed in the performance of their religious duties, and the delights of social worship; in my solitary situation I felt, for near four years together, a privation of all the sacred ordinances of Christianity, and from attendance on public worship. During that period I had very little communication with Europeans, and no personal intercourse with one kindred mind: in such situations the Christian can happily experience, in some degree, the consolations so sweetly mentioned by the pious Cowper in a letter to a religious friend in a foreign country:

"Ah! be not sad, although thy lot be cast
"Far from the flock, and in a dreary waste;
"No shepherds' tents within thy view appear,
"But the chief Shepherd is for ever near:
"Thy tender sorrows, and thy plaintive strain,
"Flow in a foreign land, but not in vain;

> " Thy tears all issue from a source divine,
> " And every drop bespeaks a Saviour thine!
> " 'Twas thus in Gideon's fleece the dews were found,
> " And drought on all the drooping herbs around."

In the southern parts of India, as I have frequently observed, are abundance of churches, and thousands of Roman-catholic Christians, who are generally converts from the lowest castes of Hindoos. In Guzerat there are very few of that persuasion, and none in this part of the province: among their priests and missionaries are liberal and intelligent men, but these are not numerous. Far be it from me to cast a reflection upon any religious profession, particularly on missionaries from a Christian society; but certainly those of the Romish church do not appear to have sown the seeds of that gospel which Paul planted and Apollos watered, and to which so great an increase was given in the days of the apostles. I would not pass an uncharitable censure, but we well know there may be zeal without knowledge; the excellent, the liberal Bernier, who was a member of their own church, thus writes of the missionaries during his residence in India in the seventeenth century.

" Je ne sçaurois certainement que je n'approuve extremement " les missions et lest bons missionaires, et entant qu'ils sont le re- " fuge et la consolation des pauvres etrangers et voyageurs, et que " par leur science, vie retenuë et exemplaire, ils confondent l'igno- " rance et la vie libertine des infidelles; ce que ne font pas tou- " jours quelques autres qui seroient bien mieux dans leurs couvens " bien resserrez, au lieu de nous venir faire dans ces päis une " momerie de notre religion, et qui par leur ignorance, jalousie,

" vie libertine, et abus de leur authorité et caractére, se font les
" pierres de scandale de la loi de Jesus-Christ : mais cela n'empêche
" pas que je n'approuve extremement les missions, et les bons
" et savans missionaires; ils sont absolument necessaires."

There was not a Christian inhabitant either in Dhuboy or the districts under my care; the Mahomedans were in all respects similar to those I have described in other places, and the Hindoos brought to my recollection the simplicity of the patriarchal age; they had not been accustomed to any intercourse with Europeans, and while under the Mahomedan dominion their religious and national customs were generally tolerated. Soon after my arrival some venerable brahmins and principal Hindoos entreated of me that the Europeans belonging to the garrison might not be permitted to molest the monkeys, nor to fire at the pelicans, cranes, and water-fowl, which resorted to the lake. They not only dwelt upon the metempsychosis, but alleged that they were extremely useful in keeping the city and tank free from dirt and nuisances, and that for ages, even during the Mahomedan government, they had never been molested. It was a capital offence in ancient Egypt to kill an ibis or an hawk; the former was venerated because it devoured the serpents and reptiles which bred in the country after the inundation of the Nile: the inhabitants of Holland are as strongly attached to the stork, because it destroys the rats, mice, and other vermin which undermine the dykes. Supposing therefore that the Hindoos had similar reasons for their prejudice in favour of monkeys and pelicans, I readily granted their request; and this compliance led to another of far more importance, and indeed to the greatest favour I could confer upon them; which was, that I would issue an order that no ox or cow might be killed in the city, nor the flesh publicly exposed to sale. They said they knew the English soldiers would have beef where it was procurable; but as those animals were esteemed sacred, and none had ever been killed in Dhuboy during the Hindoo government, nor had a Mahomedan ever dared to offer such an offence, they hoped, if I could not entirely suppress the slaughter, that I would keep the whole matter as private as possible during the hours of darkness. It would have been cruel as well as impolitic to have refused them so innocent and reasonable a request. I only wished the rest of my countrymen there had been as indifferent to this part of their food as myself, and their feelings should not have been wounded. I made some fruitless attempts to reason with the brahmins on the necessity of killing animals intended for food; they opposed the doctrine of the metempsychosis to all my arguments, and would neither admit the truth nor beauty of Pope's more rational system.

> " The lamb thy riot dooms to bleed to day,
> " Had he thy reason, would he skip and play?
> " Pleas'd to the last, he crops the flowery food,
> " And licks the hand just rais'd to shed his blood."

According to Herodotus, the ancient Egyptians believed, that on the dissolution of the body, the soul immediately entered into some other animal, and that after using as vehicles every species of terrestrial, aquatic, and winged creatures, it finally entered a second time into the human body; and that it underwent all these changes in the space of three thousand years. Very similar to these ideas, are the reveries of the modern brahmins, with whom I found it fruitless to argue upon the metempsychosis or any religious subject; their pride and self-sufficiency militated against every attempt to convince them of their errors. The brahmins of Malabar usually treated such kinds of conversation with arrogance and contempt: those at Dhuboy affected either an air of superiority, or indifference. Indeed these extraordinary beings are so highly exalted in the institutes of Menu, that it is almost impossible it should be otherwise; for thus saith this celebrated Hindoo lawgiver:

"From his high birth alone, a brahmin is an object of veneration, even to deities; his declarations to mankind are decisive evidence; and the Veda itself confers on him that character. Never shall the king slay a brahmin, though convicted of all possible crimes; let him banish the offender from his realm, but with all his property secure, and his body unhurt. Although brahmins employ themselves in all sorts of mean occupations, they must invariably be honoured; for they are something transcendently divine."

Such were doubtless, in their own estimation, the brahmins at Dhuboy, who reposed under the solemn groves, or offered sacrifices in their temples. But how shall I describe the poor out-cast Chandalas, who were not allowed to have a habitation within the city walls, and were compelled to live in wretched huts at a distance from the western gate! which, on that account, was seldom frequented by the other tribes; while the gate of diamonds, on the eastern face, was the resort of the zemindars, banians, and chief men of the city. I have described the abject condition of of these Chandalas and Pariars at Bombay and Malabar; it will scarcely be believed by a liberal-minded European, that the very same code of the benevolent Menu, which deifies the brahmins, thus condemns to perpetual and hereditary ignominy, the poor Chandala, created by the same God, and born as pure and as innocent as the brahmin.

"The abode of the Chandalas must be out of the town; they must not have the use of entire vessels; their sole wealth must be dogs and asses. Their clothes must be mantles of the deceased; their dishes for food, broken pots; their ornaments rusty iron; and continually must they roam from place to place. Let food be given to them in potsherds, but not by the hands of the giver; and let them not walk by night in cities or towns."

It cannot be supposed that with a set of men who preached and practised such doctrines, and encouraged their followers to do the same, my authority or arguments should have much influence. I did indeed wish to redress the grievances of the Chandalas, but I found it in vain to combat with the prejudices of a whole city; prejudices which are interwoven with every part of the civil and religious system of the Hindoos. What a wrong opinion have the Europeans, until very lately, formed of the brahmins, and how many are there who still see no necessity for introducing among them the purity and benevolence of the gospel! But the veil is now withdrawn, and men of enlightened minds will make a just comparison between the two religions.

Let us not imagine that because the Hindoos do not admit of converts from other religions, they have no dissensions nor schisms among themselves; nor that the brahmins are so mild with those who differ from them in religious sentiment as they have been represented. Dr. Buchanan, when speaking of the Jaina in Mysore, says that "in a quarrel among the brahmins, the party which obtained the victory, caused the priests of Jaina, with as many of their followers as were obstinate, to be ground to death in oil-mills; while the remainder, who were converted by this powerful mode of argument, received pardon from the offended brahmins." This intelligent traveller further observes, that the houses at Tonoru, where this cruelty took place, are roofed with tiles, and covered with thorns, to prevent the monkeys from unroofing them, because those mischievous animals are very numerous, and to destroy them is reckoned a grievous sin. Those very persons who applaud the brahmins for having ground the Jainas in an oil-mill, shudder with horror at the thought of a monkey being killed.

These Jainas are a very singular sect among the Hindoos; we find in the Asiatic Researches, that there are three classes of yatis, or ascetics, in this tribe, called *Anuvrata*, *Mahavrata*, *Nirvana*. "To attain the rank of *Anuvrata*, a man must forsake his family, entirely cutting off his hair, throwing away the sacred thread, holding in his hand a bundle of peacock's feathers, and an earthen pot, and wearing only tawny coloured clothes; he must reside for some time in one of the temples. He next proceeds to the second rank, *Mahavrata*; when totally abandoning any degree of elegance in his dress, he uses only a rag fastened to a string round his loins, as a *Brahmachárí:* he still retains his fan and pot; he must not shave his head with razors, but employs his disciples to pull out the hair by the roots. On the day, when this operation is performed, he abstains from food; at other times he eats only once daily, of rice put in the palm of his hand. Having, for a considerable time, remained in this state of probation, he attains the third degree of *Nirvána;* he then lays aside even rags; and, being perfectly naked, he eats, once every second day, of rice, put by others in the palm of his hand; carrying about with him the clay pot, and a bundle of peacock's feathers. It is the business of his disciples to pull out his hairs; and he is not to walk, or move about, after the sun sets. He is now called by the dignified title of *Nirvan*, and the Jainas worship him as god of their tribe, in the like manner as the images, which they worship in their temples, of their ancient *Nirváns* or *Guroos.*

"The other Jainas, who have not entered into these religious vows, are obliged to abstain from the following things, viz. eating at night, slaying an animal; eating the fruit of those trees that give milk, pumpkins, young bamboo plants; tasting honey or flesh; taking the wealth of others; taking by force a married woman; eating flowers, butter, cheese; and worshipping the gods of other religions. To abandon entirely the abovementioned, is to be a proper Jaina. The Jainas, even the young lads, never taste honey, as it would occasion expulsion from their caste; they never taste intoxicating liquors, nor any other forbidden drink."

Such are the penances and privations among the Jainas; in Dhuboy I had occasion to witness a thousand similar austerities of the devotees who frequented its sacred shrines: but I never saw one like the Brahmechary; an account of whom, with his portrait reclining on a bed of iron spikes, was communicated by Mr. Duncan, the present governor of Bombay, to the Asiatic Society. This wretched fakeer is described as fixing himself on his *ser-seja*, or bed of spikes, where he constantly day and night remains. "To add to what he considers as the merit of this state of mortification, in the hot weather he has often logs of wood burning around him; and in the cold season, water falling on his head from a perforated pot, placed in a frame at some height above him: and yet he seems contented, and to enjoy good health and spirits. Neither do the spikes appear to be in any material degree distressing to him, although he uses not the defence of ordinary clothing to cover his body, as a protection against them."

In captain Wilford's essay on the Sacred Isles in the west, communicated to the Society, is a very curious account of some of these devotees, taken from the writings of Ctesias, who accompanied Cyrus and the ten thousand Greeks, in his unfortunate expedition to Persia. Ctesias was taken prisoner, but being a physician he became a great favourite with Artaxerxes Mnemon. In describing different countries in Hindostan, four hundred years before the Christian æra, Ctesias says, " beyond the sources of the " *Sipa-chora*, is a tribe of men, who have no evacuations; they " however make a little water occasionally; their food is milk " alone, which they know how to prevent from coagulating in their " stomachs. In the evening they excite a gentle vomiting, and " throw up the whole." "This strange narrative is not without foundation. Many religious people in India, in order to avoid the defilement attending the coarser evacuations, take no other food but milk; and previous to its turning into fæces, as they say, they swallow a small string of cotton; which, on their pulling it back, brings up the milk, or those parts of it which they consider as the *caput mortuum*. This they make the credulous believe;

their disciples are ready to swear to it; and they have even deluded persons otherwise of great respectability. I suppose they conceal themselves with great address; and their evacuations cannot be very frequent, nor copious; for they really live upon nothing else but a very small quantity of milk, though certainly more, as I should suppose, than they do acknowledge; and the ceremony of the string they perform, occasionally, before a few friends. I have known many of these people: they are all hermits, who seldom stir from the place they have fixed upon: there is one near the military lines at Sicrowre, near Bernares, on the banks of the Burna; but, I believe, he is rather in too good a case for a man living upon so scanty an allowance."

I have perused, with attention and pleasure, colonel Wilks's History of Mysore, and have availed myself of his valuable information respecting landed property in India. I admire, throughout the work, his philanthropic sentiments towards the Hindoos, and gladly subscribe to many of his liberal opinions; but I candidly confess I cannot admit of *all* his reasonings on this important subject. In the following extract from the appendix the word *forcibly* is printed in italics. Although my sentiments on the cremation of a Hindoo widow, on which that humane and benevolent writer lays so *great* a stress, may differ, yet I trust our motives to promote the happiness of the Hindoos are the same. I therefore disclaim every idea of compulsion, or any weak, sinister, or improper means for their conversion to Christianity. No force, no coercive measures were employed by the Great Founder of our faith, nor by those who immediately followed the steps of heir Divine Master. How contrary to that letter from a *Mahome-*

dan prince in the work now before me, where it is expressly said, "slay the infidels without distinction, wheresoever thou canst find them" was a power given by the Almighty Avenger to his prophet Mahomed, and to no other. But the Christian apostle, the Holy Messiah, according to universal admission, was not invested by the Almighty with the power of the sword, and never did undertake a holy war." The power of working miracles, the supernatural gift of languages, and the extraordinary operations of the Holy Spirit, sealed the ministry of the first apostles; mild persuasion, impressive conviction, united to a corresponding life and practice, marked the character of the primitive teachers, and were the most powerful engines of proselytism; their successors in every age, and in every nation, must regulate their conduct by such examples, if they wish to disseminate the truth of Christianity.

I admit most of the arguments in the following quotations; they are too obvious to be mistaken by an unprejudiced mind, and convince us of the necessity of blending the wisdom of the serpent with the innocence of the dove, in undertaking the great work of religious and moral improvement among a people so rivetted to ancient usages as the Hindoos.

"Of the actual system for the administration of justice to the native subjects of British India, I wish to speak with respect; because it originated and has been continued in the purest intentions. On the political question I presume to risk but one short observation. It is impossible to separate the political tendency of laws from the genius of the government from which they emanate. The spirit of the English constitution assigns to the mass of the people an extensive control over the exercise of public authority; and deems the executive government to be the representative of the public will. This spirit pervades the whole body of its laws; these laws necessarily reflect back, and reproduce the principles from which they spring: and it is matter for grave reflection, that if this species of reaction should ever be produced in India, from that moment it is lost to this country for ever. The efficient protection of our native subjects in all the rights which they themselves consider to be essential to their happiness, is certainly the most sacred and imperious of all our duties; and it is on this express ground that our present regulations, considered as a system of jurisprudence for the south of India, appear to me to require a radical reform.

"The English civil code professes to govern the Hindoos by their own laws: the distinction of castes, which is absolutely the key-stone of Hindoo law, has unfortunately either not been recognized at all in our laws and regulations, or indirectly treated with contempt; thus insulting the higher, without gratifying the lower classes; and, added to the novelty of our forms, exciting in both the apprehension of further change. It would be absurd and unjust to impute to the authors of this system the intention of proselytism; and it can only be lamented that it has contributed, among other causes, to produce the belief of such an intention. But if, as some publications give reason to believe, such views have really been entertained by other persons, it will be incumbent on sober thinkers seriously to consider that, exclusively of the excess of visionary folly, it is a most unmanly, ungenerous, and unchristian deception, to veil this object under the pretext of respecting the civil and religious customs and prejudices of the people; for all their prejudices, all their opinions, and all their customs, from the most trifling to the most important, are absolutely incorporated with their religion, and ought all to be held sacred.

" The founder of a philosophical Utopia would certainly reject with abhorrence a system which tends to enslave the human mind, and to entail hereditary degradation on a large portion of his citizens. But we are not here discussing a speculative theory; the objects in our contemplation are not metaphysical entities to be moulded into ideal forms; but human beings, already fixed in stubborn and immoveable prejudices, to which any system founded in wisdom and humanity must necessarily conform. It is not the question, it never can be a question, whether the English or the Hindoo code of religion and jurisprudence be entitled to the preference; but whether the Hindoo law and religion, for they are one and the same, are, or are not, to be maintained, or whether we are at liberty to invade both. If we profess to govern the Hindoos by their own laws, let us not falsify that profession by tearing them up by the roots, on the pretence of pruning and amending them. They are no longer Hindoo if they are subject to innovation. Before quitting this branch of the subject, it may be useful (for the sake of illustration) to examine the reasonableness of interfering with the most exceptionable of all their institutions. It has been thought an abomination not to be tolerated, that a widow should immolate herself on the funeral pile of her deceased husband. But what judgment should we pronounce on the Hindoo, who (if any of our institutions admitted the parallel) should *forcibly* pretend to stand between a Christian and the hope of eternal salvation? And shall we not hold him to be a driveller in politics and morals, a fanatic in religion, and a pretender to humanity, who would *forcibly* wrest this hope from the Hindoo widow? To return to the question of caste. To equalize them is impossible; to attempt it, offensive beyond all endurance to those whom we would exalt, as well as to those whom we would debase; and if we possessed the power, to exercise it would be a gross and intolerable oppression. That our regulations, where they do extend, and where they have not yet reached, are considered with terror as the instruments of a foreign rule, and that the Hindoos neither do nor can feel that they are governed by their own laws, seems to have been distinctly foreseen by that able and learned officer, major Leith, judge advocate general, who aided in the first compilation of the judicial regulations of Fort St. George. In a preliminary report he deprecates the idea of sudden innovation, and observes, "that the system ought rather to grow out of the first germ, than start at once, full grown, like Minerva from the head of Jupiter, shaking a lance and ægis at the astonished native. They will arise gradually, as the best laws ever have done, out of the manners and habits of the people, meliorating, and reflecting back, the principles they have derived from them."

"If Anglo-Indian legislators would throw off a little of that, which they somewhat too largely ascribe to the natives of India, namely, the prejudice of education, they would find the rules of the proceeding prescribed by the Hindoo code (with all its numerous imperfections on its head), combined with the local customs, or common law of India, not ill adapted to the state of society to which it is intended to apply; and in the *panchaiet*, or Indian jury, which is (or rather was) universally established in the south as the common law of the land, an admirable instrument of practical decision."

To the last paragraph its intelligent author adds this note: "The "*panchaiet*, or Indian jury, is an institution so entirely neglected, "or misunderstood, that I believe its existence is now, for the first "time, presented to the notice of the English reader." I am happy to find this excellent judge passing so favourable an opinion on the only mode of administering justice I adopted during my residence at Dhuboy; as will appear in the chapter set apart for that subject, under the name of *panchaut*, or the "*decision of five*." I was delighted with so simple and effectual a mode of satisfying all parties, and in confirmation of the colonel's remark, I must observe, that it was an institution perfectly new to me, and appeared to be so to all my European visitors.

I will now conclude this quotation. "The Hindoo character, like all others, is of a mixed nature; but it is composed of strange and contradictory elements. The man who may be safely trusted for uniformly unfolding the whole truth to an European in whom he reposes confidence, may be expected to equivocate, and even to contradict every word he has said, if called on to repeat it in the presence of a third person, whom he either fears or suspects; and in one of these descriptions he usually includes all strangers. The same description of man, sometimes the same individual, who from pique, and often without any intelligible motive, will perjure himself without shame or compunction at a public trial, is faithful, kind, and respectable in the intercourse of society; and the single but notorious fact of habitual lending and borrowing of money and effects, among the husbandmen, without bond, or note, or witness, abundantly proves that this people, apparently so destitute of morals, in one view of their character, are in another habitually honest and true in their dealings; that they mutually trust, and deserve to be trusted. The more intimately they are known, the more favourable is the judgment of every good and humane European on the character of this interesting people; but fully to understand them, requires to have lived and been educated among them, as one of themselves; and I conscientiously believe, that for the purpose of discriminating the motives of action, and the chances of truth in the evidence of such a people, the mature life of the most acute and able European judge, devoted to that single object, would not place him on a level with an intelligent Hindoo panchaiet.

" The fanciful notions of internal and external purity and uncleanness (the former having a twofold division of bodily and mental) are the foundations of most of the distinctions of castes which seem so absurd to Europeans. To the question of what is the difference between such and such a caste, the first answer will certainly be to indicate what they respectively can and cannot eat; but when we consider the plausible dogma not altogether unknown in Europe, that a regular and abstemious life (which they would name the internal purity of the body) contributes to mental excellence, we may be disposed to judge with more charity of the absurdity of these distinctions. The Jungum priests, and the elect among their disciples, abstain altogether from animal food; while the Sheneveea brahmins of the Concan and the Decan indulge in fish; and many of Bengal, Hindostan, and Cashmire, eat the flesh of a fawn, of mutton, and whatever is slain in sacrifice. The brahmins of the south abhor these abominations; but the latter at least is distinctly authorized by Menu, and all the ancient Smirtis, as the most bigotted are compelled to admit."

"In the leading traits of the doctrine of the Jungum we recognize the hand of a rational reformer; one part is not so favourable. The Jungum profess the exclusive worship of Siva; and the appropriate emblem of that deity in its most obscene form, enclosed in a diminutive silver or copper shrine, or temple, is suspended from the neck of every votary, as a sort of personal god; and from this circumstance they are usually distinguished by the name of *ling-ayet*, or *lingevunt*. They profess to consider Siva as the only God; but on the subject of this mode of devotion they are not communicative, and the other sects attribute to them not very decent mysteries. It is however a dogma of general notoriety, that if a Jungum has the mischance to lose his personal God, he ought not to survive that misfortune."

Who can read Sir William Jones' dissertations on the mystical poetry ôf the Persians and Hindoos without exquisite pleasure? His comments are admirable; and his quotations from Barrow and Neker fill the soul with ecstasy. It would be a rash attempt to controvert what that elegant and experienced writer has said on the absorption of the religious brahmins: from my own knowledge of those devotees on the sacred banks of the Nerbudda, I admit it all. "A figurative language," that celebrated orientalist observes, "in expressing the fervour of devotion, or the ardent love of created spirits towards their beneficent Creator, has prevailed from time immemorial in Asia; particularly among the Persian theists, both ancient *Húshangis* and modern *Súfis;* who seem to have borrowed it from the Indian philosophers of the *Vedanta* school; and their doctrines are also believed to be the source of that sublime, but poetical theology, which glows and sparkles in the writings of the old *academicks.* It is a singular species of poetry, which consists almost wholly of a mystical religious allegory, though it seems, on a transient view, to contain only the sentiments of a wild and voluptuous libertinism. Now, admitting the danger of a poetical style, in which the limits between vice and enthusiasm are so minute as to be hardly distinguishable, we must beware of censuring it severely, and must allow it to be natural, though a warm imagination may carry it to a culpable excess; for an ardently grateful piety is congenial to the undepraved nature of man; whose mind sinking under the magnitude of the subject, and struggling to express its emotions, has recourse to metaphors and allegories, which it sometimes extends beyond the bounds of cool reason, and often to the brink of absurdity."

Situated as I was among the brahmins I had ample opportunity of witnessing the truth of those passages which the illustrious president thought necessary to lay before the Asiatic Society. I admit the truth and influence of the sublime communion to which he alludes, on some of the brahminical priesthood; yet, as I have had occasion to ask in another place, what is the religion of the millions of Hindoos, who are not initiated into their mystical reveries? Sir William Jones allows that his quotation from Barrow borders upon quietism, and enthusiastic devotion; and perhaps among Christians there may be only a few, who, like Fenelon and others of that description, attain to that holy approximation, that ineffable communion, with their Creator and Redeemer, by the influence of the Divine Spirit; but there is a simple, a practical, and a delightful path, for the humble Christian of smaller attainments; a religion which will render him useful and happy in this world, and blessed for ever in that which is to come: a religion, which expressly assures us, that to whom much is given, from him much will be required; but where only one talent is committed, the improvement of only one talent will be expected. Therefore, allowing to the brahmins all their pretensions, the Hindoo religion, when opposed to the philanthropy and benevolence of the gospel, is unsocial, proud, and uncharitable.

The sublime passages so often quoted from the Hindoo scriptures and oriental poets, excite our admiration. But the brahmins and súfis alone can comprehend them; passages far more sublime may be selected from the Old and New Testament. Nothing can exceed the energy and beauty of the prophecies of Isaiah, nothing can equal the beatitudes in the sermon on the mount; nor can any oriental imagery of the shastah and vedas be compared with the sublime and energetic language of that ancient poem, the book of Job.

The profusion of hewn stone, and remains of sculpture, scattered about Dhuboy, is astonishing; the walls and towers were built entirely of large square stones. The west front, which is the only part remaining in any degree of perfection, presents a grand view of the ancient fortifications; the terreplein, several feet broad, is supported by a colonnade of pillars, which form a casemate or covered piazza, the whole length of the wall, in a style of elegance, not only ornamental beyond any thing I have seen elsewhere, but when in repair must have afforded excellent accommodation for an India garrison, who generally prefer a covered shed or veranda to a close room. This colonnade, half a mile in length, resembles the porticos in front of the barracks at the ancient city of Pompeia; where the soldiers' names are written in a rude manner on the walls, and after a lapse of seventeen hundred years are still legible. The barracks at Pompeia surround a large court, with a portico in front of their sleeping rooms; their appearance instantly reminded me of the fortifications at Dhuboy; and the villa and gardens without the gate of Pompeia, as well as many objects both there and in Herculaneum, were completely oriental. No town in India, nor any other part of the globe, can create those peculiar sensations which absorb the spectator when he beholds two cities brought to light after being buried near two thousand years; the one under a torrent of liquid fire, the other overwhelmed by a mountain of burning ashes and volcanic productions. Herculaneum still remains in a subterranean state; but at Pompeia, cleared of ashes, pumice-stones and cinders, with the plantations and vineyards which during a lapse of ages had progressively covered them, the astonished traveller beholds temples, theatres, houses and tombs, again restored to day, and on a level with the surrounding plain! The massive covering having been removed, the modern visitor walks through the streets, visits the temples, ascends the amphitheatres, and enters the houses, shops, and porticos of the ancient Romans, with the same facility as when they were first finished. In some he finds the furniture not yet removed; in a few the skeletons of their inhabitants still remain.

It is a scene which fills the mind with new sensations, impossible to describe, or previously to conceive.

But the immediate object which caused me to take this retrospective view, was the Roman villa just mentioned. On entering the portal I fancied myself in one of the modern mansions of an oriental city, and particularly the durbar which I so long occupied in Dhuboy. Like the Asiatic houses, the Pompeian villa consisted of several ranges of apartments, surrounding a large area, with a fountain and garden in the centre; each floor had a veranda, or portico overlooking the garden, and shading the rooms, leading also to the closets, baths, and store-rooms similar to those in India: these had been then lately cleared, and discovered the tracery of the flower-beds, and channels from the fountain, all perfect. In the extensive cellars which encircle the area, under the summer apartments, I saw several wine jars, some fixed in the lava, others standing loose against the wall; many of them contained the dried lees of red wine, which even then retained a fragrant odour.

In clearing the rubbish from one of these cellars the workmen discovered eight skeletons of the unhappy family crowded together against the door, which opened outwards into the area; and, from the accumulation of lava, could not be pushed forwards: thither these devoted persons had fled for refuge from the burning atmosphere above; some of the females were adorned with bracelets of gold and jewels; the master of the house stood next the door with one hand on the key, and a purse of gold in the other.

Engraved by J. Greig.

THE GATE of DIAMONDS, at DHUBOY.

Jam. Forbes. 1780.

Published by Richard Bentley 8, New Burlington St. 1834

Engraved by J. Shury

Specimen of HINDOO SCULPTURE on the Gate of DIAMONDS at DHUBOY.

Published by Richard Bentley, 8, New Burlington St. 18..

In the paintings discovered at Herculaneum and Pompeia, are many near resemblances to the houses and gardens in India, and much oriental costume in other respects; but these real objects were far more impressive; especially the soldiers' guard-rooms and porticos just mentioned, which are so very similar to those at Dhuboy, that I could not omit the comparison.

The western wall and colonnade at Dhuboy are the only remains of the ancient fortifications now entire; the other faces having been razed to the ground by order of a Mahomedan prince who took the town many years ago.

The Bhauts, and oral historians of the country, say that these fortifications, with the tank and Hindoo temples adjoining, cost nine crores of rupees; upwards of ten millions sterling. This is not improbable, when we consider the extent and beauty of the walls and corridores, the grandeur of the double gates, and the amazing expense of bringing such massive stones from the distant mountains; for not the smallest pebble is to be found in that part of Guzerat. The city-gates are all strong and beautiful; there is a double gate in the centre of each face, with a spacious area between, surrounded by a corridore and rooms for the guards. But the eastern portal, called by way of eminence the *Gate of Diamonds*, and the temple connected with it, present the most complete and elegant specimen of *Hindoo* taste I ever saw. In proportion of architecture and elegance of sculpture it far exceeds any of their ancient or modern structures I have met with; and the latter is superior to the figures at Salsette and the Elephanta. This beautiful pile extends three hundred and twenty feet in length, with proportionate height. Rows of elephants richly caparisoned support the massy fabric; the architraves and borders round the compartments of figures are very elegant, and the groups of warriors, performing martial exercises, on horseback, on foot, and on fighting elephants, approach nearer to the athletic gladiators and classical bas-reliefs of ancient Greece, than any performances in the excavations of the Elephanta, or the best finished temples I have seen in Hindostan. The warlike weapons of the soldiers, with their armour, as also the jewels, chains, and ornaments in the caparisoned horses and elephants, are admirably finished; there is likewise a profusion of lions, camels, birds, and serpents, too numerous to discriminate. In one compartment, a man and woman, standing under a plantain-tree, with an infant at their feet, are very conspicuous; it forms a separate group, resembling the general representation of Adam and Eve in paradise. The serpent, which forms so distinguished a feature in the Hindoo mythology, and is usually introduced with our first parents, made no part of this sculpture, although a prominent subject in other places.

In the sculpture of the eastern portal the cobra di-capello was very distinguishable; and not only this species, but a variety of other large snakes abounded in the city and its environs, especially in the banian-groves without this beautiful gate. The ruinous buildings near the durbar were so infested by serpents of almost every description, that I frequently employed the charmers to withdraw them. The cobra di-capello, like those mentioned at Baroche, were considered as the guardian genii of my garden. The brahmins and Hindoo astrologers of Dhuboy on hearing my escape from the hooded-snake, and the cobra minelle found in such numbers in my bed-chamber at Bombay, began their astrological calculations, made abundant use of the astrolabe, and in due time recorded me on their cabalistical tablets as a very lucky man; for which I was indebted to my friends and protectors in the coluber tribe. Tacitus says, Nero in his infancy was supposed to have been guarded by two serpents. According to Murphy, Suetonius explains the origin of this fable, from a report that certain assassins were hired by Messalina to strangle Nero in his bed, in order to remove the rival of Britannicus. The men went to execute their purpose, but were frightened by a serpent that crept from under his pillow. This tale was occasioned by a serpent's skin being found near Nero's pillow; which, by his mother's order, he wore for some time upon his right arm, enclosed in a golden bracelet.

In the Indian Antiquities, a work of deep research and great merit, the author ingeniously remarks, " that it is impossible to say in what country the worship of serpents first originated. The serpent was probably a symbol of the *κακοδαιμων*, or evil genius; and those whose fears led them to adore, by way of pacifying the evil dæmon, erected to the serpent the first altar. In succeeding periods, its annual renewing of its skin, added to the great age to which it sometimes arrived, induced the primitive race to make it the symbol of immortality. Serpents biting their tails, or interwoven in rings, were thenceforwards their favourite symbols of vast astronomical cycles, of the zodiac, and sometimes of eternity itself. In this usage of the symbol we see it enfolding all the statues of gods and deified rajahs in the sacred caverns of Salsette and Elephanta. Symbols also being the arbitrary sensible signs of intellectual ideas, in moral philosophy, the serpents, doubtless from what they themselves observed of it, and from the Mosaic tradition concerning its being more subtle than any other animal, became the emblem of wisdom. An ancient Phœnician fragment, preserved in the Œdipus Ægyptiacus, fully explains the notion which the Egyptians and other pagan nations entertained of this compound hieroglyphic, the GLOBE, WINGS, and SERPENT, which decorated the portals of their proudest temples. Jupiter, says the fragment, is an imagined sphere; from that sphere is produced a serpent. The sphere shews the divine nature to be without beginning or end; the serpent, his word, which animates the world and makes it prolific; his wings, the Spirit of God, that by its motion gives life to the whole mundane system."

The principal image in the temple at the east gate of Dhuboy is said to have diamond eyes; from their magnitude I doubt their reality: the brahmins have probably exchanged those magnificent ornaments for stones of inferior value. Whether this portal was dignified with the appellation of the gate of diamonds from those brilliant eyes of the deity, or from its costly architecture, I cannot say; but I have no doubt that this immense work, with the sanctity annexed to it, as well as to the temple itself, is indebted for its celebrity to its eastern situation, as much as for its ornaments. Possibly had it not been erected in that relative aspect it would not boast of such magnificence. Whether this gate was peculiarly appropriated to the entrance of the ancient Hindoo rajahs, and brahmins of the higher order, or whether opened only for the admission of religious processions, I could not learn from tradition.

We know from ancient history that the east was generally considered to be a more sacred aspect than the other cardinal points;

whether from the sun rising in that quarter of the heavens, or from what other cause is unnecessary to inquire. Many passages from sacred and profane authors might be adduced in support of this idea, none perhaps more striking or appropriate than an occurrence in the visions of Ezekiel; when "a man appeared with a measuring-line, and brought him to the gate of the temple at Jerusalem, whose prospect is towards the east, and measured it round about: he measured it on the east, and west, and north, and south sides, five hundred reeds each, with the measuring-reed; he measured it by the four sides; it had a wall round about, five hundred reeds long and five hundred broad; to make a separation between the sanctuary and the profane place. Afterwards he brought me to the gate, even the gate that looketh towards the east: and behold the glory of the GOD of Israel came from the way of the east; and his voice was like the voice of many waters; and the earth shined with his glory; and the glory of the Lord came into the house by the way of the gate whose prospect is toward the east. Then said the Lord unto me, this gate shall be shut; it shall not be opened; and no man shall enter in by it: because the Lord, the God of Israel, hath entered in by it, therefore it shall be shut! It is for the prince; the prince, he shall sit in it to eat bread before the Lord: he shall enter by the way of the porch of that gate, and shall go out by the way of the same."

The eastern gate of Dhuboy was not only a venerated part of the city, but the general morning rendezvous of the brahmins and principal inhabitants; shady trees protected them from the heat, and on the verdant slope without the exterior portal, heedless of all the coluber genus, or trusting to the reputed benevolence of the warning lizard, they enjoyed a listless indolence, or entered on the political news of the day, a favourite topic with most of the castes in India. Under these trees were some rude altars of single stones; uncouth, and apparently unhewn; smooth by age and the friction of the worshippers, especially an ordeal stone under a banian-tree, daily strewed with flowers, and anointed with oil, where the citizens generally assembled for their morning discussions. This scene reminded me of Nestor at Pylos, and shews a great similarity of manners.

"The old man early rose, walk'd forth, and sate
"On polish'd stone before his palace gate;
"With unguents smooth the lucid marble shone,
"Where ancient Neleus sat, a rustic throne;
"But he descending to the infernal shade,
"Sage Nestor fill'd it, and the scepter sway'd."   ODYSSEY.

A public well without the Gate of Diamonds was a place of still greater resort; there most travellers halted for shade and refreshment. The women, as already mentioned, frequent the fountains and reservoirs morning and evening to draw water. Many of the Guzerat wells have steps leading down to the surface of the water, others have not; nor do I recollect any furnished with buckets and ropes for the convenience of a stranger; most travellers are therefore provided with them, and halcarras and religious pilgrims frequently carry a small brass pot, affixed to a long string for this purpose. The Samaritan woman, in the memorable conversation with our

SAVIOUR, says unto him, "Sir, thou hast nothing to draw with, and the well is deep; from whence then hast thou that living water?" Nothing is more common than for strangers to enter into conversation upon such occasions. Happy was the meeting of the woman of Sychar with the holy traveller at Jacob's well. An assemblage of pilgrims at an oriental reservoir, often brings to mind the interview in Samaria. When at Rome I purchased a picture on this subject, by Guercino, large as life; reckoned one of the finest works of that master: meekness and dignity are happily blended in the Saviour's countenance, and the whole composition is a chef d'ouvre of the Italian school. I spent much of my time with the amiable Angelica Kauffman, while finishing the large picture of our Saviour uttering those endearing words, "Suffer little children to come unto me, and forbid them not: for of such is the kingdom of GOD!" The marked countenance of the disciples, maternal love pressing forward with infants at the breast, the innocence of the children already embracing his knees, and the tender sympathy of the surrounding spectators, were all admirable; but in the character of the DIVINE REDEEMER Angelica transcended her usual excellence, and formed a union of majesty and meekness not easy to conceive. The expression of majesty, or dignity, alone, was comparatively easy to a mind accustomed to sublime ideas; meekness and humility still more so; to combine them with propriety required all the efforts of her transcendent genius. Angelica told me she had often dwelt with pleasure on my picture by Guercino, it had in some degree been a model for her own. A learned friend, eminent in his profession, on seeing it at Stanmore Hill, wrote the following extempore lines, which I trust he will forgive me for inserting.

Soon as the silken curtain I undraw,
My soul is fill'd with reverential awe;
Emotions various agitate my breast,
With fear, grief, joy, alternately imprest.
When the frail fair *Samaritan* I view
Trembling with conscious guilt, I tremble too!
Like her, I seem a wretched sinner, brought
Before that God, who knows man's inmost thought,
With shame abash'd, back from myself I start,
And keen remorse and sorrow pierce my heart.
But when that image meets my ravish'd sight,
Where softness, grace, and dignity, unite
Meekness with majesty, I think I see
My God himself cloth'd in mortality!
His eyes beam mercy, while his lips reprove,
Tempering rebuke with gentleness and love:
His hand uplifted, points the way to heaven;
I hear his voice—"Repent and be forgiven!"
Desponding fears no more my peace destroy,
Sorrow's black gloom, Hope ripens into joy!
But, if a mere resemblance here pourtray'd,
The child of Art, the effect of light and shade,
Can to my mind such strong sensations call,
O! what must be the Great Original! B. I. S. 1797.

Having described the eastern gate of Dhuboy, and the interesting scenery in its vicinity, I may observe that the Bhauts and Churruns, the only historians of Guzerat, account for this expensive and sumptuous portal and the other magnificent structures in the city, by the following story; which is probably founded on fact, though blended with fable. Their traditions relate that, many centuries ago, a Hindoo rajah, named SADARA JAI SIHNG, the "LION OF VICTORY," reigned in Putton, the *Paithana*, or *Pattana*, of the ancient Greeks; a city built on the banks of the river *Godavery*, at a great distance from Dhuboy.

According to the privileged custom of oriental monarchs, this rajah had seven wives, and many concubines; the first in rank, and his greatest favourite, was called RATANALEE, the "LUSTRE OF JEWELS," an additional name conferred upon her, expressive of transcendent worth and superior beauty; in which, and every elegant accomplishment, she excelled all the ladies in the haram. She thus preserved an ascendancy over the rajah, notwithstanding she had no child, and several of the rest had presented him with princes. The intrigues and jealousies among the secluded females in the eastern harams are well known; they prevailed powerfully at Putton, where the ladies were all jealous of Rattanalee, and used every means to alienate the rajah's affection from his favourite; but when they found that she also was in a state of pregnancy, their hatred knew no bounds. According to the superstitious customs of the Hindoos, they employed charms and talismans to prevent the birth of the child; and the beloved sultana, superstitious and credulous as themselves, imagined their spells had taken effect, and that while she remained in the palace, her infant would never see the light.

Impressed with these ideas, she departed with a splendid retinue to sacrifice at a celebrated temple on the banks of the Nerbudda, and after a long journey arrived late in the evening at a sacred grove and lake, about ten miles from the river, on the very spot where Dhuboy now stands; there the princess pitched her tents, intending to conclude her journey the next morning. In this grove dwelt a Gosannee, who had renounced the world, and passed his life in religious retirement. On hearing of Rattanalee's arrival he requested to be admitted into her presence; a request which is seldom refused to those holy men: he desired her not to proceed any further, as that grove was sacred, and there in a few days she would be delivered of a son. The princess followed his advice, and continued in her encampment until the birth of her child; who, at the Gosannee's desire, was named Viseldow, or "the child of twenty months."

This pleasing news was soon conveyed to the rajah, who declared young Viseldow heir to his throne; and finding his mother delighted with the spot where she had obtained the blessing, and fearful of returning among the ladies of the haram, he ordered the lake to be enlarged, the groves extended, and a city erected, surrounded by a strong fortification, and beautified with every costly decoration. The most eminent artists were engaged to build this famous city, and over them was placed a man of superior abilities, who lived to complete the immense work, thirty-two years after its commencement. At that time Viseldow had succeeded his father on the throne of Putton, but generally resided at the place of his nativity; where, on dismissing the several artists, he made them suitable presents; but desirous of more amply gratifying the man to whose superior taste it was indebted for such extraordinary beauty, he desired him to name a reward for his services. The architect respectfully replied, that being happy in the prince's favour he wanted neither money nor jewels; but as the place had not yet received any particular name, he entreated it might be called after his own, Dubhowey, which was immediately granted, and with a slight alteration is the name it still retains.

There is a story something similar to this, in the Ayeen Akbery, respecting Bunsrajh, the founder of the Guzerat monarchy, in the one hundred and fifty-fourth year of the hejira; it mentions Putton as having been built by that prince, whose mother was delivered of him in the wilds of Guzerat, where a hermit took charge of him.

Dhuboy for a long time was inhabited only by Hindoos, no Mussulman being permitted to reside within the walls, nor under any pretence to bathe or wash in the tank; but a young Mahomedan stranger, named Sciad Ballah, on a pilgrimage with his mother Mamah-Doocre, in their way to Mecca, alighted at a caravansary, without the gates of Dhuboy; and Sciad Ballah, having heard much of its magnificence, walked in to gratify his curiosity. After viewing the curious gates and temples on the borders of the tank, and ignorant of any prohibition to the contrary, he rashly ventured to bathe in the sacred lake: the brahmins, deeming the water polluted, prevailed on the rajah to punish the delinquent by cutting off his hands, to deter others from following his example: he was then turned out of the city with disgrace; and thus covered with shame, and weak with the loss of blood, he could but just reach his mother at the caravansary, and there expired.

These strangers were Mahomedans of distinction, then on their way to Surat to embark for the Red Sea, from the interior parts of Hindostan. Mahmah-Doocre, after the first paroxysm of grief, laid aside her pilgrimage, and vowed revenge. She immediately returned to her own country, and sued to her sovereign to redress this disgrace and cruelty to her family; he immediately ordered a large army to march under the command of his vizier against Dhuboy. The siege continued for several years; at length famine raging in the city, the garrison having no hopes of foreign assistance, made a sally, and fought with enthusiasm: a dreadful slaughter ensued, but the besiegers were at length victorious; the principal Hindoos fled to a distant country, and the Mahomedans entered the city. On viewing the strength of the works, the vizier determined to destroy them: three sides of the fortress were immediately razed to the ground; the beauty and elegance of the west face, and the magnificence of the four double gates preserved them from his fury; they remain to this day splendid monuments of the architectural taste of the ancient Hindoos.

After the destruction of Dhuboy, the Mahomedans returned to their own country, and the city remained for many years in a state of desolation. Mahma Doocree, the lady on whose account the expedition had been undertaken, came with the army against Dhuboy, and dying during the siege, was revered as a saint, and buried in a grove near the gate of diamonds, where her tomb still remains. Near it a perforated stone, already mentioned, is used for ordeal trials, and I was often obliged to consent to this experiment in favour of injured innocence, from the faith which the present inhabitants of Dhuboy, both Hindoos and Mahomedans, place in the sanctity of this heroine. The monument of Sciad Ballah is near that of his mother.

When the Moguls finally conquered Guzerat, Dhuboy once

more became populous, and remained under their government upwards of two centuries; it then fell into the hands of the Mahrattas, who rebuilt the walls in their present heterogeneous condition; under them it continued until the beginning of 1780, when, during the Mahratta war with the English, general Goddard appeared before it at the head of an English army from Bengal. While he was preparing for a siege, the pundit with the Mahratta troops evacuated the city in the night, and the next morning the English took possession. General Goddard having established a garrison, marched to the conquest of Ahmedabad, and I was appointed to take charge of this new acquisition, and to collect the revenues, still retaining my situation as a member of the council at Baroche, where I occasionally resided.

The circumstance of giving a name to a city on any particular occasion, or of changing the name on some extraordinary event, frequently occurs in ancient history, as we find at Alexandria, Constantinople, and many other places: in India it is equally prevalent; Ahmedabab, Hyderabad, and Aurungabad derive their name from their founder or conqueror. And although the former name of Dhuboy, if the spot had any peculiar appellation, is no longer remembered, I should suppose it must have been the "*city of waters;*" for in the rainy season it is completely insulated by large lakes, so that the cattle swim in and out of the gates every morning and evening. A similar passage occurs in the reign of David; when the Israelitish monarch sent Joab, his principal general, to besiege Rabbah, a royal city of the Ammonites. After the conquest, Joab sent messengers to David, and said, "I have fought against Rabbah, and have taken the city of waters; now therefore gather the people together, and encamp against the royal city, and take it; lest I take the city, and it be called after my name."

I had not been many weeks in Dhuboy, before it was surrounded by the Mahratta army, consisting of near an hundred thousand horse and foot, who encamped within sight of the walls, although not within reach of our cannon. The Dhuboy garrison consisted only of three companies of Bombay sepoys, commanded by three European officers, a few European artillery-men and lascars, with five byracs of Arabs and Scindian infantry. Our situation was very unpleasant; but finding from the halcarras and spies sent into the enemy's camp, that they entertained a much higher opinion of our strength, we were in hopes the city might be defended until we received a reinforcement from Baroche.

Two English gentlemen, with whom I was intimately acquainted, were at that time hostages in the Mahratta camp; one in the civil service on the Bombay establishment, the other a military officer. The former contrived to send me secretly a few words concealed within the tube of a very small quill, run into the messenger's ear, to inform me of the enemy's determination to recapture Dhuboy; advising me, as I could expect no relief from Baroche, and general Goddard's army was pursuing a different direction, to make the best terms possible, and deliver up the keys to the Mahratta sirdar, as all resistance would be vain. My library at Dhuboy was very scanty; the Annual Registers and Encyclopedia were its principal treasures. I consulted the commanding officer, and looked over various articles of capitulation, that in case of necessity we might at least have made honourable terms; and having no artillery officer, nor engineer, we studied the treatises on fortification, gunnery, and similar subjects to strengthen the ramparts, repair the towers at the diamond gate, and render the old Mahratta guns of some service. Fortunately at this critical period, the approach of general Goddard, with his conquering army from Ahmedabad, was announced; the Mahrattas instantly broke up their encampment, and retreating towards Poonah, the general marched to Surat.

It having been suggested to me that authentic official information, connected with the subject, introduced with brevity, would be interesting and satisfactory, I shall transcribe part of my public correspondence after I had been a year at Dhuboy, and had put the fortifications into tolerable repair: premising that in my retired situation, among people strangers to Europeans, and with very few artificers from Baroche, my Encyclopedia was of wonderful utility; the Indians thought it contained all knowledge, from building a castle to making a gun-carriage, and were constantly consulting it; and so ingenious and persevering were the Indian artificers, that in a few months after my arrival I had furnished the durbar with chairs, tables, sofas, and other necessary articles, after the latest fashion from Europe, finished entirely by the natives of Guzerat.

I shall in the first place make a few extracts from my instructions from the chief and collector-general of Baroche and its dependencies, on my being appointed collector of Dhuboy, to shew the moderation and justice which universally prevailed on such occasions in India.

" As I have appointed you collector of the Honourable Company's revenues at Dhuboy, and its districts, you will please to proceed immediately thither, with the troops intended for its garrison, as per enclosed return; which general Goddard will reinforce with a company of Bombay sepoys from his army: and then the garrison will be abundantly sufficient, in the opinion of those who should be judges, to defend it against any attack of the country powers. Sundry guns and stores are also sent for the use of Dhuboy, accounts of which will be given you by the storekeeper.

"General Goddard has left in Dhuboy four companies of Bombay sepoys, to garrison it until our detachment arrives, when they will join his army; and on your arrival the officer commanding these sepoys will deliver over charge of it to you; you must accordingly take charge of the fort, and all its dependencies, which in any respect belonged to, or were under the government of the peshwa, his officers, or agents; but cautiously avoid, until hostilities are actually commenced against Futty Sihng, to interfere with, or in any shape molest his people, or their concerns. I also enclose you a list of the Arabs and Scindians, consisting of five byracs, entertained as part of the garrison for Dhuboy, specifying their respective pay. They will proceed thither with the detachment from Baroche.

"As Dhuboy was taken by force of arms, and did not surrender on any articles of capitulation, in course whatever houses or property belonged to the peshwa, his officers, agents, or servants, are become the property of the Honourable Company; and as such, must be taken charge of by you, and not given up without orders from me.

"The whole of the purgunna is to be considered as the Honourable Company's property, until the claims any person or persons may have on it for vajefa, pysita, or any other established custom, are regularly produced; and properly and fully proved on a strict inquiry, which will be made hereafter. At present the grand point is to collect all the outstanding revenue that can be done with justice and reason. You will therefore, without delay, please to make the necessary inquiry as to the cultivation and produce of the lands this season; and what has already been recovered from them, and what they can still bear to pay; and acquaint me with the result of your inquiry.

"I am exerting my endeavours, as you must yours, to get the Dessoys, Patells, and Ryots, who have absconded, or are absent from their villages, to return home, and pursue their business; and to them, and all the other subjects of the Company in your districts, you will please to give all assurances of protection and favourable treatment.

"Enclosed is a list of the civil and revenue establishment which I think right for Dhuboy; you will please to appoint the several people wanted: if you judge any addition necessary, acquaint me, and it shall be made. A junadar with five and twenty horse will attend you for the protection of the purgunnas, or any other service you may require. The number of Malzupty sepoys necessary for the collection I cannot determine; you will therefore employ as many as you find requisite; observing in this, and all other circumstances, the greatest frugality.

"As Bhaderpoor and its villages belonged to the Mahratta government, we should have possession of it; and having given this opinion to general Goddard, he has written to me, to take charge of this district; you will therefore send proper persons so to do, in the name of the Honourable Company, and annex it to Dhuboy. In respect to the inhabitants, revenues and appointments, you will proceed agreeably to my instructions for the Dhuboy purgunna.

" Your expenses will be paid by the Honourable Company; in them I need not to you recommend frugality.

(Signed) ROBERT GAMBIER,

As Chief of Baroche, and Collector General of all its dependencies, &c.

Baroche,
26th January, 1780.

Two months after taking possession of the Dhuboy and Bhaderpoor districts I received directions to occupy the purgunna of Zinore, and the fortress of Ranghur, in a commanding situation on the banks of the Nerbudda, which had been ceded by Futty Sihng to general Goddard, in behalf of the Company, on settling a peace with the Guykwars in Guzerat. These places were garrisoned only by a small party of Arabs and Scindians.

After the Mahratta army had entirely left the country, and the Ryots were returned to their respective villages and agricultural employments, peace and plenty once more blessed the purgunnas intrusted to my care. And in consequence of orders from Bombay to the Board of Revenue at Baroche, directing them to transmit the most exact statement of the revenues in the several dependant districts, with a particular account of the produce, population and commerce of those lately acquired by general Goddard,

I sent the following particulars of the purgunnas under my management to the Collector General of Baroche.

"The purgunna of Dhuboy contains eighty-four villages, exclusive of the capital. Four of these villages, in consequence of the late troubles, are entirely deserted, and a few of the remainder very thinly inhabited. The greater part are as populous as can well be expected, when we consider the situation of this province for some years past. The cultivation during the last season has been as much attended to, and the crops as favourable as I could hope for after the desertion of the country during general Goddard's campaign; when more than half the villages were burnt to the ground, and the Ryots were not able to rebuild their cottages, or cultivate the land, until both armies left the country, only a little before the commencement of the last rainy season.

"During those troubles, the villagers, with their cattle and the most portable of their effects, took refuge under the walls of Brodera, Dhuboy, and other fortified towns. Many fled to the Rajepipley mountains; from whence, notwithstanding all my endeavours, they are not yet returned; nor can it be expected until they are assured of peace and safety. This prevents my being more particular respecting the population and state of agriculture in the Dhuboy purgunna: but, from the knowledge I have acquired during a year's residence on the spot, I have every reason to flatter myself, when the country is entirely restored to tranquillity, and the Company's government firmly established, that agriculture and population will both flourish in a great degree, as the soil is generally rich, and very productive.

"Notwithstanding the preceding impediments during the last

season of cultivation, I have the pleasure to add, that the Company's share of the revenue from the crops for the present year, as settled at the late jumma-bundee, amounts to a lac and twenty five thousand rupees; which I am assured is equal to any collected for several years in the Dhuboy purgunna, and greatly exceeding the usual revenue. Last year, from unfavourable rains and subsequent troubles, the assessment did not amount to sixty thousand rupees. The rains this season were remarkably favourable, and the crops generally answered every expectation. I have also the satisfaction to add, that of the lac and twenty five thousand rupees settled for the Dhuboy purgunna, not two hundred remain to be recovered.

"The produce of the Dhuboy district consists of batty, bajeree, juaree, and smaller grain; with some cotton, mowrah, seeds for oil in great variety, and shrubs for dying. Batty may be termed the staple grain of this purgunna; the others bear only a small proportion, and wheat is seldom sown.

"The city of Dhuboy is two miles, two furlongs, and twenty poles in extent; the fortifications form nearly an exact square, and, like most of the Indian works, consist of a single wall, flanked with small towers, within musket shot of each other, and a ditch which in most places is very shallow. To the south the wall is well built of stone, and in excellent repair; has now a new thin brick parapet, and a terreplein broad enough for the free passage of troops. To the west there is a good stone-wall, and brick parapet, in the same manner; but the terreplein, which has been the terrace over a kind of casemate, or colonnade of hewn stone, which extends along all that face, is now impassable; the stone beams are broken, and the roof fallen in. The north side has been originally of the same construction: but the stone casemate has been totally removed, and its place supplied with earth, which has been so much washed away by the rain, that in many places there is only room for one man on the terreplein; and in some, no footing at all. The parapet of this face is only of mud, and in many places entirely broken down. The east side is in the worst repair of any; it has, like the rest, a stone wall, but there is hardly any terreplein, and the parapet is almost washed away; it has this advantage, that the ditch is deep, and retains water most part of the year.

"The number of inhabitants in Dhuboy is about forty thousand, mostly Hindoos, including a very large proportion of brahmins. There are three hundred Mahomedan families; but no Parsees have yet settled here.

"The manufactures chiefly consist of coarse dooties, sent from hence to be dyed at Surat for the Mocha and Judda markets; no very fine cottons are wove here; the common sort dyed in the city are generally for home consumption. Ghee and the coarse cottons called dooties are the staple commodities of Dhuboy. The customs collected in the capital, and at the naukas, or smaller custom-houses in the purgunna, seldom exceed sixteen thousand rupees a year.

"Dhuboy is the only fortified town in this district. There was a small gurry at Verah, which has been almost washed away by heavy rains, and is now a scene of ruin. Chandode and Nundaria are now added to the Dhuboy purgunna; the revenues of these villages amount this year to four thousand rupees, and the customs exceed fifteen hundred. Chandode has no fortification; being esteemed a place of great sanctity by the Hindoos, and much respected by all other tribes. The detachment of horse kept for the security of the Dhuboy districts, are particularly useful about Zinore and Chandode, situated near the Gracias, a most insolent and cruel set of banditti.

"The Zinore purgunna contains fifty inhabited villages; the town of that name is open, large, and straggling; tolerably populous; situated on the steep banks of the Nerbudda, the deep gullies which nearly encompass it are the only defence. The trade and manufactures are similar to those at Dhuboy; so is the produce of the country, except that it bears less rice, and a larger proportion of cotton.

"During the troubles last year, the Zinore villages suffered the same cruel fate as those in the Dhuboy purgunna. The Ryots sought for safety in other places, and many are not yet returned. The cultivation was nevertheless forwarded as much as possible, and the jumma-bundee for this year settled at ninety thousand rupees; a revenue seldom exceeded under the Guykwar government of Futty Sching: this amount is nearly recovered. The customs of Zinore and the Naukas, are usually about three thousand rupees per annum.

"The small compact gurry at Ranghur, strongly situated on the banks of the Nerbudda, eight miles from Zinore, is now included in that purgunna.

"Bhaderpoor, although dignified as a separate purgunna, does not with its whole district annually produce so much as one of the best Dhuboy or Baroche villages. The principal town situated on the banks of the Oze, is little more than seven miles from Dhuboy; some of its villages only three. There are sixteen inhabited, many desolated from the incursions of the Bheels and Gracias. The produce is similar to that of the Dhuboy purgunna; the revenue this year, which exceeds most under the Mahratta government, is only sixteen thousand rupees: the customs in tranquil times amount to three or four thousand rupees per annum.

"In Bhaderpoor is a small gurry for the protection of the town. It contains the custom-house, and a few other low buildings, of poor materials; which were burnt down by the Mahrattas, with a considerable part of the gurry, when they found it would become English property. I have repaired the whole at a small expense; and in all respects have endeavoured to fulfil the duties in the several districts intrusted to my care, with fidelity to my honourable employers, and to the benefit and happiness of the subjects in their late acquisitions.

(Signed) JAMES FORBES,
Collector of Dhuboy, &c.

Dhuboy,
13th January, 1781.

In the course of the preceding year I put the fortifications and public buildings at Dhuboy into the best repair in my power, at a small expense, and sent the following answer to some remarks made by the chief of Baroche on my accounts.

"I now return the Dhuboy accounts, rectified according to your instructions; and I flatter myself the following remarks will be a satisfactory answer to that part of your letter, desiring me to assign my reasons for the high charges under the head of fortification and house repairs.

"The building up the large breach on the south face of the town, in length nine hundred and twenty-six feet, was by far the most expensive work; but so indispensably necessary, that I could not avoid representing it to you immediately on our taking possession of Dhuboy; and obtained your consent for instantly repairing it. A subadar's guard, which our weak garrison could very ill spare, was required to be constantly posted there, and a much stronger guard at the time we were so annoyed by the Mahratta army. This work included several towers; which, with a strong outer wall of brick and chunam, has been constructed on the old stone foundation, with a retaining wall and rampart.

"A magazine was no less requisite the city afforded no building fit for that purpose, either from its structure or situation. I expended near three hundred rupees in repairing a pagoda and contiguous shed near the large tank, to serve as temporary magazines for our ammunition from Baroche, and a quantity of loose gunpowder found on our taking possession of Dhuboy: but as the water in the rainy season rises higher than the floor of these buildings, they would then have been totally useless. They were also very near several houses communicating with the town; and two fires happening in that neighbourhood after our arrival, I lost no time in procuring the plan for a small magazine from captain Jackson of the artillery, to be built as cheap as possible in a proper place.

"Strengthening the works at the Herau-Durwajee, or Diamond-Gate, filling up contiguous breaches with strong masonry, making embrazures for nine guns, and erecting a flag-staff on the inner tower of the east-gate, were expenses that could neither be avoided nor delayed; the whole wall on that face being made of mud, without either brick or stone, is entirely weak and defenceless, without this strong gate-way, and the angular towers to flank it. To these timely repairs we certainly were much indebted when the enemy repeatedly advanced on that side, from knowing its weak state under the Mahrattas. One of our first steps was to put the Gate of Diamonds in order, and mount nine guns on its ramparts; by which we several times compelled their advancing cavalry to make a hasty retreat.

" In the area between the eastern outer and inner gates, I erected sheds for the accommodation of the regular and local sepoys, doing duty in the garrison; having previously been dispersed in the open streets, or violently possessing the houses of the inhabitants, which occasioned continual disturbances. These were finished before the setting in of the monsoon, when their situation would otherwise have been still more distressing, and for their accommodation I also repaired some part of the colonnade in the interior of the west wall. The five byracs of Arabs and Scindians, constantly posted on the walls, were exposed to every inclemency of the weather, without a place of shelter: their own jamadars and the English commanding officer made so many complaints of their situation, that I ordered the four large angular towers to be covered in, and the terrace then afforded them excellent accommodation.

" Unavoidable expenses for repairs almost daily occurred, when the enemy approached the weak parts of the fortress; but all these, with cleaning out the ditch on the north face, where it was entirely filled up, fell short of one thousand rupees.

"The durbar had for many years been in so ruinous a state, that the Mahratta pundit would not reside there; it was scarcely habitable when colonel Keating wintered here in 1775, from that time it had been converted into smiths'-shops, powder-mills, and other conveniences, from the natural aversion of the Hindoos to reside in a house that has been inhabited by Europeans. I have been as frugal as possible in rendering it commodious for myself, and have repaired the houses allotted to the English officers, serjeants, and artillery-men, and the caravansary used for an hospital.

"The foregoing remarks will I trust be satisfactory; and convince you that nothing has been undertaken which could be avoided, and that every thing has been done at as small an expense as possible.

(Signed) JAMES FORBES."

Dhuboy,
31*st January,* 1781.

As the estimate which I afterwards delivered to the chief of Baroche for further repairs to the fortifications at Dhuboy, recommended by general Goddard and colonel Kyd, (engineer in the Bengal army, when the general and his staff were with me during the rainy season in 1781), is very short, and contains the price of bricks, mortar, labour, and other articles, I annex the estimated account for the information of the reader, and have put the amount into English money, as well as in the Bombay currency of rupees, quarters, and reas. By this will be seen the great difference in price, of building in India and England, especially in the article of labour; which also extends proportionably in all manufactures, and the various branches of agriculture. In the following estimate the usual profit which the Company allowed to their paymasters and storekeepers, is included in the charges.

Estimate of the expense in taking down the mud wall in the fortifications at Dhuboy, and rebuilding it with bricks and chunam, on the ancient stone foundation, being in length 3520 feet; including the retaining wall and the parapet in this measurement.

	Rupees.
Bricks, thirty lacs, 3,000,000, at 2 rupees 2 quarters, about 6*s.* per million	7,500
Chunam, (mortar) 10,560 moondah, at 1 rupee 1 quarter, or 3*s.* per million	13,200
Bricklayers 4,520, at one quarter of a rupee, or 7½*d.* per day	1,130
Biggarees, (labourers) 8,600, at 50 reas, or 3¾*d.* per day .	1,075
Master bricklayers, at half a rupee, 15*d.* per day . . .	90
Stone-cutters . . . ditto . . . ditto	450
Pacaulies, (water carriers) ropes, baskets, iron utensils, and other necessary articles, about 106*l.* 5*s.*	850
Rupees .	24,295
£. sterling .	3,036

I have inserted the preceding documents and accounts, not only to gratify the wishes of some particular friends, but to convince my readers in general, that there was a regular system in every department of the Company's service in India; a system of simplicity, truth, and virtue, on a plain path, in which moderation, and clemency were the predominant features, at least as far as local circumstances admitted: and as I have every reason to believe that this system was generally adopted, I have enjoyed a peculiar pleasure in transcribing the above passages from manuscripts, long since consigned to oblivion.

Virtus, repulsæ nescia sordidæ,
Intaminatis fulget honoribus:
Nec sumit aut ponit secures
  Arbitrio popularis auræ. HOR. L. 3. Ode 3.

With stainless lustre Virtue shines;
  A base repulse nor knows, nor fears;
Asserts her honours, nor declines
  As the light air of crowds uncertain veers.

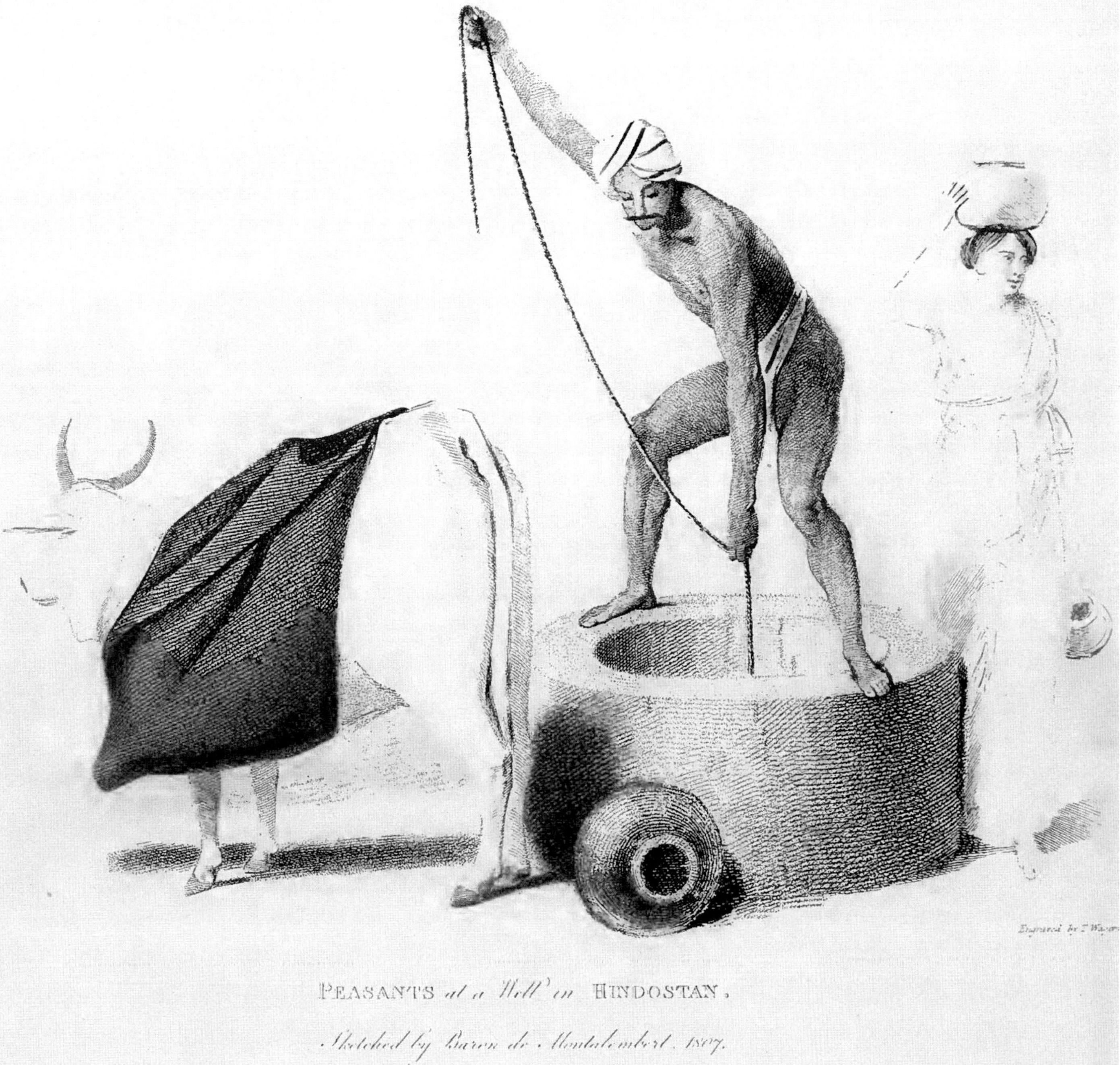

Engraved by T. Wageman

PEASANTS at a Well in HINDOSTAN.

Sketched by Baron de Montalembert, 1807.

Published by Richard Bentley 8 New Burlington St 1834

INDIAN SQUIRREL *and* TAMARIND

CHAPTER XXIV.

ADMINISTRATION OF JUSTICE IN THE CITY AND DISTRICTS OF DHUBOY;

TRIAL BY PANCHAUT; EXTRAORDINARY ACCOUNT OF DEMONS AND NECROMANCY IN INDIA;

ANECDOTES RELATING TO HIDDEN TREASURE, AND OTHER SINGULAR CUSTOMS.

1781.

- - - - - " if our virtues
Did not go forth of us, 'twere all alike
As if we had them not. What's open made to JUSTICE
That JUSTICE seizes." SHAKESPEARE.

" Let us reflect upon *sixty millions* of human beings, either absolutely subjects of the East India Company, or under their influence; beings who for countless ages, certainly not less than twenty centuries, have had their minds debased by the grossest and most disgusting superstitions, and their feelings blunted and confused by a strange and inconsistent mixture of cruelty and humanity; of cruelty extending to the murder of parents and children, with stony-hearted apathy; of humanity exaggerated in the preservation of noxious reptiles at the public expense; with the most affected aversion to the taking away of life. These and greater abominations constitute the picture which India offers to the British philanthropist, and call upon us emphatically in the present extended state of our dominion, to consider the responsibility we have assumed."

BRITISH REVIEW.

CONTENTS.

—one similar at Surat—charmers of serpents—susceptible of music—sacred serpents—anecdote of a naga, or hooded snake—ordeal trials permitted at Dhuboy—account of one—general ordeals—Dherna, a most extraordinary kind of arrest, and punishment—Koor equally singular and cruel—Hindoos buried alive—story of a suttee, or a self-devoted Hindoo widow reclaimed—ablutions and other customs in India—salt the symbol and pledge of hospitality—anecdotes to illustrate.

CHAPTER XXIV.

In a short time after my arrival at Dhuboy, I became tolerably reconciled to its recluse situation, which afforded me very little intercourse with my countrymen: in other respects I was far from leading a solitary life; for the administration of justice, collecting the revenue, superintending the agriculture of five large towns, and a hundred and fifty populous villages, which were under my care, gave me constant and anxious employment.

I dedicated one day in the week, and more when necessary, to the administration of justice, in which I was assisted by four principal brahmins; the cazee, and three Mahomedans, conversant in the laws of the Koran, with some respectable merchants, and the heads of other castes. These persons advised me in doubtful cases, and especially on points relating to the religious ceremonies and customs of the Hindoos. The carpet of justice was spread in the large open hall of the durbar, where the arbitrators assembled: there I always attended, and, agreeably to ancient custom, referred the decision to a panchaut, or jury of five persons; two were chosen by the plaintiff, two by the defendant, and the fifth by myself, from among these elders. I had, by this means, the satisfaction of pleasing a hundred thousand inhabitants; who only made one appeal to the superior courts at Baroche or Bombay.

I was delighted with the simplicity of this mode of proceeding. From having been an alderman and sheriff at Bombay, and for some years worn the black gown as a pleader in the courts of justice at that presidency, I was not entirely unacquainted with English law: but had I equalled Blackstone in knowledge of British jurisprudence, it would have availed little among a people completely attached to their own customs, and influenced by the prejudices of caste. I was therefore happy to accommodate myself to their usages. I believe I may truly say, that not a present was ever made to an individual belonging to the adawlet; nor was a court-fee under any description ever exacted. This mode of justice was something similar to the statute ordained in the Levitical law. "If there arise a matter too hard for thee in judgment, being matters of controversy within thy gates, then thou shalt come unto the priests the Levites, and unto the judge, and shall inquire of them, and they shall shew thee the sentence of judgment: and thou shalt observe to do according to the sentence of the law which they shall teach thee; and according to the judgment which they shall tell thee, that shalt thou do."

In the inner court of the durbar, immediately fronting the open side of the hall of justice, was a sacred pepal-tree, and in an adjoining square a noble banian-tree. These places were esteemed holy while Dhuboy continued under the peshwa government of Poonah, and a brahmin pundit resided at the durbar; on becoming the abode of an Englishman, the building lost its reputed sanctity; the trees still retained their claim to veneration: they afforded a sort of sacred shade to the Hindoos who were summoned to the adawlet, and proved at least a useful shelter to other castes.

I was far from discouraging this idea respecting such umbrageous canopies in the torrid zone. It prevented their destruction, and added to the ornament and refreshment of the city. Among the ancient Scythians, a stately tree with out-spreading branches was considered an emblem of the godhead, and an object of worship. Trees and groves were either worshipped or consecrated by most pagan nations; and from them the same idolatrous custom was introduced among the Jews, who were reproached by the prophet for the oaks which they had desired, and for the gardens, or groves, which they had chosen. Not only the Scythians, but the Persians, Druids, and many other people, rejected enclosed temples for the worship of God, as too narrow a limit for the adoration of a Being who filled immensity. The modern brahmins seem in many instances to adopt the same idea; they most probably all derived their religion from the same source, and the most enlightened among these various tribes have united in their adoration

> " To Him, whose temple is all space,
> " Whose altar, earth, sea, skies;
> " One chorus let all beings raise,
> " All Nature's incense rise!

An ingenious writer in the Asiatic Researches asserts, apparently on well-grounded authority, that from Noah and his descendants, who established themselves on the mountains of Taurus in Higher Asia, "the Hindoo religion probably spread over the whole earth. There are signs of it in every northern country, and in almost every system of worship. In England it is obvious; Stonehenge is evidently one of the temples of Boodh; and the arithmetic, astronomy, astrology; the holidays, games, names of the stars, and figures of the constellations; the ancient monuments, laws, and coins; the languages of the different nations; bear the strongest marks of the same original. The brahmins of the sect of Brahma were the true authors of the Ptolemaic system; the Boodhists, followers of Budha, the authors of the Copernican system, as well as of the doctrine of attraction; and probably the established religion of the Greeks, and the Eleusinian mysteries were only varieties of the two different sects."

In whatever light the reputed sanctity of the trees at the Dhuboy durbar may be viewed in Europe, to me they were of great advantage. Under their sacred shade the ordeal trials were performed; the Hindoo witnesses examined; and the criminals were allowed a solemn pause, while waiting for their trial; a pause, perhaps, doubly solemn and impressive, from standing under the immediate emblem of the godhead.

I generally kept minutes of the causes which came before me, in case of reference or appeal. They were often trifling, sometimes ludicrous. I shall insert two or three which occurred in the same morning, as characteristic of the singular situation in which I was placed.

A certain blind man, well known in Dhuboy, died during my residence there. Although deprived of one sense, he seemed to enjoy the others in greater perfection: among various talents he could generally discover hidden treasure, whether buried in the earth, or concealed under water, and possessed the faculty of diving and continuing a long time in that element without inconvenience. As he never commenced a search without stipulating for one third of the value restored, he had, by this occupation, maintained an aged father, a wife, and several children. The old man complained, that several persons for whom his son had found money, refused to make good their promise; and particularly a goldsmith, who on being summoned before the court, acknowledged the truth of the story, but thought a third part of the amount too large a proportion. The goldsmith had reprimanded his wife for misconduct: being a woman of spirit, she took the first opportunity of his absence to collect as much of his money and valuables as possible, and threw them, together with herself and her own jewels and ornaments, into a well. As they had not lived very happily together, the goldsmith on his return, was not much concerned about his wife, but regretting the loss of his treasure he made diligent search for her body, which was found in an adjoining well, divested of all her ornaments. Surprized and disappointed, he knew not what further to do, when a confidential friend of his wife told him the deceased had taken off her gold chains and jewels, and tying them up in a bag with his own valuables, threw them into another well, but where it was she knew not; having alleged two reasons for her conduct, that he might lose his property, and be deprived of the means of procuring another wife, which he would find difficult without the jewels. The blind man was sent for, and after a long search, found the bag in a distant well, but could not prevail on the goldsmith to give him his share; and since his decease his father had been equally unsuccessful. The court of adawlet decreed him one third of the property.

Next came two respectable brahmins, a man and his wife, of the secular order; who, having no child, had made several religious pilgrimages, performed the accustomed ceremonies to the linga, and consulted the diviners, and recluse devotees, in hopes by their prayers and sacrifices to obtain the desired blessing. A woman skilled in divination promised the wife a son if she would drink a potion composed of the pure essence of jewels. This she consented to, and produced all her pearls, diamonds, and precious stones, which her chemical friend deeming insufficient, persuaded her to borrow more from her relations: these were deposited in a small vase, hermetically sealed, and, with many superstitious ceremonies, placed in a jar of holy water, where it was to remain eight days, without molestation, or the secret being communicated. Two days after this consecration, the woman told the brahmin's wife she was going to a celebrated temple on the banks of the Nerbudda, to perform some additional ceremonies; if she did not return before the expiration of the time, she might open the vase, and would then discover the jewels under the surface of an essential oil; which she was immediately to swallow, and in due time her wishes would be accomplished. On the appointed day the deluded wife found only an empty vase in the jar of holy water; and learned that her deceiver had fled to a distant country. The unhappy pair now petitioned that I would write to the rajah to deliver the culprit up to justice.

The third in succession was a tandar, or petty officer of a district; who appeared with a banian merchant who had plunged into a well, to drown himself; but having been discovered, timely assistance restored suspended animation, and he was brought before the court. On being asked his reason for committing this rash action, he coolly replied, that several people owed him considerable sums of money, and would not pay him: whereas he was only indebted to one man, who threatened to imprison him if he did not discharge it; which being unable to do, and unwilling to act with the same cruelty to his debtors, he thought it better to lose his life, than his good name; and therefore resolved to leave them all, and enter upon another stage of existence. This affair was soon compromised to general satisfaction.

Most of the disputes which came before the paunchaut at Dhuboy were for infringing the rules of caste, encroachments upon sacred territories, misbehaviour of women, or similar offences; which were generally settled by the brahmins. What gave me the greatest trouble and uneasiness, was to prevent, as far as in my power, the suicides frequently committed by young women in a state of pregnancy. A crime generally practised by the higher class of Hindoo widows; who having been married in infancy, and losing their husbands in childhood, were, by the cruel and impolitic laws of Menu, prevented from marrying a second husband, and consequently led into imprudences. Some of these unfortunate females, conscious of bringing a disgrace on their family, thus terminated their own existence and that of their unborn infant; their bodies were often found in the public wells of the city, and villages in the purgunna, but none of the brahmins in the panchaut, nor any Hindoo officer took the smallest trouble to prevent these shocking occurrences. The suicides were at last so frequent, that I was under the necessity of issuing an order, to be affixed at the market-place and city gates, that the body of any female found in a well or tank, within the Dhuboy districts, should be exposed naked for twenty-four hours before it was taken to the funeral pile. This had so far the desired effect, that after the proclamation of the edict, either no more suicides were committed, or they were carefully concealed from my knowledge, as I never had occasion to make an exposure. Suicide is not only sanctioned among the Hindoos, but on certain occasions is deemed meritorious. Major Moor mentions, that among the five most eligible modes, is that of going into the sea near the mouth of the Ganges, and there praying and confessing sin, until the alligators or some other monster devours the penitent.

While writing on this subject, I shall insert a singular petition presented to me when acting judge in the court of adawlet at Baroche; which, however ludicrous or trifling it may appear to an European, strongly characterizes the superstition of the Indians, and the difficulty of accommodating English laws to a people under such extraordinary prejudices, and who believe in a race of beings whose existence we do not admit of. I shall only premise that the heroine of the story was the wife of a rich and eminent merchant at Baroche, of a very repectable family among the Parsees; and that all the persons necessarily convened to investigate this mysterious affair, were astonished at my entertaining any doubts about it.

"To JAMES FORBES, Esq.

Presiding in the Court of Adawlet, at Baroche.

The humble petition of Ruttonjee-Monackjee, a Parsee merchant, inhabitant of Baroche,

Most humbly sheweth,

"That your petitioner, with all respect and submission, begs leave to represent to your worship, that Framjee Nanabhy's wife and your petitioner's daughter were for many years intimate friends, and lived near each other in this city.

"Some time ago the said Framjee's wife had two devils entered into her body, which devils were sisters. One day your petitioner's daughter went to her friend's house, where she found her burning frankincense on a fire, and performing some magical ceremonies; soon afterwards the devils began to speak, and angrily asked why they were called up; telling her at the same time that their sacrifices had been neglected and their daily offerings of flowers, cocoa-nuts, and fruit, discontinued. The devils then vehemently cried out, "for this we will destroy, we will kill, we will eat." On which Framjee's wife immediately made the proper offerings at the altar of the devils, and promised no more to offend. The devils then declared they were satisfied, and shewed your petitioner's daughter much amusement; and the said Framjee's wife, by means of the devils within her body, performed many conjuring tricks, and curious exploits, with which your petitioner's daughter was greatly delighted.

"It is however well known to your petitioner, and all who enter into these mysteries, that Framjee's wife committed a great fault in performing these ceremonies before a stranger, who had not been initiated, and which she had been enjoined to keep secret. For this reason, and because your petitioner's daughter had been present at those magical rites, one of the devils left Framjee's wife, and entered into your petitioner's daughter; who, on coming home from that visit, fell down upon the bed, without sense or motion, and continued in that state for some hours. On coming to herself, her parents inquired the cause of her illness: she answered she could not tell; and sunk again into silence and stupidity.

"In this melancholy situation your petitioner's daughter continued for two months; at the expiration of which time she told her friends that a devil from Framjee's wife had entered her body, and tormented her for food and sacrifices; saying she would destroy her if she did not furnish every thing necessary, as Framjee's wife had supplied both her and her sister; that if she would treat her in all respects as her sister was treated, she never would hurt her, because the devils were sisters, and there must be no difference in their treatment. From that day the devil in your petitioner's daughter was supplied with necessaries and sacrifices to her liking, and all remained in peace and quietness.

"Some time afterwards, as Framjee and his wife were sitting at home together, the latter burnt incense, and performed the usual ceremonies to call up her devil: she accordingly made her appearance; when Framjee desired her to cause the devil, which had so long been in your petitioner's daughter, to come and dwell again in the body of his wife. On which the devil replied that her sister could not leave your petitioner's daughter, who now treated her with good things, and performed her daily sacrifices.

"Your petitioner has likewise a female relation, named Johye, who is skilled in these mysteries, and understands all the conjuring business; she was a great friend to Framjee's wife, but because she would not assist her in getting the devil to leave your petitioner's daughter, and return into her own body, she quarrelled with the said Johye, and accused her falsely before your worship, in the Court of Adawlet, of having performed certain magical ceremonies, by which she almost conjured her only son to death. On Framjee's son being carried on his bed to your garden house, and shown to you in those dreadful fits which left him without any appearance of life, you was pleased to hear all the stories and accusations of Framjee and his wife against the said Johye, and to order her to be confined in the chowkey of the adawlet until the next court day, when she is to be tried upon this false accusation.

"But your petitioner begs leave to say, that this is all a false story against the said Johye; for it is God who has been pleased to afflict Framjee's son with a sickness almost unto death; and it is not in the power of Johye to cure him, although Framjee has assured you that she can; and you have, in consequence of his assertion, ordered her to take off the spell, and to effect his cure. And further as your petitioner knows that his daughter will die whenever the devil leaves her body, he begs leave to inform you, that the said Johye cannot assist Framjee's wife in calling her out, and sending her again into her own body.

"This being the case with respect to the said Johye, your petitioner requests that you will be pleased to release her from confinement, as he will be bound for her appearance next court day in the Adawlet; together with her son Hormuz, whom Framjee has also accused of being an accomplice in this conjuring business.

"And your petitioner will ever pray for your long life and happiness. RUTTONJEE MONACKJEE."

Baroche,
8th January, 1782.

As the spirits in the original petition are called devils, and I did not choose to alter any part of this singular production, except to correct the orthography of the Hindoo translator, so I have inserted that term, and copied it in all other respects from the petition which was presented to me as judge in the public court; but I believe the original word means those genii, or spirits, who form a class of middle beings in the creed of most Indians, whether Hindoos, Mahomedans, or Parsees. Every Persian and Arabian tale is embellished with their adventures. The Mahomedans firmly believe in their agency; and the Hindoos are taught that two of these genii attend upon every mortal, from the moment of his existence until his death; that to the one is committed the record of his good actions; to the other the report of his transgressions, at the tribunal appointed for judgment.

On these subjects it is difficult even for a person of more experience than myself to expatiate; the acute Dr. Fryer, however, affords some assistance. After describing the sacrifice of a dunghill-cock under a banian-tree, by the chief of a Hindoo town, he says "the blood was sprinkled upon the dancers, who giving a great shout, cried out that the devil must be pacified with blood; God with prayers. Some of these people sell themselves to wickedness; nourishing a familiar in their families, appearing to them upon their command, and undergo fiery afflictions to have the most hurtful devil. Besides those diseases that are said to be devils put into one another: about which, as many as I have met with, I have been curiously inquisitive, their phænomena, or energies, are discussed by natural causes, and as often cured by natural means: but, on the contrary, it is allowed where they resist them it is suspicious. And the devil, without doubt, cannot more easily work on any than the weak and simple; and on that account may probably delude and over-awe these people that give themselves up to him wholly out of fear; having not so much virtue, fortitude, and cunning, to resist and check their cunning, as the wiser sort. As for the visible appearance of a devil or dæmon, which they say is common among them, I am convinced it may be credible; but in the meanwhile rage and melancholy madness, assisted by the infernal powers, may create great illusions to a fancy fitted for such an operation; and they may think they see things which in reality are not so."

All history, ancient and modern, presents grounds for these phænomena: the scriptures of the Old and New Testament clearly assert the fact, as in the case of Saul with the woman of Endor, and in many other passages. That such dæmons existed in our Saviour's time none can doubt; had they not been common among the heathen nations in preceding ages, the Israelites would not have had these solemn injunctions. "There shall not be found among you any one that useth divination, or is an observer of times, or a consulter with familiar spirits, or a necromancer; for all that do these things are an abomination to the Lord."

Dr. Francis Buchanan mentions a man who was supposed to be possessed by one of these evil spirits in Mysore; which caused great uproar in the village, and was at length appeased by the brahmins' prayers, and strewing consecrated ashes over the invalid. Dr. Buchanan proves that this man was subject to the epilepsy, and that the recurrence of the fit had been occasioned by a violent paroxym of intoxication. That I have no doubt was the cause in this instance, but I am of opinion that the effects I have alluded to, proceeded from other causes, although I cannot undertake to explain them. The petition of the Parsee merchant was entered on the records of the court of Adawlet at Baroche, and I preserved it among my manuscripts, on account of the impression it then made upon my mind, and the agitation it caused in a large city, inhabited by many thousand Hindoos, Mahomedans, and Parsees, widely differing in religious sentiments, but uniting in the belief of this supernatural agency. When these facts are compared with many other circumstances, more or less connected with them, throughout these volumes, respecting the ignorance, superstition, and prejudices of the natives in general, their introduction may perhaps not be thought irrelevant to the subject of Indian jurisprudence.

Since the commencement of this selection from my original manuscripts, I have endeavoured to omit such passages as did not appear generally interesting; and by abridging others as much as possible, to avoid prolixity. But if a writer on foreign countries were to suppress every thing which could not be brought to the standard of reason, and to withhold local anecdotes, apparently trifling, which often very strongly mark the national and individual character, his narrative would be comparatively dull, and want that zest which distinguishes the traveller from the sedentary composer: at the same time it must be allowed, that after a long series of years, the traveller who wrote from first impressions, and committed to paper all that then engaged his attention, will find it necessary to expunge many incidents which at the time were interesting to himself, though at a subsequent period they might not be deemed so by general readers.

Few persons have had more experience of the Indian character than Lord Teignmouth. Being elected President of the Asiatic Society, after the much-lamented death of Sir William Jones, he thus addresses them in his first paper: "*Man* and *Nature* were proposed, by our late President, as the comprehensive objects of our researches; and although I by no means think that advantage should be taken of this extensive proposition, to record every trivial peculiarity of practice, habit, or thinking, which characterizes the natives of India, many singularities will be found amongst them which are equally calculated to gratify curiosity, and to attract the notice of the philosopher and politician. Of all studies, that of the human mind is of the greatest importance; and, whether we trace it in its perfection or debasement, we learn to avoid error, or obtain models for improvement, and examples for imitation. In pursuing customs and habits to the principles from which they are derived, we ascertain by the sure rule of experience, the effects of natural or moral causes upon the human mind. The characters of the natives of India, notwithstanding all that has been published in Europe, are by no means well understood there; and a careful and accurate investigation of them, with a due discrimination of habits and usages, as local or general, would afford a subject for a curious, useful, and entertaining dissertation."

After these general observations, the President instances several very extraordinary facts respecting the brahmins; some of which I have mentioned at Baroche. He then introduces a story from the judicial records, in which five women were put to death for the supposed practice of sorcery. "In the year 1792, three men of the caste of *Soontaar*, in one of the Bengal districts. were indicted for the murder of these five women: the prisoners without hesitation confessed the crime with which they were charged, and pleaded in their defence, that with their tribes it was the immemorial custom and practice to try persons notorious for witchcraft. That for this purpose an assembly was convened of those of the same tribe, from far and near; and if, after due investigation, the charge was proved, the sorcerers were put to death: and no complaint was ever preferred on this account to the ruling power. That the women who were killed had undergone the prescribed form of trial, were duly convicted of causing the death of the son of one of the prisoners by witchcraft, and had been put to death by the prisoners, in conformity to the sentence of the assembly.

"To ascertain with a degree of certainty the persons guilty of practicing witchcraft, the three following modes are adopted.

First, branches of the saul tree, marked with the names of all the females in the village, whether married or unmarried, who have attained the age of twelve years, are planted in the water in the morning, for the space of four hours and a half; and the withering of any of these branches is proof of witchcraft against the person whose name is annexed to it. *Secondly*, small portions of rice enveloped in cloths, marked as above, are placed in a nest of white ants; the consumption of the rice in any of the bags, establishes sorcery against the woman whose name it bears. *Thirdly*, lamps are lighted at night; water is placed in cups made of leaves, and mustard-seed oil is poured, drop by drop, into the water, whilst the name of each woman in the village is pronounced; the appearance of the shadow of any woman on the water during this ceremony, proves her a witch.

"Such are the general rules for ascertaining those who practise witchcraft. In the instance which I have quoted, the witnesses swore, and probably believed, that all the proofs against the unfortunate women had been duly verified. They assert in evidence, that the branches marked with the names of the five women accused, were withered; that the rice in the bags, having their specific names, was devoured by the white ants, whilst that in the other bags remained untouched; that their shadows appeared on the water on the oil being poured upon it whilst their names were pronounced; and further that they were seen dancing at midnight, naked, by the light of a lamp, near the house of the sick person. It is difficult to conceive that this coincidence of proof could have been made plausible to the grossest ignorance, if experience did not shew that prepossession will supersede the evidence of the senses."

What connexion the oriental sorcery may have with the necromancy of Homer and other ancient writers, I cannot say. The Grecian bard asserts its antiquity in several instances, and especially in the most ancient of all denominations, the evocation of the dead; by customs and ceremonies, similar perhaps to those used by the infernal agent for calling up Samuel at the desire of Saul.

> "There, in a lonely land, and gloomy cells,
> "The dusky nation of Cimmeria dwells;
> "There the wan shades we hail,
> "New wine, with honey-tempered milk, we bring,
> "And living waters from the crystal spring;
> "O'er these we strew'd the consecrated flour,
> "And on the surface shone the holy store.
> "Thus solemn rites and holy vows we paid,
> "To all the phantom nations of the dead.
>
> ---
>
> "Know to the spectres that thy beverage taste
> "The scenes of life occur, and actions past;
> "They, seal'd with truth, return the sure reply,
> "The rest repell'd, a train oblivious fly."

Dacier, on these passages, proves that this kind of necromancy prevailed before Homer's time, among the Chaldeans, and spread over all the oriental world. Æschylus introduces it in his tragedy of Persa; and thus it appears that there was a foundation for what Homer writes, and that he only embellishes the opinions of antiquity with the ornaments of poetry.

From the story of Saul and the woman of Endor, there can be no doubt of the general belief and practice of this kind of necromancy in Palestine, derived most probably from the surrounding nations. In that instance we find that the woman herself had a familiar spirit; and by that means obtained the power of conversing with departed spirits [from the human body]: similar to that is the belief so universally entertained throughout Persia, Arabia, and India, of the existence of genii, demons, and familiar spirits, under different denominations. Harmer, on this singular subject, says, " the sacred and profane writers, believing the reality of the same thing, use exactly the same language, and apply the same terms in precisely the same sense. An afflicted father brings his wretched son to our blessed Lord, and thus in accosting him describes the case of the child: 'Master, I beseech thee, look upon my son, for he is my only child; and lo, a spirit taketh him, and he suddenly crieth out; and it teareth him, till he foameth again; and bruising him, hardly departeth from him.'

" That the same form of speech is used by heathen writers, and the same effects described, when they speak of supernatural influence, the following account from Herodotus will make sufficiently evident. Speaking of Scyles, king of the Scythians, who, having received a Grecian education, was more attached to the customs of the Greeks, than to those of his own countrymen, and who desired to be privately initiated into the bacchic mysteries, he adds, " Now because the Scythians reproach the Greeks on account of these bacchanals, and say, that to imagine a god driving men into paroxysms of madness is not agreeable to reason; a certain Borysthenian, while the king was privately performing the ceremonies, went out, and discovered the matter to the Scythian army in these words. " Ye Scythians ridicule us because we celebrate the mysteries of Bacchus, and the god possesseth us; but now this same *demon* (ΔΑΙΜΩΝ) possesseth your king, and he performs the part of a Bacchanalian, and is filled with fury by the god.' HERODOTUS.

This passage is truly remarkable. The identical expressions used by the evangelist are also used by Herodotus. A demon, (δαιμων), or spirit, is the agent in the Greek historian, and in the case mentioned in the text; in both cases it is said the demon takes or possesses the persons, and the very same word λαμβανει is used to express this circumstance by both historians. They both also represent these possessions as real, by the effects produced in the persons. The heathen king rages with fury through the influence of the demon, called the god Bacchus; the person in the text screams out, is greatly convulsed, and foams at the mouth. The case in the sacred text was certainly a real possession; and therefore when the Jews saw that, by the superior power of Christ, the demon was expelled, they were all astonished at the majesty of GOD!

Virgil has left us a description of a demoniacal possession of this kind, where the effects are nearly similar.

" ——— ait, deus, ecce, deus! cui talia fanti
" Ante fores, subito non voltus, non color unus,
" Non comptæ mansere comæ; sed pectus anhelum,
" Et rabie fera corda tument: majorque videri,
" Nec mortale sonans, adflata est numine quando
" Jam propiore Dei.———
" ——— At Phœbi nondum patiens immanis in antro
" Bacchatur vates, magnum si pectore possit

" Excussisse deum. Tanto magis ille fatigat
" Os rabidum, fera corda domans, fingitque premendo. ÆNEID 6.

" I feel the god, the rushing god! she cries—
" While thus she spoke, enlarged her features grew,
" Her colour chang'd, her locks dishevell'd flew;
" The heavenly tumult reigns in every part,
" Pants in her breast, and swells her rising heart;
" Still spreading to the sight, the priestess glow'd,
" And heav'd impatient of th' incumbent god.
" Then, to her inmost soul, by Phœbus fir'd,
" In more than human sounds she spoke inspir'd." PITT'S VIRGIL.

These are remarkable instances, and mutually reflect light on each other: the sacred historian explaining the profane, and the profane illustrating the sacred. I am indebted to Harmer's observations for many of the preceding illustrations of this singular subject, which I shall conclude with an extract from the life of the late Dr. Townson, by archdeacon Churton; it deserves the attention of every unprejudiced mind, as it places the hypothesis in a fair light, and is ably defended by the writer. It may be necessary to premise that it was Dr. Townson to whom Lord North addressed himself when the Divinity chair of the university of Oxford became vacant by the death of Dr. Wheeler, in 1783. Lord North, then chancellor of Oxford, thus writes to Dr. Townson: " Upon the death of Dr. Wheeler, the king commanded me to look out for a proper successor; by which words his majesty understood some person confessedly well-qualified for the Divinity chair, whose promotion should be acceptable to the public at large, and, particularly, to the university of Oxford. I have since endeavoured to execute his majesty's commands; and, after the most minute inquiries, I cannot find any person in the kingdom, who corresponds so exactly to his majesty's definition of a Divinity Professor, as Dr. Townson; a gentleman, whose character is universally beloved and esteemed, and whose general learning, and particular knowledge in theology, has been acknowledged in the most distinguished manner by the university where the professorship is now vacant. You will, therefore, I hope, give me an opportunity of acquiring credit to myself, of promoting theological knowledge, and of giving satisfaction to the public and to his majesty, by accepting a situation which, by the public testimony of the University of Oxford, and by the general consent of all who are acquainted with you, you are the properest person in England to fill.

(Signed) NORTH."

This character, then, so illustrious for learning and piety, on a special occasion, composed and used the following prayer by the desire of the sufferer.

" O Almighty and everlasting God! whose blessed Son Jesus Christ did give to his apostles and other ministers of his word, power over unclean spirits, grant, O Lord, that if any evil spirits have afflicted this thy servant, they may be driven away from him, and be suffered no more to hurt or come near him. Hear, O Lord, our humble supplication in the name and through the mediation of Jesus Christ our Lord. Amen."

On this prayer his excellent biographer remarks, that " Dr. Townson was well aware the hypothesis on which it proceeds, though consonant to the sentiments of our best divines, is not the current opinion of the day. But what is unfashionable is not always false. It is thought by some to be in all cases a sufficient proof that nothing beyond natural disease has happened, because, when by medical aid bodily health has been restored, the mind is again perfectly free and tranquil. He esteemed this argument by no means satisfactory. There are persons who will converse with you coolly and rationally on any subject whatever, who yet have occasionally propositions darted into their mind (as they believe and express themselves) as distinct from their own train of thoughts, as if they were pronounced by another person. To allege that the body occasions these things, is surely to assign an effect without a cause; or, which is the same thing, without an adequate cause; for it is not, I hope, the body that creates thoughts and forms propositions. To say again that the mind itself is the sole agent in the business, is to argue against the consciousness and conviction of that mind; for the person thus molested shall at the same instant be talking with you cheerfully on a subject totally different; shall be reading, or praying. If these momentary interruptions are seldom experienced but when the body is more or less indisposed, and cease when it has regained the full tone and vigour of health, this only shews that a disordered body was the predisposing occasion or organ, but does not prove it to have been the immediate or efficient cause. It will not be denied that there are malignant beings, who watch every opportunity, and eagerly seize every permitted mode, of assaulting us; and where then is the absurdity of supposing they may be able to harass us, when one part of the machine is disordered, in a different manner or degree, from what is in common cases possible, when the whole moves in perfect harmony? When a wicked monarch was troubled by a more wicked spirit, the melody of the harp composed and refreshed him, and he was well, and his foiled assailant departed from him. In what I have stated, I am assured, I represent facts; and I know, as to the probable cause of those facts, I express his sentiments, whose opinions, as well as actions, so far as it is material to record the one or the other, it is my duty to exhibit with all fidelity. We cannot pronounce with certainty what is merely natural disease, what demoniacal possession, and what the occasional molestation of the powers of darkness; for we have not, as bishop Newton has justly remarked on the subject, that miraculous gift, the discerning of spirits; but it is right surely to pray for deliverance from the more extraordinary degrees of temptation or trouble, as well as from those which are less uncommon; provided it be done with a condition expressed, that the case be what to us appears probable; and a better prayer for the purpose will not easily be devised, than that which precedes and occasioned these remarks."

Soon after my appointment to Dhuboy, I witnessed an extraordinary occurrence, and committed the particulars to paper a few hours after it happened.

The discovery of money and jewels, concealed in receptacles within the thick walls and subterraneous cells in oriental houses, is well known: such treasures are also frequently found in obscure spots in fields and gardens. A town is seldom conquered without such a discovery; and it is not uncommon to find similar deposits in the country. That such concealments were believed among the ancients, we learn from many historians; especially from an anecdote in Tacitus, respecting Nero becoming the dupe of fortune, and incurring the derision of the public, from believing the visionary schemes of Cesellius Bassus, a native of Carthage; a man of a crazed imagination, who relied on whatever occurred to him in his distempered dreams. This man arrived at Rome, and, by the influence of money well applied, gained admission to the emperor. The secret, which he had to communicate, was, that on his own estate he had found a cavern of astonishing depth, in which were contained immense stores of gold, not wrought into coin, but in rude and shapeless ingots, such as were used in the earliest ages: besides these were vast heaps and massive columns of pure gold; which were supposed to have been deposited there by Dido, when she fled from Tyre, and founded the city of Carthage. The result of the story is well known; I have only mentioned the anecdote in corroboration of existing circumstances in India; where, from time immemorial, it has been the custom for sovereigns and great men to make immense collections of gold and precious stones. The treasures belonging to some of the ancient Hindoo rajahs almost exceed belief. Nadir Shah's plunder at the court of Delhi excites our wonder; and the treasuries of the late Tipoo Sultaun afford a recent instance of these accumulations. The Iliad and Odyssey abound with descriptions of royal wealth; and sacred history informs us, that Hezekiah, king of Judah, shewed the ambassadors of the Babylonish monarch all the house of his precious things; the silver, the gold, and the spices; the precious ointments, and all the house of his armour.

But what comes nearest to the point in my own adventure is, an anecdote related by d'Herbelot, of a Persian king who, from want of attention to his finances, was reduced to great difficulties, and knew not how to replenish his exhausted exchequer. Walking one day in an unfrequented part of his palace, he saw a snake put his head out of a hole in the wall; on which he ordered it to be killed. His attendants accordingly broke down a part of the wall, in search of the serpent; it eluded their vigilance, but, in so doing, they discovered a secret receptacle, containing treasure to a great amount, which had been concealed there by another prince, and relieved the monarch from his necessities.

After this preamble, I have more courage in relating the adventure which occurred during a journey from Baroche to Dhuboy; when I stopped, with a small escort, for water and refreshments at Nurrah, a large ruined village about six miles from the capital. It had been plundered and burnt not long before, by the Mahratta cavalry, when general Goddard took Dhuboy. The principal house at Nurrah, a mansion far beyond the general style of Hindoo buildings, had belonged to a man of family and opulence, who emigrated during the war, and died in a distant country; the house and gardens were then in a state of desolation. I received private information, that under a particular tower in this mansion was a secret cell, known only to the owner and the mason who constructed it; that very man gave me the intelligence; adding it was purposely formed to contain his treasure without the knowledge of his family, and was afterwards closed with strong masonry.

We accompanied the informer through several spacious courts and extensive apartments, in a state of dilapidation, until we came to a dark closet in a tower, at one corner of the mansion:

this was a room about eight feet square, the diameter of the interior of the tower, some stories above the supposed receptacle of the treasure. In the floor of this closet we observed a hole in the bricks and chunam, of which it was composed, sufficiently large for a slender person to pass through. We enlarged the opening, and sent down two men by a ladder. After descending several feet they came to another chunam floor, with a similar aperture; this also being enlarged and torches procured, I perceived from the upper room that it was a gloomy dungeon of great depth. I desired the men to enter it and search for the treasure, which they positively refused, alleging that throughout Hindostan, wherever money was concealed, there existed one of the genii, in the mortal form of a snake, to guard it. I laughed at their credulity, and enforced the order for their immediate descent with some energy. My attendants sympathized in their feelings, and, under a deep impression of fear, seemed to wait the event in a sort of awful expectation. The ladder being too short to reach the floor of this subterraneous cell, I ordered strong ropes and additional torches to assist their descent. They at length reluctantly complied, and, by the lights held in their hands, during a slow progress down the ropes, we could distinguish, through the gloom, the dark sides and moist floor of the dungeon. They had not been many seconds in search of the treasure, when they called out vehemently that they were enclosed with a large snake, and their cries, ascending from this dismal abyss, were most horrible. I still remained incredulous, and would not suffer the ropes for facilitating their escape to be lowered until I had seen the serpent. Their screams were dreadful, and my resolution inflexible; until at length, by keeping the upper lights steady, I perceived something like billets of wood, or rather more resembling a ship's cable coiled up in a dark hold, seen from the deck; but no language can express my sensations of astonishment and terror, when I saw a horrid monster rear his head, over an immense length of body, coiled in volumes on the ground; and working itself into exertion by a sort of sluggish motion. What I felt on seeing two fellow creatures exposed by my orders to this "fiend of vengeful nature," I must leave to the reader's imagination. There was not a moment for reflection; down went the ropes, and we drew up the panting terrified wretches speechless; but, to my inexpressible joy, no otherwise affected than by the cold perspiration and death-like state produced by fear, which soon subsided. Some hay being then thrown down upon the lighted torches left in the cavern, consumed the mortal part of the guardian genius, as we afterwards took up the scorched and lifeless body of a large snake; but, notwithstanding a minute search, no money could be found. The proprietor had doubtless carried off his treasure when he fled to a foreign country. As the cells in the tower were all very small and deep, and the walls of strong masonry, it appears wonderful how this snake had subsisted. Toads have been discovered alive in the centre of large blocks of marble, without any aperture, and in the midst of a solid trunk of oak; how either those reptiles, or the coluber genii of India, subsist in their singular abode, I must leave to the investigation of the curious.

My upper servant, then with me at Nurrah, was of the Parsee tribe; an intelligent man, unprejudiced, and not tinctured with superstition. He told me that one of his countrymen at Surat, in repairing a house a few years before, had found a considerable sum of money in a similar receptacle; guarded in the same manner by a large cobra di capello, or hooded-snake, of which several persons were witnesses. This Parsee was a man of consequence, and head-broker to the Dutch factory at Surat. Such an accumulation of wealth made a great noise in the city; but instead of destroying the extraordinary centinel, he brought it a bason of milk, and burnt incense, which caused it to retire while he removed the treasure; one half of which he wisely presented to the nabob, and dedicated part of the remainder to charitable purposes. After this adventure he was considered to be a lucky man, and prospered in all his undertakings.

I wished very much for one of the ancient psylli, or a modern snake-charmer, in my train at Nurrah, to have called forth the serpent who had guarded the treasure confided to his care until its owner most probably carried it away, but forgot to liberate the centinel. Having acted faithfully in his trust, his life ought to have been spared. I have mentioned the power of music over the dancing-snakes at Bombay, and the fatal accident which ensued there; I have since had many opportunities of witnessing the effect of these charmers upon the serpents in Guzerat; my garden at Dhuboy was infested with them, and I have every reason to believe they were attracted from it to follow these musicians. It may appear extraordinary in Europe, but as I have already observed, there is an allusion to it in the Hebrew poetry; and the ancients were doubtless well acquainted with their power, if any such they possess. Medea is said to have charmed the dragon which guarded the golden fleece by the melody of her voice; and similar effects are mentioned in Virgil's Æneid:

> " Vipereo generi, et graviter spirantibus hydris
> " Spargere, qui somnos cantûque manûque solebat,
> " Mulcebatque iras, et morsus arte levabat.
>
> " His wand and holy words the viper's rage,
> " And venom'd wound of serpents could assuage." DRYDEN'S VIRGIL.

Herodotus mentions that in the vicinity of Thebes there were sacred serpents not at all troublesome to men; and also that in the citadel of Athens there was a large serpent in the temple which continually defended it; and of this they had such an entire conviction, that they offered it every month cakes of honey, which were always consumed. Bryant observes that the symbolical worship of the serpent was in the first ages very extensive, and was introduced into all the mysteries wherever celebrated.

Dr. Buchanan, describing his journey through the Mysore, says that he was shewn the pit where Sedasiva, who flourished there in the fifteenth century, and erected a temple to Iswara at Kilida, found a treasure, and a sword, which were the commencement of his good fortune. "To this spot he was conducted by a naga, " or hooded serpent, sent for the purpose by some propitious deity. " While Sedasiva was a asleep in a field, the naga came, and " shaded his head from the sun, by raising up as an umbrella its " large flat neck. The young man was awaked by a shriek from " his mother, who in looking after her son found him under the " power of the monster. He immediately started up to escape,

" but was opposed by the serpent, until he consented to follow " it quietly, and was conducted to the place where the treasure was " hid. Here the snake began to bite the ground, and make signs; " at length Sedasiva, having dug into the earth, found a cave filled " with treasure, and containing a sword. Such are the fables by " which the Hindoo chiefs endeavour to gain the admiration and " respect of their countrymen, whose credulity indeed renders the " means very adequate to the end proposed."

Among other curious circumstances in my administration of justice at Dhuboy, I was sometimes obliged to admit of the ordeal trial. In the first instance a man was accused of stealing a child covered with jewels, which is a common mode of adorning infants among the wealthy Hindoos. Many circumstances appeared against him, on which he demanded the ordeal: it was a measure to which I was very averse, but at the particular request of the Hindoo arbitrators, who sat on the carpet of justice, and especially at the earnest entreaty of the child's parents, I consented. A cauldron of boiling oil was brought into the durbar, and after a short ceremony by the brahmins, the accused person, without shewing any anxiety, dipped his hand to the bottom, and took out a small silver coin, which I still preserve in remembrance of this transaction. He did not appear to have sustained any damage, or to suffer the smallest pain; but the process went on no further, as the parents declared themselves perfectly convinced of his innocence.

In a former chapter I related some particulars respecting the ordeal trial on the Malabar coast, where it is much used. During my abode among the northern Hindoos I found it universally credited, and more or less used under all the governments in Guzerat. They are permitted to practise it in several different modes, both under their own rajahs, and the Mahomedan princes. These ordeals are by fire, water, poison, rice, the balance, and boiling oil. I have already described the trials by water, and by rice, I shall now confine my remarks to that by boiling oil, as being most customary in the Dhuboy districts, and the only method which came under my own observation.

In general, on the day appointed for the trial, many religious ceremonies are used by the brahmins, and the prisoner; the vessel is consecrated, and the ground on which the fire is lighted, is previously covered with cow-dung; a substance much employed in religious ceremonies by the Hindoos. When the oil is sufficiently heated, a leaf of the holy pippal (ficus-religiosa) is put into the vessel, and when it has evidently felt the effect of the fire, a solemn prayer is offered by the superior brahmin; the accused is then ordered to take out the ring or coin which had been placed at the bottom of the vessel. There are some instances where the prisoner has been terribly burnt; and there are many others, equally well attested, where the hand and arm received no injury.

Voltaire, in writing on the ancient ordeal in Europe, says, that in the dark ages they were possessed of a secret to pass unhurt through many of these singular trials; especially that of plunging in boiling water, which consisted in rubbing the body over with spirit of vitriol and alum mixed with the juice of onions. Whether this was efficacious in those days I leave to the determination of antiquarians; in the Malabar ordeals, especially those permitted by the English government, I know that every possible care was taken to prevent deception.

The practice called *Dherna,* is not only known, but used in many places in Guzerat; it appears to me as singular as any custom among the *Bhauts,* or any other extraordinary people among whom my lot was cast; and seldom did a day pass without my hearing something extraordinary concerning them. As I cannot describe the *dherna* from my own experience, I shall introduce lord Teignmouth's account of it, as another instance of the wonderful power the brahmins have obtained over the minds of the Hindoos.

"The inviolability of a brahmin is a fixed principle of the Hindoos; and to deprive him of life, either by direct violence, or by causing his death in any mode, is a crime which admits of no expiation. To this principle may be traced the practice called *dherna,* which may be translated *caption,* or *arrest.* It is used by the brahmins to gain a point which cannot be accomplished by any other means; and the process is as follows. The brahmin who adopts this expedient for the purpose mentioned, proceeds to the door or house of the person against whom it is directed, or wherever he may most conveniently intercept him; he there sits down in *dherna,* with poison, or a poignard, or some other instrument of suicide, in his hand; and threatening to use it if his adversary should attempt to molest or pass him, he thus completely arrests him. In this situation the brahmin fasts; and by the rigour of the etiquette, which is rarely infringed, the unfortunate object of his arrest ought also to fast; and thus they both remain until the institutor of the *dherna* obtains satisfaction. In this, as he seldom makes the attempt without resolution to persevere, he rarely fails: for if the party thus arrested were to suffer the brahmin sitting in *dherna*, to perish by hunger, the sin would for ever lie upon his head. This practice has been less frequent of late years, since the institution of the court of justice at Benares in 1783; but the interference of that court, and even that of the resident there, has occasionally proved insufficient to check it; as it has been deemed in general most prudent to avoid for this purpose the use of coercion, from an apprehension that the first appearance of it might drive the sitter in dherna to suicide. The discredit of the act would not only fall upon the officers of justice, but upon the government itself. The practice of sitting in dherna is not confined to male brahmins only; as is proved and exemplified in the conduct of *Beenoo Bhai*, the widow of a man of the brahminical tribe."

The same intelligent writer mentions another singular and cruel custom called the *koor*. This term is explained to mean a circular pile of wood, which is prepared ready for conflagration; upon this, sometimes a cow, and sometimes an old woman, is placed by the constructors of the pile; and the whole is consumed together. The object of this practice is to intimidate the officers of government, or others, from importunate demands; as the effect of the sacrifice is supposed to involve in great sin the person whose conduct forces the constructor of the koor to this expedient. A woman who had been placed upon the *Khoor* in a dispute between three brahmins in the province of Benares, was saved by the timely interposition of authority, and the attainment of the object by the temporary intimidation. She was summoned to appear before the English superintendant of the province, but absolutely refused to attend him; declaring that she would throw herself into the first well, rather than submit. She was nearly blind from age, and the summons was not enforced."

The conduct of the bhauts and brahmins at Neriad, which I have particularly mentioned in the campaign in Guzerat, was exactly similar to the khoor described by lord Teignmouth, and proceeded from the peshwa of the Mahrattas making what they deemed an unjust demand.

Many other extraordinary customs prevailed in the purgunnas under my charge; which I do not particularize, from a consciousness that in England they would have a very suspicious appearance.

The cremation of Hindoo widows with the bodies of their deceased husbands, is now no longer doubted; but, it is more difficult to believe, that men in the prime of life, and surrounded by every blessing, should voluntarily desire to immolate themselves to their deities, and be buried alive; which is no uncommon sacrifice among the tribe of Gosannees and other Hindoo devotees. A short time before I took charge of Dhuboy, a young man insisted on being interred alive near the temple at the Gate of Diamonds; and soon afterwards another performed the same sacrifice about half a mile without the English districts, because I refused him permission to do it in his native village; for neither is this self-immolation, the cremation of women, nor any other act of suicide allowed of within the company's territories. These solemn sacrifices are always performed in the presence of many witnesses, and during the celebration of various religious rites and ceremonies by the brahmins.

On such a sacrifice being announced, a large crowd assemble;

a round pit is dug, of a depth sufficient for a man to stand upright, into which the self-devoted victim descends, and the earth is gradually thrown on, until it entirely covers him. A tomb of solid masonry is immediately erected over his head, and solemn rites and flowery offerings are performed at stated periods, in memory of a saint who is supposed to have rendered an acceptable sacrifice to the destructive power, or some other deity in the Hindoo mythology.

In some particular castes, the Hindoo widows, instead of burning themselves on the funeral pile of their husbands, are buried alive with the dead body. The deluded female, with the utmost composure, seats herself near the deceased in an upright posture; when the earth is gently filled around her, until it reaches her mouth; it is then thrown on in large quantities, that she may be the sooner suffocated.

Instances occur of the Suttee, or Hindoo widow who has thus devoted herself to death, being reclaimed; but they are very uncommon. Sir Charles Malet has communicated to me an event of this kind, which happened during his embassy at Poonah, on the 5th of September 1792, as related in the following extract from his diary.

" An extraordinary incident happened this day. A sepoy of my guard, of the *Mharatta*, or *Columbee* tribe, died; his wife immediately declared herself a suttee; that is, resolved to devote herself to the flames with his body: she accordingly assumed the yellow garment, the turban, the mirror, and all other insignia usual on such occasions. When informed of her resolution, I desired the officer of the guard, captain H——, to endeavour to divert the suttee from her intention, and in case of failure to acquaint me with the result. He soon communicated his despair of success, and I desired her to be brought to me.

"I found her a healthy young woman, about twenty-two years of age, in a state of mind firmly resolved on sacrificing herself with her dead husband, whom she incessantly and passionately invoked, with every endearing expression. The scene was singular and affecting: I scarce knew how to commence the difficult task of soothing grief so poignant, or of diverting a resolution founded on despair. In the course of my endeavours I found the poor suttee had no relations at Poonah; her father and mother lived in her native village, at some distance. I discovered likewise that her husband's death had exposed her to the dread of absolute distress. The first subject furnished a strong counteracting power to the passionate grief that possessed her mind, and by proper application awakened a new sensation: which, followed up, produced a flood of tears, the first symptom of relaxation from determined grief; such as must have been the despairing sorrow of Niobe! A counteracting passion being thus excited, the dread of distress was soothed by assurances, properly introduced, of maintenance in the means of devoting her future life to the discharge of religious ceremonies at the shrine of her household gods, in honour of her husband's memory; which would be more grateful to the gods, and acceptable to him, than sacrificing herself on his pyreal pile.

"After these and a variety of other arguments, which occupied nearly three hours, in the course whereof gentle restraint was sometimes imposed on occasional fits of passion and anguish, she was at length persuaded to suspend her fatal purpose, until the arrival of her parents; to whom a messenger was dispatched in her presence, with a letter, and money for the expenses of their journey to the capital. The Hindoos attach the merit of the most sublime and holy heroism to this self-devotion; but the resolution once suspended, is seldom resumed, and was not in the present instance.

"I am sorry to remark, that I really believe the Hindoo spectators were rather grieved and mortified, than pleased at our success in saving this poor creature from the flames."

These human immolations shock an Englishman in every point of view: animal sacrifices are no longer common on the Hindoo altars; but the morning offering of fruit, flowers, and meal, to the benevolent deities, create a pleasing sensation in the mind of the worshipper, the priest, and the European spectator; the latter at least beholds an innocent and grateful sacrifice, the brahmin finds it a beneficial one, and the humble devotee rejoices in having performed his daily duty at the altar of gratitude, for blessings daily enjoyed.

I am not certain whether the Hindoos have any religious ceremony, or libation, before their meals, like the libamina of the Romans, or the Christian's grace; that ablution precedes their repast is well known; it is also introduced among the Mahomedans, and adopted by some Europeans. Although, after a dusty journey among the Hindoo villages in my districts, I might neither drink out of their cups, nor wash my hands in their basons, yet would the women gently pour water from their jars into my hands, contracted into the form of a cup; and held sloping to the mouth: this is a common method for the Indians of different castes to take water from each other. Pouring water over the hands to wash, instead of dipping them into a bason, has been always an oriental custom; we frequently meet with it in ancient manners. Elisha poured water upon the hands of his master Elijah: Moses washed Aaron with water, and poured the anointing oil upon his head, to sanctify him. When I dined with the Dutch governor at Cochin, three female slaves, neatly dressed, attended each of the guests before the dinner was put on the table; one girl held a silver bason decked with flowers, to contain the water, which another poured upon his hands, from a silver vase; and a third offered a clean napkin on a salver. At the English tables two servants attend after dinner, with a gindey and ewer, of silver or white copper; the former is adorned with fresh-gathered flowers, stuck in a perforated cover, to conceal the water which is poured from the latter over the hands of each guest.

Whether the Hindoos annex any sacred idea to salt, I am not certain; the Mahomedans assuredly do throughout Asia. It is common among all the castes of India, and adopted by the English, to say of an ungrateful or perfidious man, that "he is not worth his salt." It is a sacred pledge of hospitality among all the followers of the prophet. Numerous instances occur of travellers in Arabia, after being plundered and stripped by the wandering tribes of the desert, claiming the protection of some civilized Arab, who, after once receiving him into his tent, and giving him salt, instantly relieves his distress, and never forsakes his guest until he is placed in safety. The tale of the forty thieves in the Arabian Nights Entertainment, presents a singular instance of the effect of eating salt, even in the mind of a robber and a murderer. When Morgiana, the faithful slave of Ali Baba, had in the character of a dancer struck a dagger in the heart of a merchant, his guest, and excited the horror of her master for such an act, she threw off her disguise, and told Ali Baba, that in the pretended merchant Coja Hussain, she had destroyed his cruel enemy, the captain of the robbers: to convince him of the truth of her assertion she discovered under his robe the murdering poignard, and asked her master this simple question, which caused *her* suspicion of his pretended friend: "Do you not recollect that he refused to eat salt with you? Can you require a stronger proof of his malicious intentions?"

This Arabian story is confirmed by a real anecdote in d'Herbelot, of Jacoub ben Laith, then a celebrated robber, but afterwards the founder of a dynasty of Persian monarchs, called Soffarides; who in one of his exploits having broken into the royal palace, and collected a large booty, was on the point of carrying it off, when he found his foot kick against something which made him stumble. Imagining it might be an article of value, he put it to his mouth, the better to distinguish it. On tasting he found it was a lump of salt, the symbol and pledge of hospitality; on which, he was so touched, that he retired immediately without carrying away any part of the spoil. The next morning occasioned the greatest surprise in the palace; Jacoub was taken up and brought before the prince, to whom he gave a faithful account of the whole transaction, and by this means so ingratiated himself with his sovereign, that he employed him, as a man of courage and genius, in many arduous enterprizes; in which he was so successful as to be raised to the command of his troops; whose confidence and affection to their general, made them, on the prince's death, prefer his interest to that of the heir to the throne, from whence he afterwards spread his extensive conquests.

Salt was equally emblematical and sacred among the Greeks; Homer says " they sprinkle sacred salt from lifted urns."

> " With water purify their hands, and take
> " The sacred offering of the salted cake." ILIAD.

Drinking water in an Arab's tent has the same good effect as eating salt. It was so in the time of the crusades, when the sultaun Saladine allowed his prisoner Lusignan, king of Jerusalem, to drink water in his presence; on the captive monarch offering the cup to one of his lords, equally thirsty, the sultaun prevented his drinking, because he meant to put him to death. However we may view the transaction in a political light, it adds no honour to Jael's character, that she treacherously murdered an unfortunate prince who had fled to her tent for protection; and " when he asked for water, she gave him milk; and brought forth butter in a lordly dish."

CHAPTER XXV.

STATEMENT OF THE CULTIVATION, PRODUCE, AND REVENUE, IN THE PURGUNNA OF DHUBOY AND SUBORDINATE DISTRICTS; WITH SKETCHES OF THE ZEMINDARS, REVENUE-OFFICERS, AND ABUSES IN THE REVENUE DEPARTMENT.

1781.

> Such themes as these, the rural Maro sung
> To wide imperial Rome, in the full height
> Of elegance and taste, by Greece refin'd.
> In ancient times, the sacred plough employ'd
> The kings and awful fathers of mankind:
> They held the scale of empire, rul'd the storm
> Of mighty war; then, with victorious hand,
> Disdaining little delicacies, seiz'd
> The plough; and, greatly independent, liv'd! THOMSON.

CONTENTS.

General state of agriculture in Guzerat—soil—produce—various crops—cotton—batty--juarree--bahjaree, and smaller grains—shrubs and seeds for oil—palma-christi—bhang—tobacco—betel—poppy, opium—sugar-cane—double crops—enclosures—morning beauties in India—best mode of preserving health—Guzerat villages described—tanks and wells—allusions in scripture to living waters and verdant scenery—hospitality to travellers in Guzerat—peasantry—right of landed property—mode of cultivation, and appropriation of the produce—massaulchee—illustration of a parable—washerman—cullies, or farm yards—oppression of the zemindars—Hindoo and Mosaic charities—unfavourable traits in the brâhmin character, and the Hindoo religion—human sacrifices—contrasted with Christianity—reflections on this subject—jughires and different tenures in Guzerat—scale of oriental despotism—anecdote of cruel oppression at Tatta—Mahratta cruelty in the sheep-skin death—Dr. Robertson, on landed property in India—extracts from Wilks's History of Mysore—Hindoo bill of sale of land—lease of land at Baroche—instructions on taking charge of Dhuboy—minute respecting landed property, and farming in Guzerat—remark from Bombay—replication from Baroche—conclusion in favour of leases to respectable farmers in India.

CHAPTER XXV.

THE administration of justice, collection of the revenues, and superintendence of the districts under my charge, especially during the seasons of seed-time and harvest, required frequent excursions into the country, and afforded me an opportunity of observing the state of agriculture in the Guzerat province, and the manners and customs of the peasants in some of its remote purgunnas. In that delightful part of Hindostan are "no antres vast, nor deserts idle," all is fertility and plenty; the soil, generally rich and loamy, produces valuable harvests of batty, juarree, bahjerce, and other grain, with cotton, shrubs for oil, and plants for dying. Many parts yield a double crop, particularly the rice and cotton-fields, which are both planted at the commencement of the rainy season, in June. The former is sown in furrows, and reaped in about three months: the cotton shrub, which grows to the height of three or four feet, and in verdure resembles the currant-bush, requires a longer time to bring its delicate produce to perfection. They are planted between the rows of rice, but do not impede its growth, or prevent its being reaped. Soon after the rice harvest is over, the cotton-bushes put forth a beautiful yellow flower, with a crimson eye in each petal; this is succeeded by a green pod filled with a white stringy pulp; the pod turns brown and hard as it ripens, and then separates into two or three divisions, containing the cotton. A luxuriant field, exhibiting at the same time the expanding blossom, the bursting capsule, and the snowy flakes of ripe cotton, is one of the most beautiful objects in the agriculture of Hindostan. Herodotus says, the Indians, in his time, possessed a kind of plant, which instead of fruit, produced wool of a finer and better quality than that of sheep, of which the natives made their clothes: this plant was no doubt the same as the (gossypium, Lin.) or modern cotton of India. The medium price of this valuable commodity when I was at Baroche and Dhuboy was from seventy to eighty rupees the candy, or from eight to nine pounds sterling for seven hundred and forty English pounds weight of cotton. Batty, or rice, from eighty to ten rupees a culsey, a weight equal to six hundred pounds; most of the other grains in Guzerat were of a similar value.

Juarree, or cush-cush, (holcus-sorghum, Lin.) is a fine large grain, growing to the height of eight or ten feet: each ear contains many hundred seeds, sometimes two thousand; the stem generally bears more than one head of corn, but the uppermost is always one of those royal ears, which, like the largest head of the heliotrope, greatly exceeds the rest in size and beauty. This grain in many respects resembles the maiz and guinea-corn, and forms a chief article of food in the Guzerat province.

Bahjeree (holcus spicatus, Lin.) is another valuable grain, growing in the manner of the juarree; of an inferior size, and only eaten by the poor. Providence has been peculiarly bountiful to the natives of Guzerat, in a variety of other useful grains. Codra,

[illegible] NS [illegible] ZERAT.

[illegible] DUTA [illegible] [illegible]

3 CODRA, [illegible] 4 CHINA. [illegible]

chena, buntee, and bowtah, all of a nutritious quality, and grateful to the peasants, are planted in June, and the harvest is finished in September: they are generally two or three feet high; when ripe, their golden, purple, and varied tints, give the country a rich apapearance; as do the leguminous classes, of tuar, mutt, gram, and other pulses. Tuar (cytisus cajan, Lin.) when taken from the skin, like the split pea, is called dohll, and forms, with rice, a principal part of the best Indian dishes. Mutt, and gram, (dolichos-biflorus, Lin.) are the most nutritious food for cattle: the Guzerat cows are very fond of the capaussia, or cotton-seed; it makes them give abundance of rich milk, and costs only four or five rupees the culsey. The large villages breed a number of milch-cows and buffaloes, as ghee, or clarified butter, for foreign consumption is a principal staple in the Guzerat markets. They also rear the best oxen for the service of the vanjarrahs, or merchants, so often mentioned, who travel with large caravans of these animals; they are also bred in many parts of Hindostan, for the purpose of transporting salt and other merchandize from the sea-coasts, to the interior towns at a distance. They will carry a load, according to their size and strength, from two to three hundred pounds, and travel ten or twelve miles a day for a great length of time. The food of these animals is straw, grass, capaussia, and oil-cakes, after the oil is expressed from the nuts.

The variety of shrubs and plants which are cultivated for oil in that part of India, add much to its general beauty. The natives never burn candles, and in the inland districts, where the cocoanut does not thrive, large tracts are set apart for the seeds from which they extract oil: those in the greatest esteem are the gingeli, or Sesamum; and the erinda, ricinus Palma-christi. The latter oil is used medicinally with great success; an outward application of the leaves is often efficacious; when previously heated, and rubbed with oil, I have known it to give great relief in the gout. The consumption of vegetable oils for many millions of lamps which are lighted every night, for anointing the body, culinary purposes, and religious ceremonies, is very great throughout the whole of India, where I believe animal oil is never used.

Mustard-seed is in great estimation for pickles, and similar purposes, but more so for its oil, which is expressed in great abundance. Hemp and flax are cultivated by many villages, not for the fibres, converted in Europe to such valuable manufactures; they are thrown away, or burnt as useless: but for the valuable oil produced from the seeds, and an intoxicating drug called *bhang*. The usual mode of expressing the oil from the different seeds is to put them into a cylindrical trough, or large mortar; a bullock driven round the simple machine, keeps the pestle in action, until the oil is extracted; after which, the remainder forms a nutritious food for horned cattle. Besides the annual plants for this purpose, the mawah, and some other large ornamental trees, produce nuts and fruit, from which they obtain oil of a good quality.

Tobacco is cultivated in most parts of India; it requires a good soil, and attains the height of two or three feet. The hairy stalk is covered with large leaves, which are carefully picked off when they change colour and scent the air; they are then dried in the shade, and preserved for use. Tobacco is an annual plant, of delicate appearance; the blossoms of a pale rose colour, and

The MAHWHAW Tree of GUZERAT.

W. Hooker fecit — Jam. Forbes Bhaderpoor 1782.

sometimes of a darker tint, grow in clusters, like the cowslip, at the top of a stately stem, abundantly enriched with leaves of varied and beautiful verdure. This plant, so common throughout India, Persia, and China, is doubtless indigenous to Asia, as well as to America.

The areca, or betel-nut tree, does not thrive in Guzerat. Betel-leaf (piper betel, Lin.) so highly esteemed by the natives, is cultivated in most of the Indian provinces; abundantly so in Guzerat. I have already mentioned it, and shall here only observe, that this beautiful creeper climbs upon small poles, like hops; a betel-garden, kept free from weeds, and well watered, is a beautiful object. The cooler the situation, the more luxuriant are the plants; for which reason the gardeners often raise a clump of plantain trees at the end of each bed, as they are known to cause additional coolness in the atmosphere. The betel requires constant care; it does not attain perfection until the fourth year; but continues to repay the cultivator's trouble, for at least six or seven years, by a plentiful crop of leaves, which are always a staple commodity in the bazar. The betel is produced by cuttings, planted four or five in a hole, and from the first requires great attention.

Ginger and turmeric abound in the Dhuboy purgunna: like the betel, they are planted in rows in large gardens, from cuttings of the roots, put into the earth at the commencement of the rainy season; in December and January following they are ready for taking up and drying. There are a few poppy-gardens in Guzerat; the natives are fond of mixing the seeds in cakes and confections. The opium poppy (papaver somniferum, Lin.) thrives best in Malwa, and is a great article in the commerce of Eujeen. The opium oozes from incisions made at the top of the plant, in a white milky juice; which, when congealed, is gathered for sale, and frequently adulterated. Opium from the poppy is a drug perfectly distinct from bhang, which is made from the hemp already mentioned. Both are used as a substitute for spirituous liquors; their intoxicating effects are very similar, and equally injurious to the constitution.

The sugar-cane grows to the height of eight or nine feet, with a spreading tuft of leaves; the cane is three or four inches in circumference. Like the bamboo, and other arundinaceous plants, it is intersected by numerous joints, which do not impede the circulation. The stem, covered with a hard rind, contains a spongy pith, full of juice; which in Bengal, Java, and other places is manufactured into sugar; in the western provinces of India it is seldom brought to such perfection. The natives either purchase foreign sugar, or are content with jaggree, a coarse kind of molasses made from the boiled juice of the cane; it is also cut into small pieces, and sold, like fruit, in the bazar. Honey, wax, drugs, and a variety of medicinal plants, are produced, more or less, throughout Hindostan.

It is necessary to make a distinction between the double crops in the agriculture of Guzerat, and the double harvests in the Concan and Malabar. I have just mentioned two respective crops of rice and cotton, in the same field, in Guzerat. The two harvests in Malabar, during my residence in Travencore, were exactly as Dr. Fryer has described them in the style of the seventeenth century: “ At the period when the rains invade India, they put a stop to journeying, voyaging, and all warlike operations, until the middle of August, when the earth is discovered,' and the rice begins to ripen; all this while it floated in the water, which it rejoices in. This is the first harvest, natural and uncompelled, because of the rain. The other crop ripens about March, with great pains of bringing water by gutters into their sown-fields: which, notwithstanding, yields not so plentiful a crop as the first."

The lands in the Dhuboy districts are generally more enclosed than the Baroche purgunna; the hedges, frequently shaded by large mango and tamarind trees, are formed by different kinds of euphorbia, and a variety of bushes, shrubs, and creeping plants, in the rainy season profusely covered with blossoms of every mingled hue, which they more or less preserve through a few succeeding months. Their early fragrance is delicious; the nightly dews, impregnated by the odours, exhale their short-lived sweets, and render a morning walk delightful. Those who do not *then* enjoy them, may truly say,

> We lose the prime, to mark how spring
> The tender plants, how blooms the citron grove,
> What drops the myrrh, and what the balmy reed;
> How nature paints her colours, how the bee
> Sits on the bloom, extracting liquid sweet. MILTON

Such beauties are lost on those who do not rise at an early hour in India: the heat soon becomes too powerful for rural excursions. It is late in the evening before the atmosphere becomes cool; the plants have lost their freshness, and every thing appears through a different medium.

My first improvement in the garden at Dhuboy, was to make

a bathing room, under an umbrageous banian-tree, close to the principal well. Bathing is generally considered to be one of the greatest luxuries in India. Early rising, the cold bath, a morning walk, temperate meals, an evening ride, and retiring soon to rest, are the best rules for preserving health in India; and, wherever circumstances permitted, this pleasing routine was my general practice. An amiable medical writer has since given the same advice to the British youth in India, clothed in the pleasing dress of poetry.

" The peaceful evening draws her sober shade
    Round the green summits of Malaya's hills;
While meek-ey'd Contemplation, pensive maid!
    My bosom with a secret rapture fills.

The gentle sea-breeze scarce is heard to blow,
    The tall areca waves no more its head,
The shady plantain in the vale below
    Hangs pensive o'er the modest Hindoo's shed.

Beneath the humble roof, their frugal meal
    Behold Hindostan's tawny sons prepare;
No wish for other dainties do they feel,
    Than their own simple vegetable fare.

Rash youth, beware! advice attend:
Soon as Aurora gilds the eastern skies,
    And birds in pearly dew their plumage lave,
Dispel your slumbers, from your couch arise,
    And fearless plunge into the briny wave.

Next where the towering hills their umbrage lend,
    And fragrant champahs scent the morning gale,
On the swift steed your devious courses bend,
    And health from every passing breeze inhale.

But when the sun, with fierce meridian ray,
    Pours the bright torrent of ethereal fire,
When ravening birds, and prowling beasts of prey,
    Seek the green shade, or to the den retire;

Then, stretch'd at ease in plantain-shelter'd bower,
    Poetic fiction, or the classic page,
May oft beguile the tedious sultry hour,
    And the ripe cocoa's juice his thirst assuage.

——— Observe the Hindoo, whose untutor'd mind,
    All false seductive luxury disdains;
To nature's wants his wishes are confined,
    While Health her empire o'er his frame maintains.

His modes of life, by ancient sages plann'd,
    To suit the temper of his burning skies,
He, who the climate's rage would long withstand,
    Will wisely imitate, nor e'er despise!" J. Johnson.

The villages in the Dhuboy purgunna generally consist of thatched cottages, built of mud, and a few brick houses, with tiled roofs; a small dewal, a mosque, and sometimes a choultree, are the only public buildings. Near the large villages there is generally a tank, or lake, where the rain is collected, for the use of the cattle in the dry season; when, for the space of eight months, not a shower falls, and no water is to be met with except in these reservoirs: they are often enclosed with strong masonry, and their banks adorned by banian, mango, and tamarind-trees, to shade the weary traveller, and lessen evaporation. The tanks are constructed at the expense of government, or by an assessment on the villages; they also contribute to the masonry of a good well, and cistern for the cattle, when the large reservoirs fail. Sometimes these useful works are private acts of charity from a rich individual, as instanced in the noble works of Govindsett, in the Concan. Large wells, with a grand flight of steps down to the water, are not uncommon in remote situations where travellers, merchants, and caravans are obliged to pass, far from other supplies.

These are unspeakable blessings in the torrid zone, and have consequently been celebrated in the songs of the oriental poets, and in the sacred page; where we find the most beautiful and natural allusions to refreshing fountains and sacred groves happily illustrating spiritual joys. "The glorious Lord will be unto us a place of broad rivers and streams; in the wilderness, waters shall break forth, and streams in the desert; the parched ground shall become a pool, and the thirsty land springs of water. When the poor and needy seek for water, and there is none, and their tongue faileth for thirst, I, the Lord, will hear them; I, the God of Israel, will not forsake them; I will open rivers in high-places, and fountains in the midst of vallies; I will plant in the wilderness the cedar, the myrtle, and the oil-tree; I will set in the desert the fir-tree, the pine, and the box-tree."

Those trees are not indigenous to Hindostan, but my districts afforded as great a variety: mangos and tamarinds were planted near the villages, for general use, or were the property of individuals, who enjoyed their produce, after a small deduction for government. In a plentiful season, at Dhuboy, a culsey, or six hundred pounds weight of good mangos sell for one rupee; poor as well as rich enjoy the golden produce; birds, bats, and monkeys partake of that bounty, which "spreads a common feast for all that live."

Hospitality to travellers prevails throughout Guzerat; a person of any consideration passing through the province, is presented at the entrance of a village, with fruit, milk, butter, firewood, and earthen-pots for cookery; the women and children offer him wreaths of flowers. Small bowers are constructed on convenient spots, at a distance from a well or lake, where a person is maintained by the nearest villages, to take care of the water-jars, and supply all travellers gratis. There are particular villages, where the inhabitants compel all travellers to accept of one day's provisions; whether they be many or few, rich or poor, European or native, they must not refuse the offered bounty.

Thus contented and happy do the peasantry live in that garden of India, when war keeps at a distance, and their pundits and collectors do not treat them with severity; even to that they habitually submit, for they have no idea of liberty, as it is felt and enjoyed by Britons. As well may you talk of colour to the blind, or the harmony of sound to the deaf, as liberty, patriotism, and the nobler virtues, to the inhabitants of Asia, under the political and religious systems to which they have hitherto been accustomed.

The mode of apropriating the land, and collecting the revenues in Guzerat, is in many respects similar to that of the ancient Germans, on their emerging from Gothic barbarism, when the property of land was invested in the tribe or nation, and a portion of corn was allotted to every individual, by the magistrate; and corresponded to the number of his family, the degrees of his merit, and the importance of his services. Yet he derived no source of power, or influence, from a territorial property which he could not bequeath to his successor.

Thus it is in Hindostan: the lands appropriated to each village belong to the government; the ryots or peasants, who cultivate the fields, under the orders and inspection of the patell, or superior of the village, are in a manner attached to the spot. The cattle for the plough, and other services of husbandry, are sometimes the common stock of the village, oftener the property of individuals. The patell provides seed and implements of agriculture, takes care that such as are able cultivate the land, and at the time of settling the jummabunda, or harvest-agreement, with the collector of the revenue, allots to each family their portion of grain, or a share of the money for which it has been sold; according to the number of the family, the quantity of their cattle, and the extent of the land they have cultivated. Some particular fields, called pysita and vajcessa lands, are set apart in each village for public purposes; varying, perhaps, as to the mode of application, in different districts; but in most the produce of these lands is appropriated to the maintenance of the brahmins, the cazee, washerman, smith, barber, and the lame, blind, and helpless; as also to the support of a few vertunnees, or armed men, who are kept for the defence of the village, and to conduct travellers in safety from one village to another. An English reader may perhaps be surprized to see the barber in the list of pensioners: there is seldom more than one in each village; he shaves the inhabitants gratis; and as he has no exercise in the day, it is his province at night to carry a mussaul, or torch, to light travellers on the road, or for any other purpose required; no time remaining for him to attend to husbandry or to provide for his family, it is but just he should be maintained at the public expense; this is also to be applied to the washerman and the smith, who work for the village, without any other emolument. In some places, particularly in Mysore, there is an appropriation of grain to the saktis, or destructive spirits; and perhaps to many other deities who may be the objects of hope or fear in the worship of the villagers.

The occupation of massaulchee, or torch-bearer, although generally allotted to the village barber, in the purgunnas under my charge, may vary in other districts. The massaul, or torch, in India, is composed of coarse rags, rolled up to the size of an English flambeau, eighteen or twenty inches long, fixed in a brass handle: this is carried in the left hand; in the right the massaulchee holds a brass vessel containing the oil, with which he feeds the flame as occasion requires. By these means a bright extensive light is kept up. A great number of torch-bearers are assembled at the Hindoo festivals, especially weddings; they give a brilliant effect to the spectacle, and illustrate the parable of the ten virgins. It is introduced in another place, though not for the purpose of mentioning the mode of supplying the oil, which is thus clearly ascertained. The wise virgins took oil in the vessels with their lamps; the foolish omitting that necessary store, their vessels failed them when they most needed a supply. I have sometimes, during a midnight journey in the ravines and nullahs between Baroche and Dhuboy, infested by wild beasts, and wilder men, been in a perilous situation from a failure of oil in a tract where there were no villages to replenish the vessels.

It may appear equally extraordinary to an European to see the washerman mentioned among those who have a stipulated portion of grain. The Hindoo females in general do not wash either their own or their husbands' clothes: a public washerman, attached to each village, performs that office, which I believe is hereditary in his family; and for this duty he receives his portion of grain from the *cullies.* The washing in India, both for Europeans and natives, is performed without doors; if possible near a running stream; if not, on the margin of a lake, where the linen is beat violently against flat stones, or large blocks of wood, placed for the purpose: this mode of cleansing soon destroys the linens of Europe; but has no bad effect on the Indian cottons.

The *cullies* just noticed, are farm-yards, or receptacles at the different villages, for the general produce of the lands at the close of harvest. There the cotton, oil-seeds, and all kinds of grain are accumulated for the inspection of the zemindars, and officers of government, previous to the assessment for the revenue, and usual appropriations. The cully contains the thrashing floor, where the corn is trampled upon by oxen, the immemorial custom in the east. Here also are large receptacles for cotton, formed by digging holes in the earth, lined with cow-dung, and filled with cotton as picked from the bushes; which are then covered with clods of dried earth, rubbed over with a cement of cow-dung, to preserve the contents from the weather.

In some places the cattle and implements of husbandry belong to individuals, who receive their proportion of land from the patell, to cultivate at their own expense, and to furnish their cattle and seed-grain. At the settling of the jummabunda, they pay their proportion of the village assessment to government, and then dispose of their grain, cotton, and fruit, without being accountable to the patell; for between the patell and the collectors belonging to government, are a set of venal corrupt men, called zemindars, who by a powerful influence in every district, take an advantage of both parties; these men, in fact, ought to be only intelligent clerks and accomptants, conversant in the revenue department; and, from being acquainted with its forms and usages, should settle accounts between the collectors and patells, and see that justice is done on both sides. But so much is this office abused, that the zemindars are permitted to advance money to the patells and cultivators, to purchase cattle, seed, and other things wanted at the commencement of the rainy season, at the exorbitant interest of three and three quarters per cent. per mensem, or at the rate of five and forty per cent. per annum; though it is always lent by the month. For the security of money thus advanced, the produce of the land is mortgaged to the zemindars, who, at the time of settling the Jummabunda, assume the new title of minutedars; which is a name and an office by right only belonging to the seraffs (bankers) and monied men of the district; who, by a proper agreement, and for a reasonable consideration, take upon themselves to pay the sum assessed by the collectors, to the officers of government. The pernicious practice of permitting the zemindars, who have already too much influence, to be the minutedars also, extends their power to a dangerous length; and is productive of the worst consequences to the cultivators. The cunning, chicanery, and wickedness of the minutedars cannot easily be described, or comprehended, by a generous mind, unused to their artful wiles; yet pysita-lands are set apart in almost every village for these oppressors, who share with the industrious peasants and proper pensioners, the allotments before mentioned; and I must own, when I cheerfully acquiesced in every distribution to the poor, the maimed, and helpless objects of compassion, it was a painful imposition to reward these wretches for their cruelty and oppression. It is pleasing to reflect how similar were many of the Hindoo appropriations to the charities enjoined by the Mosaical law. "If there be among you a poor man within any of thy gates, thou shalt not harden thine heart, nor shut thy hand from thy poor brother; but shalt open thine hand wide unto him, and to the stranger, and the fatherless, and the widow: that the Lord thy God may bless thee. When thou beatest thine olive-tree, thou shalt not go over the boughs again; when thou gatherest the grapes of thy vineyard, thou shalt not glean it afterwards; when thou cuttest down thy harvest, and hast forgotten a sheaf in thy field, thou shalt not go again to fetch it; these shall be for the stranger, the fatherless, and for the widow; that the Lord thy God may bless thee!"

In different districts of Guzerat are different modes of cultivation, collecting the revenues, and distributing the crop. Those that I have alluded to were usual in the purgunnas under my management. In some parts of Hindostan, exclusive of the larger jaghires to princes and great officers, whole villages with all the lands belonging to them, are appropriated to favorites of the reigning sovereign, to dancing-girls, or celebrated devotees. One of the most beautiful and flourishing villages I ever saw, had, with its surrounding districts, been given to a set of dancing-girls;

another, of similar population and fertility, belonged to a tribe of Gosannees, or Hindoo mendicants.

Besides the portions of grain set apart for the charitable purposes already mentioned, in many places before the final allotment of the crops between the government and cultivators, a considerable quantity of grain is appropriated for the gods, brahmins, astrologers, and others, not particularized in my division. The gods and brahmins are every where well fed; not only from the general stock of grain, but by the fruits, meal, and dainties offered every morning in the temple. The story of Bel and the dragon was not confined to Babylon; it is daily realized in India, where it would be happy if all the offerings and sacrifices were as innocent. But surely a religion which tolerates lasciviousness, and dedicates the delicate virgin to lingam, or the lustful priests of Jaggernaut, requires some reformation. This is an unpleasant subject; but such expositions are necessary in the present system of false philosophy and general toleration. Thus writes the amiable Bernier, in the seventeenth century.

" Les brahmens, ces fourbes prennent une jeune fille, des plus " belles qui se trouve entre-eux, pour etre l'espouse de Jaggernaut; ils la laissent la nuit dans le temple, ou ils l'ont transportée " en grande ceremonie, avec l'idole; luy donnant á entendre que " Jaggernaut viendra dormir avec elle; et luy ordennent de luy " demander si l'aunée sera fertile &c. cependant un de ces imposteurs entre lá dedans la nuit, par une petite parte de derriere, " joüit de cette fille, et luy fait acroire tout ce que bon luy semble; " et le lendemain qu'on la transporte de ce temple dans un autre,

" avec la mesme magnificence, qu'onl'avoit portée sur ce chariot de
" triomphe, á côté de Jaggernaut son epoux, ces brahmens luy font
" dire hautement au peuple, tout ce qu'elle à appris de ces fourbes,
" comme l'ayant appris de la bouche mesme de Jaggernaut."

Such is the faithful account of an unprejudiced traveller a hundred and fifty years ago: it is well known this infamous practice still continues! Silence from those who have obtained the same knowledge, should not sanction such infamous proceedings, under the idea of vindicating a "harmless religion," if a religion can be so called, which allows of infanticide; encourages a young mother to deprive her infants of maternal care, and sacrifice herself on the funeral pile of her husband; which ordains a child not four years old to be betrothed to a man of forty; and, should he die before the marriage is consummated, dooms her to virgin-widowhood, and domestic degradation, for the remainder of her life. The murder of female infants among whole tribes of Hindoos, and the painful cremation of widows, cannot be included in that description; neither are their sacrifices confined to flowers, fruit, and herbs, nor yet to that of animals. It is proved, by late researches into Hindoo mythology, that human victims were formerly offered by the brahmins to the destructive powers; probably, in that sense, now every where discontinued. But what can be said by their modern advocates for the sacrifice of those pilgrims who annually resort to the temples of Jaggernaut, and are encouraged by the brahmins to place themselves under the enormous wheels of the idol's triumphal car, and thus be crushed to death, amidst the shouts and acclamations of a deluded multitude attending the procession? Surely these are as much human sacrifices as those offered at the shrine of Moloch, or the sanguinary rites in the mysterious groves of the Druids.

A religion which admits of such shocking practices, and many other enormities which might be adduced, cannot have proceeded from a pure and holy God. He has revealed himself under a very different character; as a God, glorious in holiness, fearful in praises; a God merciful and gracious; slow to anger, and plenteous in mercy! The divine and moral laws under the Mosaical dispensation I shall not enter upon; we learn from a royal teacher what was then required of a religious man. "Lord, who shall dwell in thy tabernacle, and who shall rest upon thy holy hill? He that walketh uprightly, and worketh righteousness, and speaketh the truth from his heart: he that backbiteth not with his tongue, nor doeth evil to his neighbour; in whose eyes a vile person is contemned; but he honoureth them that fear the Lord. He that sweareth to his neighbour, and disappointeth him not, though it were to his own hinderance. He that putteth not out his money to usury, nor taketh reward against the innocent." Similar to this is the prophetical language. "Wherewith shall I come before the Lord, and bow myself before the High God? Shall I come before him with burnt-offerings, with calves of a year old? Will the Lord be pleased with thousands of rams, or with ten thousand rivers of oil? Shall I give my first-born for my transgression, the fruit of my body, for the sin of my soul? He hath shewed thee, O man, what is good: and what doth the Lord require of thee, but to do justly, to love mercy, and to walk humbly with thy God?"

Love breathes through the whole Christian dispensation. "Thou shalt love the Lord thy God with all thy heart; and thy neighbour as thyself. A new commandment give I unto you, that ye love one another." What jurisprudence ever reached this excellent system? "Whatsoever ye would that men should do to you, do ye even so to them." It supersedes every moral code; and were the world at large actuated by the spirit of that single precept, what a happy world would it be! Charity, seraphic guest, when implanted in the christian's heart, how dost thou exalt human nature! "Thou sufferest long and art kind, thou enviest not, seekest not thy own, art not easily provoked, thinkest no evil!" What a heavenly portrait! Scarcely can it be believed that any person acquainted with both systems, would wish to establish the contracted scheme of Hinduism, the limitation of brahminism to castes and sects, in opposition to this divine and universal system of faith, hope, and love! nay even to endeavour to exalt it above this heavenly religion, by saying, "when it does as much for the lower orders of society in Europe, as the Hindoo system has done in India, they will vote for its establishment." I cannot withhold my sentiments, feeble as they may be thought, against such powerful opponents. To endeavour to counteract them is a duty I owe to truth, to feeling, to my country, and to fallen India, once called the "land of virtues!"

I have been asked by one of the most amiable men I know, and one of the most valuable friends I ever possessed, why I trouble myself so much about the Hindoos: why not allow mothers to destroy their infants, widows to immolate themselves with their husbands, and brahmins to pour boiling oil into the ears of the lower castes who hear the Shastah? This gentleman lived upwards of twenty years in India, and, like many other others, saw no impropriety in such conduct; or he would have been among the first to reprobate it, and attempt a change. But as I know he speaks the sentiments of numerous philanthropists, I shall answer the question in the language of the excellent. Cowper

> " Much.—I was born of woman, and drew milk,
> " As sweet as charity, from human breasts.
> " I think, articulate, I laugh and weep,
> " And exercise all functions of a man.
> " How then should I, and any man that lives,
> " Be strangers to each other?
> " nor can I rest
> " A silent witness of the headlong rage
> " Or heedless folly by which thousands die,
> " Bone of my bone, and kindred souls to mine."

There is a sweet simplicity, a pure and holy joy in the Christian religion, unknown to other creeds. It needs not external pomp, nor splendid decoration to captivate the soul. They may be appropriate and necessary in a national church: and very far be it from me to lessen the influence of any mean whatever, which tends to encourage piety or convert a single soul to the path of peace! The brahminical, as well as the papal hierarchy, knew how much the human mind is influenced by mysterious pageantry. Bigotry, or some other cause, unnecessary to develope, led the one to prevent the poor from reading the holy scriptures, and the other to pour boiling oil into the ears of the Soodra or Chandala who heard the Shasta; but in this happy country, where the gospel is every where preached, and the Bible every where read, a British ploughman can tell us in strains of poesy, peculiarly his own, that religion, in a lovely form, is to be found where neither the aid of sacred music is employed, nor the splendid ornaments of religious worship are adopted.

> " The cheerfu supper done, wi serious face,
> " They, round the ingle, form a circle wide:
> " The sire turns o'er, wi patriarchal grace,
> " The big ha-Bible, ance his father's pride:
> " His bonnet reverently is laid aside,
> " His lyart haffets wearing thin an bare;
> " Those strains that once did sweet in Zion glide,
> " He wales a portion with judicious care;
> " And, " Let us worship God !" he says with solemn air.
> " They chant their artless notes in simple guise;
> " They tune their hearts, by far the noblest aim. BURNS.

The share of the territorial revenue appropriated to the brahmins, has caused a digression from the general subject. The charitable distributions, and jaghires of landed property in Guzerat, are various and extensive; not only small villages, and particular fields are set apart for the maintenance of religion, and charitable purposes, large districts and whole provinces have been sometimes assigned by sovereigns in jaghire to their favourites. As mentioned in the Mahratta history, these jaghiredars hold their lands upon the feudal system. The revenue is their own; they assess their subjects as they please, and have an uncontrolled power of life and death in their dominion. For these honours and advantages they pay an annual tribute, or maintain a stipulated number of troops for public service. Under these chieftains are pundits, duans, and oppressors of various denominations; who all agree in extorting from the poor ryots every thing they possibly can, to enrich themselves: that, in conformity to the general system, they may be able to answer the exactions of their superiors; who view the growing wealth of their ministers with an eager eye; and when sufficiently accumulated, seize their persons, and claim a large share of the spoil.

This system of oppression so completely pervades all classes of society under every form of oriental government, that it is almost impossible, out of the British dominions, to find an Asiatic of any caste or tribe, who, like the English *country gentleman*, in the middle walk of life enjoys his patrimonial inheritance, surrounded by domestic happiness and rural pleasures. Such a character is now probably confined to this favoured island: however it may be comparatively known in other European states, it certainly would present a most uncommon spectacle among the Asiatics. A system of oppression prevails from the throne to the zemindar, whom I have frequently heard give the order for a patell and head farmer to be unmercifully flogged, as representatives of the village they were ruining by their extortions. This system ascends by a regular scale from these brahmin and banian zemindars to the imperial despot upon the musnud; who, like the Babylonish monarch of old, allows of no other alternative to those that obey or disobey his unjust decrees, than that in the former case, they should receive gifts, and rewards, and great honour; and for the latter they should be cut in pieces, and their houses made a dunghill: who, one day, fell upon his face and worshipped Daniel, commanding an oblation of sweet odours to be offered unto him, and the next condemned his three friends to a fiery furnace for not worshipping his golden image. Or of his immediate successors, one of whom clothed his virtuous minister with scarlet, and put a chain of gold about his neck, as a reward for his services; and the other, who at the instigation of his wicked counsellors ordered him to be thrown into a den of lions! Such was despotism two thousand years ago, such it continues at this present day!

That absolute power hardens the heart, in whatever climate or country it is permitted, cannot be doubted. We need not confine our remarks to Asia: some of the cruel and wanton acts of tyranny exercised by the feudal barons in Europe, over their bondmen and villains, are too shocking for the modest page. Oriental despotism proceeds on different grounds, though acting from the same principle; lust and revenge predominated in Europe, dominion and avarice in Asia. It would be painful to describe the various modes of oppression within my own knowledge; I shall only mention one anecdote in confirmation of what I have lately alluded to; it happened at Tattah, on the banks of Indus, where one of my friends was the English resident at the prince of Scindy's court. Tattah, the capital of those princes, has for many years been in a declining state, occasioned by wars and revolutions. The little commerce it enjoys since the English factory has been withdrawn, is in the hands of the Hindoo merchants; the principal officers in the commercial and revenue departments are also Hindoos. The prince and his court are Mahomedans, who, like other oriental despots, permit these officers to amass wealth by every means in their power, and then seize their prey.

The collector of the customs was a Hindoo of family, wealth, and credit. Lulled into security from his interest at court, and suspecting no evil, he was surprised by a visit from the vizier, with a company of armed men, to demand his money; which being secreted, no threatenings could induce him to discover. A variety of tortures were inflicted to extort a confession; one was a sofa, with a platform of tight cordage in net-work, covered with a chintz palampore, which concealed a bed of thorns placed under it: the collector, a corpulent banian, was then stripped of his jama, or muslin robe, and ordered to lie down on the couch: the cords bending with his weight, sunk on the bed of thorns; those long and piercing thorns of the baubul or forest acacia, which being placed purposely with their points upwards, lacerated the wretched man, whether in motion or at rest. For two days and nights he bore the torture without revealing the secret; his tormentors fearing he would die before their purpose was effected, had recourse to another mode of compulsion. When nature was nearly exhausted, they took him from the bed, and supported him on the floor, until his infant son, an only child, was brought into the room; and with him a bag containing a fierce cat, into which they put the child, and tied up the mouth of the sack. The agents of cruelty stood over them with bamboos, ready at a signal to beat the bag, and enrage the animal to destroy the child: this was too much for a father's heart! he produced his treasure, and on his recovery was sent for to court, invested with a sirpaw, or robe of state, and exalted to a high situation in another province; there to accumulate more wealth, and, at a future period, be again subject to the capricious fiat of a needy despot.

Another act of tyranny sometimes practised by the Mahrattas, is called the sheep-skin death. On this occasion the culprit is stripped naked, and a sheep being killed, the warm skin of the animal is immediately stretched to the utmost, and sewed tight over the prisoner's body; he is then conducted to the flat roof of the prison, and exposed to the fervour of a tropical sun, the skin contracting by the heat, draws with it the flesh of the agonizing wretch; until putrefaction, hunger and thirst terminate his sufferings.

When we compare the benevolent precepts of the gospel, and the conduct of its professors, with such practices, the superiority of its doctrines, and the moral dignity of a christian must be allowed a glorious pre-eminence! The divine rule, of doing unto others as we would they should do unto us, outweighs the whole code of Menu, and all the moral precepts of the Koran. I had not so many opportunities of being personally acquainted with the rapacity of the Mahomedans, as of the venality and corruption of the Hindoos, either in the Cutcheree court, or the Adawlet; but I imagine there is very little difference, especially in the revenue department. Orme's scale of cruelty and oppression is equally true under both governments: although the climax presents a sad picture of human depravity, its truth must be confirmed by every impartial observer. "The havaldar plunders the village, and is himself fleeced by the zemindar; the zemindar by the phousdar; the phousdar by the nabob, or his duan. The duan is the nabob's head slave; and the nabob compounds on the best terms he can make with his soubah on the throne. Wherever this gradation is interrupted bloodshed ensues!"

I am so unwilling to be thought actuated by prejudice against the Indians in general, and especially the Hindoos, among whom I so long resided, that I endeavour to avail myself of every valuable and authentic proof in support of my assertions; whether from the living or the dead, from sacred or profane history, from ancient annals or modern travels. As I may perhaps have elsewhere observed, I no longer feel myself at liberty to conceal my sentiments on the moral and religious conduct of the Hindoos, and particularly of the brahmins: although I confess my partiality towards them in many respects.

> " Seize upon TRUTH where'er 'tis found.
> " On Christian or on Pagan ground;
> " The flower's divine where'er it grows:
> " Neglect the thistle, but assume the rose." WATTS, *from memory.*

Dr. Robertson observes, that " the accounts given by ancient authors of the condition and tenure of the renters of land in India, agree so perfectly with what now takes place, that it may be considered almost as a description of the present state of its cultivation. In every part of India, where the native Hindoo princes retain dominion, the ryots, the modern name by which the renters of land are distinguished, hold their possessions by a lease, which may be considered as perpetual, and at a rate fixed by ancient surveys and valuations. This arrangement has been so long established, and accords so well with the ideas of the natives, concerning the distinctions of castes, and the functions allotted to each, that it has been inviolably maintained in all the provinces subject either to Mahomedans or Europeans; and to both, it serves as the basis on which their whole system of finance is founded.

In another part the same intelligent writer says, " it is now known that what the sovereign receives from land varies greatly in different parts of the country; and is regulated by the fertility or barrenness of the soil, the nature of the climate, the abundance or scarcity of water, and many other obvious circumstances. One particular with respect to the administration of revenue in Bengal merits notice, as it redounds to the honour of the emperor Akber, the wisdom of whose government I have often had occasion to celebrate. A general and regular assessment of revenue in Bengal was formed in his reign; all the lands were then valued, and the rent of each inhabitant and of each village ascertained. A regular gradation of accounts was established. The rents of the different inhabitants who lived in one neighbourhood being collected together, formed the account of a village; the rents of several villages being next collected into one view, formed the accounts of a larger portion of land; the aggregate of these accounts exhibited the rent of a district; and the sum total of all the districts formed the account of the revenue of the whole province."

To the preceding remarks by Dr. Robertson, I had added many of my own observations and answers to my own inquiries, during my residence in Guzerat. They were attended with more difficulty and deception from the zemindars than I was at first aware of, and from not being brought to any satisfactory proof are now suppressed. My sphere was limited, and my sources of information slender when compared with recent publications on landed property in India, by gentlemen of superior attainments; none throw more light on that thesis than colonel Wilks's History of Mysoor; to which I must refer for full information, as the generality of my readers would probably not deem it a very interesting subject; although it is one which from the higher powers seems to require a minute investigation, and the maturest deliberation. The result of the Mysoor Researches proves the difficulty attending such inquiries. After several excellent discussions on landed property, the author conducts us to regions remote from the first impressions of the northern conquerors of India, in Trichinopoly and Tanjore, sometimes united and sometimes separate, "the latter principally containing the town of *Cambacenum*, the ancient capital of the Chola race; one of the oldest Hindoo dynasties of which any traces have hitherto been discovered in those lower regions, and from which the whole coast in later times took its name. Tanjore in 1675 fell into the hands of Eccojee, brother of Sevajee, the celebrated founder of the Mahratta empire.

"Throughout all its revolutions this country remained under a Hindoo government, with the exception of the very short period that it was possessed by Mahomed Ally; and the whole province exhibits at this day every character that constitutes a highly respectable proprietary right. A late report says, that immemorial usage has established, both in Tanjore and Trichinopoly, that the occupants, whether distinguished by the names of *Meerassdar* or *Mahajanums*, have the right of selling, bestowing, deriving, and bequeathing their lands in the manner which to them is most agreeable." The landed property is in the hands of men who feel and understand the full rights and advantages of possession; who have enjoyed them, in a degree more or less secure, before the British name was known in India; and who, in consequence of them, have rendered populous and fertile the extensive provinces of Tanjore and Trichinopoly.

"This class of proprietors are not to be considered as the actual cultivators of the soil; the far greater mass of them till their lands by the means of hired labourers; or by a class of people termed *Pullers*, (perhaps the same as those called *Pooleahs* on the Malabar coast.) These are of the lowest class, and may be considered as the slaves of the soil. The landed property of these provinces is divided and subdivided in every possible degree; there are proprietors of four thousand acres, of four hundred acres, of forty acres, and of one acre.

"The occupants and meerassdars, above described, are far from being mere nominal proprietors; they have a clear, ample, and unquestioned proprietor's share; amounting, according to the same authority, to the respectable proportion of twenty-seven per cent of the gross produce; a larger rent than remained to an English proprietor of land, who had tythes and land-tax to pay, even before the establishment of the income tax.

"One hundred and fifty is the whole produce of a fixed portion of land, on which the calculation is made; of which eighteen goes to the general charges, and one hundred and thirty-two remains to be divided between the government and the proprietor. The government receives $59\frac{51}{125}$, or fifty-five per cent. and the proprietor $72\frac{57}{125}$, or fifty-five per cent. This latter amount is again to be divided between the proprietor and his *paragoodie*, an independent labourer, who receives a fixed share of the produce; and out of it defrays the expenses of cultivation; his share of the above seventy-two is thirty-eight, and the proprietor's thirty-four; the former being twenty-eight per cent., and the latter twenty-seven per cent., upon the whole sum to be divided, viz. one hundred and thirty-two. The difference is remarkable (as it necessarily must be from the facility of culture) between the expenses of cultivation, and maintenance of the farmer's family, in this province and in Canara; viz. twenty-eight per cent. and fifty per cent."

I shall close this part of the subject with the translation of a bill of sale of some land in India, written originally in the Tamul language, introduced in those valuable researches. It affords a very satisfactory specimen of those deeds among the natives of India.

"Be it propitious!

"On this fortunate day, Monday the 16th of the month Ahvany, of the year (of the cycle) Kahlyuktee, in the year of *Salinahan* 1720, and of the *Cali Yug* 4899, being the third day of the increasing moon, under the auspicious conjunction and happy influence of the constellation Ashanattee and Magarum: *Kistna Sawmey Pilla* of Cunnatoor, the son of *Vencatachelum Pilla*, for himself and his house executes this deed of sale of land to *Cumance Sawmey Pillà*. That is to say: of the twenty-eight established shares of Cunnatoor, I have made a full and complete sale to you of my own two shares therein, for one hundred chuckrums; and you having paid, and I having received the said one hundred chuckrums for the said two shares: therefore possess the *Nunja, Punja*, (wet and dry lands) trees, groves, gardens, hillocks, water, wood, stone, and treasures; the well that points beneath, the tree that points above, *together with all property belonging in common thereto*, within its four boundaries. Your children, from generation to generation, are free to bestow, or exchange, or to dispose of it at their pleasure. Possess and enjoy it as long as the sun and the moon, the earth and its vegetables, the mountains and the river Cauvery, exist; and all prosperity attend you. Thus it is subscribed by me *Kistna Sawmey Pilla*, with my full consent to *Cumaun Sawmey Pilla*. This deed is written by *Mootoo Sawmey*, the village *Conicopoly*."

(Signed) KISTNA SAWNEY.

Witnesses

ARNACHELUM,
SUNKALINGUM,
SHUMMOGUM.

That the inhabitants of Baroche, when under the English government, were considered to possess landed property in their own right, appears from a lease of some lands which I obtained for the term of ninety-nine years, from Lullabhy, the celebrated zemindar at Baroche; not drawn up in such strong terms as the preceding deed of sale, but equally binding on all parties concerned in the transaction.

"This indenture, made on the 25th day of June, in the eighteenth year of the reign of our sovereign Lord George the Third, and in the year of the Christian æra 1778, between Lullabhy Daaldass, mozmundar of Baroche, in behalf of himself and of all his family, by due and regular authority so invested, on the one part; and James Forbes, senior merchant in the service of the United Company of merchants of England trading to the East Indies, and a member of the council at Baroche, residing in that city, on the other part; Witnesseth, that the said Lullabhy Daaldass, in behalf of himself and every branch of his family aforesaid, in consideration of the sum of fifty rupees, lawful money of Baroche, to be annually paid to him, the said Lullabhy Daaldass, his heirs, executors, administrators, or assigns, by the said James Forbes, or his assigns, doth covenant and agree, to let unto the said James Forbes, his heirs, executors, administrators, and assigns, a spot of ground, situated on the west side of the city of Baroche; bounded on the north by the house and garden of the said James Forbes; on the east by the garden and house occupied by Charles Brome, Esq.; on the south by the river Nerbudda; and on the west by the garden of James Cheape, Esq. containing seven begahs, more or less, together with all the wells, water-ways, trees, hedges, and all appurtenances whatsoever to the said ground appertaining or belonging. To have and to hold the said land for the full and just term of ninety-nine years, from the date aforesaid, for the annual consideration of fifty rupees before specified," &c. &c.

During the Mogul government it was considered that all the land of the empire belonged to the sovereign, but the lands in the provinces were subject to the respective nawabs, or nabobs. With them, or their representatives, Orme observes, the farmers agreed for the cultivation of such an extent, on reserving to themselves such a proportion of the produce. This proportion was settled according to the difficulty or ease of raising the grain; and seldom exceeded one third.

The landed property in Guzerat was certainly as generally considered to belong to the respective governments of the province, whether English, Mogul, or Mahratta. My instructions, on being appointed collector of Dhuboy and the adjoining purgunnas, clearly authorised me so to consider them. Before the expiration of the first year after those districts had been intrusted to my management, the governor and council of Bombay thus addressed the Board of Revenue at Baroche:

"We direct that you give us your opinion, fully and explicitly, whether letting out the lands to farm in a public manner, for a certain term, or continuing the present method by jummabundy, may be the most eligible method of collecting the revenues, especially in times of tranquillity."

To this the majority of the Board at Baroche sent the following answer.

"*Minute of Messrs. Callander, Brome, Forbes, and Dalton, the majority of the Board of Baroche, in answer to the Governor and Council's commands, respecting farming the Purgunnas of Baroche and its dependencies.*

"THAT having maturely weighed and reflected upon this very important subject, with its various connections, they highly and decidedly disapprove of the proposed mode of farming; as contrary to all the Company's real interest in this country, and in no wise necessary, either from the extent or situation of their possessions. They are clearly of opinion, that in its consequences it will become oppressive, and extremely disgusting, to the ryots, and subjects in general; ruinous to the Company's revenue, by removing the regular check in that department; and giving a scope and opportunity to the most corrupt practices. And from the knowledge they have of the few persons in these parts capable of being either real, or even nominal, farmers, and the mode of collecting in kind, that it must terminate in monopolies of the most dangerous and distressing nature, particularly all sorts of grain, to the ruin of the country; they are therefore of opinion, that the present mode by jummabundy, although liable to exceptions, is far preferable.

(Signed)

ALEXANDER CALLANDER,
CHARLES BROME,
JAMES FORBES,
JOHN DALTON.

Baroche,
29th December, 1780.

The Board of Revenue at Bombay being of opinion that the preceding minute required a further explanation, desired us to specify what scope or opportunities farming the lands could give for corrupt practices; or if, as we represented, there were so few persons capable of becoming farmers, how there was a possibility of having nominal farmers? They also desired we would explain the exceptions to the present mode of assessment by Jummabundy; and what methods occurred to us to obviate those objections.

In answer to which we addressed the following letter to the Board at Baroche.

To ROBERT GAMBIER, Esq.

Chief, &c. Members of the Board of Revenue at Baroche.

Gentlemen,

In obedience to the commands of the Honourable the Governor and Council at Bombay, we are now to give the required explanations of our minute on the subject of farming the Honourable Company's lands; but previously we deem it incumbenton us to disclaim all collusion which our Honourable superiors seem to suspect.

In answer to the first point we have to observe, that contracts for farms, from the want of a sufficient number of responsible persons in this place, cannot be managed in the manner the Honourable board may expect. Once, on public trial even of single small villages, competitors could not be found; and the first and principal part of the business will therefore be necessarily transacted in a sort of private manner, and through the administration of a set of corrupt zemindars. Add to this the constant and unavoidable dependance of the farmers on the same persons who grant the leases, for effectual support in their farms; and we imagine what has been already said, without enlarging, will be sufficient to give the preference to the mode of jumma-bundy. But no farm having, to our knowledge, ever taken place, it was impossible we could mean any reflection on the present collector-general, or sub-collectors; but as they might be hereafter introduced, we gave our opinion that it would be lodging a dangerous power in the hands of any set of men.

In explanation of the second point, we have only to remark, that the want of competitors and persons capable of being farmers bona fide, will, in our opinion, give rise to nominal farmers. And by our minute in council, we meant only to express, that however the lands may be divided, in order to avoid monopolies, the farms will fall into the hands of a very few individuals; although perhaps covered under the ostensible names of other persons who have no real interest in them.

Here we desire to be understood, that whatever we have said respecting farming, is merely local to Baroche and its districts: for with a more extended territory, and under different circumstances, farming may be expedient and necessary.

We cannot take upon us to explain all the exceptions that may be made to the present mode of collection by jumma-bundy; or to any other system of revenue, but what we alluded to in our minute, were the three following. First, the disadvantages incident to annual rents, which in all countries have been found unfavourable to improvements in cultivation. Secondly, the great uncertainty both on the part of the sircar and ryot, notwithstanding any division that may be adopted; and the continued dependance thereby occasioned, both in the officers of government, and landholders, on a worthless set of men called zemindars; which creates to them a very prejudicial influence. Lastly, the peculiar situation of the collector-general, or sub-collector. If the jummabundy unfortunately falls low, they are suspected to have sacrificed the Company's interests; and if, trusting to their own judgment, they push it high, contrary to the opinion and inclination of the zemindars, the ryots are led to be dissatisfied, and the whole immediately cry out OPPRESSION. These inconveniences appear to us to be inseparable from that mode, nor do we know any way to obviate them.

We are respectfully,
Gentlemen,
Your very obedient servants,

ALEXANDER CALLANDER,
CHARLES BROME,
JAMES FORBES,
JOHN DATON.

Baroche,
24th February, 1781.

I shall conclude the subject of landed property and assessments in India, (which to many may perhaps have been uninteresting,) with this remark, I am decidedly of opinion, upon my own knowledge, founded on practice as well as theory, that, however sanctioned by long habit and established custom, the mode of assessment by jumma-bundy, in the districts under my cognizance, failed, in many essential points, to produce the good effects which might reasonably have been expected, could we have found men of humane character, and responsibility to conduct the business. A better mode would be, were men of moral conduct and probity to be found, to grant such leases as would give the farmer a secure and permanent interest in the land he cultivates; and such a tenure would be the only means of preventing the abominable fraud, plunder, and oppression, which the ryots suffer under the zemindars, and the whole mass of native officers, employed in the cutcheree, or revenue department. Such farmers as I allude to were not to be met with in the Company's territory, nor, I believe, throughout the whole province of Guzerat while I resided there.

CHAPTER XXVI.

A DESCRIPTION OF BHADERPOOR; THE CULTIVATION AND FOREST SCENERY IN THAT PURGUNNA; AND THE MANNERS AND CUSTOMS OF ITS INHABITANTS.

1781.

Far as Creation's ample range extends,
The scale of sensual, mental, powers ascends;
Mark how it mounts to Man's imperial race,
From the green myriads in the peopled grass;
What modes of sight betwixt each wide extreme
The mole's dim curtain, and the lynx's beam!
Or smell, the headlong lioness between
And hound sagacious on the tainted green!
Of hearing, from the life that fills the flood,
To that which warbles through the vernal wood!
The spider's touch, how exquisitely fine!
Feels at each thread, and lives along the line!
In the nice bee, what sense so subtly true,
From pois'nous herbs extracts the healing dew?
How instinct varies in the groveling swine,
Compar'd, half-reasoning elephant, with thine! POPE

CONTENTS.

jugglers—Hindoo drama—Arab and Scindian infantry in India—hawking—fighting rams—hospitality of the Arabs—power of music on antelopes in a spectacle at Poonah—its effect on different animals—destruction of monkeys by tigers—cruelty of Bheels and Gracias—presentation of a Gracia's head—cruelty of the ancients in collecting the heads of their enemies, extending down to Hyder Ally—death of an Indian female from Futty Sihng's seraglio—Hindoo soothsayers, and diviners—wilds of Baderpoor—royal sports of the Mogul princes—description of a tiger-hunt by Sir John Day.

CHAPTER XXVI.

HAVING described the city and inhabitants of Dhuboy, the administration of justice, and collection of the revenues in that district, I will now more briefly mention the subordinate purgunnas intrusted to my management.

The nearest of those districts was called Bhaderpoor; it contained a small town of the same name, and sixteen inhabited villages. As the capitals were within a few miles of each other, I frequently visited it, and sometimes resided there at the commencement of the harvest immediately after the rains; when the roads, not only in the Bhaderpoor purgunna, but many other places, were so destroyed by the preceding heavy rains and floods, that it was impossible to travel without sending precursors to see that the hills of sand and mud were levelled, and the chasms and ravines filled up, before a wheeled carriage could pass. This, by the custom of the country, is performed gratuitously for governors and persons in office; and at this season travellers of every description, whether in a palanquin or on horseback, must have the highways mended before they undertake a journey. During the rainy season they are generally impassable, and frequently invisible, from inundation. On the halcarra, or harbinger, arriving at a village with an intimation that a man of consequence is on his way thither, a proclamation is issued to repair the road as far as the next village, and so in continuance. In a light soil it is a work of no great expense, and soon accomplished.

This established custom elucidates a beautiful passage in the evangelical prophecy respecting the coming of the Messiah, preceded by John the Baptist, as a harbinger, in the spirit and power of Elias, to prepare the way of the Lord, and make his paths straight; when every valley was to be exalted, and every mountain and hill to be made low; and the crooked to be made straight, and the rough places plain.

Another passage occurs in the same prophet, not easily comprehended by an English reader, which is clearly illustrated by a common practice among the peasants in Hindostan, particularly in the unenclosed parts of my districts. At the commencement of the rainy season they plant abundance of melons, cucumbers, and gourds, which are then the principal food of the inhabitants. They are not sown in garden-beds, as in Europe, but in open fields, and extensive plains, liable to depredation by men and beasts. In the centre of the field is an artificial mount, with a hut on the top, sufficiently large to shelter a single person from the inclemency of the weather. There, amidst heavy rain and tempestuous winds, a poor solitary being is stationed day and night, to protect the crop from thieves of various descriptions, but especially from the monkeys, who assemble in large bodies to commit depredations. From thence the centinel gives an alarm to the nearest village, and the peasants come out and drive them off. Few situations can be more unpleasant than a hovel of this kind, exposed for three or four months to thunder, lightning, and rain. The prophet, no doubt, alludes to it in that passage deploring the desolation of Judea; "the daughter of Zion is left as a cottage in a vineyard; as a lodge in a garden of cucumbers; as a besieged city!"

During these periodical rains, and for a few weeks after, the aspect of the country is verdant and beautiful. At other seasons the russet hue generally prevails; the autumnal tints, which give so much beauty to the English woods and groves, are little known in the torrid zone; but there is sufficient variety in the verdure of the trees and plants to produce a pleasing contrast. In the Bhaderpoor purgunna are many noble burr-trees, extensive mango topes, and abundance of the mowah (bassia butyracea). This is a valuable tree, indigenous to many parts of India, and particularly flourishing in my districts; it attains the size of an English oak, grows in almost any soil, and from the beauty of the foliage, makes a conspicuous appearance in the landscape; its timber is very desirable, from being proof againt the destructive teeth of the termites; those formidable ants, it is said, are unable to eat it. The leaves are large and shining; and the flowers, which grow in full bunches, of so rich a nature, that when gathered and dried in the sun, they resemble Malaga raisins in flavour and appearance. These blossoms are ate in various ways, either as a preserved fruit, or to give an acidity to curries and other savoury dishes; but their greatest consumption is in the distillery of arrack, of which there are many kinds, from rice, jaggaree, tari, and sugar: this, by way of distinction, is called mowah-arrack, and is so strong and cheap a spirit, that the lower class of natives drink it to great excess; its consequences are as pernicious as the same deleterious liquors in Europe. In a plentiful season, a good tree produces from two to three hundred pounds weight of flowers; the proportionate quantity of spirit I cannot ascertain. The flowers are never entirely gathered; those that remain on the tree are succeeded by a fruit, or shell containing a pulp of delicate whiteness; from which is extracted an oily substance like butter, or ghee, which keeps a long time, and for family use answers all the purposes of those valuable articles. The kernel, or seed of the fruit, contains an oil of inferior quality and a more rancid flavour; it does not congeal, and is chiefly used by the poor.

The palmyra, or brab-tree, flourishes on the banks of the Nerbudda and many Guzerat rivers. The cocoa-nut tree does not grow in the interior districts, nor is it abundant on the sea coasts so far north. The palmyra, like the rest of that beautiful genus, gives an oriental costume to the landscape, and is a tree of long duration; it sows itself from the seed contained within its semi-transparent fruit, when it falls from the tree, or is dispersed by birds and monkeys. A palmyra-tree, when in perfection, yields daily about three quarts of tari, or palm-wine; which when boiled down produces a pound of coarse sugar, called jaggaree. This also is made of a better quality from the juice of the sugar-cane, which grew plentifully in several parts of my purgunnahs. No finer sugar was manufactured, but a great number of canes were daily sold in the bazars for the fresh juice, which the natives are very fond of. The cane is planted by joints, in regular rows: when arrived at maturity, such as have escaped the depredation of wild hogs (and of elephants where they are indigenous) are cut down; the juice

Engraved by J. Greig

The wedded BANIAN TREE, or the PALMYRA and BURR TREE united

drawn on Salsette

expressed by a mill constructed with great simplicity, and the boiled into jaggaree.

The bamboo, (bambusa, Lin.) flourished near the rivers in the Bhaderpoor districts; it is a beautiful and very useful plant, common in most parts of India and China: it does not attain the largest size in Guzerat; but there the thick stems and smaller branches are converted to various purposes; building, furniture, baskets, and utensils. In Malabar, those of large dimensions are formed into arches, by training them, while vegetating, over an iron frame of the shape required, to support the canopies of palanquins. Some bamboos, of large diameter and a lofty arch, are valued at five or six hundred rupees.

I mentioned the wedded-banian-tree at Salsette; it is not uncommon in this part of Guzerat, and causes a singular variety in vegetation. Colonel Ironside describes a very curious one in the province of Bahar, among the other banian-trees, which he says are creepers; as is the peipal, or ficus religiosa, which often springs round different trees, particularly the palm; and observes that the palmyra growing through the centre of a banian-tree looks extremely grand; it frequently shoots from old walls, and runs along them. On the inside of a large brick well, one of these trees lined the whole circumference of the internal space, and thus actually became a tree turned inside out. Under this tree sat a fakeer, a devotee. He had been there five and twenty years, but did not continue under the tree the whole time; his vow obliging him to lie, during the four coldest months, up to his neck in the Ganges; and to sit, during the four hottest months, close to a large fire.

A banian-tree thus inverted is uncommon, but their general

usefulness and beauty, especially in overshadowing the public wells and village markets, can only be known by those who live in a sultry climate: the best wells in Bhaderpoor are similar to the Bowrees, already described; and possibly the wells in Palestine were of the same construction, from a circumstance mentioned in sacred writ. "Jonathan and Ahimaaz being suspected at Enrogol, came to a man's house in Bahurim, which had a well in the court; whither they went down; and the woman took and spread a covering over the well's mouth, and spread ground corn thereon; and the thing was not known."

Cheap as every common necessary of Indian life was in Dhuboy, they were still more so at Bhaderpoor; few indeed were the wants of the inhabitants in that lonely district: a couple of yards of cotton cloth tied round the middle, was all the clothing of the common men; some wore a turban. A single piece of coarse cotton, several yards in length, put on in graceful folds, was the usual dress of the females. A thatched hut, containing a few earthen pots for cookery, a large jar of unburnt clay to hold grain, another of burnt clay for water, and a glazed pot for oil, comprized the stock of a villager. The oil is produced from various seeds planted for the purpose; expressed, like the kernel of the mowah, by mills of the simplest structure.

The construction of all the machines for the arts and manufactures in India are light and simple: in these respects the Asiatics are far behind Europeans, and, as frequently mentioned, are averse to imitation or improvement. Colonel Wilks relates an anecdote of the ingenuity of Shahjee, father of Sevajee, the founder of the Mahratta empire, from which some conjecture may be formed of the general state of the arts and sciences in India, at the commencement of the seventeenth century. "The minister Jagadeva Row had made a vow to distribute in charity the weight of his elephant in silver; and all the learned men of the court had studied in vain the means of constructing a machine of sufficient power to weigh the elephant. Shahjee's expedient was certainly simple and ingenious in an eminent degree. He led the animal along a stage prepared for the purpose, to a flat-bottomed boat; and marking the water line removed the elephant, and caused stones to be placed in the boat, sufficient to load it to the same line. The stones being brought separately to the scales, ascertained the true weight of the elephant, to the astonishment of the court at the wonderful talents of Shahjee."

Sugar-canes, mangos, and bringals, always formed a principal part of my villagers' presents when I halted at the public well. Although too great a part of the Bhaderpoor purgunna was uncultivated, in the other districts I had seldom occasion to look out for gardens or pleasure grounds to pitch my tent or erect my summiniana, or shamyana, the whole country being generally a garden. A corn-field, considered in its full extent, affords one of the most gratifying objects in nature: not much less interesting, and more beautiful to the eye, are the fields of cotton already mentioned. I then omitted one of my occupations respecting this valuable production. I had generally large commissions annually to purchase cotton at Baroche for the Bombay merchants, to be sent from thence to Bengal and China. For this purpose the English gentlemen at Baroche made their contracts with the cotton dealers, who received it from the villages every evening; and early on the ensuing morning weighed the cotton gathered the preceding day to the brokers, by whom it was immediately packed in bales for foreign markets. As these brokers, and native cotton-dealers of every description, play into each others hand, and use all possible means to cheat an European, we found it very difficult to counteract their cunning. One of their principal frauds was that of exposing the cotton, spread out on cow-dung floors, to the nightly dews, and then weighing it early the next morning in a moist state to the receivers. This occasioned a great loss in the weight of a candy, containing five hundred and sixty pounds, when it became dry. To prevent it as much as possible, I often paid an unexpected visit at day-break to at least a hundred of these small cotton-merchants; when, by placing a handful of the cotton taken up indiscriminately from the floor, upon the cheek, it was easy to discover whether it had been exposed to the dew to increase its weight. Like Gideon's fleece, spread upon the floor, with an honest dealer the cotton was perfectly dry; if in the hands of a rogue, you might like him wring out a bowlful of water.

Notwithstanding so many late encomiums on the Hindoo character by respectable writers, it will I believe be generally allowed by those who have dealt much with Banians, and merchants in the large trading-towns of India, that their moral character cannot be held in high estimation; since they are guilty of all the arts of craftiness, duplicity, and cunning that can be practised without the pale of the law. A modern writer has asserted that "no "people ever exhibited more suavity of manners, or more mild-

" ness of character; and that the Christian religion has not done
" so much for the lower orders of society in Europe, as that of
" Brahma appears to have done for the Hindoos."

I cannot acquiesce in these opinions, and others of a similar nature, unnecessary to introduce; a residence of many years among the brahmins, and a constant intercourse with those employed in the revenue department, afforded me great opportunity of becoming acquainted with the Hindoo character, from the religious and lay brahmins, to the lowest of the banian tribe. On my return to Europe I had the pleasure of a long intimacy with the venerable and respectable governor Holwell, one of the first who published an account of these people, under the name then better known of *Gentoos*; that benevolent man was esteemed very partial to the natives of India, and had investigated their character more than was usual at that period. Yet this is *his* portrait of them. " The Gentoos, in general, are as degenerate, crafty, superstitious, " and wicked a people, as any race of people in the known world, " if not eminently more so, especially the common run of brah- " mins; and we can truly aver, that, during almost five years that " we presided in the cutchery court of Calcutta, never any murder " or other atrocious crime came before us, but it was proved in " the end a brahmin was at the bottom of it."

I have no pleasure in making these quotations, but when so opposite a character is held forth by modern writers, truth and candor compel me to confirm them by my own observations; the same opinion was formed of these people by Dr. Fryer, a century before governor Holwell's publication. "The banians at Surat make all the bargains, and transact all money business; and though you hear, see, and understand them, yet you shall be choused, they looking you in the face; for, as a piece of superstition, they must put their hands under a cloth, or mantle, when by their fingers they instruct one another, and by that sleight often contradict their tongues. These banians are the absolute map of sordidness; enduring servilely foul words, affronts and injuries, for the hope of future gain; expert in all the arts of thriving and insinuation; so that lying, dissembling, cheating, are their master-piece; their whole desire is to have money pass through their fingers, to which a great part is sure to stick; for they well understand the constant turning of cash amounts, both to the credit and profit of him that is so occupied; which these banians are sensible of, otherwise they would not be so industrious to enslave themselves."

My journies in the purgunnas made a pleasing variety in my occupations; and the little difficulties occasioned by heat, rain, or the appearance of a tiger, rendered them interesting. Travelling in a palanquin during the rainy season, I generally met with accommodation at the towns and villages in my own districts. In the warm months a friendly tamarind or banian-tree sheltered me by day; at night a small tent contained my bed, and a summiniana protected me from the evening dews; these with a camp table and chair were all the conveniences I wanted when travelling alone. The summiniana, used both by Europeans and natives in most parts of India, is an awning, or pavilion, open on all sides, supported by poles, and stretched out by cords, in any level spot in the country; often in a court or garden near the house; where we assembled after sun-set to enjoy the society of our friends, smoak a hooka, and partake of a slight supper. The ground was generally covered by a thick cotton

HINDOO FAMILY, of the BANIAN CAST

cloth, or Persian carpet: convenient furniture and cheerful lights rendered it preferable to any part of a house;' which, during the hot winds, was never cool until midnight. The summiniana differs from a tent in having a flat covering lined with chintz, and no side walls; it is neither troublesome nor expensive, but extremely useful in a hot climate; and often alluded to by ancient writers, especially in that sublime description in the sacred records, "He stretched out the heavens as a curtain; and spreadeth them out as a tent to dwell in."

One of my chief pleasures in these excursions was the occasional interviews I enjoyed with travellers of various descriptions from different parts of Hindostan, who stopped at the same choultrie, or reposed under the same banian-tree with myself. My people at Dhuboy knowing my desire for information, seldom suffered a Mahomedan fakeer or Hindoo pilgrim of any celebrity to pass through the city without an introduction to me: their narratives were generally interesting, though sometimes extravagant, in describing the miracles of saints and hermits in remote regions, where there was little probability of detection.

Of all the countries visited by these Yogees and Senassies, they were most lavish in praise of Cachemire, whither they frequently extended their pilgrimage. These narrations made me long to behold this "Earthly Paradise," formerly a kingdom, happy under its own monarchs; surrounded by lofty mountains, their summits covered with perpetual snow; the acclivities, according to their different aspects, either adorned with the trees of Europe, or decked by the perennial plants and flowers of Asia, and sometimes presenting a delightful acsemblage of both. Immense rocks, rich groves, magnificent cataracts, and murmuring cascades, produce a sublime and beautiful effect. These waters, either in roaring cataracts, or gentle streams, flow to the lakes and rivulets which fertilize the plain, and there uniting, form the celebrated Indus, one of the great rivers of Asia.

This charming diversity of mountain and valley, wood and water, cornfields, meadows, orchards, and gardens, intermingled with towns, villages, palaces, and cottages, present a scene unrivalled in any part of the world. Most travellers confirm this account, especially Bernier, who accompanied the emperor Aurungzebe and his court on a visit to this province in the year 1663; which, next to the march of Darius, was perhaps one of the most magnificent scenes of eastern pageantry ever exhibited. The number and sumptuous caparisons of the elephants, camels, horses tents, and equipage of every description, for the accommodation of the emperor, the ladies of his haram, and principal nobles of the court, were truly surprising. They were escorted by an army of thirty-five thousand cavalry, ten thousand infantry, a large train of artillery, and every splendid accompaniment belonging to the Mogul sovereigns in the zenith of power. Bernier gives an excellent description of this journey, and an account of Cachemire, which exactly corresponds with the narrations of the Hindoo pilgrims who visited Dhuboy.

" Quoy qu'il en soit Kachemire n'est plus un lac, c'est à pre-
" sent une trés-belle campagne, qui est diversifiée de quantité de
" petites colines, qui a trente lieuës de long ou environ et dix ou
" douze de large, qui est située dans l'extrémité de l'Hindoustan

" au nord de Lahor, et qui est enclavée dans le fond des mon-
" tagnes du Caucase. Les premieres montagnes qui l'entourent,
" je veux dire celles qui sont les plus prés de la plaine, sont de
" mediocre hauteur, toutes vertes d'arbres ou de pâturages, pleines
" de bêtail de toute sorte, comme vaches, brebis, chévres et che-
" vaux: de gibiers de plusiéurs especes, comme perdrix, liévres,
" gazelles, et de quelques animaux qui portent le mux; il y a
" aussi des abeilles en trés-grande quantité; et ce qui est tres-rare
" dans les Indes, il ne s'y trouve ni serpens, ni tygres, ni ours, ni
" lyons, si ce n'est tres-rarement; de sorte qu'on peut dire que ce
" sont des montagnes innocentes et découlantes de lait et de miel,
" comme étoient celles de la terre de promission." VOYAGES DE BERNIER.

Besides a description of countries, the Hindoo travellers in Dhuboy, often gave me a faithful account of men and manners, which they were very capable of estimating. For although the natives of India are seldom communicative in what relates to their religion, caste, or domestic oeconomy; and perhaps are neither ready nor willing to answer the statistical inquiries of strangers, I generally found these pilgrims very much the contrary; their minds were enlarged, and their sentiments altogether more liberal and philanthropical than the stationary Hindoos. I made a proper allowance for marvellous adventures, endeavoured to extract a little honey from every flower, and in the durbar at Dhuboy, or on the shady banks of the Nerbudda, I spent many a pleasant and improving hour with religious mendicants, both Hindoos and Mahomedans.

I was highly entertained with one visitor of this description at

Dhuboy; who seeing me engaged on public business in the durbar, inquired to which presidency I belonged. On replying that I was on the Bombay establishment, he wished me to explain the nature of the British governments in India, particularly in what manner the other Presidencies were subordinate to the governor general of Bengal. Having endeavoured so to do, the venerable brahmin told me he had lived under different governments, and travelled in many countries; but had never witnessed a general diffusion of happiness equal to that of the natives under the mild and equitable administration of Mr. Hastings, at that time governor-general of Bengal. I cannot forget the words of this respectable pilgrim; we were near a banian-tree in the durbar court when he thus concluded his discourse: "As the burr-tree, one "of the noblest productions in nature, by extending its branches "for the comfort and refreshment of all who seek its shelter, is em-"blematical of the DEITY; so do the virtues of the governor re-"semble the burr-tree; he extends his providence to the remotest "districts, and stretches out his arms, far and wide, to afford pro-"tection and happiness to his people; such, SAHEB, is Mr. Hast-"ings!" Yet, this is the man, who, by the violence of faction, intended for patriotic zeal, and conducted by a flow of eloquence seldom equalled, was arraigned for crimes the most foreign to his benevolent heart, and doomed to a trial of seven years duration: a scene unparallelled in the annals of mankind!

I never saw Mr. Hastings until his public appearance on that solemn occasion, and could then hardly conceive it possible, by any combination of ideas, or concatenation of circumstances, to believe that a man should be tried in his own country, for crimes supposed to have been committed at ten thousand miles distance; among a people who not only knew his character, but feeling the blessings which flowed from his humane and benevolent heart, considered him as an emblem of the GODHEAD!

This is confirmed by the congratulary address from the English inhabitants of Calcutta, who had witnessed the blessings of his government, and thus addressed him on his acquittal from the charges preferred against him. "We cannot but admire, Sir, the patience, fortitude, and resignation, with which you have borne a trial unexampled in its length; and a scrutiny into character, motives, and actions, the most strict and minute that ever was instituted. But, upheld by conscious innocence, you have given an example of your reliance on the justice of your cause, which, we doubt not, will carry conviction to the world and posterity, equal to the verdict of the illustrious tribunal before which you have appeared."

"Go, bid the neighbouring poor his crimes proclaim,
"Full in their answering smiles is writ his shame:
"Go to the rich, in their affection find
"The blameless history of this *monster's* mind.
"Go to his country, bid his sovereign tell,
"All, all delighted, on his virtues dwell!
"Go, launch the bark, his baseness to explore,
"And pierce the bowels of the Indian shore:
"Go, make the visit to the *Begum* race,
"Scene of his fraud, his plunder, and disgrace!
"In Asia, as in Albion, were he tried,
"Still should we find that honour is his guide."

Such are the confirmations to the traits of justice, humanity, and benevolence, communicated to me by my delighted Hindoo traveller at Dhuboy, which there distinguished the governor-general. Colonel Malcolm will not be accused of partiality to Mr. Hastings's political character; yet of that he gives this admirable summary. "In the history of British India, it is admitted, even by those who condemned part of his conduct, that Mr. Hastings, during a time of unexampled public embarrassment, and at a moment when he had to contend against those from whom he should have derived support, shewed all the active energy of a great statesman; and, by his spirited and extraordinary exertions, saved the interests of his country in India from that ruin with which they were threatened; and in which they undoubtedly would have been involved, had a man of less resolution, fortitude, and genius, held the reins of government."

I have since passed one of the happiest days which has fallen to my lot, at Dalesford, the paternal seat of this great man; where, in the bosom of his family and the pleasures of society, hospitality and benevolence, but above all, in the retrospective view of a well-spent life, he passes the evening of his days in a state of calm delight, far beyond all the wealth and honours to which his country and his sovereign deemed him entitled. Never have I beheld *otium cum dignitate* more truly enjoyed: never was I more convinced of the serenity and happiness of *mens sibi conscia recti.*

> "One self-approving hour whole years outweighs,
> "Of stupid starers, and of loud huzzas!"

I now return to the Hindoo pilgrims which occasioned this digression. Bhaderpoor, though in itself an insignificant place, and nothing in the district very interesting, afforded me occasional entertainments in meeting with travellers of various descriptions. The gurry, or little fortress, situated near the fords of the Ouze, and the pandauls, or open sheds for the collectors of customs, at the pass of the Ore, the two Bhaderpoor rivers, were the general rendezvous of travellers, in their way to the eastern hills, or coming from the interior to the sacred shrines of Guzerat, and on the latter account very much frequented by Hindoo devotees, and pilgrims of every caste. There I beheld, assembled in the same pandaul, or reposing under the friendly banian-tree, the Gosannee in a state of nudity, and the Yogee with a lark or paroquet, his sole companion for a thousand miles; the Guroo, of the first rank in the brahminical hierarchy, travelling with oriental pageantry to visit the temples and superintend the seminaries, meeting the brahmacharee, with a covered mouth and nostrils, that he may not inhale an animalcule; and a soft broom in his hand to sweep the ground, that he may not tread on an insect. There also were religious enthusiasts reduced to a skeleton by abstinence, or almost bursting under a vow of swallowing so many maunds of consecrated ghee. One resting from turning over his body in a rolling posture, another imploring food from others, by having rendered himself incapable of lowering or moving his arms in consequence of superstitious devotion. But it would be endless as well as needless to enlarge further on these enthusiasts, so often mentioned in these memoirs; except that in the eastern parts of my districts, attracted no doubt by the sacred fanes at Dhuboy and Chandode, they were more abundant than I ever saw them elsewhere, and seemed to have acquired an unusual degree of consequence. The annexed engraving exhibits two of these singular characters, drawn from life, meeting near the ford of a river; the one accompanied by his faithful lark, nearly in the state of the ancient Gymnosophists; the mouth of the other covered with a cloth to prevent the death of an insect. The next engraving represents a further variety of these deluded fanatics, also taken from nature.

Far be it from me to cast a general reflection on these mendicants, but respecting the majority, those who have had the best opportunities of knowing them, will, I am confident, coincide in Dr. Fryer's remark, made a hundred and fifty years ago, that "most of them are vagabonds, and the pest of the nation they live in: some of them dwell in gardens and retired places in the fields, in the same manner as the seers of old, and the children of the prophets did. Their habit is the main thing that signalizes them more than their virtue; they profess poverty, but make all things their own wherever they come. All the heat of the day they idle it under some shady tree, at night they come in troops, armed with a great pole, a mirchal or peacock's tail, and a wallet, more like plunderers than beggars: they go into the market, or to the shopkeepers, and force an alms, none of them returning without his share. Some of them pass the bounds of a modest request, and bawl out in the open streets for an hundred rupees, and nothing less will satisfy them. They are clothed with a ragged mantle, which serves them also for a mattress; for which purpose some have lions', tigers', or leopards' skins to lay under them; the civilest of them wear flesh-coloured vests, somewhat like our brick-makers' frocks, and almost of that colour. The merchants, as their adventures return, are bountiful towards them; by which means some of them thrive upon it. These field-conventiclers, at the

HINDOO DEVOTEES, *of the Gosaunee & Jetty Tribes*

hours of devotion, beat a drum, from them called the fakeer's drum. There are enough of these strollers in Surat, to make an army, insomuch that they are almost become formidable to the citizens; nor is the governor powerful enough to correct their insolence; for lately setting on a nobleman of the Moors, when his kindred came to demand justice, they unanimously arose in defence of the aggressor, and rescued him from his deserved punishment."

This portrait is certainly confirmed by too many of these fanatical vagabonds at the present day. On the continent they are very often complete Gymnosophists. When they visit the English settlements, some of them, from a little regard to decency, wear a slight covering. Within my recollection, a party of these naked philosophers, amounting to more than two hundred, crossed over from the temple of Vizraboy to Bombay, under a pretence of some religious visit; they were generally fine looking young men; athletic, bold, and impudent, beyond any set of Indians I ever met with: they became very troublesome even to the Hindoos, and in the English town were perfectly disgusting. The governor wished to get rid of them without offending the brahmins, who rather encouraged their visit. The fosse surrounding the fortifications, of great extent and considerable breadth, at that time required cleaning. A government order was issued for all vagabonds, mendicants, and idle persons, who could not give a proper account of themselves, to be immediately employed in cleaning out the town-ditch. The next morning not a travelling yogee, gosannee, senassee, or any one of the fraternity, was to be found upon the island.

There are doubtless many in these tribes of wandering enthusiasts who deserve a better character; and like the brahmins stationed at the temples, lead a more useful life; and are actuated by a spirit of philanthropy, sensibility, and acuteness of feeling, flowing from a humane and benevolent heart. Their religious tenets, and superstitious prejudices, lead them, doubtless, into many errors; some excite our pity, a few our censure. Among the former, I recollect a well-authenticated story of an English gentleman, extremely fond of natural and experimental philosophy being intimate with a liberal-minded brahmin, who had been educated at Benares, or some other celebrated college; they generally passed the morning together in the pleasing walks of science. The brahmin read English books, searched into the Encyclopedia, and profited by the best philosophical instruments. The gentleman, on receiving a valuable solar microscope as a present from Europe, shewed it with rapture to his Hindoo friend; and, in opposition to the scheme of the metempsychosis, discovered to him the innumerable animalculæ devoured by the brahmins on every fruit and vegetable they eat; each of which, like archdeacon Paley's canary-bird, is a cluster of contrivances: "in the single ounce of matter which composes the body of that little warbler, are instruments for eating, for digesting, for nourishment, for breathing, for generation, for running, for flying, for seeing, for hearing, for smelling: each appropriate, each entirely different from all the rest." By analogy, we have every reason to suppose, indeed we must be assured, that the same infinite wisdom and goodness has endued the minutest insect with organs, faculties, and propensities, suited to its link in the great chain of creation. The brahmin, consistent with his idea of the Hindoo metempsychosis, remains in a state of happy ignorance; he views the tint of the mango and the bloom of the fig as only the beautiful colouring of nature; and innocently slays his thousands and ten thousands at a meal of fruit and vegetables. The European philosopher, in contemplating the great scheme of Providence, beholds a super-fecundity in many parts of the animal economy; which, though of great occasional use and importance, exceeds the ordinary capacity of nature to receive or support its progeny. "All super-abundance supposes destruction, or must destroy itself. Perhaps there is no species of terrestrial animals whatever, which would not overrun the earth, if it were permitted to multiply in perfect safety, or of fish, which would not fill the ocean: at least, if any single species were left to their natural increase without disturbance or restraint, the food of other species would be exhausted by their maintenance. In almost all cases nature produces her supplies with profusion; a single cod-fish spawns, in one season, a greater number of eggs than all the inhabitants of England amount to. It is necessary, therefore, that the effects of such prolific faculties be curtailed. In conjunction with other checks and limits, all subservient to the same purpose, are the *thinnings* which take place among animals, by their action upon one another. In some instances we ourselves experience, very directly, the use of these hostilities. One species of insects rids us of another species, or reduces their ranks. A third species, perhaps, keeps the second within bounds; and birds or lizards are a fence against the inordinate increase by which even these last might infest us."

Such is the wide difference between the contracted system of the Hindoos, and the enlightened philosophy of Europe; the discussion might be extended over an ample and beautiful field; but I must return to the anecdote which caused the digression. After a full display of the wonders produced by the new apparatus, the English gentleman, instead of seeing his friend delighted, observed him to be unusually thoughtful, and at length he silently withdrew. At his next visit he requested the gentleman would sell him the microscope; to this he objected, observing that it was a present from a friend in Europe, not to be replaced, and while in his possession would afford them a mutual gratification. The brahmin offered him a very large sum of money, or any Indian commodity of equal value, in hopes of obtaining it, without effect; at last the gentleman, overcome by incessant importunity at every repeated visit, presented him with the microscope. A momentary gleam of joy flashed across the brahmin's countenance on obtaining possession of the object he had so ardently desired. They were then in a veranda overlooking a garden, with some kind of artificial rock-work composed of flints and rough stones; from which the brahmin, grasping the instrument, descended with a quicker motion than is customary with his caste into the garden; where, seizing a large stone, he laid the microscope upon the lowest step of the veranda, and instantaneously smashed it to pieces before his astonished friend could prevent it. He flew into a violent passion, and in his heat upbraided the brahmin with ingratitude, ignorance, and fanaticism. As usual with his caste, he bore it all patiently, and respectfully withdrew, saying when he was cool he would pay him a visit, and explain his reasons; justification was deemed impossible. The brahmin returning a few days afterwards, met with a polite, if not a welcome reception; and thus addressed his friend: "O that I had remained in that happy state of ignorance wherein you first found me! yet will I confess that as my knowledge increased, so did my pleasure, until I beheld the last wonders of the microscope; from that moment I have been tormented by doubt, and perplexed by mystery: my mind, overwhelmed by chaotic confusion, knows not where to rest, nor how to extricate itself from such a maze. I am miserable, and must continue so to be until I enter on another stage of existence. I am a solitary individual among fifty millions of people all educated in the same belief with myself; all happy in their ignorance! so may they ever remain! I shall keep the secret within my own bosom; where it will corrode my peace, and break my rest: but I shall have some satisfaction in knowing that I alone feel those pangs, which, had I not destroyed the instrument, might have been extensively communicated, and rendered thousands miserable! Forgive me, my valuable friend, and O! convey no more implements of knowledge and destruction!"

Could this man have been instructed in the sublime truth of religious philosophy, could he have been made the mean of imparting a true system of natural theology, happy might have been the consequences. To use the language of that excellent author who has written such a work on the evidences of the existence and attributes of the Deity, collected from the appearances of nature, the deluded brahmin would have found, that, according to his own creed, "immortality upon this earth is out of the question: that, without death, there could be no generation, no sexes, no parental relation, i. e. as things are constituted, no animal happiness. The particular duration of life assigned to different animals can form no part of the objection; because, whatever that duration be, whilst it remains finite and limited, it may always be asked, why it it is no longer. The natural age of different animals varies from a single day to a century of years. No account can be given of this; nor could any be given, whatever other proportion of life had obtained amongst them. The term of life in different animals being the same as it is, the question is, what mode of taking it away is the best even for the animal itself.

"According to the established order of nature, the three methods by which life is usually put an end to are acute diseases, decay, and violence. The simple and natural life of brutes is not often visited by acute distempers, nor could it be deemed an improvement to their lot if they were. Let it be considered, therefore, in what a condition of suffering and misery a brute animal is placed which is left to perish by decay. In human sickness or infirmity, there is the assistance of man's rational fellow creatures, if not to alleviate his pains, at least to minister to his necessities, and to supply the place of his own activity. A brute, in his wild and natural state, does every thing for himself. When his strength therefore, or his speed, or his limbs, or his senses fail him, he is delivered over, either to absolute famine, or to the protracted wretchedness of a life slowly wasted by the scarcity of food. Is it then to see the world filled with drooping, superannuated, half-starved, helpless, and unhelped animals, that you would alter the present system of pursuit and prey? This system is also to them the spring of motion and activity on both sides. The pursuit of its prey forms the employment, and appears to constitute the pleasure, of a considerable part of the animal creation. The using of the means of defence, or flight, or precaution, forms also the business of another part. And even of this latter tribe, we have no reason to suppose that their happiness is much molested by their fears. Their danger exists continually; and in some cases they seem to be so far sensible of it as to provide in the best manner they can against it; but it is only when the attack is actually made upon them, that they appear to suffer from it. To contemplate the insecurity of their condition with anxiety and dread, requires a degree of reflection which (happily for themselves) they do not possess."

On such a system the brahmin would have concluded with the religious philosopher of Europe, " that if one train of thinking be more desirable than another, it is that which regards the phænomena of nature with a constant reference to a supreme intelligent Author: to have made this the ruling, the habitual sentiment of our minds, is to have laid the foundation of every thing which is religious. The world henceforth becomes a temple, and life itself one continued act of adoration: the change is no less than this, that, whereas formerly God was seldom in our thoughts, we can now scarcely look upon any thing without perceiving its relation to him. Every organized natural body, in the provisions which it contains for its sustentation and propagation, testifies a care on the part of the Creator expressly directed to these purposes. The works of nature want only to be contemplated; when contemplated, they have every thing in them which can astonish by their greatness. For, of the vast scale of operation through which our discoveries carry us, at one end we see an intelligent

Power arranging planetary systems; fixing, for instance, the trajectory of *Saturn*, or constructing a ring of two hundred thousand miles diameter to surround his body, and be suspended like a magnificent arch over the heads of his inhabitants; and, at the other, concerting and providing an appropriate mechanism for the clasping and reclasping of the filaments of the feather of the humming-bird. One being has been concerned in all! Under this stupendous being we live: our happiness, our existence, is in his hands: all we expect must come from him! Nor ought we to feel our situation insecure. In every nature, and in every portion of nature, which we can descry, we find attention bestowed upon even the minutest parts. The hinges in the wings of an *earwig*, and the joints of its antennæ, are as highly wrought as if the Creator had nothing else to finish. We see no signs or diminution of care by multiplicity of objects; or of distraction of thought by variety. We have no reason to fear, therefore, our being forgotten, or overlooked, or neglected!"

Such is the sublime and rational system of the Christian philosopher; who, after the minutest investigation he is capable of, in the great scheme of nature, with a regulated, though fervid rapture finds his mind in a higher state of preparation for the truth and consolations of the gospel. There it is that the Christian feels himself exalted above the deist and mere natural philosopher. "An undevout astronomer is mad." It seems impossible to examine the works of nature without adoring the Great Author of nature; it seems almost equally impossible to read the volume of divine revelation in a spirit of humility and reflection, without being not "almost, but altogether a christian." In a comparison between the truths of that holy volume, and the hypotheses of the two prevailing religions in India, the allowed sublimity, as well as the acknowledged puerility, of the Vedas must recede; the morality and cruelty of the Koran must retire before the tome of divine inspiration: "Bel boweth down, Nebo stoopeth;" when the sun arises, darkness flies! On a superficial view, the doctrine of the metempsychosis appears humane and beautiful; and, until the scheme of Providence is more deeply investigated, the Pythagorean system captivates by a thousand tender suggestions. No advocate for this innocent and merciful hypothesis, has more pathetically appealed to humanity and compassion towards the brute creation than Ovid.

> " Quam malè consuescit, quam se parat ille cruori
> " Impius humano; vituli qui guttura cultro
> " Rumpit, et immotas prœbet mugitibus aures!
> " Aut qui vagitus similes puerilibus hœdum
> " Edentem jugulare potest!" Met. 15, 463.

> " What more advance can mortals make in sin
> " So near perfection, who with blood begin?
> " Deaf to the calf that lies beneath the knife,
> " Looks up, and from her butcher begs her life:
> " Deaf to the harmless kid, that, ere he dies,
> " All methods to secure thy mercy tries;
> " And imitates in vain the children's cries!" Dryden.

Plutarch, in his life of Cato, justly as beautifully observes, that if we kill an animal for our provision, we should do it with the meltings of compassion, and without tormenting it. Let us consider that it is in its own nature cruelty to put a living creature to death:

we at least destroy a soul that has sense and perception. It is no more than the obligation of our very birth to practise equity to our own kind; but humanity may be extended through the whole order of creatures, even to the meanest. Such actions of charity are the overflowing of a mild good-nature on all below us.

Situated as I was for many years among the brahmins in Dhuboy, it was almost impossible not to adopt some of their tenets, and imbibe their benevolent sentiments. There every bird that flew over the city walls found an asylum, every house was crowded with monkeys and squirrels; the trees were filled with peacocks, doves, and parrots; the lake covered by aquatic fowl, and the surrounding groves melodious by bulbuls and warblers of every description. Not a gun molested them. I prevailed with the English officers and soldiers, whenever the garrison was relieved, not to fire a shot within the fortress. I found the edict which I issued respecting the slaughter of oxen, and prohibiting their exposure for sale, procured me a favourable reception among the Hindoos in other places, and it was one cause of the brahmins presenting me the images and sculptured ornaments from their dilapidated temples mentioned in the sequel.

It was not only from the different castes and narrations of religious pilgrims travelling through my districts, that I derived the instruction and entertainment which gave rise to these philosophical discussions; I was as frequently amused at the public wells and halting places by the vanjarrahs and their families already described; and especially by the jugglers, who generally found out the encampments of these travelling merchants. There they spread their carpets, and performed feats of legerdemain superior to any I have seen in England; the most conspicuous was generally one of those women mentioned by Dr. Fryer, who hold nine gilded balls in play, with her hands and feet, and the muscles of her arms and legs, for a long time together, without letting them fall. These people also enable me to confirm another anecdote, which I could not have so scientifically described. This observing traveller says, "I saw a man who swallowed a chain such as our jacks have, and made it clink in his stomach; but on pulling it out, it was not so pleasant to the ladies, for whose diversion it was brought. I was promised also to see a fellow cast up his tripes by his mouth, stomach and all, shewing them to the beholders; but this we excused. In his stead was brought another, who by suction, or drawing of his breath, so contracted his lower belly that it had nothing left to support it, but fell flat to his loins, the midriff being forced into the thorax, and the muscles of the abdomen as clearly marked out by the stiff tendons of the linea alba, as by the most accurate dissection could be made apparent; he moving each row, like living columns, by turns."

These people were frequently accompanied by strolling comedians, who acted Hindoo plays in the style of the Fantoccini. I never saw any Indian theatricals on a larger scale; but on these occasions I have at times heard some very humorous and witty dialogues, but never witnessed a representation that offended piety, morality, or delicacy. That some of their dramatic writings merit very high encomium, we may judge from the beautiful play of Sacontala, translated by Sir William Jones. Nothing can be more innocent, or illustrative of the simplicity of ancient Hindoo manners. The stage ought every where to be a school for virtue. Addison justly remarks, that theatrical entertainments were invented for the accomplishment and refinement of human nature; and the Athenian and Roman plays were written with such a regard to morality, that Socrates used often to frequent the one, and Cicero the other.

In the preface to Sacontala, Sir William Jones observes, that "by whomsoever or in whatever age the entertainment of dramatic poetry was invented, it is very certain, that it was carried to great perfection in its kind when Vicramáditya, who reigned in the first century before Christ, gave encouragement to poets, philologers, and mathematicians, at a time when the Britons were as unlettered and unpolished as the army of Hanumat. Nine men of genius, commonly called the Nine Gems, attended his court, and were splendidly supported by his bounty. Calidas, the author of Sacontala, and the Shakespeare of India, is unanimously allowed to have been one of them. Some of his contemporaries, and other Hindoo poets even to our own times, have composed so many tragedies, comedies, farces, and musical pieces, that the Indian theatre would fill as many volumes as that of any nation in ancient or modern Europe. They are all in verse where the dialogue is elevated, and in prose where it is familiar: the men of rank and learning are represented speaking pure Sanscrit, and the women Prácrit; which is little more than the language of the brahmins melted down by a delicate articulation to the softness of Italian; while the low personæ of the drama speak the vulgar dialects of the several provinces, which they are supposed to inhabit."

I had no European officer, serjeant, or soldier, either at Bhaderpoor or Zinore, nor even a Bombay sepoy; the garrison of

Dhuboy was too weak to admit of more than a detachment to each place from the byracs of Arabs and Scindians stationed there for the general protection of the districts. The former were mostly natives of Arabia, the latter of the country bordering upon the Indus. I had frequently an escort of these people; and living so much among them under banian-trees, and open sheds, afforded me an opportunity of seeing their manners and customs. In the Arabian byracs were a few officers of high character; but in general, those who emigrate to India, and enter into the service of foreign governments, are not men of the best families; the commanders of the greatest respectability attach themselves to the Mahratta chieftains, and different princes of India, and while well paid and properly treated, form excellent subsidiary troops, brave, hardy, and faithful. Some of them, armed with matchlocks and sabres, usually marched with the little escort of cavalry which necessarily accompanied me in my rural excursions.

Similar to the usual accounts of the Arabians in their own country, I found those in the Company's service attached, hospitable, and friendly on all occasions. They take more exercise than the Indians, and those who keep horses are generally fond of field sports. For which purpose, besides the dogs and chetaus they often possess, they train hawks and falcons for the purpose of hunting antelopes and other game in the forests. As usual they carry the bird hood-winked to the chase: on discovering a herd of deer the bird is uncovered, and, after taking a general survey, singles out one as his prey; then mounting aloft he darts down repeatedly on the head of the animal, especially on the eyes, until it is so confused and wounded by the beak and talons of the falcon that it is unable to make further resistance. There the bird clings fast, until the huntsman cuts the antelope's throat, and satiates the little victor with its blood.

The Arabs were very fond of fighting-rams: one of the commanders presented me with a pair of an uncommon size and wonderful power; but they were so expensive in their food, and afforded me so little pleasure by their prowess, that I soon returned them to the donor: after every combat they were regaled with almonds, raisins and pistachio nuts, as a reward for courage, and renewal of strength. The Indians, from the prince on the musnud, to the subahdar of a small fortress, keep fighting animals. In the acme of Mogul splendour, the menageries of the emperors and great omrahs were stored with elephants, lions, tigers, and other beasts, trained for combat: those who can afford it, still retain a few for that purpose: men in inferior stations are content with fighting rams, goats, game-cocks, and quails.

The modern Arabians practise the same hospitality as Abraham, and the ancient patriarchs. D'Arvieux, travelling with a party to an Emir's camp, halted to dine under a tree at the entrance of a village; the shaik sent them eggs, butter, curds, honey, olives, and fruit. Where they passed the night they were supplied with poultry, sheep, or lambs, according to their number; sometimes alive; oftener dressed, in pilaus, stews, kabob, or kab-ab, which is meat cut into small pieces and placed on thin skewers, alternately between slices of onion and green ginger, seasoned with pepper, salt, and kian, fried in ghee, or clarified butter, to be ate with rice and dholl, a sort of split-pea, boiled with the rice. This is a savoury dish, generally liked by the English, of which I often partook with my Arabs; and sometimes, as a great delicacy, they roast a lamb or kid whole, stuffed with almonds, raisins, and spices; or pistachio nuts only, highly seasoned.

Many of these Arabs and Scindians had tame deer, antelopes, and ichneumons, which followed the byrac, and, with their dogs and horses, shared in all the variety of their wandering life. A tame antelope is a very pleasant companion; I kept one a considerable time; as also another beautiful species of deer, which I brought up from a fawn; it became perfectly familiar, and partook of every food congenial to its palate, which had not touched the lips, or been breathed upon by any of the family. The antelopes are said to have an ear for music; I do not assert it from my own experience, but it is generally believed in India: and, in confirmation, Sir Charles Malet favoured me with the following account of an entertainment given by the Mahratta sovereign, at one of his parks near Poonah, in 1792.

" The peshwa having invited me to a novel spectacle, at his *rumna*, or park, about four miles from Poonah, I proceeded thither about two o'clock in the afternoon, with the gentlemen of my party; where we found a tent pitched for the purpose, and were received at the door by some of the principal nobles. The peshwa arrived soon after; and when we were all conveniently seated on carpets, agreeably to oriental costume, four black buck antelopes, of noble mien and elegant form, made their appearance at some distance, moving gracefully before a party of cavalry, who forming a semicircle, gently followed their pace, each horseman holding a long pole, with a red cloth at the end. On approaching the tent, a band of music struck up in loud notes, and three of the antelopes entered in a stately manner. Two swings, commonly used by the Indians, being suspended for the purpose, an antelope ascended on each swing, and couched in the most graceful attitude; the third reclined on the carpet in a similar posture. On the loud music ceasing, a set of dancing-girls entered, and danced to softer strains before the antelopes; who, chewing the cud, lay in a state of sweet tranquillity and satisfaction. At this time the fourth antelope, who had hitherto appeared more shy than his comrades, came into the tent and laid himself upon the carpet in the same manner. An attendant then put one of the swings in motion, and swung the antelope for some time, without his being at all disturbed. The amusement having continued as long as the peshwa thought proper, it was closed by the game-keeper placing a garland of flowers over the horns of the principal antelope, on which he rose, and the four animals went off together.

"The peshwa informed me, that seven months had been employed to bring the antelopes to this degree of familiarity, without the smallest constraint, as they wandered at their pleasure, during the whole time, amongst large herds of deer in the *rumna;* which, although I have mentioned as a park, is not enclosed, nor has it any kind of fence. I was also assured these animals were not impelled by appetite, no grain or food of any kind having been given them: on this I am somewhat of a sceptic. The peshwa was persuaded they were thus attracted by the power of music; aided, perhaps, by some particular ingenuity of the men who profess the art of familiarizing this beautiful and harmless animal. The peshwa seemed to be much pleased with the amusement; which in innocence is suited to the tenets of the brahmins, if not to their present character."

Probably when Sir Charles wrote the preceding description, he would not have been sceptical had he read a passage in the Asiatic Researches written by Sir William Jones, which beautifully illustrates and confirms the truth of the spectacle at Poonah; I have also in my possession a Hindoo painting in water colours, very well done, where some young females are playing on instruments, and antelopes, attracted by the music, approach from the woods. The passage to which I allude is thus mentioned: "I have been assured, by a credible eye-witness, that two wild antelopes used often to come from their woods to the place where a more savage beast, Sirajudaulah, entertained himself with concerts, and that they listened to the strains with an appearance of pleasure; until the monster, in whose soul there was no music, shot one of them to display his archery. A learned native of this country told me that he had frequently seen the most venomous and malignant snakes leave their holes upon hearing tunes on a flute; which, as he supposed, gave them peculiar delight. An intelligent Persian, who repeated his story again and again, and permitted me to write it down from his lips, declared he had more than once been present when a celebrated lutanist, Mirza Mohammed, surnamed *bulbul*, was playing to a large company in a grove near Shiraz, where he distinctly saw the nightingales trying to vie with the musician; sometimes warbling on the trees, sometimes fluttering from branch to branch, as if they wished to approach the instrument whence the melody proceeded, and at length dropping on the ground in a kind of ecstasy, from which they were soon raised, he assured me, by a change of the mode. I hardly know how to disbelieve the testimony of men who had no system of their own to support, and could have no interest in deceiving me."

While the mischievous monkey, as well as the innocent dove, found an asylum within the walls of Dhuboy, the adjacent country was infested by tigers and savage beasts; who, in defiance of Pythagorean systems and brahminical tenets, waged perpetual war on the antelopes and innocent animals near the villages; even the monkeys with all their wily craftiness could not escape them. The peasants in the wilds of Bhaderpoor confirmed the stratagem used by the tiger to effect his purpose, as mentioned by Dr. Fryer. "The woodmen assert, that when the tiger intends to prey upon the monkies, he uses this stratagem: the monkies, at his first approach, give warning by their confused chattering, and immediately betake themselves to the highest and smallest twigs of the trees; when the tiger, seeing them out of his reach, and sensible of their fright, lies couchant under the tree, and then falls a roaring; at which they, trembling, let go their hold, and tumbling down, he picks them up to satisfy his hunger. That monkies are their food, their very ordure declares, scattered up and down, where is visible the shaggy coats of hair of these creatures."

As I did not always travel with the Arabs and Scindians lately mentioned, I found it necessary to be escorted, in the distant parts of my purgunnas, by a little troop of cavalry, and a number of armed peons; not so much from the fear of tigers and wild beasts, as of the Bheels and Gracias, a savage race of men who inhabit the hills and wood-lands near Bhaderpoor and Chandode. The protection I afforded the villages against their cruel depredations, irritated these savages against me; and by experience I found that the severity of the Mahratta government was more efficacious in controlling these people than British lenity. Not long after my arrival at Dhuboy, sitting at dinner with a young gentleman lately arrived from England, the chopdar introduced some peasants bearing a dish covered with a napkin, which, supposing it to contain a peacock, or part of an antelope, I desired might be put on the table. I attempt not to describe our horror and astonishment when, on lifting up the cloth, we beheld a man's head just decollated. It was the head of a savage Gracia killed during the preceding night by the vertunnees, or armed men of a village, where a party of them had made a descent to commit robbery and murder.

Nothing shocks humanity more than to read of Marc Antony's delight at seeing the heads of Cicero, and the noble Romans he had proscribed, except the idea of the two princesses in Palestine, a mother and a daughter; the one presenting, and the other receiving, the head of the Baptist in a charger. True it is, that the Persian monarchs heaped up pyramids of heads at their palace gates, and a king of Israel received them in baskets, in the same manner as Hyder Ally and his son Tippoo were regaled at breakfast with a vesselful of the ears and noses of our poor sepoys who fell into their hands. My young friend and myself were so disgusted by the sight of a single head, and so much did it militate against British feeling, that I immediately issued the most public orders to prohibit such transactions in future. With concern I found this did not prove an act of mercy to the villages, who, in consequence, became more exposed to the atrocity of these cruel banditti.

Cruelty was not peculiar to the Gracias, or the less civilized parts of Guzerat; I met with frequent instances, in various ranks of society, inconsistent with the mild tenets of Hinduism, or with common humanity. I shall mention one only, which occurred during an excursion in the confines of the Brodera purgunna, in a village contiguous to my encampment; where the women, assembling, as usual, at day-break to draw water for their families and cattle, found the body of a beautiful young woman, richly dressed, in the public well. Two strangers on horseback arrived at the coultry late in the preceding evening, and desired permission from the tandar, (an officer who has the care of a certain number of villages) to pass the night there, as travellers. They were both armed, and one of them had a large bag tied behind him: no further notice was taken of them, and before morning they departed. From subsequent inquiries I had every reason to suppose this young beauty was one of the ladies in Futty's Sihng's haram; and having incurred the displeasure of a jealous tyrant, was, by his order, thrown alive into the well; a fate similar to that of the unfortunate female mentioned in Ragobah's haram during the Mahratta campaign. I preserve a bracelet, composed of alternate beads of embossed gold and coral, taken from the arm of the ill-fated beauty in my district, in remembrance of her cruel fate.

The tandar and Hindoo police officers requested me on this occasion to send for some of the bhauts, already mentioned, or some other soothsayers, from Serulah and Chandode; who are supposed to possess the art of divination, and are in consequence the reputed prophets and seers of the country: these they pretended would inform me of the truth, and prevent an improper suspicion. But being then within a few miles of Brodera, Futty Sihng's capital, I collected many circumstances which left me no doubt of the murderer, and considering it altogether as a foreign concern, I took no further notice of the deed.

Many transactions in the administration of justice at Dhuboy brought me acquainted with the Hindoo soothsayers above-mentioned. They are an extraordinary set of people, more particularly described in a following chapter. Although I do not liken them to Samuel and the early prophets in sacred writ, (nor did they immediately resembie the augurs and diviners of Homer and Virgil) I often found them and their employers entertaining the same ideas, and following the same practice as is recorded of the seers in Palestine; especially in the little story told of Saul and his servants, who being sent in quest of some strayed asses belonging to his father, had passed through the land of Shalisha and Shalim, and found them not: he therefore purposed returning home without them, to relieve his father's anxiety for their own safety. Being then near to Ramah, the residence of Samuel the prophet, the servant said unto Saul, "Behold now, there is in this city a man of God, and he is an honourable man; all that he saith cometh surely to pass: now let us go thither; peradventure he can shew us our way that we should go. Then said Saul to his servant, but behold, if we go, what shall we bring the man? for the bread is spent in our vessels, and there is not a present to bring to the man of God; what have we? And the servant answered, behold, I have here at hand the fourth part of a shekel of silver; that will I give to the man of God to tell us our way."

Such is exactly the state of things at this day in the eastern districts of Guzerat: in every considerable town, and most of the large villages, resided one or more of these Hindoo soothsayers: who, contrary to justice and good policy, were consulted on all occasions. Saul, though wrong in his opinion of a prophet of the Most High, was perfectly right in his judgment respecting the generality of these seers. An application to a modern oriental diviner, unaccompanied by a present, would be very little attended to. The ascendancy of these people over the vulgar mind is wonderful, and in my jurisdiction was often troublesome.

The wilds of Bhaderpoor, at the foot of the eastern hills, are romantic and beautiful, finely wooded, and abounding with flowing streams at all seasons; in this respect it resembles the scriptural Jobbath, a land of rivers of waters; an appellation of a very significant meaning in the torrid zone.

But, as I have already observed, it is dangerous to visit this delightful scenery without a large party of armed men, on account of the savage animals with which they abound: the number of tigers, leopards, and panthers is immense. During the viceroyship of the Mogul princes in Guzerat, and also at a later period among some of the Mahratta chieftains, it was customary for these great men, and their numerous attendants, to pitch their tents in unfrequented tracts, for the purpose of hunting those ferocious beasts. Their encampments, especially of the Moguls, were extensive and magnificent; there they entertained their friends in a sumptuous manner during the continuance of the hunt, which sometimes lasted several weeks. Such probably has been the custom in Persia and Arabia, from the time of Nimrod to the present day. In ancient history we read of royal feasts in tents and pavilions; Olearius, who attended a Danish ambassador to the court of Persia, says "they were invited by the king to accompany him into the country on a hunting and hawking party; where, on their arrival at an Armenian village, they found tents prepared for the reception of the company. Their various colours, and the peculiar manner of the encampment, gave it a most pleasing appearance."

I have occasionally joined the European parties in their tiger hunts, as particularly mentioned in the wilds of Turcaseer. The forests on the confines of Bhaderpoor, are equally wild and infested with beasts of prey. As I can offer nothing so interesting upon this subject as a description of a tiger-hunt in Bengal, the subject of a letter from Sir John Day to Sir William Jones, which I have had many years in my possession, I shall not apologize for inserting so highly-finished a picture of this royal sport; which was given to me by a very intimate friend of the writer, and has not to my knowledge appeared in print.

Description of a tiger-hunt, upon the banks of the Ganges, near Chinsura in Bengal in April 1784.

Although you could not partake of the pleasure, I am resolved that you shall not entirely escape the fatigue of our enterprize; and with that laudable view, although we have not returned more than an hour, and at this moment a sound sleep were heaven to me, I snatch the pen to give you the following hasty and imperfect description of the business of the day.

Matters had been thus judiciously arranged: tents were sent off yesterday, and an encampment formed within a mile and a half of the jungle which was to be the scene of our operations; and in this jungle the thickets of long rank grass and reeds are in many places fifteen feet high. At one o'clock this morning thirty elephants, with the servants, and refreshments of all kinds, were dispatched; at two we all followed in fly-palanquins; at a quarter after four we reached the encampment, and having rested near two hours, we mounted our elephants, and proceeded to the jungle.

In our way we met with game of all kinds: hares, antelopes, hog-deer, wild boars, and wild buffaloes; but nothing could divert our attention from the fiercer and more glorious game.

At the grey of the dawn we formed a line of great extent, and entered a small detached jungle. My elephant (sorely against my grain; but there was no remedy, for my driver was a keen sportsman, and he and I spoke no common language) passed through the centre, but happily no tiger had at that hour nestled there. I saw, however, as I passed through it, the bed of one, in which there were an half-devoured bullock and two human skulls; with an heap of bones, some bleached, and some still red with gore.

We had not proceeded five hundred yards beyond the jungle, when we heard a general cry on our left of Baug, baug, baug! On hearing this exclamation of Tiger! we wheeled; and, forming the line anew, entered the great jungle, when the spot where a single tiger lay having been pointed, on the discharge of the first gun a scene presented itself confessed by all the experienced tiger hunters present to be the finest they had ever seen. Five full-grown royal tigers sprung together from the same spot, where they had sat in bloody congress. They ran diversely; but running heavily, they all couched again in new covers within the same jungle, and all were marked. We followed, having formed the line into a crescent, so as to embrace either extremity of the jungle: in the centre were the houdar (or state) elephants, with the marksmen, and the ladies, to comfort and encourage them. In one Mr. Zoffani with Mrs. Ramus, in the other Mr. Ramus with Lady Day, led the attack; my brother and I supported them; and we were followed by Major Bateman, Mr. Crispe, Mr. Longcraft, and Mr. Van Europe, a Dutch gentleman.

These gentlemen had each an elephant to himself. When we had slowly and warily approached the spot where the first tiger lay, he moved not until we were just upon him; when, with a roar that resembled thunder, he rushed upon us. The elephants wheeled off at once; and (for it is not to be described by any quadruped-motion we know, I must therefore coin a term for the occasion) shuffled off. They returned, however, after a flight of about fifty yards, and again approaching the spot where the tiger had lodged himself, towards the skirts of the jungle, he once more rushed forth, and springing at the side of an elephant upon which three of the natives were mounted, at one stroke tore a portion of the pad from under them; and one of the riders, panic struck, fell off. The tiger, however, seeing his enemies in force, returned, slow and indignant, into his shelter; where, the place he lay in being marked, a heavy and well directed fire was poured in by the principal marksmen; when, pushing in, we saw him in the struggle of death, and growling and foaming he expired.

We then proceeded to seek the others, having first distinguished the spot by pitching a tall spear, and tying to the end of it the muslin of a turban. We roused the other three, in close succession, and, with little variation of circumstances, killed them all; the oldest, and most ferocious of the family, had, however, early in the conflict, very sensibly quitted the scene of action, and escaped to another part of the country.

While the fate of the last and largest was depending, more shots were fired than in the three other attacks; he escaped four several assaults, and taking post in different parts of the jungle, rushed upon us at each wound he received with a kindled rage, and as often put the whole line to flight. In his last pursuit he singled out the elephant upon which Lady Day was; and was at its tail, with jaws distended, and in the act of rising upon his hind paws to fasten on her, when fortunately she cleared the jungle; and a general discharge from the hunters having forced him to give up the chase, he returned to his shelter. The danger, I believe, was not very great; but it was sufficient, when she shall be again invited, to make her say with Lord Chesterfield, when they attempted to allure him to a second fox-hunt, "*I have been.*"

The chase being over, we returned in triumph to our encampment, and were followed by the spoils of the morning, and by an accumulating multitude of the peasants from the circumjacent villages, who pressed round an open tent in which we sat at breakfast, with gratulations, blessings, and thanksgiving. The four tigers were laid in front; the natives viewed them with terror, and some with tears. There was a very affecting incident, which so fastened upon Zoffani's imagination, and so touched his heart, that he means to give it a principal place in a picture which he meditates upon the subject; and which, had YOU been with us, I should have hoped might have been also recorded elegantly and pathetically in song.

An old woman, looking earnestly at the largest tiger, and pointing at times to his tusks, and at times lifting his fore-paws, and viewing his talons, her furrows bathed in tears, in broken and moaning tones narrated something to a little circle composed of three brahmins and a young woman with a child in her arms. No human misery could pierce the phlegm and apathy of the brahmins, and with *them* there was not a feature softened; but horror and sorrow were alternately painted in the face of the female; and, from her clasping at times her child more closely to her breast, I guessed the subject of the old woman's story, and upon inquiry I found that I was right in my conjecture. She was widowed and childless; she owed both her misfortunes to the tigers of that jungle, and most probably to those which then lay dead before her; for they, it was believed, had recently carried off her husband and her two sons grown up to manhood, and now she wanted food: in the phrenzy of her grief she alternately described her loss to the crowd, and in a wild scream demanded her husband and her children from the tigers; indeed it was a piteous spectacle!

The site of our encampment was well chosen; it was a small sloping lawn, the verdure fresh, and skirted on three sides with trees; the fourth bounded by the deep bed of a torrent-river. At proper distances on this lawn, there were five large and commodious tents, pitched in a semicircle: that in which we all assembled, and passed the sultry part of the day, was carpeted, and by means of the tattces of aromatic grass, continually watered, kept at a temperature pretty near to that of an April day in England. Here we had a luxurious cold dinner, with a variety of excellent wines, and other liquors, well cooled; and while we dined the French-horns and clarionets played marches, hunting-pieces descriptive of the death of the game, and other slow movements; the tigers still lying in front, and the people still assembled, but retired to a greater distance; where they anxiously waited the signal for skinning and cutting up the slain; for with them the fat of a tiger is a panacea; the tongue dried and pulverized a sovereign specific in nervous cases, and every part applicable to some use; even the whiskers they deem a deadly poison, and most anxiously, but secretly, seek them, as the means, in drink, of certain destruction to an enemy.

As my share of the spoil, I have reserved one of the talons of the tiger which pursued Lady Day, and intend to have it set in gold, with a swivel and fillet, ornamented with diamonds, and filling it with ottar of roses, I shall sometime hence surprize her with it, and insist upon her giving it a place among the trinkets of her watch, as a trophy; the "spolia opima," torn from the body of an enemy slain in battle. I have reserved also a skin for you; which shall when cured be sent to you; and I shall hope to see it, ere many years elapse, an hammer-cloth to an handsome chariot of yours in the streets of London.

Dinner over, the tigers skinned, and their flesh and offal distributed, as soon as the sun declined, we returned to Chinsura; and here ends the history of the chase; in which I have been thus minute, that you may be tempted to accompany us in some future expedition; and if not, that you may be able to say that you have been authentically informed upon the subject by an eye-witness.

CHAPTER XXVII.

A DESCRIPTION OF ZINORE;
THE HINDOO TEMPLES AND SACRED GROVES ON THE BANKS OF THE NERBUDDA;
AN ACCOUNT OF THE NATIVE HINDOOS, AND PARTICULAR ANECDOTES OF A SINGULAR SECT OF BRAHMINS.

1781.

How sweet NERBUDDA smiles, and glides
Luxuriant o'er her broad autumnal bed!
Her waves perpetual verdure spread,
Whilst health and plenty deck her golden sides!

Thy sacred fanes I often sought,
And verdant plains, by tepid breezes fann'd,
Where health extends her pinions bland;
Thy groves, where pious Valmic sat and thought;
Where Vyasa pour'd the strain sublime,
That laughs at all-consuming Time,
And Brahmins rapt, the lofty Veda sing!

Blest Nerbudda! o'er cherish'd lands,
To Brahma's grateful race endear'd,
Throws wide her fostering arms, and on her banks divine,
Sees temples, groves, and glittering towers, that in her crystal shine.

HYMN TO GANGA, *altered.*

CONTENTS.

CHAPTER XXVII.

ANOTHER purgunna under my management, called Zinore, contained a tolerable town and fifty villages. Zinore, the capital of the district, was fifteen miles south from Dhuboy, and forty to the eastward of Baroche. Neither the public or private buildings were of much importance; but it was delightfully situated on the steep banks of the Nerbudda; with a noble flight of a hundred stone steps from the houses to the water-side, which would have added to the grandeur of a much larger city. The Hindoo temples, brahminical groves, and a few superior houses, indicate its having been once a place of consequence. When I took possession of it for the Company, it contained about ten thousand inhabitants; generally weavers of coarse cotton cloth, for the Persian and Arabian markets, with some finer baftas and muslins for home consumption. Very few of these cottons are dyed or painted at Dhuboy or Zinore; the art has attained a much greater perfection at Ahmedabad and Surat.

Cotton grows abundantly in most parts of the Zinore purgunna; the cultivation, gathering, cleaning, spinning, and weaving this valuable production, employs the inhabitants of all ages. Throughout the greater part of Guzerat we may apply Orme's remarks on the manufactures of Coromandel, that a people born under a sun too sultry to admit the exercise and fatigue necessary to form a robust nation, endeavour to obtain their scanty livelihood by the easiest labour: it is from hence, perhaps, that the manufactures of cloth are so multiplied in Hindostan. Spinning and weaving are the slightest tasks which a man can be set to; and it is observable, that the manufactures prevail most, both in quantity and perfection, where the people are least capable of robust labour. It is difficult in such provinces to find a village in which almost every man, woman, and child, is not employed in the cotton manufacture. The loom is fixed under a tree, and the thread laid the whole length of the cloth. The Hindoo weaver is not a despicable caste; he is next to the scribe, and above all mechanics. These people produce works of extraordinary niceness; and as much as an Indian is born deficient in mechanical strength, so much is his whole frame endowed with an exceeding degree of sensibility and pliantness. Orme, speaking of the silk manufactory in Bengal, says, "the women wind off the raw silk from the pod of the worm: a single pod of raw silk is divided into twenty different degrees of fineness; and so exquisite is the feeling of these women, that whilst the thread is running through their fingers so swiftly that their eye can be of no assistance, they will break it off exactly as the assortments change, at once from the first to the twentieth, from the nineteenth to the second."

At no period have the manufactures of Guzerat or the Deccan equalled in fineness and delicacy the muslins of Bengal and the eastern provinces: and yet, fine as they now are, they were formerly of a more exquisite texture. The fall of the Moguls, who spared no expense for these articles, is perhaps a principal reason for their decline. As an extraordinary instance of their curious texture, Tavernier mentions, that when the ambassadors of Shah Sefi, king of Persia, returned from India, he presented his royal master a cocoa-nut, richly set with jewels, containing a muslin turban, sixty covits, or thirty English yards in length, so extremely fine, that it could hardly be felt by the touch. Some of the Cachemirean shawls are of so delicate a fabric that they may be drawn through a wedding ring.

In the Zinore purgunna, a country little known in the annals of Hindostan, I saw human nature almost in primitive simplicity, but far removed from the savage condition of the Indians of America, or the natives of the South-sea islands. The state of civil society in which the Hindoos are united in those remote situations, seems to admit of no change or amelioration. The brahmins pass their lives in listless indolence within the precincts of the temples, with little profit either to themselves or the community. Among the inferior castes, whose minds are uncultivated, and who have no communication with the rest of the world, I found it next to an impossibility to introduce a single improvement in agriculture, building, or any useful art or science. In any nation, where the art of printing is unknown, and no books are introduced, the higher classes can enjoy but little intellectual pleasure.

I sometimes frequented places where the natives had never seen an European, and were ignorant of every thing concerning us: there I beheld manners and customs simple as were those in the patriarchal age; there, in the very style of Rebecca and the damsels of Mesopotamia, the Hindoo villagers treated me with that artless hospitality so delightful in the poems of Homer, and other ancient records. On a sultry day, near a Zinore village, having rōde faster than my attendants, while waiting their arrival under a tamarind tree, a young woman came to the well; I asked for a little water, but neither of us having a drinking vessel, she hastily left me, as I imagined, to bring an earthen cup for the purpose, as I should have polluted a vessel of metal: but as Jael, when Sisera asked for water, gave him milk, and "brought forth butter in a lordly dish," so did this village damsel, with more sincerity than Heber's wife, bring me a pot of milk, and a lump of butter on the delicate leaf of the banana, "the lordly dish" of the Hindoos. The former I gladly accepted: on my declining the latter, she immediately made it up into two balls, and gave one to each of the oxen that drew my hackery. Butter is a luxury to these animals, and enables them to bear additional fatigue.

On my first arrival at Zinore, the zemindars, as customary, paid me a respectful visit, bringing presents of money and jewels: those I refused, except one rupee; which, notwithstanding every injunction to the contrary, I did take from the head zemindar of each district under my charge. These four rupees I preserve in remembrance of the people among whom I lived, who would have been hurt at a total refusal. Although prohibited by oaths and covenants from accepting any valuable presents, I did not refuse what they sent for me and my people to the shamyanah I fixed near the bank of the river, for want of a more comfortable residence in the town. These articles so exactly resembled those which Barzillai and his friends brought to David at Mahanaim, that hardly a single word need be altered: "Shobi, and Macher, and

Barzillai brought beds, and basons, and earthen vessels, and wheat and barley, and flour, and parched corn, and beans, and lentiles, and honey, and butter, and cheese of kine, and sheep, for David, and for the people that were with him: for they said the people are hungry, and weary, and thirsty in the wilderness."

The more I saw of the Hindoos in those remote districts, the more I perceived the truth of Orme's remark, that Hindostan has been inhabited from the earliest antiquity, by a people who have no resemblance, either in their figure, or manners, with any of the nations contiguous to them; and that although conquerors have established themselves at different times, in various parts of India, yet the original inhabitants have lost very little of their original character.

A few of the Guzerat brahmins, especially at Zindore and Chandode, were men of education, who had studied at Benares, and were masters of the Sanscreet language, that inexhaustible mine of Hindoo literature, art, and science; which, Sir William Jones says, is "a most wonderful structure; more perfect than the Greek, more copious than the Latin; and more exquisitely refined than either; yet bearing to both of them a stronger affinity, both in the roots of verbs, and in the forms of grammar, than could possibly have been produced by accident; so strong indeed, that no philologer could examine them all three, without believing them to have sprung from some common source, which perhaps no longer exists."

Those towns on the banks of the Nerbudda, so famous for brahmin seminaries, contain numerous schools for the education of other boys: these are generally in the open air, on the shady side of the house. The scholars sit on mats, or cow-dung floors, and are taught as much of religion as their caste admits of; also reading, writing, and arithmetic; the two latter by making letters and figures in sand upon the floor. Education, like every thing else among the Hindoos, is extremely simple: that of the girls is generally confined to domestic employments.

Near Zinore were several monuments in memory of those devotees, so often mentioned, who bury themselves alive, in hopes of expiating their sins, or of pleasing the destructive powers by such a sacrifice; and under the lofty banks of the Nerbudda, as on the shore of the Ganges, I was told the Hindoos sometimes drown their sick and aged parents. In this respect they certainly act directly contrary to our ideas of filial affection, and common humanity; but I am willing to hope it proceeds from a good motive. Similar customs prevailed in many ancient nations. Herodotus says, when one of the Massagetæ becomes infirm through age, his assembled relations put him to death; boiling along with his body the flesh of sheep, and other animals, upon which they feast. The Hyperboreans, who eat no meat, but live entirely upon fruit, put all those to death who attain the age of sixty years. The present inhabitants of Arracan are said to accelerate the death of their friends and relations when they see them afflicted by old age, or an incurable disease; with them it is an act of piety.

From my little encampment on the banks of the Nerbudda, although accustomed to such spectacles at Baroche and Surat, I have been frequently astonished at the number of both sexes in the river during great part of the day. From Zinore to Chandode the stream is reckoned peculiarly holy; and there not only religious purity, but healing efficacy, is annexed to the ablution. Pilgrims from distant provinces resort thither for the cure of different complaints: they do not, I believe, entirely rely on the virtue of the water for convalescence, but apply also to the medical skill of the brahmins, who are the principal physicians in India.

A belief in the purification of the Ganges, Nerbudda, and other sacred rivers of India, universally prevails: all castes of Hindoos resort to them at stated periods to perform their religious ceremonies. There may be some among them, who, like Naaman the Syrian general, would say, "Are not Abana and Pharpar, rivers of Damascus, better than all the waters of Israel; may I not wash in them and be clean?" and, like him, may treat the Indian Jordan with contempt. Such a character is very rare, nor would his example have much influence in a society where ancient manners and customs, especially in religious concerns, are so tenaciously adhered to.

We recommended the cleansing virtues of the Nerbudda to an elderly mahomedan, named Shaik Edroos, who lived many years in our family. At first he waited at table, and performed little offices about our persons; but on the appearance of some spots of leprosy we excused him from that part of his employment. These spots increasing, his motley skin grew so disgusting, that we dispensed with his attendance at table, and at length procured him a situation where the disorder did not interfere with his duty; for, although Shaik was not suddenly smitten, like Gehazi, for avarice and falsehood, yet his skin gradually experienced the same effect, until, like him, he became "a leper as white as snow." The whiteness of the Indians afflicted with this disorder is so extremely disagreeable as to render the complexion of the blackest Ethiopian beautiful in the comparison. Shaik having no faith in the religious or physical effects of the Nerbudda, took a voyage up the Red-Sea, and performed a pilgrimage to the sacred shrines of his own prophet at Mecca and Medina, by which he imagined he attained no small degree of sanctity. After his return, I frequently saw him mounted on an eminence near one of the gates of Baroche, haranguing a large crowd of both sexes on religious and moral subjects, to the delight of his wondering audience, and the surprise of his quondam employers, who were ignorant of his oratorical powers.

Shaik was one of those enthusiasts who laid a great stress on having performed a pilgrimage to Mecca; and, in consequence, thought himself superior to every person in our family, which consisted of Hindoos, Mahomedans, Parsees, Roman Catholic and Protestant Christians; exclusive of the Pariahs and Chandalas who were employed in menial offices without doors. We all agreed very well; for, except our slaves, none ate in the house, nor did we furnish them with clothes, or provisions of any kind. A monthly stipend of twelve rupees to the upper servant, gradually lessened to that of the poor Chandala, who received but two; which I believe was fully sufficient in a climate where their wants are very few compared with colder regions. Shaik had seen better days; was of a good family, had served in the army, and been wounded in Ragobah's campaign in Guzerat; as a domestic servant he was not so contented as the rest, his religion not having taught him that patience and resignation, so generally practised by the Indians in consequence of their belief in a sort of unlimited predestination:

neither was he at all given to taciturnity, another striking trait in the Mahomedan character. He often amused me with his account of the hajje, or pilgrimage to Mecca, and confirmed all that is related by travellers on those occasions; especially those ceremonies and penances mentioned by Pitts, when the hajjes, or pilgrims, enter into *Hirrawen;* a ceremony from which the females are exempted; but the men taking off all their clothes, cover themselves with two *hirrawems*, or large white wrappers; "one they put round their middle, which reaches down to their ancles; with the other they cover the upper part of the body, except the head; and they wear no other thing on their bodies except these wrappers, and a pair of thin-soled shoes like sandals, their insteps being all naked. In this manner, like humble penitents, they go from Rabbock to the temple of Mecca, enduring the scorching heat of the sun until the skin is burnt off their backs and arms, and their heads swollen to a great degree. It was a sight to pierce the heart, to behold so many thousands in their garments of humility and mortification, with their naked heads, and cheeks watered with tears; and to hear their grievous sighs and sobs, begging earnestly for the remission of their sins; promising newness of life, using a form of penitential expressions, and thus continuing for the space of four or five hours.

The Hindoo temples at Zinore, though smaller and less splendid than those at Chandode, are esteemed peculiarly sacred; and some of the sculpture and paintings, as the works of modern times, are interesting, and superior to those generally met with. Among the statues of the inferior deities in the Hindoo mythology, there appear to be many allusions to Camdeo, or Kama-deva, who, Sir

William Jones informs us, "is the same with the Grecian Eros, and the Roman Cupido; but the Indian description of his person and arms, his family, attendants, and attributes, has new and peculiar beauties.

"According to the mythology of Hindostan, he was the son of Maya, or the general *attracting* power, and married to Retty, or *Affection*, and his bosom friend is Bessent, or *Spring*. He is represented as a beautiful youth, sometimes conversing with his mother and consort, in the midst of his gardens and temples; sometimes riding by moonlight on a parrot or lory, and attended by dancing-girls, or nymphs; the foremost of whom bears his colours, which are a fish, on a red ground. His favorite place of resort is a large tract of country round Agra, and principally the plains of Matra, where Krishen also, and the nine Gopia, who are clearly the Apollo and muses of the Greeks, usually spend the night with music and dancing. His bow of sugar-cane, or flowers, with a string of bees, and his five arrows, each pointed with an Indian blossom of a healing quality, are allegories equally new and beautiful."

Sir William Jones has translated a hymn to Camdeo, which is replete with beauty and oriental imagery, from which I shall only select these stanzas, as a most elegant illustration of the character of this powerful deity, and especially of his bow and arrows.

"What potent god from Agra's orient bowers
"Floats through the lucid air, whilst living flowers
"With sunny twine the vocal arbors wreathe,
"And gales enamour'd heavenly fragrance breathe?
"Hail, pow'r unknown, for at thy beck
"Vales and groves their bosoms deck;

" And every laughing blossom dresses
" With gems of dew his musky tresses.
" I feel, I feel thy genial flame divine,
" And hallow thee, and kiss thy shrine.

" God of the flowery shafts and flowery bow,
" Delight of all above and all below!
" Thy lov'd companion, constant from his birth,
" In heaven clep'd *Bessent*, and gay *Spring* on earth,
" Weaves thy green robe and flaunting bowers,
" And from thy clouds draws balmy showers;
" He with fresh arrows fills thy quiver,
" (Sweet the gift, and sweet the giver!)
" And bids the many-plum'd warbling throng
" Burst the pent blossoms with their song.

" He bends the luscious cane, and twists the string
" With bees how sweet! but ah, how keen their sting!
" He with five flow'rets tips thy ruthless darts
" Which through five senses pierce enraptur'd hearts:
" Strong *Champa*, rich in odorous gold,
" Warm *Amer*, nurs'd in heavenly mould,
" Dry *Nagkeser*, in silver smiling,
" Hot *Kitticum* our sense beguiling,
" And last, to kindle fierce the scorching flame
" *Loveshaft*, which gods bright *Bela* name.

" Thy mildest influence to thy bard impart,
" To warm, but not consume, his heart."

The temples of Guzerat abound with phallic representations; and with figures of most of the deities, who become the alternate objects of worship: for the northern brahmins, as well as those mentioned by Dr. Buchanan in Malabar, " when in sickness and distress, invoke with fear and trembling the power of Bhairava, and of the female Sactis; who were formerly, perhaps, considered by the natives as the malignant spirits of the woods, mountains, and rivers; and worshipped by sacrifices, like the gods of the rude tribes which now inhabit the hilly country east from Bengal, and whose poverty has hitherto prevented the incursions of the sacred orders of their more learned western neighbours."

In the groves surrounding the Guzerat temples, as in many other parts of India, are sacred bulls, belonging to their respective Dewals. These animals, after being dedicated with great ceremony, by the brahmins, to different deities, have a distinguishing mark set upon them, and are permitted to go whither they please; and to eat whatever they like, of grain, provender, or crops in the fields; not only without molestation, but frequently by invitation; these consecrated animals seem to be as much venerated as the Apis in ancient Egypt. Where they are not kept within the precincts of the temples, as also where they most abound, there is generally a representation of one or more of the race, sculptured in marble, stone, or petrified rice, reposing under the banian or peepal trees; living or dead they are supposed to add to the sanctity of these holy retreats. I mentioned the nearly fatal consequence of my having inadvertently strayed into one of these enclosures in Malabar: I met with no such prohibition in Guzerat, neither within my own purgunnahs, nor any other; I seldom entered the temples, but often read or made a sketch under the same banian tree with the officiating brahmin and his associates, without giving the least offence.

Such shady enclosures seem to have been an appendage to most religions. The idolatrous Israelites, in imitation of their Pagan neighbours, planted those ilex-groves in Judea, for which they were reproached by their prophets, and sacrificed to the heathen deities on the shady hills of Palestine. This extended from Asia to Europe: from the burr trees of the brahmins to the oaks of the druids. Their deities, according to Tacitus, were not immured in temples, nor represented under any kind of resemblance to the human form. To do either were, in their opinion, to derogate from the majesty of superior beings. Woods and groves were the sacred depositaries; and the spot being consecrated to those pious uses, they gave to that sacred recess the name of the divinity that filled the place which was never profaned by the steps of man. The gloom filled every mind with awe; revered at a distance, and never seen but with the eye of contemplation.

The prophetical writings contain many allusions to Hindoo customs: "they inflame themselves with idols under every green tree; they sanctify and purify themselves in the gardens, behind one tree in the midst: among the smooth stones of the stream in thy groves, even on them hast thou poured out a drink-offering, and there hast thou offered a meat-offering." These smooth and shapeless stones have been at all times an object of worship: it appears extraordinary, when we consider the elegant form of the Venus di Medici, Venus Urania, or any other statue of this celebrated Grecian goddess, that when Titus visited Cyprus, the statue of the Paphian Venus had no resemblance to the human form, but was a round figure, broad at the base, and growing fine by degrees, until, like a cone, it lessened to a point. The translator in a note on this passage in Tacitus, remarks that Clemens of Alexandria supposes the statuary had not the skill to give the elegance of symmetry and proportion; he therefore left the form and delicacy of Venus to the imagination: as Ovid says, is qua latent, meliora putat. Tacitus observes, the reason, whatever it be, is not explained; whether it has any allusion to the uncouth lingam, or any other almost shapeless stone altars of the Hindoos, I am not competent to determine.

In the out-skirts of Zinore, separated from all other inhabitants of the town, were a number of poor Chandalahs, the outcasts of society; objects of compassion to every thinking mind, from the deprivations and degradations they are compelled to submit to by impolitic and inhuman laws. Their condition appears the more humiliating, when contrasted with the luxurious brahmins, in their calm recesses, surrounded by the ramjannees, and every kind of indulgence allowed to their privileged caste: the one pampered by voluptuous indolence, the other degraded below the monkeys which surround them, and deprived of religious ordinances.

How different is the conduct of these "*transcendantly divine*" brahmins towards the poor Chandalahs, from that of Nehemiah, when the Jews returned to Palestine, from the Babylonish captivity, ignorant of the Mosaical law, and all the sublime truths of their religion. "After repairing the walls of Jerusalem, rebuilding the temple, and preparing the priests and Levites, Nehemiah and Ezra assembled all the congregation of Israel, both men and women, and all that could hear with understanding, and brought the book of the law before them; and the priests read in the book, in the law of God, distinctly, and gave the sense, and caused them to understand the meaning; and the Levites taught the people; and they wept when they heard the words of the law. And Nehemiah and Ezra said unto the people, this day is holy unto the Lord your God, mourn not, nor weep; go your way, eat of the sacrifice, and drink the sweet; and send portions unto them for whom nothing is prepared: for the day is holy, and the joy of the Lord is your strength!"

I sometimes frequented the jatterahs, or religious festivals, at the Hindoo temples of Zinore and Chandode; or rather I mingled with the motley crowd who then assembled under the sacred groves on the banks of the Nerbudda. It is unnecessary to repeat the religious ceremonies, or the sports and pastimes of the Hindoos, who, in astonishing numbers, resort to these consecrated spots on such occasions. At the jatterah of Cubbeer-Burr, near Baroche, the pilgrims, of various descriptions, often exceeded an hundred thousand, without reckoning the comedians, dancing-girls, snake-charmers, jugglers, and those of similar professions, who came to amuse them. I have elsewhere mentioned some feats of the Indian jugglers; at Zinore I saw one which surpassed every thing of the kind I had before witnessed, I mean the swallowing a sword up to the hilt. Had I not afterwards met with the same set on the island of Salsette, exhibiting before the English Chief at Tannah, I should have doubted the evidence of my senses. I witnessed the fact more than once, and was convinced there was no deception. Finding my tale generally disbelieved in Europe, I suppressed it; but having since read a clear and satisfactory account of this extraordinary transaction, drawn up by Mr. Johnson, surgeon in the navy, who in the year 1804, was an eye-witness of the performance, and having described it as a professional man, I shall transcribe the account from his memoir, instead of inserting one less scientific and satisfactory from my own manuscripts.

" Having been visited by one of these conjurers, I resolved to see clearly his mode of performing this operation; and for that purpose ordered him to seat himself on the floor of the verandah. The sword he intended to use, has some resemblance to a common spit in shape, except at the handle, which is merely a part of the blade itself, rounded and elongated into a little rod. It is from twenty-two to twenty-six inches in length, about an inch in breadth, and about one fifth of an inch in thickness; the edges and point are blunt, being rounded, and of the same thickness as the rest of the blade; it is of iron or steel, smooth, and a little bright.

" Having satisfied myself with respect to the sword, by attempting to bend it, and by striking it against a stone, I firmly grasped it by the handle, and ordered him to proceed. He first took a small phial of oil, and with one of his fingers rubbed a little of it over the surface of the instrument; then, stretching up his neck as much as possible, and bending himself a little backwards, he introduced the point of it into his mouth, and pushed it gently down his throat, until my hand, which was on the handle, came in contact with his lips. He then made a sign to me with one of his hands, to feel the point of the instrument between his breast and navel; which I could plainly do, by bending him a little more backwards, and pressing my fingers on his stomach, he being a very thin and lean fellow. On letting go the handle of the sword, he instantly fixed on it a little machine that spun round, and disengaged a small firework, which encircling his head with a blue flame, gave him, as he then sat, a truly diabolical appearance. On withdrawing the instrument, several parts of its surface were covered with blood, which shewed that he was still obliged to use a degree of violence in the introduction.

"I was at first a good deal surprised at this transaction altogether; but when I came to reflect a little upon it, there appeared nothing at all improbable, much less impossible in the business. He told me, on giving him a trifle, that he had been accustomed from his early years, to introduce at first small elastic instruments down his throat, and into his stomach; that by degrees he had used larger ones, until at length he was able to use the present iron sword.

"As I mentioned before, the great flexibility of their joints and muscles, the laxness of their fibres, and their temperate mode of life, render them capable of having considerable violence done to the fleshy parts of their bodies, without any danger of the inflammation, and other bad effects, which would be produced in the irritable bodies of Europeans; witness their being whirled round on the point of a pole, suspended by a hook thrust into the fleshy part of their backs, without experiencing any fatal consequences.

"There is, therefore, no great wonder, if by long habit, in stretching up their necks, they are able to bring the different windings of the stomach into a straight line, or nearly so; and thereby slide down the sword into the latter organ without much difficulty."

I seldom pitched my tent, or spread a shahmyana near any principal town in Guzerat, but some of these people, or a set of dancing-girls, made their appearance. They generally presented themselves in front of my mud-walled palace at Zinore, when I took up my abode in the town, during a short visit in the rainy season. The inclemency of the weather then compelled me to live in a Hindoo house, situated near the lofty bank of the Nerbudda. Unlike an oriental durbar, this building was little more than a pendall, or open hall, with two small chambers, formed of mud and unburnt bricks, between a frame of wood; an elevated bench, composed of the same materials, surrounded the front veranda, which, with the floors, and the whole interior of the house, was always washed over with a thick wash of cow-dung and water; which, when perfectly dry, had a neat and cleanly appearance; and from having no glare, was, at least in that respect, preferable to a white-wash. A cotton carpet, camp-chair, and table, were my only furniture; my travelling palankeen formed my bed, its purdoe or chintz covering my curtains. The women and children decked this humble tenement with mogrees and fragrant flowers, and brought the little necessaries I wanted. There I sometimes passed a few days very pleasantly among those innocent and simple people.

Under that description I do not include the zemindars, and officers in the revenue department, with whom I was under a necessity of passing the morning in public business: their oppressive conduct was an alloy to every gratification I should otherwise have enjoyed. The wives and daughters of these zemindars, and especially the higher classes of the brahmin women, impressed a very pleasing idea of the female character; mild, gentle, and affectionate, they seem formed to make good wives and good mothers: ignorant of the world, and the various temptations to which European females are liable, religious and domestic duties engross their chief attention. It is notwithstanding a just remark of the Hindoo women, who are often mothers at twelve years of age, and wrinkled before they are thirty, that "they are flowers of too short a duration not to be delicate, and too delicate to be lasting."

Although I am so frequently under the necessity of reproaching the corrupt zemindars, I have much greater pleasure in bearing witness to many amiable traits in the Hindoo character; who, notwithstanding the natural prejudices of caste, religion, and habit, generally shewed an affectionate and grateful attachment to their English employers. Yet so contradictory is their character, that superstition leads them to most extraordinary deviations, from every thing that is humane, gentle, and praise-worthy. As already observed, the brahmin who shudders at killing an insect, feels no compunction at pounding a brother to death in an oil-mill because he differs from him in religious opinions. As a late traveller remarks, "there is no end to the delusions of superstition, nor any bounds to the cruelties to which it can instigate people the most gentle and timid with which history has made us acquainted. Some are persuaded to regain their lost rank in society by precipitating themselves naked from a great height upon spikes and edged weapons; others pierce their skin with a hot iron; in short, cruelties too horrid for recital, and too extravagant to obtain belief, daily provoke our pity and indignation, amidst a people famed for humanity in every part of the world. In almost every action of his life, the Hindoo is under the immediate influence of his superstition: his prayers are offerings to his gods; his purifications and ablutions in the river; his dressing and eating his victuals; the objects which he touches; the companions with whom he associates, are to him all intimately and equally connected with religion, and the everlasting welfare of his soul. If there is any part of his conduct with which his religious ideas have no concern, it is his moral character. In doing justly, or loving mercy, he is apparently left to act as he pleases: but, if in the most trivial action he violate the rites of superstition, he is, in this life, deprived of all the comforts of society, and in the next condemned to animate the body of some noisome reptile, or contemptible animal." DR. TENNANT.

There were a few families of the Bhauts, or Churrans, in Zinore; but Serulah, one of the largest and wealthiest villages in the purgunna, belonged exclusively to that singular cast of people, particularly mentioned at Neriad; and occasionally in other parts of these memoirs. The Bhauts gave me no trouble in collecting the Company's share of their revenue, and appeared in all respects a worthy, honourable tribe, highly deserving of the confidence placed in them by the princes of Guzerat, and the various inhabitants of their dominions. This caste were more or less historians, heralds, prophets, and soothsayers. In the two last characters they, perhaps, a little interfere with the brahmins and Hindoo devotees, abounding in Zinore and Chandode. I may have mentioned a sheet of paper, now in my possession, seventy-two feet in length, containing the calculations and predictions of the Dhuboy brahmins and astrologers, on my destiny. I preserve it as a curiosity; but neither curiosity nor inclination have made me yet wish for a translation.

Among many things suppressed from my original manuscripts, were several particulars respecting these Indian soothsayers, or fortune-telling brahmins, as they are generally called by the English. It is a subject as unsatisfactory, and difficult to investigate, as was that of the Parsees possessed by the demons at Baroche. Not to gratify my own inclination, but at the particular desire of some discerning friends who had read them in my letters, and whose names would add respectability to any publication, I have selected three anecdotes on that subject, from many others well known in India. I chose these in particular, because, let the prediction itself stand on what basis it may, I was acquainted with the principal persons concerned in each occurrence; and because several eminent persons, now living in England, are ready to attest the truth of the narration.

I have frequently mentioned the augurs and soothsayers, common in ancient history, sacred and profane. There are in modern India some brahmins, who, like the magicians of Egypt and the astrologers of Chaldea, are supposed to "have within them the spirit of the holy gods, and light, and understanding, and wisdom, in shewing hard sentences, and dissolving of doubts:" this is as certain as that such persons existed in Babylon when Daniel was consulted by the Chaldean and Persian monarchs. The men I now speak of are in no respect similar to the necromancers at Baroche, nor do they at all resemble the Jiggerkhars, or liver-eaters mentioned in the Ayeen-Akbery, whom I consider to be of the same kind as those persons among the Parsees at Baroche, who called up demons or genii by some extraordinary agency. Abul Fazel, in the Ayeen-Akbery, says, "one of the wonders of this country is the Jiggerkhar, or liver-eater: one of this class can steal away the liver of another by looks and incantations; other accounts say, that by looking at a person he deprives him of his senses, and then steals from him something resembling the seed of a pomegranate, which he hides in the calf of his leg; after being swelled by the fire, he distributes it amongst his fellows to be eaten; which ceremony concludes the life of the fascinated person. A Jiggerkhar is able to communicate his art to another by learning him the incantations, and by making him eat a bit of the liver-cake. Those jiggerkhars are mostly women; it is said that they can bring intelligence from a great distance in a short space of time; and if they are thrown into a river, with a stone tied to them, they nevertheless will not sink. In order to deprive any one of this wicked power, they brand his temples, and every joint in his body, cram his eyes with salt, suspend him for forty days in a subterraneous cavern, and repeat over him certain incantations." Such is the account given by Abul Fazel, vizier to the great Akber.

In confirmation of such kind of people having at all times been known in Asia, Pietro della Valle mentions many extraordinary anecdotes; I select one, because similar complaints were often occurring in my districts, unnecessary to detail at so remote a time and distance, but which occasioned much trouble and murmuring in the jurisprudence of the smaller purgunnas subordinate to Dhuboy, especially when they appealed to me for a decision by panchaut.

" This sort of witchcraft, which the Indians call eating the heart, is not a new thing, nor unheard of elsewhere; many persons practised it formerly in Sclavonia; and Pliny, upon the report of Isigones, testifies that this species of enchantment was known among the Triballes, and many other people whom he mentions, as it is at present among the Arabians who inhabit the western side of the Persian gulph, where this art is common. The way in which they do it is only by the eyes and mouth, keeping the eyes fixed steadily upon the person whose heart they design to eat, and pronouncing certain diabolical words; by virtue of which, and by the operation of the devil, the person, how hale and strong soever, falls immediately into an unknown and incurable disease, which consumes by little and little, and at last destroys him. This takes place faster or slower as the heart is eaten, as they say; for these sorcerers can either eat the whole or a part only; that is, can consume it entirely and at once, or bit by bit, as they please. The vulgar give it this name, because they believe that the devil, acting upon the imagination of the witch when she mutters her wicked words, represents to her the heart and entrails of the patient, taken as it were out of his body, and makes her devour them."

"The old woman who gave rise to these observations, at first made some difficulty to confess her guilt; but seeing herself pressed with threats of death, and being led, in fact, to the public square, where I saw her with a sick young man whom she was accused of having brought into his deplorable state, she said, that though she had not been the cause of his complaint, perhaps she could cure it, if they would let her remain alone with him, in his house, without interruption; by which she tacitly confessed her witchcraft: for it is held certain in those countries, that these wicked women can remove the malady which they have caused, if it be not come to the last extremity. Of many remedies which they use to restore health to the sufferers, there is one very extraordinary, which is, that the sorceress casts something out of her mouth like the grain of a pomegranate, which is believed to be a part of the heart that she had eaten. The patient picks it up immediately, as part of his own intestines, and greedily swallows it. By this means, as if his heart was replaced in his body, he recovers his health by degrees. These things can be only in appearance, by the illusions of the devil; and if the afflicted actually recover their health, it is because the same devil ceases to torment them."

This anecdote so corresponds with the occurrences in the Zinore purgunna, and there seems so much probability in that part respecting the devil acting upon the imagination of the sorcerer, as to give him the idea of eating the heart of the devoted sufferer, as in some degree settles that point. The real illness, dreadful convulsions, and premature death of the wretched beings subject to such diabolical influence, I can only ascribe to the terrors of an affrighted hypochondriac, and the powerful effects of imagination, which are known to operate strongly upon weak minds in more enlightened countries than Guzerat. Be that as it may, the frequency of these spectacles in the districts under my care, were painful, disgusting, and, situated as I was, irremediable. There was no deceit in the afflicted persons brought on their beds into my presence, bedewed by parental tears, imploring a relief I could not give. I seldom saw them in an early stage of this cruel disorder; perhaps hope was encouraged, and other means used for their recovery, before they were brought before an English gentleman invested with authority to give redress. That certainly was the case at Baroche; consequently the wretched beings I generally saw, were, like the Parsee youth, brought on his bed to our garden-house at Baroche, emaciated, agonizing, foaming at the mouth, the tongue hanging out, and the eyes starting from their sockets. Or, to make use of the pathetic language of an afflicted father, addressed to our Saviour on a similar occasion, "Master, I beseech thee, look upon my son, for he is mine only child: and lo! a spirit taketh him, and teareth him; and he foameth, and gnasheth with his teeth, and pineth away: and oft times it casteth him into the fire, and into the waters, to destroy him!" That all-powerful Being, who went about doing good, and healing all manner of sickness; who restored a daughter tormented by a similar spirit, to the faithful Syrophenician woman, rebuked this diabolical spirit, healed the child, and delivered him again to his father!

Having discussed this subject in a former chapter, it is unnecessary to enlarge; although such things must be viewed in Europe with doubt and incredulity, to a person in a public station in India, who wishes to act with clemency, moderation, and justice, they cause sensations not easy to describe, and create doubts difficult to resolve.

Another troublesome set of people in that part of Guzerat, were the soothsayers and astrologers, who have very great influence over the minds of millions, who, more or less, believe in unlimited predestination. Such, no doubt, were the sorcerers mentioned by the prophet. "Let now the astrologers, the star-gazers, the monthly prognosticators, stand up and save thee from the things that shall come upon thee! They shall not deliver themselves; they shall wander every one to his quarter; none shall save thee!" Such persons abound in all parts of India; but there are among the brahmins a select few, who seem to differ from all the descriptions of people beforementioned; they seem also perfectly distinct from the fortune-telling brahmins, and pretended astrologers, who, like the gypsy tribe in Europe, are well known in India. Those I now speak of seem to be gifted with a talent possessed only by a very few of the quiet, retired, literary brahmins. To one of these I shall now confine myself; he was a man well known to many of my contemporaries in India, and I have occasionally met with him at Bombay, Surat, and Cambay, where I believe he chiefly resided.

I shall relate three anecdotes in confirmation of the penetrating spirit, preternatural gift, or whatever term may be allowed for the talent which this man possessed. I shall detail them as they were commonly told, without any remark or comment of my own, for which I confess my incapacity: as a christian I must hesitate in believing things so apparently contradictory to revealed religion; as a member of the society in which they happened, and where they were generally believed, I know that the predictions were made long before the events happened, and were literally accomplished. As a traveller I have told them in England, and found it so difficult to impress any thing like conviction, that I no longer mentioned them, and suppressed them in the latest copies from my manuscripts; for the reasons just assigned, I rather reluctantly introduce them into these volumes.

On my arrival at Bombay in 1766, Mr. Crommelin, the governor of that settlement, was under orders to relinquish his situation at the beginning of the following year, and then to return to England. Mr. Spencer, the second in council, was appointed his successor in the Bombay government. The affairs of a distant settlement, especially after a lapse of many years, must be uninteresting; but in the present instance it is necessary briefly to mention them.

The occurrences in Trinidad, Ceylon, or New South Wales, engage the attention of few readers in England, even within a few months after they happen; but it is very different on the spot, where locality gives them an interest; and the more remote and insulated the situation, the more important are the passing events.

I arrived in India during a profound peace; there were then neither king's ships nor troops in that part of the world. Over-land dispatches were not common, and a packet by sea seldom arrived. Bombay had very little communication with England, except on the arrival of the Indiamen in August and September, a period expected with no small anxiety. Such being the general situation and character of that small settlement, I found it on my arrival in 1766 peculiarly agitated. Society was divided into three parties: one who paid their court to Mr. Spencer, the rising sun; another gratefully adhered to Mr. Crommelin; the third were affectionately devoted to the interest of Mr. Hodges, whom they deemed an injured character, deprived of his just right as successor to the government.

Mr. Crommelin went out a writer to Bombay in 1732, Mr. Hodges in 1737, Mr. Spencer in 1741. At that time supercessions in the Company's employ were little known; faithful service and a fair character, if life was spared, generally met with reward. I shall not enter upon the political or commercial system of India at that period. Previous to Lord Clive being appointed governor of Bengal, in 1764, Mr. Spencer had been removed from Bombay to Calcutta, and for some time acted as provisional governor of Bengal; ten years before the appointment of a governor-general and supreme council in India, when the four presidencies were entirely independent of each other. On Lord Clive's nomination to the government of Bengal, Mr. Spencer was appointed by the court of directors to return to Bombay, with the rank of second in council, and an order to succeed Mr. Crommelin in the government of that settlement in the month of January 1767. This supercession and appointment was deemed an act of injustice by the company's civil servants in general on that establishment, and a peculiar and personal injury by Mr. Hodges in particular, who was then chief of Surat, second in council, and next in regular succession to the government of Bombay, which he looked upon as his right, being senior to Mr. Spencer by four years.

Indignant at Mr. Spencer's supercession, and chagrined by his disappointment in the government of Bombay, Mr. Hodges addressed a spirited letter from Surat to the governor and council, complaining of injustice in the court of directors, with whom, as an individual, he was not permitted to correspond. This, therefore, was the only regular channel by which he could communicate his sentiments, and seek redress. The governor and council of Bombay deeming his letter improper, and disrespectful to his employers, ordered him to reconsider it, and make a suitable apology; which not being complied with, he was removed from his honourable and lucrative situation as chief of Surat, sent down to Bombay, and suspended the company's service; thither he accordingly repaired to settle his private affairs, and afterwards to proceed to Europe. The government of Bombay sent a dispatch to the court of directors by the way of Bussorah and Aleppo, informing them of these proceedings. This was the situation of that settlement at the breaking up of the monsoon in 1766.

After this necessary preamble, I can with more propriety, introduce the brahmin who occasioned the digression, and with whom Mr. Hodges became acquainted during his minority in the company's service. This extraordinary character was then a young man, little known to the English, but of great celebrity among the Hindoos, and every other description of natives, in the western part of the peninsula. I believe Mr. Hodges first saw him at Cambay, where he was appointed the English resident soon after the expiration of his writership. The brahmin expressed an affectionate regard towards him, and, as far as the distinction of religion and caste allowed, the friendship became mutual and disinterested. The brahmin was always justly considered as a very moral and pious character; Mr. Hodges was equally well disposed: his Hindoo friend encouraged him to proceed in that virtuous path which would lead him to wealth and honour in this world, and finally conduct him to eternal happiness. To enforce these precepts, he assured him he would gradually rise from the station he then held at Cambay, to other residences and inferior chiefships in the company's service; that he would then succeed to the higher appointment of chief at Tellicherry and Surat, and would close his Indian career by being governor of Bombay. Mr. Hodges not having been enjoined secrecy, spoke of these brahminical predictions among his associates and friends from their very first communication; and their author was generally called Mr. Hodges's brahmin. These predictions for some years made but little impression on his mind. Afterwards, as he successively ascended the gradations in the company's service, he placed more confidence in his brahmin, especially when he approached near the pinnacle of ambition, and found himself chief of Surat, the next situation in wealth and honour to the government of Bombay.

When, therefore, Mr. Spencer was appointed governor of that settlement, and Mr. Hodges dismissed from the chiefship of Surat, and suspended the service, he sent for his brahmin, who was then at Pulparra, a sacred village on the banks of the Tappee, on a religious visit. Mr. Hodges received him at the chief's garden-house, where he was sitting in the front veranda. He immediately communicated to him the events which had lately taken place, to the disappointment of all his hopes and future expectations; and that he was then on the eve of his departure to Bombay, and from thence to England. It is said Mr. Hodges slightly reproached him for a pretended prescience, and for having deceived him by false promises. The brahmin, with an unaltered countenance, as is usual with his tribe on all such occasions, coolly replied, "You see this veranda, and the apartment to which it leads; Mr. Spencer has reached the portico, but he will not enter the palace. He has set his foot upon the threshold, but he shall not enter into the house! Notwithstanding all appearances to the contrary, you will attain the honours I foretold, and fill the high station to which he has been appointed. A dark cloud is before him!"

This singular prophecy was publicly known at Surat and Bombay; and the truth or falsehood of the brahmin was the subject of discussion in every company. Mr. Hodges's faith in his prediction seemed to have very little influence on his conduct; for, in obedience to the orders of his superiors, he had returned from Surat to Bombay, and was preparing for his voyage to Europe.

Thus were affairs situated at Bombay in the month of November 1766, at which time an express arrived from England, after a wonderful celerity over the Persian desart, and a sea voyage equally favourable, from Bussorah to Bombay. The packet contained a letter from the court of directors to the president and council, in answer to their representation respecting Mr. Hodges's conduct; mentioning, in the first place, that on a review of Mr. Spencer's proceedings while governor of Bengal, he appeared so blameable, that they had thought proper to annul his appointment to the government of Bombay, to dismiss him from the company's service, and order him to proceed to England without delay. Although the conduct of Mr. Hodges had been improper, they were pleased to pass it over; and, in consideration of his long and faithful services, his good character and well-known abilities, they had taken off his suspension, and ordered him to succeed to the government of Bombay on Mr. Crommelin's resignation in the month of January following. All which accordingly took place. Mr. Spencer embarked for England in the same ship in which I arrived in India in December; and Mr. Crommelin sailed in January, leaving Mr. Hodges in complete possession of the government.

Such was the fact: on causes and effects I cannot argue; on preternatural gifts I cannot enter. I must leave these discussions to those who can account for the conduct of the witch of Endor, the genius of Socrates, the spirit which appeared to Eliphaz, or the apparition to Brutus. It is almost needless to remark the ascendancy of this brahmin over the mind of Mr. Hodges during the remainder of his life; nor is it to be wondered at, that the new governor undertook no important step without consulting his brahmin. The public sale of the company's staple commodities from Europe, consisting of the cargoes of all the Bombay ships of the season, was then annually advertised to commence at a specified time, and to be continued during several successive days under a large tent pitched for the purpose on Bombay-green, where the governor and council always attended in person, with the ware-house-keeper, and samples of the broad cloth and metals for sale. Notice of these sales was sent to the principal trading towns on the adjacent continent, and merchants resorted from thence and many other parts of India. During the government of Mr. Hodges I have known this sale deferred to a future period because the day appointed was pronounced unlucky in the Hindoo calendar; and the cause of the procrastination was thus registered in the Bombay diary and consultations, and transmitted to Europe.

In the third year of his government Mr. Hodges fell into a declining state of health; a sea voyage being recommended as one mean of his recovery, I have seen him stand under a burning sun at the water-side, with a stop-watch in his hand, waiting for the lucky moment to set his foot in the boat which was to convey him to the frigate in which he was to sail at some future period equally propitious by the brahminical calculations. I must here remark, that Mr. Hodges's brahmin never promised him any thing beyond the government of Bombay, he never foretold a return to his native country, nor the happiness which an exile naturally expects after a long absence; on the contrary, it was well known, during his life, that a mysterious veil was said to obscure the prospect after an era in the Hindoo calendar corresponding with the beginning of A. D. 1771.

Sea voyages not affording the relief expected, and medicine having but little effect on the governor's indisposition, he determined to try the waters at the hot-wells of Dazagon, formerly described. For this purpose, in February 1771, he sailed to Fort Victoria, with a confidential physician and a few friends, carrying with him a moveable house, tents, and equipage, for a long continuance at the wells. He landed at Fort Victoria rather benefited by the voyage, and his convalescence increased by the pure western breezes on the lofty hills at that settlement, where he purposed to remain until the accommodations were ready at Dazagon. On the 22d of that month, when the sun declined, he ordered his palankeen to be prepared as usual, that he might take the air on the sea-side. Suddenly changing his mind, he said to his physician, and a friend of mine then in company, "I shall not go out this evening; it will be a critical night with me." To which, seeing him in his customary state of health, they paid no particular attention. An aged Indian woman, who had lived with his deceased wife, and nursed their only child, then attended him. He had been many years a widower, and his son was then in England for education. Retiring to his chamber he went to bed, and gave strict orders to this servant to let no person disturb him. As governor, and an invalid, he had been accustomed to many attentions; the gentlemen of his family were anxious to know if he wanted any thing, and the physician wished to see him. The trusty female obeyed his orders, and for some hours suffered none to approach him. All being quiet, and the nurse asleep, after midnight one gentleman opened the muslin curtain at the foot of the bed, and seeing the governor in a meditating attitude, with his eyes fixed stedfastly upwards, and his finger on his lip as in deep thought, he silently withdrew, fearful of a reprimand for the intrusion. Towards morning, hearing no call for medicine or assistance, so contrary to former practice, the gentleman, accompanied by the physician, once more approached the bed, and beheld the patient exactly in the same situation. On speaking they received no answer, and the doctor venturing to feel his pulse, found he had been dead several hours. His remains were carried to Bombay, and buried in the church with the honours due to his high station.

The second anecdote relates to the same brahmin, and was as well known to the inhabitants of Bombay as the former. I have suppressed all family occurrences in these volumes, and generally curtailed every thing immediately respecting myself. I might otherwise have mentioned that I landed at Bombay in my seventeenth year, unknown, friendless, and forsaken, except by the worthy character who commanded the ship which carried me to India. His kindness during the voyage was unremitted, and for a period of forty-six years I have enjoyed his friendship. He still lives a fine instance of *green old age*, and now near fourscore, is the delight of the elegant circle in which he moves. On leaving England I might, like most other youth who enter the company's service, have had letters of recommendation from the directors, for the chairman and deputy were my father's friends, and offered an appointment either at Bengal, Madras, or Bombay. A relation, who was then going out as chief supracargo to Mocha, fixed it for the latter, that I might sail in the same ship with himself, and proceed entirely under his care without other patronage. He promised to be my guardian and protector, and introduce me properly at

Bombay. He lost his health and spirits during the voyage, and on reaching our destined port was no longer the same character we had known in England. From his forgetfulness and inattention I remained on board until the day after the captain and every other passenger had left the ship, to enjoy the pleasures of land, after a voyage of eleven months. While the officers and men were busily employed in unloading the cargo, I found myself a solitary, deserted being, without a letter to offer, or the knowledge of a single individual on the island.

Having occasionally heard my guardian mention the name of a gentleman with whom he intended to reside until the ship sailed from Bombay to Mocha, on landing I inquired for his house, and was told that a noble colonnade overlooking the sea, under which I then stood, formed a part of his mansion. With an anxious heart and trembling steps I ventured up a broad flight of stairs leading to this colonnade, from whence I saw the family sitting at their dessert in a large saloon to which it opened. My guardian gave me a sort of reprimand for the intrusion, but introduced me as a young gentleman, with the appointment of a writer, who had left England under his protection, and whom he meant to have sent for from the ship when he had provided a lodging. His friend pitied my situation, and felt for the cool reception of a bashful youth from one who had promised to extend over him the wings of parental love. If the reception of one was cool, that of the other was truly warm: he *then* took me by the hand, and for forty years never let it go; he immediately introduced me to his wife and family, encouraged me by the kindest attention, supplied me with money, and told me to consider his house as my own. So I ever found it in India, and for twenty years after my return to England, where I trod the walk of private life; while my friend, with an ample fortune, and abilities equal to his station, filled a seat in parliament, became a director and chairman of the East India company, and purchased one of the finest estates in Hertfordshire, where he lived many years a blessing to all around him. To him I was entirely indebted for my appointment to Baroche, and consequently for the independence I now enjoy. From the first hour I saw him until the day of his death, at the venerable age of fourscore, he was indeed my friend! A heart overflowing with a grateful recollection of departed worth, has caused a little deviation from the story of the brahmin, to which I now return.

The lady sitting at the head of my friend's table when I made my bashful entry, was a widow at the time he married her. Her first husband died when she was very young, leaving two children, a son and daughter. The latter remained with her mother, the former was sent to England for education, and at the age of sixteen embarked for Bombay with the appointment of a writer, some years prior to my arrivai there. The ships of that season all reached the island in safety, except the one in which this young gentleman sailed, which at length was deemed a missing ship, and her safety despaired of. A mother could not so easily give up hope; her usual evening walk was on a sandy beach, forming a bay on the western side of the island, in full view of the ocean. Maternal anxiety frequently cast a longing eye to that quarter where the ships from Europe generally appeared. The shore of that bay was also the place where most of the Hindoos erected the funeral pile and burnt their dead. This ceremony is attended by brahmins, and Mr. Hodges's brahmin, then at Bombay, was occasionally among them. Observing the mother's anxiety, he asked her the cause; the lady being a native of India, and well knowing his character, inquired in his own language why a man so extraordinarily gifted should be ignorant of her tender solicitude. The brahmin was affected, and said, "I do know the reason of your sorrow; your son lives; the ship will soon arrive in safety, but you will never more behold him!" She immediately mentioned this conversation to her friends. A signal was made not long after for a ship from Europe: on the pilot reaching her his private signal indicated the missing ship; boats were sent off to bring the passengers on shore. The expected son was not forgot; his mother's friends went on board, and were informed that he had remained at the Brazils, where the ship having been long detained for repair, the jesuits converted this promising youth to the church of Rome. Instead therefore of conducting him to his expecting parent, they only delivered her letters replete with affectionate expostulations and entreaties that she would follow his example, and enter into the true church. A mother's disappointment is easier to conceive than describe. Her son continued at Rio de Janeiro, and occasionally wrote to her, until the suppression of the jesuits in the pontificate of Clement XIV, on which occasion, with many other members of that society, he was sent from South America to the prisons of Portugal, and no more heard of.

His sister, who remained with her mother at Bombay, grew up beautiful and amiable, and married a gentleman in the civil service, by whom she had a large family. He succeeded Mr. Hodges in the government, and held that station thirteen years. Long before his own return to England it became necessary for his wife to proceed thither to superintend the education of the children. Her mother resolved to accompany her to a country in which both were strangers, neither having before left the land of their nativity. *Her* husband followed them within four years: the governor remaining in India, there heard the melancholy news of his wife's death in England. This was a stroke her fond mother was little able to sustain; a bereavement which seemed to admit of no consolation. The downy wings of time, the balmy comforts of religion, aided by every effort of an affectionate husband, were of no avail in extricating her from a state of apathy and despair.

Not long after this event, an intimate friend of the family having remitted a considerable sum of money from India by bills on Portugal, went to Lisbon to recover them. Walking near a prison in that city, he was supplicated for charity by a voice from a subterraneous grate; and being addressed in English made it the more impressive. Not content with affording transient relief, he entered into conversation with the prisoner, and found he was the long lost son of his disconsolate mother. The intelligence was immediately conveyed to England, and tenderly communicated to his sorrowing parent, with the addition that her husband had already remitted money to Lisbon, and exerted such means for his deliverance that there could be no doubt of his speedy restoration to her maternal arms. This extraordinary news *did* shed a momentary gleam of joy on her countenance, but it was soon succeeded by renewed pangs of sorrow, and a continued exclamation of "O the brahmin! the brahmin!" Her husband, by every tender assiduity, endeavoured to rouse her from melancholy by assurances that every difficulty was removed, that the Almighty having in infinite wisdom thought proper to deprive her of one child, had mercifully restored another in this unexpected manner, whom she had long considered dead. All seemed to produce no effect, even on a religious mind, of which resignation and indifference seemed to have taken mingled possession. Every prospect set before her of future joy and comfort only produced a monotonous repetition of "The brahmin! the brahmin!"

The friend at Lisbon, when all was happily accomplished, lost no time in communicating to her son that his mother lived, was married to a gentleman of fortune and respectability, and both were waiting to welcome him to their parental roof;—that their interest and liberality had procured his liberty, which he was the happy instrument of effecting, and was then come to conduct him from a scene of misery to life, and light, and joy! Although the communication was made in the most considerate manner, the sudden transition seemed too much for human nature. Like the venerable patriarch, his spirit fainted, for he believed it not! or scarcely believed the reality of his emancipation from those dreary walls where he had for years been excluded from the light of the sun and fresh air; or, to use the pathetic language of Sterne, "in all that long and dismal period the western breeze had not once fanned his blood; he had seen no sun, no moon, in all that time; nor had the voice of friend or kinsman breathed through his lattice!" The spirit of Jacob revived; he lived to see his long-lost son riding in the second chariot of Egypt, and next to Pharaoh in royal splendour. Not so the liberated captive from the dungeons in Portugal; "hope deferred had made his heart sick," "the iron had entered into his soul!" "He had ate no pleasant bread, neither flesh nor wine came into his mouth, nor had he anointed himself with oil; his comeliness was turned into corruption, and he retained no strength!" The sudden transition from hopeless despair in the dungeon's gloom to the *sight of the sun*, the *fanning* of *the breeze*, and the sympathy of *friendship*, were too much for his emaciated frame. He faintly uttered the effusions of a grateful heart, and expired!

Thus was the brahmin's prediction to his mother, uttered full thirty years before, completely fulfilled!

The last anecdote which I shall relate respecting this extraordinary man, is very short. Some months previous to my first leaving India, a gentleman and his wife arrived from England at Bombay. He having been appointed to a lucrative situation at Surat, proceeded thither by an early opportunity, leaving his wife in a friend's family until he should have procured a house, and made suitable provision for her reception at Surat. They were both young, and had an only child. In a few weeks she followed him to Surat. The evening before she embarked, sitting in a mixed circle of gentlemen and ladies, anticipating her approaching happiness, the same brahmin came into the veranda with the gentleman of the house, who was high in station at Bombay. He introduced him to the company, and in a sort of jest asked him to tell the destiny of the happy fair-one lately arrived from Europe. To the surprise of the whole company, and particularly so to the object of inquiry, he gave her a penetrating and compassionate look; and, after a solemn pause, said to the gentlemen in the Hindoo language, "her cup of felicity is full, but evanescent! a bitter potion awaits her; for which she must prepare!" Her husband had written that he should come in a barge to Surat bar to accompany her on shore. He did not appear; but a friend of mine went on board to announce to her his dangerous illness: he was then in the last paroxysm of a fever, and expired in her arms! I came home a passenger in the same ship with the widow and another lady, who endeavoured to alleviate her sorrow by every tender assiduity. The name of a brahmin was never mentioned at table, nor any thing relating to Hindoo astrology. The anniversary of her husband's death happened during the voyage, and was indeed a day of woe!

On these singular anecdotes I do not attempt to comment; many respectable characters who knew the parties, still live to attest the truth of the prediction long before the fulfilment. If any thing of the kind was permitted among the heathen nations of antiquity, it may still exist in Hindostan, where arts and science, learning and philosophy, and the sublimest poetry, were encouraged by the native sovereigns at a time when Greece and Rome were involved in darkness, and Egypt herself was probably in a state of comparative barbarism. The mahomedan conquests and other causes have sadly degraded, not only the philosophy and science of the Hindoos, but totally destroyed the simplicity of a religion which there can be no doubt was then essentially different from modern brahminism. If there should still remain any of that priesthood who adore God in his unity, and cherish the sublime ideas then inculcated, it is perhaps not easy to determine the limits of their researches, or the gifts and talents they possess.

"Such were thy strains, VYASA, saint and sage,
The immortal Berkeley of that elder age!

Like him, with flames of holiest rapture fir'd,
To thoughts sublime thy daring mind aspir'd;
And, nature opening to thy ardent glance,
Saw God alone through all the vast expanse.
Mysterious theme! Beneath the peipal shade,
His aged limbs the rev'rend brahmin laid;
The snow-white zennar o'er his shoulder flow'd,
Full on his brow the holy ointment glow'd;
The pointed cusa deck'd his green retreat,
And Ganges' billow kiss'd his sacred feet.
Serene he view'd the laughing scene around,
Bright Magadh's vales with floating chawla crown'd;
The sun-shine calm on Casis' turrets shed,
And clouds reposing on Heemalas head;
Then all entranc'd, recall'd his wandering eye,
And fix'd the gather'd beams on Deity:
From height to height his musing spirit soar'd,
And speechless thought th' unutter'd name ador'd;
Till words unconscious flowing from his tongue,
He swell'd the strain, and mystic measures sung!

C. Grant.

END OF VOL. II.

T. Bensley, Printer,
Bolt Court, Fleet Street, London.